B

Once They Moved Like the Wind

Cochise, Geronimo, and the Apache Wars

David Roberts

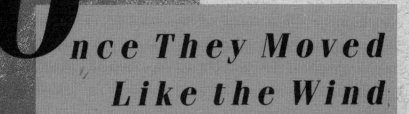

SIMON & SCHUSTER
New York London Toronto
Sydney Tokyo Singapore

SIMON & SCHUSTER
Simon & Schuster Building
Rockefeller Center
1230 Avenue of the Americas
New York, New York 10020

Designed by Karolina Harris
Manufactured in the United States of America

10 9 8 7 6 5 4 3 2 1

Library of Congress Cataloging-in-Publication Data
Roberts, David, date.
   Once they moved like the wind : Cochise, Geronimo, and the Apache wars /
David Roberts.
   p.   cm.
   Includes bibliographical references (p.   ) and index.
   1. Cochise, Apache chief, d. 1874. 2. Geronimo, 1829–1909.   3. Apache
Indians—Biography.   4. Apache Indians—Wars. 5. Apache Indians—History.
I. Title.
E99.A6C575 1993
973'.04972—dc20
[B]   93-7112   CIP
ISBN 0-671-70221-1

*To the living Apache
of Arizona, New Mexico,
and Oklahoma—
In sorrow at what they lost,
and awe at what they saved*

Contents

■

Once I moved about like the wind. Now I surrender to you and that is all.

—Geronimo

on surrendering to General George Crook

Preface

■

At the end, in the summer of 1886, they numbered thirty-four men, women, and children under the leadership of Geronimo. This small group of Chiricahua Apaches became the last band of free Indians to wage war against the United States government. The "renegades," as white men called them, were mercilessly pursued by five thousand American troops (one-quarter of the U. S. Army) and by some three thousand Mexican soldiers. For more than five months Geronimo's band ran the soldiers ragged. The combined military might of two great nations succeeded in capturing not a single Chiricahua, not even a child.

The odyssey of those fugitive Apaches ran its course, to be sure, as a hopeless cause. Yet in its melancholy inevitability, the struggle of Geronimo's band wrote a logical end to a quarter century of betrayal and misunderstanding. For their refusal to give in, the Chiricahua were punished as no other native people in U. S. history has ever been.

The story of the Chiricahua resistance is one of the most powerful of American narratives. In its essential features, it sings the perennial themes of both epic and tragedy, as the ancient Greeks defined those genres. Hundreds of books have been written about the Apaches, yet few seem to have grasped the basic shape of their story. All too often the telling bogs down in the details of troop deployments and Indian raids. The human character of the struggle's protagonists—both white and Apache—goes unilluminated.

Like most cultural tragedies, the war between the United States and the Chiricahua was founded on fundamental errors of perception.

Scouts, soldiers, and statesmen came away from years of experience with the Apache convinced they had probed to the core of his nature. What these "experts" saw, of course, was the shimmer of their own befuddled preconceptions. A sampler of their pronouncements—the examples could be multiplied indefinitely—makes rueful reading today.

They hurl themselves at danger like a people who know no God nor that there is any hell.

—SPANISH MISSIONARY *(ca. 1660)*

In character they resemble the prairie wolf—sneaking, cowardly, and revengeful. They are always ready to assassinate women and children.

—TRAVELER SAMUEL WOODWORTH COZZENS *(1858)*

The most rascally Indian on the continent. Treacherous, bloodthirsty, brutal with an irresistible propensity to steal.

—INDIAN AGENT GEORGE BAILEY *(1858)*

An [Apache] only knows two emotions, fear and hate.

—LIEUTENANT WALTER SCRIBNER SCHUYLER *(1873)*

A miserable, brutal race, cruel, deceitful and wholly irreclaimable.

—GENERAL JOHN POPE *(1880)*

The cowardly Apache creeps upon his victim like a snake in the grass; if he can capture him he invariably tortures him to death, but otherwise he scalps and mutilates him in the most horrible manner, and has never been known to show the smallest trace either of humanity or good faith.

—EXPLORER WILLIAM A. BELL *(1870)*

None of the Pacific Coast Indians can count much beyond ten, but the Apaches can count to 10,000 as easily as we do.

—ARIZONA HISTORIAN *(1884)*

They are the keenest and shrewdest animals in the world, with the added intelligence of human beings.

—MAJOR WIRT DAVIS *(1885)*

An [Apache] can stoically suffer death without so much as a grunt, while imprisonment is a terror to him.

—NEWSPAPER REPORTER *(1886)*

The cardinal failing of most accounts of the Apache resistance has been an inability to comprehend its doleful history from the Chiricahua point of view. No chronicler today would echo the racist calumnies of the nineteenth-century witnesses quoted above. But since the 1960s, our guilt-ridden culture has indulged in a reverse stereotype, a sentimental idealization of the American Indian—the noble sage, living in harmony with the land—that represents a comparable failure of the imagination.

Thanks to the labors of such scholars as Grenville Goodwin, Morris Opler, Keith Basso, D. C. Cole, Angie Debo, and the remarkable Eve Ball, non-Apaches are in a better position than ever before to understand the Chiricahua tragedy from the Apache point of view. Nor can we continue to excuse the cardboard cutouts, however striking, that substitute in our narratives for the real men and women who waged that struggle.

Cochise himself will always seem somewhat elusive: it is hard to probe beneath the legend, borne out in detail after detail, of the finest Apache leader on record. In recent years, however, there has been a movement to downplay Geronimo's importance, to minimize his deeds as overrated. Revisionist scholars compare him unfavorably to such less celebrated Apache leaders as Juh and Victorio.

This book resists such revisionism. In part because he lived into the twentieth century, Geronimo left us a rich trove of anecdote and testimony. No more interesting or contradictory figure crossed the stage of Western history in the second half of the nineteenth century. To be sure, as his detractors point out, Geronimo was not even a chief; yes, he could be manipulative, vain, vengeful, and cruel; granted, at times he verged on the comic or the pathetic. For all that, Geronimo stands astride the desert Southwest, haunting our collective nightmare of Manifest Destiny. As most of the living Apache see him today, so this narrative attempts to paint him: as one of the heroes of American history.

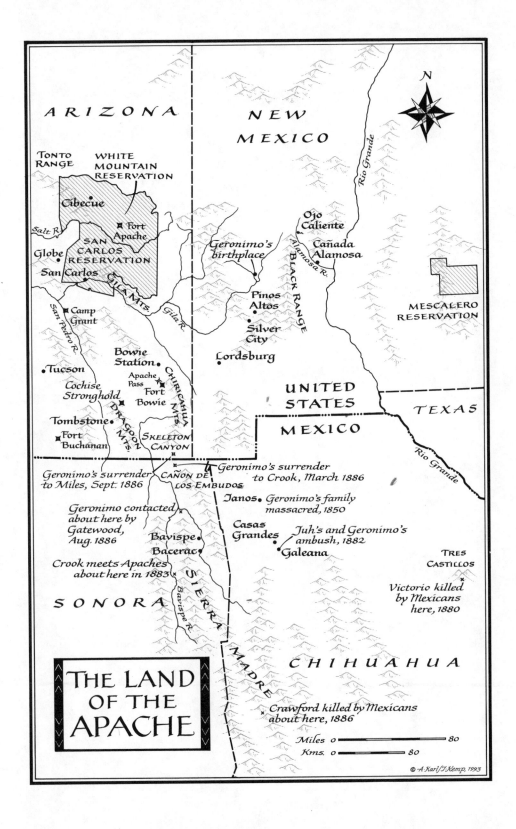

THE LAND
OF THE
APACHE

ARIZONA

NEW MEXICO

TONTO RANGE

WHITE MOUNTAIN RESERVATION

Cibecue

Fort Apache

Salt R.

SAN CARLOS RESERVATION

Globe

San Carlos

GILA Mts.

Gila R.

Camp Grant

San Pedro R.

Bowie Station

Tucson

Cochise Stronghold

Apache Pass

Fort Bowie

CHIRICAHUA Mts.

DRAGOON Mts.

Tombstone

Fort Buchanan

SKELETON CANYON

Geronimo's surrender to Miles, Sept. 1886

CAÑON DE LOS EMBUDOS

Geronimo contacted about here by Gatewood, Aug. 1886

Geronimo's surrender to Crook, March 1886

Janos

Geronimo's family massacred, 1850

Bavispe

Bacerac

Crook meets Apaches about here in 1883

Bavispe R.

SIERRA MADRE

SONORA

CHIHUAHUA

Geronimo's birthplace

Ojo Caliente

Cañada Alamosa

Alamosa R.

BLACK RANGE

Pinos Altos

Silver City

Lordsburg

UNITED STATES

MEXICO

TEXAS

Rio Grande

MESCALERO RESERVATION

Casas Grandes

Galeana

Juh's and Geronimo's ambush, 1882

TRES CASTILLOS

Victorio killed by Mexicans here, 1880

Crawford killed by Mexicans about here, 1886

Miles 0 — 80
Kms. 0 — 80

© A. Karl/J. Kemp, 1993

I

Cochise's
Will

One

■

Cut the Tent

*I*t was not a confrontation between equals.

The host, sitting tense and rigid inside the canvas army tent, his dark blue trousers dusty from a five days' march, was Second Lieutenant George N. Bascom. A full beard tapered to a V beneath his chin, failing to mute the earnest, callow face beneath. Heavy eyebrows overhung the bright stare of a zealot. A Kentuckian by birth, Bascom was about twenty-five years old; two years earlier, he had graduated from West Point. Having served in Indian country for less than four months, he had just been handed his first opportunity to prove his mettle.

His guest, still drinking the coffee Bascom had served, was twice the lieutenant's age. Tall for an Apache at five feet ten inches, he bore hit taut-muscled 175 pounds with formal dignity. His dark black hair hung to his shoulders. From each ear dangled three large brass rings. A sharply bridged nose, high cheekbones, and a high forehead accented the gravity of his countenance. He never smiled.

He was the greatest Apache of his day. His own people, the Chiricahua, regarded him with awe and fear, "his glance being enough," noted a white observer, "to squelch the most obstreperous Chiricahua of the tribe." Seventy-five years afterward, an Apache who had been a boy of four at the time remembered being shown the great leader's tepees, by a man who said that "it was as much as anyone's life was worth to even look toward them."

The Chiricahua called him Cheis, or "oak"—invoking not the tree or the wood itself so much as the strength and quality of oak. Anglos added a prefix to the name, and turned it into Cochise.

It was February 4, 1861. Bascom had pitched his camp on a shrubby bank of Siphon Canyon, just east of the low pass leading from the Sulphur Springs Valley to the San Simon Basin in what is now southeastern Arizona. Dead leaves lay in wind-blown patches along the dry stream bed. It was cold, with snow in the offing: within the week, a blizzard would sweep in from the west.

Arriving at Siphon Canyon the day before, Bascom had dissembled to the station keepers of the Butterfield Stage Line, whose stone headquarters stood about a mile away. The lieutenant had claimed that with his fifty-four soldiers of the Seventh Infantry he was headed for the Rio Grande, far to the east. He desired Cochise's visit, he said, merely to offer the hospitality of his tent.

The Chiricahua chief was a cautious man. All his life he had fought an on-and-off war against the Mexicans, for whose treacheries and pusillanimities he felt a weary contempt. But these White Eyes—so the Apaches called the Anglo-Americans who had started flooding into their homeland from the east—these White Eyes were different. Despite his anger at their arrogant invasion, Cochise was willing to try coexistence. He had befriended the Butterfield employees at the nearby station; he may even have contracted to supply firewood to the stage line.

Thus he came to Bascom's tent in an amicable mood, bringing with him his brother, two nephews, his wife, and two young children. And the lieutenant had served him dinner and coffee.

Suddenly this stripling in his blue uniform turned accuser, demanding that Cochise return the cattle he had stolen and the twelve-year-old boy he had abducted. At once Cochise professed his ignorance of the raid Bascom was attributing to him. He offered, however, to find out who the perpetrators were and to negotiate for the return of the boy and the cattle. But Bascom had his eyes on phantom laurels: he announced that Cochise and his relatives would be held hostage until the stolen property was redeemed. By design, his soldiers had surrounded the tent.

Cochise reacted instantly. Seizing a hidden knife, he cut a long slash in the canvas wall of the tent and sprang through the hole. The startled bluecoats fired. Some fifty bullets creased the February air, as Cochise dashed through the bushes up the hill behind camp. As the gunpowder fumes began to settle, the soldiers saw him running still, wounded in the leg but beyond their bravest thoughts of pursuit. So quickly had he made his escape, that at the top of the hill Cochise still clutched his coffee cup.

The chief's six relatives, however, had been captured. An hour later, Cochise came in sight on another hilltop and asked to see his brother. Bascom's answer was a burst of rifle fire from his troops. According to one eyewitness, Cochise "raised his hand and swore to be revenged." He cried out that "Indian blood was as good as white man's blood," then vanished.

In the failed maneuverings of the next two weeks—the product of Bascom's adamantine will—the script was written for twelve years of misunderstanding and terror in the Southwest.

The boy whose kidnapping launched this debacle was known in 1861 as Felix Ward. His life would wind in and out of the Apache wars for the next quarter century. Though never more than a marginal actor, he would play a sinister and crucial role, like some minor figure in a Greek tragedy upon whose ordinary deeds heroes stumble and go wrong. He remains one of the most enigmatic characters in the long Apache chronicle. He would live on in Arizona until his death in 1915, without bothering to share the secrets of his life with anyone who might have recorded them. A pioneer who studied him in his decline in 1906 described him as "a wandering, aged, unkempt dependent on the government."

Felix Ward was what used to be called a half-breed. Because he had red hair and had been adopted by an Irish-born rancher named John Ward, many people thought the boy was half-Mexican and half-Irish. The truth seems rather that he was the son of an Apache father and a captive Mexican mother. After six years she managed to flee her Apache masters, taking her boy with her. Eventually she became the common-law wife of John Ward, who had started a ranch on Sonoita Creek, about forty miles southeast of Tucson.

The boy had a blind left eye, cocked up and to the left. Some said it was a birth defect; others claimed it was the result of a youthful fight with a bear. One day in January 1861, Felix was captured by Indians, who also took twenty head of cattle. Some say the boy had run away from an alcoholic stepfather who beat him; others, that he wandered off from the ranch while dutifully hunting a stray burro.

In high dudgeon, John Ward reported his loss at Fort Buchanan, eleven miles north of his ranch. Although Cochise was camped at the time fully eighty miles away, Ward was convinced that it was his band of Chiricahuas who had robbed him. Soldiers from the fort claimed to follow the depredators' trail toward the Chiricahua country. Thus Bascom was sent out on his fateful errand.

His contemporaries' opinion of John Ward was none too high. Some claimed he had been driven out of California by the Vigilance Committee; an early Arizona historian summed him up as "in all respects, a worthless character." Apaches later surmised that the abducted stepson "was probably not of as much importance to Ward as were the cattle taken from him." It did not help matters that Ward rode with Bascom, and may have served as his interpreter.

For thirteen years after the confrontation in Siphon Canyon, the whereabouts of Felix Ward remained unknown to whites. The Apaches knew what had happened to him, though. Cochise had told Bascom the truth. It was members of an entirely separate tribe, a group of Western Apaches, who had seized the boy and the cattle, and for the rest of his childhood, Western Apaches raised the boy as one of their own. In 1874 Felix Ward resurfaced with the name Mickey Free, when he offered his services as scout and interpreter to the army. In these roles, as well as later duty as an official "spy," he performed his dark mischief.

An oldtimer who worked with Mickey Free in 1880 thought him "an indolent creature . . . a more repulsive object could not be imagined." He had grown up to be a short, slender man in shabby clothes, wearing a habitual sneer, who let his long, dirty hair hang over his bad eye. He had, all agreed, a mean disposition. It is easy to feel pity for this outcast, suspended in the tension among three different cultures and three languages, including Spanish from his Mexican mother. The Apaches, who knew him best, distrusted him entirely—he was "incapable of loyalty," judged one who knew him well. In part their antipathy sprang from his innocent role as a twelve-year-old captive: he was, in their words, "the coyote whose kidnapping had brought war to the Chiricahuas." But whites had little better to say: the opinion of the chief of scouts under whom he served "could not be printed in polite words."

The mischief Mickey Free performed was real and far-reaching, and all the more unfathomable for its lack of an evident motive. Perhaps, like Shakespeare's Iago, he nursed a secret wound, a hatred of the world instilled by the wrongs done him in his youth, which drove him to return the harm, just for the pleasure of watching things fall apart around him.

Before dusk that February 4, Bascom broke camp in Siphon Canyon and moved his soldiers a mile upstream to the stage station. Judging that he had a fight on his hands, the lieutenant longed for the security of stone walls. The next morning, leading a large band of warriors, Cochise appeared on a nearby hill; but instead of attacking, the chief proffered a white flag. Led by Bascom and Cochise, two groups of four negotiators each met at a spot some 125 yards from the station. Cochise pleaded for the release of his relatives. Bascom promised their freedom "just so soon as the boy was restored." To no avail, Cochise again protested that he had not the slightest knowledge of Felix Ward.

Watching the futile parley from the station was a veteran Butterfield driver, James Wallace. Almost a decade older than Bascom, he had twenty times more experience with Apaches; he spoke some Apache and counted Cochise as a friend. Exasperation with the officer's intransigence must have driven him to action. With two other Butterfield employees, Wallace hurried out to take over the discussion.

This development alarmed the Apaches, but it also gave them an opportunity. Some warriors hiding in a nearby ravine attempted to seize the Butterfield men. Wallace was captured, but the other two broke free and sprinted back toward the station. At the first disturbance, Cochise and his trio of allies fled for cover. Bascom ordered his soldiers to fire, and Apaches on the hillsides to the south returned their volleys. One of the Butterfield men was shot in the back but was pulled to safety. The other was less fortunate. Bascom's jittery soldiers knew as little as their leader did about Indians. No one had told them that Apaches virtually never attacked a fort. Now, as the third Butterfield man reached the station wall and desperately clambered over, the soldiers mistook him for the enemy, and shot him dead at point-blank range.

That night the addled troops saw distant fires and heard the wailing cries of what they thought was a war dance. They steeled themselves for a battle on the next day. But at noon on February 6 Cochise appeared once more on a hilltop, leading Wallace, whose arms were tied behind his back, by a rope looped around his neck. Again he pleaded with Bascom to free his relatives, offering now to trade his hostage for them. And again the stubborn young man refused.

For Cochise, as for all Apaches, the ties that bound him to his family were of the strongest sort. A black rage had gathered in his breast toward this impudent youngster with his blue uniform and his silly beard. Cochise would gladly have unleashed his warriors. But he still hoped to rescue his wife, his children, his nephews, and his brother. The closest tie of all was to that younger brother, Coyuntara, a great fighter and raider whose name had long struck terror in Mexican hearts. For the chance of saving Coyuntara and the others, Cochise would bear the American's arrogance yet a while longer.

His scouts had spotted a wagon train, loaded with flour for the New Mexico markets, approaching the pass from the west. The team of three Americans and nine Mexicans had no inkling that anything was amiss. That evening Cochise's Apaches laid an ambush just below the summit on the eastern side. The wagon train blundered into the trap, and the dozen men were captured in minutes.

For Mexicans not a whisper of pity sounded in Cochise's soul. Time and again they had deceived and betrayed his people, had even put a bounty on the head of Apache women and children. His nine Mexican captives were of no use to Cochise now. He turned them over to his men, and perhaps to his women, who knew what to do. They tied the Mexicans by their wrists to the wagon wheels, then set fire to the wagons and burned their prisoners to death.

The three additional white hostages, Cochise believed, ought to even the odds in the bargaining with the American lieutenant. That evening, the chief ordered Wallace to write a note: "Treat my people well," it said in English, "and I will do the same by yours." On the same hill where only that noon Cochise had shouted down to Bascom, the note was tied to a stake and left for the Americans to retrieve.

Confusion veils the record at this point. According to one account, the note was not discovered for two days—a crucial delay. Yet Bascom's own official report states that he read the note the same day it was left. In any event, Bascom did nothing—and by his passivity, doomed the hostages Cochise held.

Why, one wonders, did Bascom refuse to believe that Cochise spoke the truth about his ignorance of the abducted boy? Some witnesses reported that as Bascom turned down the trade for Wallace, an older, savvy sergeant at his elbow pleaded so forcefully for accepting the deal that Bascom arrested him for insubordination. Was it, as one scholar suggests, that the lieutenant construed his written orders (which were imperiously phrased) as demanding the sternest possible treatment of Cochise, guilty or innocent? Or did Bascom have the kind of mind that tolerates no ambiguity, that sees the clutter of fact as a mere distraction from the purity of its own theory? Having decided that Cochise had the boy, did Bascom see all the chief's protestations, his desperate countermeasures, only as confirmation of his guilt?

Or was it, more pathetically, simply a matter of saving face before his soldiers (had they marched five days for nothing?), of keeping oriented the compass of ambition that had steered him through West Point to his destiny in the desert?

With Bascom's failure to respond to the note, Cochise gave up all hopes of negotiating: he would try to reclaim his relatives by force. He retreated south into the Chiricahua Mountains to plan his strategy.

For two days, not an Apache was seen near the Butterfield station. On February 8, two men drove the herd of army mules to the spring six hundred yards from the station. Just as the soldiers dared to hope the Indians had left for good, a large party of Apaches, naked to the waist and covered with war paint, charged from the hilltops. The soldiers fired and fought their way back to the station, but lost all fifty-six mules. This raid, however, was chiefly a diversionary tactic: a few minutes later, another band of Indians started firing on the station from the opposite side.

The stone walls served their purpose. Cochise's hundred-odd men might have stormed the station and killed most or all of the fifty-four soldiers, but at too great a cost. When the odds were merely favorable, as opposed to overwhelming, Apaches declined to attack. Cochise's party withdrew toward the south.

For all his bluster face-to-face with Cochise, Bascom now shrank into a feckless inertia. If during the two-day lull before the Apache attack he had allowed himself to think the Indians had fled, now Bascom behaved as if he was surrounded by a horde of savages who watched his every move. In reality, the Chiricahuas were riding toward Mexico.

For six days Bascom kept his men cooped up in the stage station, while he dithered and did nothing. He failed even to send out scouting parties to see if Apaches indeed lurked about. On February 7, he had managed to send a courier to Fort Buchanan requesting reinforcements. Now—humiliated perhaps by the loss of all his mules—Bascom was content to wait for other soldiers to come to his rescue.

At last they arrived, seventy dragoons from two companies under an officer who outranked Bascom. On February 16—eight full days after the last hostilities—this enlarged force scouted through the hills surrounding the pass. They found no Apaches.

Two days later a detachment heading back west over the pass noticed buzzards circling in the air. What the soldiers found beneath the scavenging birds shocked them badly. The bodies of Wallace and the three Americans from the ambushed wagon train had been mutilated, punctured again and again by Apache lances. Wallace's corpse could be identified only by the gold fillings in his teeth. Bascom could not tell whether the mutilations had occurred before or after death.

On their way to relieve Bascom a week earlier, a party from Fort Buchanan had stumbled upon three Coyotero Apaches driving cattle they had stolen in Mexico. The fifteen soldiers gave chase and captured the Indians. These men had nothing to do with the confrontation twenty-five miles to the east; they were not even of the same tribe as Cochise's Chiricahuas. Yet, as perhaps they began to divine, their luck had run out.

In outrage at the mutilated remains found near the pass, Bascom's superior officer decided to hang the adult men he was holding prisoner. This meant not only Coyuntara and Cochise's two nephews, but the three Coyoteros, who were guilty of no crime more serious than rustling in another country. To his credit, Bascom opposed the executions, but was overruled by his superior.

Four mature oak trees stood near the fresh graves of Cochise's victims. Bascom led the six Indians to the spot. Through an interpreter, he explained what was about to happen. The Apaches pleaded to be shot instead of hanged, and to be given whiskey. Bascom refused both entreaties. One man "begged piteously for his life," but another —perhaps Coyuntara—started dancing and singing, and declared himself satisfied "as he had killed two Mexicans in the last month."

Bascom bound his captives hand and foot. Six soldiers tossed their lariats over stout oak boughs. The nooses were placed around the

Apaches' necks, and the six men were lifted into the air—"so high . . . that even the wolves could not touch them." Months later their skeletons still dangled from the ropes.

Cochise's wife and two children were released. One of them, Naiche, would grow up to be the last chief of the free Chiricahuas.

In his official reports, Bascom distorted and omitted much, and in several instances lied outright. Rather than admit that Cochise had cut his way out of the tent and dashed to safety, Bascom claimed he had released the chief on his own promise to try to find Felix Ward and to return in ten days. Instead of admitting that the Butterfield agent had been shot by his own men, Bascom implied his death had come at Apache hands. He took no responsibility for the loss of all his mules.

Bascom had also lost two men, with several others wounded. The lieutenant estimated that his troops had killed between five and twenty Chiricahuas (the Apaches later admitted to four). For his efforts, Bascom was officially commended and quickly promoted to first lieutenant and then to captain. He would not long enjoy his honors: only a year after his showdown with Cochise, he was killed in a battle in New Mexico.

Among Apaches, the catastrophe at Siphon Canyon grew to be a famous event. Generations of fathers would tell the story to their children, until it passed almost into the realm of folklore, becoming known simply as "Cut the Tent" or "Cut Through the Tent."

One of Cochise's warriors in 1861, who helped burn the nine Mexicans to death, was a crafty, intelligent man of about thirty-eight. As the flames licked closer to the bound wagoneers, he may have relished their hysterical cries; he might even have lanced or cut their bodies while the men were still alive. For on account of a single event already a decade in his past, this warrior harbored a hatred of Mexicans even more passionate than Cochise's. Unknown as yet to Americans, he was named Goyahkla, "One Who Yawns."

The Mexicans called him Geronimo.

Two

■

The Black Pot

Cochise's fury over the hangings was boundless. It was characteristic, however, that he planned his revenge in methodical fashion. For about a month after the soldiers had hanged his relatives, he bided his time in Mexico, organizing a war party. It was not until late April 1861, more than two months after the Bascom affair, that he struck.

In Doubtful Canyon, a favorite Apache defile on the New Mexico–Arizona border, through which ran the Butterfield stage line, Cochise ambushed a mail coach. All nine white men—driver, passengers, and escort—were killed. Cochise subjected two whom he captured alive to a gruesome torture. Their feet were tied to tree limbs so that the men hung upside down, their heads eighteen inches from the ground. Then their arms were tied at full length to pickets. Small fires built beneath their heads burned the men slowly and excruciatingly to death.

Every week or so from April through June, Cochise and his warriors attacked small parties of whites. The Apaches rode all over southeastern Arizona, their targets forming no pattern that American soldiers could fathom. When Cochise's men attacked an isolated ranch, they would smash doors and windows, break dishes and utensils, rip open mattresses, and strew food supplies about. They killed everyone they found, including small children, and stripped their bodies. Typically they pierced a corpse with hundreds of lance thrusts.

As Cochise's campaign waxed into early summer, his forces grew. The first raids may have been waged by as few as thirty warriors; by June he commanded almost a hundred. Agitated survivors swore that they had fought a much larger horde: it was not uncommon for whites to report that five hundred to six hundred warriors rode with Cochise. However, in the entire history of the Apache conflict, no war party ever numbered more than two hundred.

An Arizona pioneer reckoned the toll of Cochise's revenge at one hundred fifty deaths in the first sixty days. Looking back half a century later on the full twelve years of warfare between Cochise and the Arizona Territory, one of the state's first historians claimed, "Bascom's stupidity and ignorance probably cost five thousand American lives and the destruction of hundreds of thousands of dollars worth of property."

That death tally is undoubtedly too high. The historian's summation, moreover, epitomizes an old myth: that before Bascom performed his folly, Cochise had determined to live in harmony with the White Eyes. But Cochise's biographer, Edwin R. Sweeney, documents an escalating series of frays between the chief and American settlers beginning in late 1859, almost a year and a half before the Bascom affair. James Tevis, a gold miner turned Butterfield agent who left a flamboyant and unreliable account of early dealings with Apaches, claimed that he attended a large Indian council in 1859 at which a number of chiefs debated what to do about the Americans. Cochise, according to Tevis, advanced a "policy of extermination."

The myth of Cochise centers on his stoic gravity, painting him as a sage and statesman, "the Abraham Lincoln of Indians," in the sardonic phrase of a modern commentator. Tevis, who knew the chief well, called him "the biggest liar in the territory." That verdict is shot through with culture-bound preconceptions: Apaches valued honesty as a cardinal virtue, and Cochise's integrity was legendary among his people. Yet in the heat of his 1861 rampage, the chief was not above using deceit to kill White Eyes, as when he rode up to a pair of miners with his rifle laid sideways across his saddle, raised his hand in the peace sign, then shot a bullet through the body of one of the men without lifting his gun.

Tevis, who at different times was Cochise's confidant and prisoner, portrays him as a man of powerful authority and will, made freakish and unpredictable by a volcanic temper, a hypersensitivity to insult, and a childish vanity linked to an instinctive sadism. When Tevis, as station agent, kicked Cochise out of the building while the stagecoach unloaded, the chief flew into a rage and demanded a horseback duel at fifty yards—Tevis with his six-shooter against Cochise with only his lance. The chief proposed odds so one-sided against himself because he was inordinately proud of his deadly skill with the lance. In the event, Tevis backed down. To rub in the disgrace, Cochise forced the agent to care for his six-year-old son for a whole day—a woman's work, in Apache eyes, humiliating for a man to perform.

Later, as Cochise's bound captive, Tevis witnessed the torture death of two of his friends in the same manner as the chief had used in Doubtful Canyon: the men were hung head-down from trees and roasted over a slow fire. Cochise seemed then to relent, offering Tevis horse meat to cook and eat; but no sooner had the agent eaten than Cochise forced him to stand, his hands tied, upon the hot coals of the campfire until his boots burned through. Before Cochise could finish his cruel work, Tevis reported, a sympathetic Apache freed him in the night.

The summer of 1861 was alive with lightning storms, far more frequent and violent than normal. For the Apaches, lightning was the visible manifestation of powerful supernatural beings called the Thunder People. Once the Thunder People had hunted on behalf of the Apaches, supplying all the game they needed. Flashes of lightning were their arrows, of which the chipped flints found all over the homeland were remnants. But at some point in the past, Apaches had come to take the hunting for granted; to punish this ingratitude, the Thunder People had withdrawn their supernatural aid.

Lightning was thus a profoundly ambiguous phenomenon. To fend off the danger of being struck by it, Apaches used charms: when lightning split the sky, they wore sage in their hair, made sure nothing red was near their persons, refused to eat, and uttered a spitting noise to show respect. When lightning struck nearby, it left a pungent powder in the air (perhaps the ozone an electric discharge releases); if a person inhaled the powder, he could fall ill from lightning sickness.

Yet lightning could be a force for good, and Apaches prayed directly to it. A whole class of shamans specialized in lightning, and during the summer of 1861 they bent their efforts to driving the White Eyes, particularly the soldiers, out of the country. The main obstacle to their success was that the presence of iron tended to negate the shamans' power—and the soldiers possessed an abundance of iron. Only one lightning shaman had a power that could counteract the baleful influence of iron. A very old man, he died during the winter of 1861–1862. Because of his age, the death seemed natural and inevitable at the time. Only much later did the Apaches wonder if his passing had turned the course of events.

So the summer full of lightning seemed a wonderful portent. Soon, in fact, the White Eyes began to leave. Ranchers deserted their spreads; budding mining camps turned into ghost towns. As early as March, the Butterfield line had ceased its service. On July 10, all the soldiers left Fort Breckenridge (on the San Pedro River, north of Tucson) and marched to the only remaining fort in Arizona—Buchanan, from which Bascom had set out on his ill-starred mission in January. A mere eleven days later, the soldiers walked out of Buchanan, burned it to the ground, and headed east into New Mexico.

The Apaches rejoiced. Cochise's policy of extermination had succeeded brilliantly. The paradise of long ago, which the elders evoked around the campfire at night—a time when the people had ranged carefree across the land that Ussen, their god, had made for them— seemed at hand once more.

Though gratified, Cochise was not greatly surprised. A decade earlier, when his Chiricahuas had gone to war against the Mexican state of Sonora, a similar abandonment had ensued.

By late 1861, only two pockets of white settlement remained in Arizona: a negligible mining camp at Patagonia, and the town of Tucson, which had shrunk to a population of two hundred. Cochise laid plans to wipe these communities from the face of the earth.

Tucson at the time was perhaps the most lawless and violent town on American soil. "If the world were searched over," wrote a contemporary witness, "I suppose there could not be found so degraded a set of villains as then formed the principal society of Tucson. Every man went armed to the teeth, and street-fights and bloody affrays were of daily occurrence." Added another: "Innocent and unoffending men were shot down or bowie-knived merely for the pleasure of witnessing their death agonies." Cochise's bloody plans for Tucson might well be abetted by the internecine carnage of the town itself.

Through the fall of 1861, the Apaches luxuriated in their power and freedom. They continued to kill stragglers who had not made their escape from Arizona quickly enough. Then, in the winter, strange news arrived from the east. The word came from those sometime allies of the Chiricahua, the Mescalero Apaches, whose homeland lay on the slopes of Sierra Blanca, far east of the Rio Grande. Mescalero raiders pushing south into Texas had come across a band of White Eyes. Obviously these men were soldiers, yet they wore gray clothes instead of the familiar blue, and they carried a flag no Apache had ever seen before. Within weeks, it became apparent that the White Eyes had divided into two armies—gray and blue—and were fighting each other.

Cochise never fully absorbed the implications of this irony. A decade later, he still believed that his reign of terror had driven nearly all the White Eyes out of Arizona in 1861. His depredations had in fact taken their toll, but more significant in the depopulation of the territory were the mortar shells launched into the air on April 12, 1861, at Fort Sumter, so far east of Arizona that it lay beyond the compass of the Apache cosmos. It was the Civil War that had emptied Forts Breckenridge and Buchanan.

The notion that a people might subdivide into groups to kill each other was not alien to Apaches. Over the centuries, various Apache tribes had made war against one another, and they had all raided against the Navajos, a people ethnically close to themselves. Even within an Apache tribe, factions formed that burst into mutual violence.

Through early 1862, a western campaign of the Civil War zigzagged across New Mexico. Tucson was full of southern sympathizers; with the abandonment of the forts, Arizona declared itself a Confederate Territory, and was recognized as such by Jefferson Davis's congress in Richmond. In June, to squelch this rebellion, Union troops marched on Tucson from California.

Thus the Apaches had to give up their dream that the White Eyes had withdrawn for good from their homeland. Still, one could hope that the grays and blues might kill each other off in sufficient numbers to leave the survivors too weak to repel Apache attacks. Whatever it ultimately meant, the Civil War seemed at first a good thing for the Indians.

In May 1861, while Cochise was laying waste to homesteads in Arizona, another band of Apaches had begun to devastate the settlements of western New Mexico. These raiders were close cousins to Cochise's men, though they preserved a distinct cultural identity. Anglos named them the Warm Springs Apaches. Some ethnographers would eventually lump them with Cochise's people, calling them all Chiricahuas; others would distinguish between the Warm Springs and the "true" Chiricahuas. The sacred homeland of the New Mexico band encircled a hot spring near the head of the Cañada Alamosa, a small western tributary of the Rio Grande. The Warm Springs Apaches called themselves Chihenne, or "Red Paint People," after the ruddy clay they found near the spring, with which they daubed their faces. Cochise's Chiricahuas called themselves Chokonen—a name with no ready translation.

The chief of the Chihenne was Mangas Coloradas, now about seventy years old, or some twenty years Cochise's senior. Among his people, he was a giant—six feet four inches tall, weighing some 250 pounds. If by 1861 Cochise was the preeminent Apache leader, so Mangas had been in the 1840s. The earliest white explorers who encountered him described him in terms of awe. "As noble a specimen of the Indian race as I had ever seen," concluded one; "the poetic ideal of a chieftain," claimed another; "the greatest and most talented Apache Indian of the nineteenth century," wrote a third.

Uniquely in the known history of the Apaches, Mangas had sought to confederate the separate tribes by allying the Chihenne with the Mescalero, White Mountain, and Coyotero Apaches, and perhaps even with the Navajos. To cement an affiliation with the Chokonen, he had married his daughter to Cochise. As well as being a master of intertribal diplomacy, Mangas was a military tactician of genius. He was also —as an Apache chief had to be to retain the following of his warriors —a champion in one-to-one combat. His relentless torment of white settlers enhanced his reputation for ruthlessness. The same explorer who called Mangas the greatest Apache of the century also wrote, "The life of Mangas Colorad[as], if it could be ascertained, would be a tissue of the most extensive and afflicting revelations, the most atrocious cruelties, the most vindictive revenges, and widespread injuries ever perpetrated by an American Indian."

Two events in particular had set Mangas against the Americans. The first, which occurred in 1837, when what is now New Mexico and Arizona still belonged to Mexico, was the work of a scalphunter and entrepreneur from Kentucky named John Johnson, "as black-hearted a murderer as ever disgraced the frontier," in the words of one scholar. Johnson was motivated, not by any injury he had received at Apache hands, but either by a Mexican promise of booty in recovered livestock or by the bounty newly offered by the state of Chihuahua: 100 pesos for the scalp of an Apache man, 50 for a woman's, 25 for a child's.

At the head of a party of Missouri fortunehunters, Johnson lured a group of Apaches in to trade near the copper mines at Santa Rita del Cobre. A sack of pinole, or cornmeal, was laid on the ground, and the Apaches were invited to help themselves. As they did so, a concealed cannon filled with scrap metal fired point-blank into their midst, while the Missourians assisted the slaughter with their rifles. At least twenty Apaches were killed, including an important chief.

Not only was Mangas a relative of the chief, but, according to latter-day Apaches, he was present at the Santa Rita debacle. Having hesitated, mistrustful, at the edge of the crowd gathering up the pinole, he fled the massacre on foot, carrying the infant son of the chief in his arms.

The second event, clinching Mangas's antipathy to whites, occurred fourteen years later, in 1851. At Pinos Altos, only a short distance from Santa Rita (both localities lie within a few miles of present-day Silver City, New Mexico), Anglos had discovered gold. Apaches were bewildered and dismayed by the passion with which Spaniards, Mexicans, and Americans alike grubbed in the ground for the yellow metal. One chief told his people, "The White Eyes are superstitious about gold. Their lust for it is insatiable. They lie, steal, kill, die, for it."

To the Apaches, this obsession was unfathomable. Gold was too soft to be useful: you could make neither bullets nor arrowheads from it. The substance was, moreover, sacred to Ussen, a symbol of the sun. The same chief explicated the taboo against mining: "We are permitted to pick it up from the surface of Mother Earth, but not to grovel in her body for it. To do so is to incur the wrath of Ussen. The Mountain Gods dance and shake their mighty shoulders, destroying everything near."

Thus the influx at Pinos Altos, which lay near the heartland of the Chihenne, alarmed Mangas: not only were the miners a threat to Apache sovereignty but their subterranean toil might unleash earthquakes. The old chief took it upon himself to persuade the white men to look elsewhere for gold. One by one he sought out the leading

miners, told them of vast deposits he knew of in Mexico, and offered
to guide them there. Instead of trusting Mangas, the prospectors took
it into their heads that he hoped to lure them off singly and kill them.
On his next visit, they seized him, tied him to a tree, and beat him
savagely with an ox whip while they filled his ears with taunts. "It was
the greatest insult that could be inflicted even on an ordinary Indian,"
wrote one historian. "And Mang[a]s Colorad[as] was a great chief."

In May 1861, Mangas focused his retributive fury on the Pinos Altos
area, all but laying siege to the gold camp. In July, Cochise joined him.
The two chiefs and their warriors made a base camp southeast of
Pinos Altos, on the slopes of Cooke's Peak, where a vital spring lay.
Here they ambushed and slew about one hundred passing soldiers
and miners. The Apaches ruled the country; but an all-out attack on
Pinos Altos led by Mangas failed to dislodge the stubborn miners.

Even as Mangas and Cochise stood on the verge of driving the last
White Eyes from their land, it was becoming apparent that the war
between blues and grays would have severe consequences for the
Apaches. Not only were they caught, as it were, in the crossfire, but
the leaders of both armies, their hearts hardened by warfare, adopted
policies toward the Indians that were more stringent than any yet
proposed by American officers.

By June 1862, the troops from California had occupied Tucson and
reestablished Forts Breckenridge and Buchanan. In order to come to
the aid of the beleaguered Union general in New Mexico, they prepared for a long march eastward along the former route of the Butterfield line. By feigning peace with a credulous and talkative lieutenant
leading an advance scout along the route, Cochise learned the soldiers' plans in detail.

The Chiricahua chief plotted his boldest strike yet against the Americans. To ensure victory, he enlisted the aid not only of Mangas Coloradas but of several other of the fiercest Apache leaders. Among them
was the young Geronimo, who, as a Bedonkohe Apache, was neither
a Chokonen nor a Chihenne. Nonetheless he had led war parties for
both Cochise and Mangas, and often acted as liaison between the two
great chiefs.

In mid-July, a command of sixty-eight soldiers, followed by a supply
train of forty-five men leading 242 head of livestock, left their camp
east of Tucson and headed for Apache Pass, as the Anglos had named
the gap in the Dos Cabezas Mountains where Bascom had confronted

Cochise seventeen months before. Cochise and Mangas watched them come. The Apaches knew that as the soldiers crossed forty miles of desert under the summer sun, they would not find a single drop of water. By the time they reached Apache Pass, they would be desperately thirsty.

Cochise and Mangas let the troops march unimpeded all the way to the abandoned Butterfield station, only six hundred yards short of the spring. Then from scores of stances hidden behind stony battlements piled up on the neighboring hills, the Apaches opened fire. The attacking force, which numbered close to two hundred, may have been the largest single war party ever assembled by the Chiricahuas. (The captain in charge of the supply train later swore that seven hundred Indians had taken part in the fight.)

On the brink of succumbing to a massacre, the Americans managed to deploy a pair of weapons with which the Apaches were unfamiliar. These were twelve-pounder cannons, howitzers mounted on wheels, which launched shells that exploded on impact. In the chaos of the gunfire, it took the soldiers a while to position the howitzers and find the range of the Indian breastworks. Once they did, the shells began to do their work, and the Apaches were forced to flee.

The battle lasted three hours. Two soldiers were killed, with two more wounded. The American commander estimated nine Indians dead. The captain in charge of the supply train claimed that an Apache later told him that sixty-three Indians had lost their lives in the fray— a preposterous number. In the twentieth century, Apache descendants swore that not a single warrior had died at Apache Pass.

It was the first true battle between American soldiers and Apaches. In prospect, it had seemed to Cochise and Mangas a sure triumph; thanks to the howitzers, it turned into a demoralizing failure. Almost a century later, the son of a chief who had fought there said, "After they turned cannon loose on us at Apache Pass, my people were certain that they were doomed."

As soon as the battle was over, the American commander sent six men back to warn the oncoming supply train. They were intercepted by a mounted party led by Mangas. A private leading a played-out horse was separated from his companions. The Apaches shot his horse; the private lay behind its body, watched the circling Apaches fire at him, and anticipated his death. But he had a good rifle, a breech-loading carbine, and he determined "to kill at least one Apache" before they killed him. He singled out a tall, prominent-looking man and fired what he later confessed was a lucky shot. The carbine ball entered the chest of Mangas Coloradas, severely wounding him. His warriors rushed to his aid, leaving the private to his miraculous escape.

The Apaches carried Mangas all the way to the town of Janos, in Mexico—a distance of 120 miles in a straight line. At Janos resided an Anglo doctor in whose talents, uncharacteristically, the Apaches had great faith. They handed Mangas, who was near death, over to the doctor, and told him that if he failed to save the chief, they would kill everyone in the village. Mangas recovered.

Having seized the spring at Apache Pass, the Union soldiers never again relinquished it. By July they had erected a fortress on the hill overlooking the spring from the south. Fort Bowie would become the headquarters of the American campaign against the Chiricahuas.

The Civil War continued to flare across New Mexico. At first, the Confederates got the better of the struggle. In early 1862, Jefferson Davis appointed John Robert Baylor governor of the new territory. A balding, fanatical Kentuckian, Baylor had forged his ideas about Indians while fighting Comanches in Texas. The Apaches, he insisted, were "cursed pests." Within weeks of taking office, he issued orders as to how to deal with them:

> You will . . . use all means to persuade the Apaches or any tribe to come in for the purpose of making peace, and when you get them together kill all the grown Indians and take the children prisoners and sell them to defray the expense of killing the Indians. Buy whiskey and such other goods as may be necessary for the Indians. . . . Leave nothing undone to insure success, and have a sufficient number of men around to allow no Indian to escape.

To his credit, Jefferson Davis eventually rescinded Baylor's orders and removed the man from the governorship.

Baylor's Union counterpart was the equally fanatical James Henry Carleton, who had led the troops from California. In the words of a modern historian, Carleton was "a devout Christian, a good family man, and a gentleman" who "had become obsessed with a psychopathic hatred of Apaches." By the fall of 1862, Carleton was ensconced at Fort Stanton, near present-day Ruidoso, New Mexico, in the heart of the Mescalero Apache country. It was thus against Mescaleros, rather than Chiricahuas, that Carleton crystallized his Indian policy: "All Indian men of that tribe are to be killed whenever and wherever you can find them. The women and children will not be harmed, but you will take them prisoners." Unlike Jefferson Davis, Abraham Lincoln never canceled Carleton's policy or fired him because of it.

Carleton's summary command was addressed to the colonel in charge of his Indian war, Kit Carson. Though privately appalled by the policy, Carson was instrumental in bringing about Carleton's grandest and most infamous "solution"—the concentration camp at Bosque Redondo, on the plains of eastern New Mexico. To this open-air prison Carson drove the Navajos on their Long Walk; there they sickened and died of smallpox in close proximity to their ancient enemies and fellow captives, the Mescaleros.

Thus within three months after the battle at Apache Pass, both Union and Confederate governments had adopted official policies of extermination. The Chiricahuas took note.

After his recovery, Mangas returned to the vicinity of Pinos Altos, from which the miners had finally fled. In January 1863, a party of gold seekers led by an oldtime mountain man named James Reddeford Walker arrived in the area. Their journey had been under such constant surveillance by the Apaches that the prospectors had developed a hair-trigger agitation. Walker determined to seize an important Apache as hostage against attacks as the party pushed farther west. The giant chief of the Chihenne was an obvious candidate.

According to Geronimo, who told the story half a century later, the prospectors made a preliminary feeler, telling Mangas that they would give his people blankets, flour, and beef in exchange for peace. Mangas promised to return with an answer in two weeks.

None of the other Apache leaders trusted the White Eyes' offer. All of them, including Geronimo, pleaded with Mangas not to go back to Pinos Altos.

From the distance of more than a century, it is hard to comprehend the old chief's motives in January 1863. Apaches have carried down the memory that after his wounding at Apache Pass, Mangas had fallen into a mood of depression and decreased energy. Yet for all the wrongs he had suffered from Americans, he still seemed to believe it was possible to live at peace with them.

There had always been, perhaps, a streak of the fatalistic, even of the self-destructive, in Mangas's character. And the country near Pinos Altos, for which he cared so dearly, seemed to act as a magnet for that flaw. Why else, at around the age of sixty, had he allowed the miners to seize, bind, and whip him there twelve years before? Perhaps there was something of King Lear in him, weary of life and responsibility, longing to surrender his throne. Perhaps something of Socrates, delivering himself up to his enemies and submitting to their punishment.

In any event, with but three or four warriors, Mangas returned to Pinos Altos to parley. Only one reliable account exists of what transpired there, that of a somewhat disaffected member of the Walker party. On the morning of January 18, the prospectors hoisted a white flag. Mangas and his men drew cautiously near. Because the negotiations took place in broken Spanish, it is likely that they embodied serious misunderstandings. "After a long and tedious indulgence of prudential precautions by both parties," Mangas dropped his guard and drew closer. Suddenly the prospectors raised their rifles, pointed them at the chief, and indicated he was their prisoner.

Mangas was told that his warriors were free to go, and that if the Apaches left the gold seekers alone during the next "ten moons," the chief himself would be returned in safety. "He talked to his people in gutturals toward the last," observed the Walker party witness, "so that we could not understand him, and his face wore an air of care and perplexity."

Whether Walker was sincere in the terms he proffered for Mangas's release quickly became moot. Under Brigadier General Joseph West, a detachment of Carleton's California column was camped nearby. West immediately took charge of the valuable captive.

> The General walked out to where Mang[a]s was in custody to see him, and looked like a pigmy beside the old Chief, who also towered above everybody about him in stature. He looked careworn and refused to talk and evidently felt that he had made a great mistake in trusting the pale face on this occasion.

West was aware, of course, of the Indian policy Carleton had espoused five months earlier. He let his soldiers know what he expected of them.

On a dark and bitterly cold night, guarded by a pair of soldiers, Mangas lay on the ground beside a campfire, wrapped in an inadequate blanket. The witness, who was on sentry duty, saw what happened next. The soldiers heated their bayonets in the fire, then burned the chief's legs and feet with them. Mangas rose on his left elbow and bellowed in Spanish that he was no child for them to play with. In response, the guards lowered their rifles and fired six shots into the chief's body. Mangas died at once.

In the morning, a soldier used the cook's butcher knife to scalp the chief: wrapping the long hair around his trophy, he put the scalp in his pocket. At noon, Mangas's body was thrown into a gully and perfunctorily buried. A few nights later, several soldiers disinterred the chief. They cut off his head and boiled it in a pot. The skull was sent to an eastern phrenologist, who measured it and reported the cranial capacity larger even than Daniel Webster's.

West subsequently reported that Mangas had been shot trying to escape.

The Apaches who had warned Mangas not to return to Pinos Altos waited and waited, but no word came to them. Perhaps the Walker party slew Mangas's companions as well: so the Apaches came to believe. Eventually, from other sources, vague news of Mangas's martyrdom filtered back to his people. Somehow the news contained the information that the soldiers had boiled Mangas's severed head in a big black pot.

This revelation deeply stirred the Chiricahua sense of horror. Apaches believed that a person traveled in the afterlife in the physical state in which he had died. The Chiricahuas pictured their great chief wandering headless through eternity.

Many years later, Geronimo would say that the betrayal and murder of Mangas Coloradas was "perhaps the greatest wrong ever done to the Indians."

Three

■

Torture

*I*n the 1970s, an ethnohistorian who surveyed Chiricahua Apaches living in New Mexico and Oklahoma discovered a remarkable fact: many more of them knew about Bascom's perfidy to Cochise and the soldiers' murder of Mangas Coloradas than remembered Pearl Harbor. This, even though the betrayals of the two great chiefs had taken place more than a century in the past, during which span Chiricahua culture had gone through a wrenching upheaval.

The impact of Mangas's murder and beheading was particularly profound. Three generations afterward, reliable Chiricahua spokesmen swore that mutilation of white victims by Apaches had been rare before Mangas's martyrdom: it was only in response to the mutilation of their own chief's body that Apaches began to butcher white corpses. The spokesmen maintained further that Apaches never tortured their victims—that mutilation was performed only after death.

To what extent the Apaches practiced torture and mutilation remains a vexing and inflammatory question, one that scholars have by and large ducked. Yet it is crucial to any understanding of the hatred between whites and Indians in the Southwest.

The testimony of many contemporary white settlers is unreliable. Nineteenth-century Arizonans were convinced, for instance, that

Apaches scalped all their victims. Yet in fact scalping was performed infrequently by Apaches, and only as a measure of the bitterest revenge: "There was no greater punishment for one's enemies." On the other hand, Mexicans and mountain men scalped Apaches wholesale after 1835, trading their grisly trophies for the bounties offered by the states of Chihuahua and Sonora. Over the decades, Apaches were far more often the victims than the perpetrators of scalping.

Yet the insistence by latter-day Apaches that torture was not performed and that mutilation of the dead largely postdated Mangas's betrayal is likewise unreliable. There are simply too many firsthand accounts to the contrary.

Ignaz Pfefferkorn, an eighteenth-century German traveler who published a book about Sonora, described Apache life with an accuracy it would take twentieth-century anthropology to confirm. In 1795 he wrote,

> In the fury of the onslaught they kill everyone in sight, and their cruelty is so great that they will inflict wound after wound, just as though their lust for blood were insatiable. I have buried victims whose bodies were unrecognizable, so gashed were they from head to foot by lances.

Another eighteenth-century observer of Sonora, a Jesuit whose name has not come down to us, wrote in 1763 of the "savagely cruel" Apaches: "An innocent [Mexican] child five or six years old, that I found, told me that his father had been killed, leaving him tied to a tree."

Samuel Woodworth Cozzens, an American adventurer who spent much time with Apaches from 1858 to 1860 (three to five years before Mangas's death) described at second hand an Apache "sacrifice" of a young Mexican girl that had taken place two years before his visit:

> After fattening her for several months, keeping her very quiet, and in ignorance of her fate, they brought her, on the morning when the sacrifice was to be made, to the place of torture. Here, placing her between two trees, they suspended her by ropes tied around her wrists, so that her feet, which were firmly fastened together, were about three feet from the ground. A fire was then kindled beneath her, and as the flames reached her flesh, scream after scream issued

from the lips of the poor victim. One after another of these *brave* Apaches plucked a burning brand from the fire and applied it to the quivering flesh of the wretched girl, till finally death released her from her terrible sufferings. The body was then hacked to pieces with sharp stones, the pieces burned upon the fire, and the ashes scattered to the winds.

This sounds like the fevered fantasy of a Victorian romance writer. Yet Morris Opler, the twentieth-century ethnographer of the Chiricahua, was told by an Apache about the traditional treatment of suspected witches:

They find out from the shaman if a person is a witch. Then they force him to tell if he did it. . . . They string the witch up by the wrists so his feet are off the ground. . . . I have heard people, when strung up to a tree by their hands, admit that they were witches. They never let them go if they prove it on them. Then a fire is built under the witch, and he is burned. Burning destroys a witch's power for future harm, but what he has already accomplished is not undone. Witches do not burn up quickly; they keep on living a long time.

Cozzens, who had read no Apache ethnography, reported that the burning of the Mexican girl was "to propitiate the Great Spirit, whose wrath had manifested itself by visiting upon them the small-pox."

From the Apache point of view, what seemed to whites the gruesome torment of innocent victims was a proper and necessary procedure for dealing with evil loosed in the world. There was nothing sadistic about burning a witch. As Opler's informant indicated, Apache belief in the reality of witchcraft was so pervasive that, strung from a tree, the accused sometimes confessed—not to solicit pity, for in doing so he sealed his doom. The same thing happened in seventeenth-century Salem, Massachusetts.

Yet the prevalence of torture and mutilation cannot be laid entirely to a vigilance against witches. The anthology of first- and secondhand accounts of Apaches' brutal treatment of white captives reads like a pastiche of all the "savage redskin" scenes from a generation of grade-B Western movies. As James Tevis saw firsthand, Cochise sometimes hung men head down over slow fires and burned them to death. He also tied them spread-eagled to wagon wheels before burning. And he liked, we are told, to drag naked victims across the ground behind a horse.

Other Apaches, according to whites who found the dead bodies, cut the hearts out of their victims (some insisted the Indians cooked and ate the hearts); staked them out to ant hills with their mouths propped open with sharp skewers; tied them to cactuses with wet rawhide that contracted as it dried in the sun; tied them naked to trees and shot arrows into them; slit their skin in strips from neck to heel; cut their corpses to pieces; cut off limbs one by one until the victim bled to death; smashed heads and testicles with rocks. Wrote one Arizona pioneer who had buried his share of settlers, "A favorite mode of mutilating a dead body is to ornament the mouth with the emasculated priapus." Sometimes the details were purported to come straight from the Apache who had performed the torture: "Old Eskimi[n]zin says he buried an American alive in the ground once and let the ants eat his head off."

Apaches often turned captives over to their women, who were reputed to be even crueler torturers than the men. One pioneer maintained that survivors of an 1880 Apache attack "saw squaws stick pieces of wood into [the victims'] bowels while alive, then crush their heads to a jelly with rocks."

Blinkered by their ethnocentrism, white observers struggled to explain torture in Apache terms. "Their savage and bloodthirsty natures experience a real pleasure in tormenting their victim," wrote John C. Cremony, a scout and soldier who knew Apaches well. "Every expression of pain or agony is hailed with delight, and the one whose inventive genius can devise the most excruciating kind of death is deemed worthy of honor."

More than a century later, can we account for Apache torture any more convincingly than Cremony did? The very effort may be naive. During the last several thousand years torture has been far more universal, more "normal," than we readily acknowledge. One survey of the phenomenon concludes, "Every nation has practised torture at one time or another in its history."

It bears keeping in mind that although mutilation did not begin with Mangas's death, it may have grown more vicious in response to decades or even centuries of Apache mistreatment at the hands of Spanish and Mexican intruders. The Apaches' enemies practiced their own kind of torture. Apache children growing up in the 1870s absorbed the lore of Hispanic atrocities, such as the fate of a Chiricahua named Chinchi, whom Mexicans dragged behind a horse through fields of prickly pear until he died.

Anglo-Americans too came to be known for their ruthless treatment of Apache victims. American soldiers not only scalped Indians, they cut off their ears and genitals. One of their nastier pastimes was to turn body parts into souvenirs: bridles, for instance, braided out of scalped Apache hair, and decorated, according to an early settler, "with teeth knocked from the jaws of living women." In his first year of army duty in Arizona, John Gregory Bourke, who would become as strong a champion of Apache rights as any American who ever fought against them, was given as a keepsake the scalp and ears of a dead Apache warrior. With the thoughtless bravado of a twenty-four-year-old lieutenant fresh out of West Point, Bourke framed the ears and hung them on his wall and turned the scalp into a lamp mat. One day a friend came into Bourke's room, saw the trophies, and reacted with horror. Instantly Bourke grasped "how brutal and inhuman I had been," and had the ears and scalp buried.

White men killed Apache babies, and even justified the killing under the eugenic aphorism, "Nits make lice." In 1864 a group of Arizonans decided to hunt Apaches on the Verde River. Among their number was an escaped convict known as Sugarfoot Jack. After the party burned to the ground a hastily abandoned village of wickiups—the shelters made of brush in which the Apache lived—this desperado found an infant who had been left behind. He tossed the baby onto the fire, then stood and watched it burn. A little later he found another small child. According to a witness, Sugarfoot dandled the baby on his knee, tickled it under the chin, then pulled out his gun and shot it in the head, "bespatter[ing] his clothes and face with infant brains."

Throughout the centuries of their contact with Spaniards and Mexicans, captured Apaches—especially women—were often sold into slavery far to the south. To be imprisoned, locked in a small room behind bars, seemed to Apaches a torture every bit as heinous as Cochise's crueler mortifications may have struck Americans. To be forcibly carried into exile, out of the land that Ussen had made for the Apaches, was comparably odious. Among the most powerfully felt stories handed down from one generation to the next were those of brave women who escaped slavery and made their way on foot, navigating by instinct and memory, hundreds of miles back to the homeland.

The horror white men felt when they came upon bodies mutilated by the Apaches was stirred by the bald evidence of pain—prolonged, acute, ingeniously devised—employed only to shunt the victim toward his inevitable death. The Apache attitude toward pain was altogether different from the American's. Pain was a fact of life, and to greet it stoically and endure it silently was the mark of character. From early childhood, boys were schooled in pain. They would be taught, for instance, to place dry sage on their skins, set fire to it, and let it burn to ashes without flinching. In winter, they had to go out at dawn and roll a ball of snow with bare hands until called away from the task. In foot races, laggards were lashed by adults.

Along with an incomparable training in endurance and athletic skills, this tutorship in pain turned a boy into a potential warrior. At an early age, boys were paired off for hand-to-hand fights that ended only with the drawing of blood. In teams of four, they shot stones with slingshots at each other. Later they made small bows and arrows with sharp wooden points and played at warfare. (One of Opler's informants recalled a playmate whose eye had been put out in such combat practice.)

As well as enduring pain, boys were taught to inflict it. They were given captured birds and animals to torture, and their inventiveness was rewarded. The emphasis on torture in Apache life remains shocking to modern sensibilities, despite our latter-day faith in cultural relativism. But from the Indian point of view, an ordeal by pain was part of the order of things.

Revenge, for an Apache, was not a lawless rampage of individual will, but a sacred social duty. Nor was it necessary to kill the particular enemy who had caused the harm: others of his people would do. "When a brave warrior is killed," one Chiricahua told Opler, "the men go out for about three Mexicans. They bring them back for the women to kill in revenge." Mutilation intensified the punishment, for just as Mangas must walk eternally headless, a dismembered enemy would travel through the afterlife in that condition.

What we call torture had for Apaches something of the character of a sacramental act. It was a test of the courage of an enemy warrior. Apaches appreciated great bravery in a hopeless cause, and a white man who fought vigorously to the end was sometimes accorded a special honor: his slayers skinned his right hand and his stirrup foot in testimony to his prowess.

Had things always been thus, back beyond the sixteenth century in that uncertain time when an Athapaskan people, with dogs but no horses, flint arrowheads but no iron, had first wandered into the Southwest from their ancestral domain in the Canadian north? Or had the Apaches, the most adaptable of tribes, learned their deadly severities from the descendants of those masters of cruelty, the Spanish conquistadors? The question, in all likelihood, will never be answered.

Four

■

The Unknown Cochise

*W*ith the demise of Mangas Coloradas in 1863, Cochise stood unrivaled among the leaders of the Chiricahua—not only in Apache hearts, but in the grudging recognition of white settlers. Wrote a pioneer who served as U. S. Representative for the Arizona Territory, "Cochise was undoubtedly the bravest and most skillful Apache leader that the Americans ever had to cope with." A brigadier general said the same thing in quite different words when he called Cochise "the very worst Indian on the continent."

Cochise's biographer, Edwin R. Sweeney, summarizes the chief's military achievement:

For twelve years he successfully eluded troops and volunteers from four states and two countries [i. e., the territories of Arizona and New Mexico, which were formally separated in 1863, and the states of Sonora and Chihuahua]. His allies were his ancestral mountains and the territorial boundary line, which he used adroitly, leapfrogging back and forth when heavily pressured. . . . [He] was involved in countless raids, skirmishes, and fights; was surprised and attacked in his camp on occasion; was wounded several times; and allegedly was killed on a dozen occasions, give or take a few. Yet he survived, which was a testament to his stubborn persistence in the face of white subjugation. . . . On the whole, he seems to have performed better than any other Apache.

Like all great Indian chiefs, Cochise led his men into battle, refusing to shy from personal combat. The Chiricahuas felt only contempt for American generals who led from the rear. Indeed, Cochise fought with an abandon so reckless that whites might have called it arrogance; it seemed to stem from a conviction that his skills made him invulnerable. The duel he proposed against James Tevis—lance against six-shooter—is one instance. After a battle between American troops and Chiricahuas, a scout who had got off many shots at the chief marveled at his riding technique: the shots missed because Cochise would slip to the side of his horse, hang on its neck, and use its body as a shield.

Cochise's sanctuary was the Dragoon Mountains in southeastern Arizona. A range of low peaks (the highest is 7,519 feet), the Dragoons stand in severe isolation, surrounded on all sides by sagebrush desert and alkali flats. For this reason, the mountains made a perfect stronghold: no enemy could camouflage its approach, since the clouds of dust its horses raised could be seen forty miles away from Dragoon summits. Though small in extent, the range is warped into a labyrinth by thousands of weathered granite spires, cliffs, and crevices, making it an ideal place for hiding and ambush. Army officers sometimes knew that Cochise was camped in the Dragoon Range; because of its natural defenses, they never dared attack him there.

The stronghold's springs seeped reliably year-round. The slopes were covered with piñon pines, mesquite, alligator juniper, catclaw mimosa, lechuguilla, mountain and banana yucca, and scrub oak. Besides the small game they hunted, the Apaches ate piñon nuts, juniper berries, the fruit of the banana yucca, acorns, and mesquite beans. As he raided, Cochise ranged far south into Mexico or east to the Rio Grande, but he tended to circle back to the Dragoons, as if there, and only there, he might replenish the power that made him invincible against the White Eyes.

By the end of 1862, the last Confederate forces had been routed and driven out of New Mexico. Yet as the Civil War wound on in the East, the Union government formed no coherent policy toward the Apaches. As early as 1860, a far-sighted Indian agent had proposed a reservation for both the Chiricahua and Mescalero Apaches, but his idea was ignored. Neither President Lincoln in Washington nor the territorial governments of Arizona and New Mexico seemed capable of grappling with the Apache question.

In this vacuum, it was Carleton's policy of extermination that held sway. With no more Confederates to fight, in 1863 the general turned his army loose on the Apaches. In his fanatic optimism, Carleton expected to drive the Chiricahuas for good into Mexico, and he predicted publicly that he would complete the conquest by Christmas.

After all, a single scorched-earth mission under Kit Carson had defeated virtually the whole Navajo nation and sent a demoralized people trudging toward their concentration camp at Bosque Redondo in eastern New Mexico, far from their homeland. Navajos died by the hundreds on the Long Walk. Even more easily, Carleton had forced the Mescalero Apaches to give up their own homeland and to join the Navajos farming the miserable soil at the Bosque. The water of the Pecos River was too alkaline to drink safely; the land was so deforested that women had to walk twelve miles for firewood. But by 1864, with more than nine thousand Mescaleros and Navajos in custody, Carleton could delude himself that he had all but solved "the Indian problem."

The general underestimated the Apache spirit. Outnumbered at least nine to one by their Navajo enemies, cheated by crooked agents and suppliers, starving on inadequate rations, the Mescalero welded an underground resistance. After the summer of 1865, when the crops failed for the second year in a row at Bosque Redondo, they decided to take action. As C. L. Sonnichsen, historian of the Mescalero, describes it,

> In secret councils the plan evolved. No white man knew anything about it, and no white man knows anything about it yet. Just before winter set in, in 1865, they were ready. On the third of November, during the night, every Apache who could travel arose and vanished. In the morning only the sick and crippled were left, and within a few days they vanished too.

Carleton's pride was mortified. The Mescalero were never again driven back to the Pecos. Three years later, recognizing the failure of the prison camp, officials dismantled Bosque Redondo, and the Navajos were allowed to return to their homeland.

If Carleton misjudged the Mescalero will, he utterly failed to appre-

ciate the tenacity of the Chiricahuas. His extermination policy back-
fired in another way as well, for it forced peaceful Indians to go on
the warpath along with the "hostiles."

Vigorously though Carleton pursued the Apaches, his tactics were
not harsh enough for the white settlers of Arizona, who began to form
their own companies of mercenaries and volunteers to hunt redskins.
The Yavapai Rangers were a representative group: in 1866 they trailed
a peaceful party of Apaches near Prescott, attacked them in their camp,
and killed twenty-three; only "a dusky maiden of some twenty summers" escaped. In the same year the cold-blooded murderer of a
Walapais chief was acquitted by a grand jury "with a unanimous vote
of thanks."

One of the most effective of these volunteers was a rancher named
King Woolsey, who hated all Apaches. An early traveler in Arizona
happened to come across some of Woolsey's handiwork: after killing
an Apache chief, the rancher had hanged him from a tree as an ex-
emplum for his tribe.

> The body was dried and shrunken, and of a parchment color. One
> of the feet and both hands had been cut off or torn away by coyotes.
> The head was thrown back, and the eye-sockets glared in the sun. A
> horrible grin seemed fixed upon the mouth, and when a slight
> breeze gave motion to the body I was startled by the ghastly but life-
> like expression of the face as it slowly turned and stared at the bright
> blue sky.

Another of Woolsey's feats came to be jauntily alluded to as the Pinole
Treaty. Mixing strychnine with pinole (corn meal mixed with flour
from mesquite beans), he offered the stuff to some peaceful Apaches,
who ate it. At least a dozen of them died.

In 1864, Woolsey led a group of volunteers and Maricopa Indians,
traditional enemies of the Apache, on a scout for stolen cattle. After
two weeks the gang found a large encampment of Apaches who may
or may not have been responsible for the missing livestock. Woolsey
feigned peace and lured the leading men into a parley, offering them
a blanket to sit on. Realizing that though the Indians spoke some
Spanish, they did not understand English, Woolsey brazenly told each
of his men which Apache to shoot when he gave the signal. Raising
his hat with one hand, he unleashed a massacre. Perhaps twenty-four
Apaches were killed, with the loss of only one white man.

For such deeds, Woolsey was acclaimed a hero. After his death in 1879, a historian saluted the rancher as "the most notable, the most enterprising and the most courageous of all the great host of trailblazers who first penetrated Arizona."

The situation worsened with the end of the Civil War. Pernicious though Carleton's campaign of extermination was, the conduct of U. S. Army troops in pursuit of Indians was generally more reasonable than that of volunteers such as Woolsey: there was more of an effort to distinguish between "good" and "bad" Apaches, to punish the actual perpetrators of a raid rather than the handiest scapegoats.

After the war, however, the army steadily shrank in size. At the time of Lee's surrender at Appomattox in April 1865, the Union army numbered 200,000 men. In 1866, Congress reduced the standing army for the reunited country to 54,302; by 1874, it had dwindled to 25,000. Gear and weapons grew obsolete, but went unreplaced by more modern matériel. With the end of conscription, the army became entirely dependent on volunteers; in the chaotic years of Reconstruction, the ranks were swelled with criminals, vagabonds, and men fleeing dubious pasts. Desertion was so common that in 1891, the Secretary of War gloomily concluded that fully one-third of all army men had "gone over the hill" in the past twenty-four years.

Meanwhile, the white population of Arizona grew fast. The U. S. census for 1860 listed only 2,421 citizens; by 1870, the number was 9,658, which included 4,348 of Mexican origin and about 2,100 troops. The number of Apaches during the same years is much harder to ascertain. The best estimates place the combined population of the various tribes at between 6,000 and 8,000. In 1864, there were thus more Navajos at Bosque Redondo than there were Apaches in the world. One traveler who tried to enumerate each Apache tribe in 1867 came up with a total figure of only 3,625; concluding that Apaches were a dying race, he mused, "Already the total population, as far as it can be estimated, is so small as to appear at first to be beneath our notice."

Of the six thousand to eight thousand Apaches, somewhere between one thousand and two thousand were Chiricahuas, including both Cochise's Chokonen and the Chihenne who had been led by Mangas. Among the latter, after Mangas's death, a number of chiefs and leaders rose to prominence. The most important was Victorio. Tall, immensely strong, with an adamantine gaze, he was remembered seventy years later by a Chihenne who had been a small boy in the chief's prime as "the most nearly perfect human being I have ever seen."

Eventually Victorio would become a paragon among Chiricahua leaders. His biographer, Dan L. Thrapp, calls him "America's greatest guerrilla fighter." In his last, desperate campaign, he would become the Apaches' most heroic martyr.

But in 1865, Victorio sought an end to the war against the White Eyes. At the end of March, he led his people to a rendezvous with one of Carleton's lieutenants on the Mimbres River in southwestern New Mexico. Well acquainted with the Mescaleros' misery at Bosque Redondo, he refused to take the Chihenne to that prison on the Pecos. If his people would be allowed to live on the Gila or Mimbres Rivers, however, he would pledge their peace.

The lieutenant wanted to know about Cochise. Victorio admitted that he had talked with his Chokonen peer, had tried to persuade him that peace was possible. But Cochise "does not wish it," said Victorio, "and will never be friendly more."

In the inflexible mind of General Carleton, the Chihenne must accept the Bosque or continue to face extermination. Nothing came of Victorio's overture, and his people continued to roam across their heartland, outside the orbit of American law and order.

Before 1861, a handful of white men had gained the acquaintance of Cochise. Some, like James Tevis, could even claim a rudimentary grasp of the chief's character. But Bascom's seminal blunder had put an end to such familiarity. Cochise became a furious enigma. To cross paths with him, for a white man, was to run a good chance of getting killed. In the absence of more intimate testimony, whites were left to divine his motives from the bodies they found decomposing on the prairie. So the Cochise legend grew. It was his name, his faceless terror, that jolted settlers awake out of bad dreams in the Arizona night.

As if to shape the terror by quantifying it, chroniclers tried to reckon Cochise's toll. One suggestible traveler swore that in a single four-mile stretch of Cooke's Canyon, New Mexico—the stretch where Cochise and Mangas had often lain in ambush—some four hundred Mexicans, emigrants, and soldiers were killed between 1862 and 1867. Charles Poston, the Arizona Representative, estimated 425 deaths at Apache hands between 1856 and 1862—"being at that period about one half the American population." Poston was further able to compile a list of the names of 170 victims during the years 1865 to 1874: a "partial list," he hastened to add. Of course Cochise was not the cause of all these deaths; but after Mangas disappeared, the Chokonen chief got the lion's share of the credit. One settler swore that in only three years, Cochise had killed thirty-four of his friends.

The terror focused, too, on the eerie way Apaches fought. In the Civil War that had just concluded with so great a loss of life, orderly rows of blue- and gray-coated soldiers had marched, to bugles and drums, toward the smoke of each others' guns. This was war as the Americans understood it. Apaches, however, struck in seemingly random, individual attacks, then scattered and hid. "Chase them and they slink into the ground or somehow vanish," complained one soldier, "look behind and they are peeping over a hill at you." An Apache moved without sound, and his arrow arrived without report. Even in winter, when they went into battle, Apaches stripped to their loincloths; such nakedness seemed more terrifying than the grimmest armor.

If Americans had had the faintest ideas of Chiricahua social structure, Cochise's campaign would have been more fathomable. But whites could hardly tell one tribe from another, and in that ignorance the most far-fetched notions bloomed. An 1858 traveler insisted that until a few years before, there had been only one Apache tribe, the Pinals, with Cochise as chief; recently, he swore, the Pinals had spontaneously subdivided into smaller bands. Carleton himself, even as he set out to drive Cochise from the country, thought he was a Pinal chief, not a Chiricahua. Another theory of the day had it that Cochise led a mob of vagabonds, deserters from other tribes.

Such ideas were far from harmless: they fueled the engine of the Arizona conflict. Had Bascom, for instance, even for a moment seriously considered that the cattle thieves he chased eastward from Fort Buchanan might not have been Chiricahuas—might have been Apaches of whose doings Cochise had no knowledge—the debacle of "Cut the Tent" need not have happened.

Yet Apache ignorance of how the White Eyes' society worked led to comparable miscalculations and sorrows. The Indians could not imagine the size, diversity, and sheer population of the United States. Only when the first Apaches took train trips east to meet officials in Washington did the number and power of their enemy strike home—with a deeply demoralizing impact. Thus the confusions born of overlapping jurisdictions within the American government seemed like sheer double-talk and trickery to the Apaches. How could the chief of "Arizona" say one thing, the chief of "New Mexico" another? Was the army in charge on the reservation, or the Indian agent (who was an employee of the Interior Department)? If there was a "Great Father" in Washington who wanted peace, why did he not arrest the King Woolseys who murdered Apaches with impunity?

Intensifying the misunderstanding between whites and Indians was the eternal problem of language. Only a handful of whites ever learned more than a smattering of Apache, a complicated tongue in which glottal stops and pitch have semantic meaning, while vowels may be short or long and nasalized or not. Before the late 1880s, few Apaches knew any English. After almost three centuries of contact with Spanish and Mexicans, many Apaches spoke passable Spanish. A certain small percentage of American settlers and soldiers also spoke Spanish. Typically, then, a parley between an American officer and an Apache chief involved a pair of interpreters who converted the words of each into Spanish. The drift in meaning was inevitably immense, even without factoring in the motivations of interpreters who softened one part of a speech, hardened another, or censored altogether yet other parts, for fear of being blamed as the messenger. Through long and disastrous experience, the Apaches came to form a fixed distrust for certain interpreters.

From 1865 through 1868, the killing of Americans proceeded apace. Cochise became the arch Apache fiend, blamed for atrocities from the Rio Grande to the Prescott diggings. Only in 1991, after a painstaking study of Mexican records, did the scholar Edwin R. Sweeney demonstrate that during most of those three years, Cochise was not even in the United States. Beset with problems of which the White Eyes had no inkling, he lay low in Mexico most of that time. One of the threats Cochise felt most keenly during those years came at the hands of peoples of whose existence American officers were virtually unaware. Ancient Indian enemies of the Apache to the south—Tarahumaras, Yaquis, and Opatas—were pushing into the Sierra Madre, driven north by their own fights with Mexican soldiers. It was the Chiricahuas' duty to drive them back south, out of their own favorite refuge and hunting ground.

Meanwhile, who was responsible for the raids, the ranch burnings, the ambushes in Arizona and New Mexico for which Cochise got the blame? That the Chiricahua might have other formidable leaders besides Cochise was a turn of fate Americans were not eager to countenance. So far the names, the identities of these shadowy "hostiles" were unknown to the white settlers. By 1868, no one in Arizona had heard of Geronimo. Only in the next decade would these stalwarts emerge in the American consciousness, and only in the 1880s would the Southwest realize, in dismay, that there seemed to be an endless supply of Chiricahua leaders who would not give up, who would fight against odds that other Indians judged to be hopeless.

By 1869, Cochise had returned to his beloved Dragoon Mountains. Through that year and the next, the killing of white settlers intensified. Whole mining towns gave up the struggle, the survivors fleeing to safer places such as Tucson. Army patrols managed to engage Cochise's band now and again; sometimes they slew one or two of his warriors, but more often, they made weary marches across parched basins in futile pursuit of the ghost of an Apache trail.

Meanwhile Carleton had been put out to pasture. There was a new President in Washington, and though Ulysses S. Grant had fought the Confederates with unyielding determination, now, unlike Abraham Lincoln or Andrew Johnson before him, he was proposing a "peace policy" to deal with the Indians.

The citizens of Arizona had had enough. In early 1871, the Territorial Legislature drafted a "Memorial and Affidavits Showing Outrages Perpetrated by the Apache Indians" for the years 1869 and 1870. Item by item, this somber document listed every head of cattle stolen, every mining claim abandoned, along with the deaths of about two hundred Americans. Each complaint was formally sworn to by an Arizona citizen, who typically appended an editorial word or two:

CHARLES A. SHIBEL, *sworn,* and says he resides at Tucson in this Territory; is Assistant Assessor of Internal Revenue; that the following depredations by the Apache Indians have come under his observation the past year:

In August, 1870, while coming from Camp Goodwin to Tucson, on the Rio Grande mail road, he found the mail coach destroyed and the following persons murdered and *mutilated:* John Collins, Wm. Burns, and two U. S. soldiers. They were *scalped,* one partially burned, and another with his eyes gouged out; and he believes this Territory is now in almost a defenseless condition.

The memorial was sent to the U. S. Congress with a strenuous plea that "the Government will demand and aid in subduing our hostile foe, and thereby reclaim from the savage one of the most valuable portions of our public domain."

Congress was moved. Despite Grant's peace policy, the army decided to strike at the heart of the Apache resistance. That heart, everyone knew, was Cochise himself. For the job of hunting him down, destroying his band, and capturing or killing the chief himself, Lieutenant Howard Cushing was thrust to the fore.

Cushing was the best Indian fighter the army in Arizona had. He had already killed more Apaches—mostly Mescaleros and Pinals—than any other officer. He was, said John G. Bourke many years later, "the bravest man I ever saw." By 1871, Bourke would remember, Cushing's "determination, coolness, and energy . . . had made his name famous all over the southwestern border."

On April 26, with a column of crack soldiers, Cushing set out from Fort Lowell, near Tucson, and headed southeast. Five days later, on the Santa Cruz River a few miles inside Mexico, the party caught sight of burning grass in the distance. Cushing assumed that part of Cochise's band was signaling the remainder in their mountain camp.

The lieutenant had formed something of an obsession with Cochise. Now, he was confident, the Chiricahua chief was almost in his clutches. Cushing marched his column back north across the border, following moccasin tracks. In the Whetstone Mountains, he pounced upon the enemy.

Five

■

1871

*O*n the morning of May 5, 1871, Cushing's patrol crossed the Babocomari River, headed north. Everywhere the soldiers rode, the grass was burnt to the ground; in places it was still aflame. The army horses were beginning to wear down from inadequate feeding.

Two miles north of the river, the patrol discovered the track of a solitary Apache woman and her pony, apparently headed toward Bear Springs in the Whetstones. Cushing dispatched three men to pursue the trail, while he brought the rest of his column up close behind.

The advance party followed the dusty footsteps into a deep canyon. Sergeant John Mott, in charge of the trackers, grew suspicious. Unlike most Apaches, the woman seemed to be making no effort to disguise her tread; indeed, where she might have stepped from stone to stone, she left clear moccasin prints in the dirt. The encroaching canyon walls made Mott apprehensive. Was the trail leading the men into a trap? All at once Mott made a decision: veering sharply from the trail, he led the two privates as he climbed the left wall out of the canyon.

It was too late. From a hidden arroyo behind him some fifteen Indians emerged. Mott turned and saw an even larger band cutting off his escape route ahead. The Apaches opened fire, seriously wounding one of the privates and killing the other's horse.

Mott stood his ground and returned the fire, but he was helpless to warn Cushing of the trap. The three men expected to die, but for some reason the Apaches preferred to toy with them: one warrior rode right up to the able-bodied private and snatched the hat from his head. This brazen deed was a characteristic piece of Apache virtuosity, a gratuitous display of skill and nerve in combat. But it also seems likely that the Indians, who had watched every step of the patrol's approach, intended to lure Cushing to the rescue of his otherwise doomed scouts.

And Cushing came. Incredulous at surviving the first attack, Mott pleaded for flight. But Cushing, gauging the situation as simply another test of his courage, ordered a charge. Three more army horses went down. Cushing's men had gained only twenty yards when the man next to the lieutenant was struck in the face by a bullet that then emerged from the back of his head. Now it was the Apaches' turn to charge. As Mott wrote afterwards, "It seemed as if every rock and bush became an Indian."

Mott had his back turned when he heard Cushing cry out, "Sergeant, Serg[ean]t, I am killed, take me out, take me out!" Mott whirled around in time to see the lieutenant pitch forward on his face. With considerable courage of his own, the sergeant ordered another man to help him carry Cushing toward safety. The two men managed to drag the lieutenant only ten or twelve paces when another well-aimed Apache bullet struck Cushing in the face. The men dropped the officer's body and "turned to sell our lives as dearly as possible."

For a mile, the Apaches kept up a running fight, as Mott's column struggled down the canyon. It seemed, however, that with the death of the lieutenant, the Indians had accomplished their aim. At last they let the rest of the soldiers go.

Walking and riding through the night, abandoning exhausted pack mules, Mott's men staggered westward to Camp Crittenden (the former Fort Buchanan). Besides the lieutenant, the patrol had lost only two men, with a third severely wounded. But the army's finest Apache fighter had been coaxed into a trap, then slain with selective precision. The war in Arizona and New Mexico would continue for another fifteen years, but the Apaches would never again kill an officer of equal rank.

For almost a century after this dramatic battle, historians assumed that it was Cochise who had directed the fight against Cushing. In his official report, Mott had left a description of the enemy leader and his tactics:

> The Indians were well handled by their chief, a thick, heavy set man, who never dismounted from a small brown horse during the fight. They were not noisy or boisterous as Indians generally are, but paid great attention to their chief, whose designs I could guess as he delivered his instructions by gestures.

No one would ever have called Cochise a "thick, heavy set" man, nor were his battle tactics those of the leader Mott described. But Mott's document languished unknown in the National Archives.

Eventually Apache scholar Dan L. Thrapp rediscovered Mott's account, which he published in 1967. Pondering the brief description of the leader who set the trap for Cushing, Thrapp speculated that the Apache tactician might have been a chief named Juh. Thirteen years later, with the publication of Eve Ball's *Indeh,* Thrapp's canny guess was confirmed by the direct testimony of Juh's son.

In 1871, Juh's identity was unknown to white Americans. Though a Chiricahua chief, he was neither one of Cochise's Chokonen nor one of Mangas's Chihenne. His people were the Nednhi, southernmost of the Chiricahua subgroups, whose heartland lay in the high Sierra Madre of northern Mexico. The Nednhi were to remain throughout the Apache wars the most mysterious, the "wildest" of the Chiricahua.

Juh is a corrupt Spanish rendering of an Apache name, pronounced *Ho.* Juh's son said that his father's name meant "he sees ahead." Others interpreted it as "long neck"; yet another insisted that the name "doesn't meant anything. He was called that because he stuttered. . . . [He] could hardly talk at all when he became excited."

Juh's stuttering had everything to do with Geronimo's rise to prominence. Although they were of different subtribes, Juh and Geronimo grew up together, playing at war and peace side by side. As a young man, Juh married Geronimo's favorite sister, Ishton, a tall, beautiful Apache whose own name meant *"The* Woman." The liaison, which made the two men brothers-in-law, was strengthened around 1869, when Ishton nearly died in childbirth. At the time, Juh was away fighting Mexicans. Geronimo climbed a mountain and prayed for his sister; later generations insist he maintained his vigil for four days and nights. On the fifth morning, he received an answer when an invisible

Power spoke to him: "The child will be born and your sister will live; and you will never be killed with weapons, but live to old age."

Because of his severe stutter, Juh often found it difficult, once he became chief, to address his warriors. He came to rely on Geronimo as his spokesman. The gestures that Sergeant Mott observed, with which the chief directed his troops in disciplined combat, may have taken the place of verbal commands Juh could not utter.

By 1871, Juh was in his forties. A Chihenne boy who first beheld the great man in the Nednhi heartland in the Sierra Madre remembered him seven decades later as over six feet in height and stockily built.

A powerful, symmetrical irony hovers over Cushing's downfall, one that whites could not know until after the publication of *Indeh* in 1980. Cushing had made it his personal vendetta to hound Cochise to his death, and as he crisscrossed Arizona killing Apaches, he was convinced that he was close to cornering his worthy adversary. At the same time, Juh—a chief Cushing had never heard of—had made it his own mission to bring the gallant and cocksure lieutenant to his downfall.

Juh's antipathy had formed when he learned of an army attack on a camp of peaceful Mescaleros in New Mexico, apparently led by Cushing. The soldiers had left everyone dead except for two women, both shot in the leg. When the comrades of the dead set about burying their bodies, the soldiers stole their horses.

Enraged by this treacherous attack, Juh developed a personal obsession with Cushing. He sent out scouts who spied on the lieutenant's maneuvers. Three times Juh engaged Cushing's column in indecisive skirmishes—the very firefights in which the lieutenant thought he was closing in on Cochise. At last Juh lured Cushing into his trap in the Whetstones.

As Juh's son recalled many years later, "Other White Eyes were killed, too; I don't know how many. We weren't all the time counting the dead as the soldiers did. Juh wasn't much interested in the troops —just Cushing."

Meanwhile, where was Cochise? With his return to his stronghold in the Dragoon Mountains in 1869, after three years in Mexico, southeastern Arizona suffered a new outbreak of Chokonen terror. By now there were nine thousand whites living in Arizona, including twenty-one hundred troops parceled among fourteen posts—by far the strongest military presence the territory had ever seen. Yet the army was powerless to ferret out Cochise, or even to drive him back into Mexico.

In February of that year, the Chiricahua chief did an unusual thing. On the fringes of the Dragoon stronghold, he allowed an American captain to approach and talk. The colloquy yielded the first direct insight any American had had into Cochise's thoughts for eight years, since Bascom's folly had driven the chief on his campaign of revenge.

Though Cochise remained defiant, sorrow and bitterness weighted his words. "I lost nearly one hundred of my people in the last year, principally from sickness," he told the captain. "The Americans killed a good many. I have not one hundred Indians now. Ten years ago I had 1000. The Americans are everywhere, and we must live in bad places to shun them." Cochise admitted he had been wounded twice during the years since Bascom had tried to capture him. Once he was shot in the neck, and once in the leg: "I had a bad leg for some time afterward."

No real peace offer emerged from this conference, however, and the raids and killing continued on both sides. A year later, Cochise was reported slain near Dolores, Sonora. "The worst Indian who ever strung a bow or pulled a trigger is defunct," crowed an Arizona newspaper.

But Cochise was very much alive. At the end of August 1870, he came in to Camp Mogollon (today Fort Apache), far to the north in the territory of the White Mountain Apaches. The several accounts of the parley that ensued differ so greatly that we must suspect the usual confusion wrought by nervous or slipshod interpreters. According to one eyewitness, Cochise "said he had been fighting the Americans for thirteen years, and now was tired and wanted to sleep. The troops had worried him, killed almost all of his band. He thought we were about even, and would like to come on the reservation." Another version of the meeting had the chief "ostentatiously" wearing the gold chain of a murdered American colonel as he sneered that "the troops were cowards and the Americans were liars. . . . He would go on killing as long as he pleased."

Yet Cochise had indeed grown weary of the endless fighting. By 1870 he was about sixty years old. For the first time in almost a decade he wanted to hear what the Americans had to offer. In October, William Arny, a civilian special agent appointed as an instrument of President Grant's peace policy, arranged the largest conference yet gathered between hostile Apaches and representatives of the U.S. government. The meeting ground was Cañada Alamosa, near the sacred hot spring at the center of the Chihenne country in western New Mexico.

Victorio, chief of the Chihenne, had for five years kept his ear out for a workable settlement on a reservation. Between Cochise and Victorio, there was regular communication and great mutual respect. Arny was delighted when, by his reckoning, 790 Apaches under twenty-two chiefs showed up to talk at the Cañada; and he was astounded to find Cochise and 96 Chokonen among them.

Yet this propitious meeting came to naught, thanks in part to the cultural blinders that Arny, like so many of his countrymen, could not help wearing. His true attitude toward the Chiricahua is exposed in his report on the conference, where he refers to them as "the most savage, barbarous, and uncivilized Indians on the continent." In the same sentence in which he blames them for having "torn out, cooked and eaten the hearts of some persons" and "burned at the stake stage passengers and other prisoners," he indicts them for having "retarded the mining operations of one of the richest portions of the United States."

Face-to-face with Cochise, Arny prepared to read his commission from Grant, which he called a "paper . . . written by the Great Father . . . to his children." Cochise waved off the document and insisted on man-to-man talk.

"The Great Father wants a good peace and [Apaches] must stop the killings and stealing and go upon a reservation," said Arny.

"The Apaches," Cochise answered, "want to run around like a coyote, they don't want to be put in a corral."

"The Great Father didn't want to put them in a corral," Arny insisted. "He wants them to eat and dress like a white man, have plenty of everything and be contented."

If the government had made good on its sometime promise to establish a reservation around Ojo Caliente, Cochise might have been willing to settle there. But the bureaucrats in Washington would not have it: the Chiricahua, they decided, must settle far beyond the Rio Grande, near Fort Stanton, in the country of the Mescalero. These eastern Apaches remained allies and friends of the Chiricahua, but to live for good in the Mescalero heartland would mean intolerable exile from their own country.

Cochise rode back to Arizona. As the year 1871 began, he returned to his raiding and ambushes, and troops from several posts set out with renewed zeal to hunt him down. In April, the Chokonen chief was thought to be in the Huachuca Mountains, not far from the Whetstones. But on May 5, when Cushing, thinking he was closing in on Cochise, was instead killed by the Apaches led by Juh, Cochise was probably far to the south, in Mexico.

The complexity of the Chiricahua bands was unknown to the American officers. It seemed in 1871 that Cochise was the last great renegade: if only his iron resistance could be broken, either by killing him or by persuading him to accept the reservation, then the Apache wars might come to a quick conclusion. The very existence of a younger generation of Chiricahua leaders—men such as Juh and Geronimo, whose antipathy for the White Eyes was even fresher and more vital than Cochise's—was beyond American comprehension.

Learning of Cochise's several parleys with American agents and officers, the citizens of Arizona howled their dismay that the chief had not been seized or shot. But Cochise would never again repeat his mistake with Bascom. When he came with his warriors to an American camp to talk, they kept their mounts and their weapons, their distance from the wooden or adobe buildings in which the White Eyes preferred to negotiate. Had Arny or the others tried to seize Cochise, many white lives would have been lost.

Once more, in September 1871, Cochise came in to Cañada Alamosa to talk. Thanks to the observant memoir of one participant, this meeting affords us the best glimpse into the soul of the great chief we are ever likely to get. After the general in charge had made his case for coming in to the reservation, Cochise stood and addressed the White Eyes. The participant left a keen description of the chief:

> Evidently he was about fifty-eight years of age, though he looked much younger; his height, five feet ten inches; a person lithe and wiry, every muscle being well developed and firm. A silver thread was now and then visible in his otherwise black hair, which he wore cut straight around his head about on a level with his chin. His countenance displayed great force of character, and his expression was a little sad. He spoke with great ease, and gesticulated very little for an Indian.

For once the interpreter must have been competent, for he could hardly have invented Cochise's eloquence. The speech the chief made that September day is the longest single utterance of Cochise's ever recorded:

The sun has been very hot on my head and made me as in a fire, but now I have come into this valley and drunk of these waters and washed myself in them and they have cooled me. Now that I am cool I have come with my hands open to you to live in peace with you. I speak straight and do not wish to deceive or be deceived. . . .

When God made the world he gave one part to the white man and another to the Apache. Why was it? Why did they come together? Now that I am to speak, the sun, the moon, the earth, the air, the waters, the birds and beasts, even the children unborn shall rejoice at my words. The white people have looked for me long. I am here! What do they want? They have looked me for long; why am I worth so much? If I am worth so much why not mark when I set my foot and look when I spit?

Something of the formal beauty, of the strophes and antistrophes, of Apache oratory transcended the gulfs of culture and language; even as Cochise spoke, the listeners were moved. He balanced the arrogance of his pride as a warrior with lamentation: "I am no longer chief of all the Apaches," he continued. "I am no longer rich; I am but a poor man. The world was not always this way."

Cochise's heart was heavy with the sense of Apache doom in the face of the innumerable White Eyes. It was a note that would be sounded again and again through the following decades. "When I was young I walked all over this country, east and west, and saw no other people than the Apaches. After many summers I walked again and found another race of people had come to take it. How is it? Why is it that the Apaches wait to die—that they carry their lives on their finger nails? . . . The Apaches were once a great nation; they are now but few."

Along with the demise he presaged for his people, Cochise foresaw his own, seemed even to long for it. "I have no father or mother," he spoke. "I am alone in the world. No one cares for Cochise; that is why I do not care to live, and wish the rocks to fall on me and cover me up."

The U.S. government had now proposed another reservation site, on the Tularosa River far to the northwest of Ojo Caliente. In closing, Cochise rejected this locale, just as he had refused to join the Mescaleros near Fort Stanton. "I want to live in these mountains; I do not want to go to Tularosa. That is a long ways off. The flies on those mountains eat out the eyes of the horses. The bad spirits live there. I have drunk of these waters and they have cooled me; I do not want to leave here."

As early as 1859, the government had established a reservation in Arizona for Pima and Maricopa Indians, along the Gila River just south of present-day Phoenix. Yet by 1871, no official reservation for Apaches had been devised. In the years after 1866, five temporary "feeding stations" had been set up near Arizona military camps. In their dealings with these stations, the Apaches gradually grew accustomed to the reservation idea. In embryo, it seemed a volatile bargain: in exchange for settling near an army camp and agreeing not to raid or steal, the Indians accepted rations, clothing, and protection from lawless white settlers.

Increasing numbers of Apaches, mostly from the White Mountain, San Carlos, and Tonto tribes, entered into this quid pro quo. There was good reason to do so, for the rapid spread of Anglos across Arizona had made it increasingly difficult for Apaches to wrest their living from the land. Winter was always the hardest season.

At the junction of Aravaipa Creek and the San Pedro River, about fifty-five miles by trail north of Tucson, Camp Grant had been built in 1859. In February 1871, the camp had for three months been under the command of Lieutenant Royal Whitman. A native of Maine, the descendant of Mayflower pilgrims, Whitman had served with distinction in the Civil War. He was thirty-seven years old, reputed to be fond of the bottle, but open-minded and intelligent. Under the most trying circumstances, he would prove to be one of those rare frontier figures, a military man who felt deep compassion for the Apaches. These qualities would cost him dearly in the public eye.

One day in February, five old women hesitantly approached the camp, carrying a white flag of truce. Whitman received them kindly, and learned that they were in search of a young boy, the son of one of the women, who had been captured on the Salt River the previous autumn. According to Whitman, the boy had been so well treated that now he did not wish to return to the Apache life.

Nevertheless, a bridge of trust with a hitherto "wild" group of Apaches had been built. Eight days later, a larger party came in to Camp Grant to buy manta—horse-blanket material from which they might make clothing—"as they were nearly naked." A few days after that, twenty-five Apaches arrived, led by a chief named Eskiminzin, who told a doleful story. He was the leader of the Aravaipa Apaches, a band that had dwindled to 150. The American soldiers had so harried his people that they felt safe nowhere. They were starting to die of starvation and disease.

At first Whitman urged that Eskiminzin take his people north to the White Mountains, where a large reservation was about to be established. New to the country, Whitman underestimated, as did nearly all Americans, the importance of tribal homelands. "That is not our country," Eskiminzin demurred; "neither are they our people. We are at peace with them, but never have mixed with them." There were no mescal plants in the White Mountains, the chief explained, and for the Aravaipa, mescal was the staff of life. The women uprooted the hardy cactuses, pruned their pointed leaves as one might the leaves of an artichoke, buried the hearts of the plants in the ground, and cooked them for a day and a night. For generations, Eskiminzin's people had lived in and around Aravaipa Canyon, upstream from Camp Grant, where there was always enough mescal.

Whitman lacked the authority to make a truce with the Aravaipa Apaches on his own. But his feelings had been stirred, and he told Eskiminzin that if he brought in his people, the army would feed them while Whitman sought permission from his superior officer for a more permanent arrangement.

On March 1, Eskiminzin returned with all his people. Other bands also came in, so that soon 510 Indians were camped within half a mile of the army post. Whitman issued food and clothing to the destitute Apaches, then offered them a cent a pound for all the hay they could harvest. Within two months, the Indians had supplied 300,000 pounds of hay.

Meanwhile, Whitman had sent a detailed report to General George Stoneman, who had been in charge of the Department of Arizona since the previous summer. Stoneman had so little taste for the territory, and so poor an understanding of the Apache threat, that he made his winter headquarters in California. It took six weeks for Whitman to receive a reply; to his disgust, he opened the envelope to find that his report had been returned by a clerk complaining that Whitman had violated protocol by failing to enclose a cover note specifying the contents. As far as the lieutenant could tell, Stoneman had not even read his urgent appeal.

Meanwhile, the natural distrust of Eskiminzin's people was ebbing away. They were comforted to be camped on the creek that ran through their heartland, reassured by the proximity of its twisting side-canyons, which they knew better than any other people on earth.

Aravaipa Canyon is one of the most haunting and idyllic places in Arizona. For twenty miles, the creek carves a corridor through ruddy conglomerate rock, leaving vertical walls that tower as high as 800 feet. The geology is tortured and chaotic (one tributary gorge was later named Hell Hole by ranchers), but traveling the length of the canyon requires only an easy horseback ride on sandy soil. Giant sycamores line the clean, sweet waters of the creek, one of the few in Southern Arizona that flow twelve months of the year. Huge saguaro cactuses crowd the dry terraces above the upper canyon floor.

Aravaipa offers the only natural route traversing eighty miles of mountains that separate the San Simon valley on the east from the San Pedro on the west. Many Apache tribes used it as a shortcut, but for Eskiminzin's people, it was sacred land, the mother country. More than five centuries before them, the cliff-dwelling Mogollon had felt a kindred attachment to the place; their ruins stare from small cave shelters the length of the canyon.

William Bell, an adventurer who was one of the first white men to ride through the canyon, found his six days in Aravaipa an overwhelming experience. "The gloomy grandeur of such a place was not good for the nerves," he wrote; "and we feared terribly an Indian attack, where the advantages of position were so much against us." Yet Bell's description of Aravaipa is a paean to its beauty—to deer drinking from the stream, beavers building dams, quails and kingfishers darting among the underbrush, "grotesque old mezquits of most unusual size" and "fine branches of mistletoe [hanging] from many of the trees."

In April 1871, the waters of Aravaipa Creek at its junction with the San Pedro dried up, swallowed by the parched earth around Camp Grant. This happened, as the Apaches knew, every spring; but only five miles upstream, at the mouth of the canyon, the water would run clear through the driest summer. Eskiminzin asked permission to move his people those five miles upstream, to a terrace above the south bank of the river where they had often camped.

Whitman reluctantly agreed. He was well aware that news of his unofficial reservation had reached the citizens of Tucson, who cursed him for his supposed pusillanimity. Five miles away, the Apaches would be much harder to supervise or protect. And through daily contact with Eskiminzin's people, he had grown fond of them. He was still so thoroughly a man of his century as to conceive his duty to be "helping to show them the way to a higher civilization." But, as he later wrote, "I had come to feel respect for men who, ignorant and naked, were still ashamed to lie or steal, and for women who would work cheerfully like slaves to clothe themselves and children, but, untaught, held their virtue above price." Remarkably, Whitman had come to recognize the individual faces of all 510 Apaches under his care.

The moral character of Tucson had improved little in the previous decade, although its citizens were beginning to lay the cornerstones of the town's reputation as the most prosperous in Arizona. Through the end of 1870 and the first three months of 1871, they had been outraged by sporadic Apache depredations. Most of these took place far from Camp Grant—in Tubac and on Sonoita Creek, for instance, well south of Tucson.

The townspeople had compiled their "Memorial and Affidavits" listing their grievances, but government response was slower than they wished. Meanwhile the apparently weak-spined Lieutenant Whitman, fresh to the territory, was coddling hundreds of Apaches up at Camp Grant, feeding them as a reward for their crimes.

Bascom and Cushing had blundered toward their fates in part because they failed to appreciate how many different tribes and bands, operating in complete independence from one another, made up the Apache people. One wonders to this day how sincerely the citizens of Tucson believed that the Aravaipa Apaches were the ones who had killed ranchers on Sonoita Creek. Afterward ringleaders cited "evidence," all of it since proved spurious.

The Tucsonians formed a Committee of Public Safety. William S. Oury, the principal American, was a man after the heart of King Woolsey. He had fought at sixteen in the Texas "revolution," narrowly missing the Alamo. Now he became the chief rabble-rouser urging vigilante action against the Apaches. Meetings were called at the Tucson courthouse, but, as Oury later wrote in mock-heroic disdain, "Many valiant but frothy speeches were pronounced, and many determined resolves were resoluted; but nothing definite was done beyond a list being gotten up and signed by some eighty-odd valiant and doughty knights resolved to do or die; but in a few days . . . the valor of all THESE PLUMED KNIGHTS seemed to have oozed out at their finger ends, and everything was at a standstill."

Oury's counterpart in the Mexican community of Tucson was a man named Jesus Elias, already renowned as an Apache fighter. One night, the two civic leaders ran into each other on the streets and started talking. Elias was certain that some renegades he had recently chased had come from Camp Grant. At the end of their late-night conversation, the men had a plan.

Organized in great secrecy, a vigilante mob of 146 men made a rendezvous on the afternoon of April 28 on Rillito Creek, just north of Tucson. There were only six white Americans in the group (a dearth that embarrassed Oury), along with forty-eight Mexicans and ninety-two Papago Indians, traditional enemies of the Apache. Avoiding the main trail to Camp Grant (today's Highways 89 and 77), the vigilantes headed east through Cebadilla Pass and followed the bed of the San Pedro River, traveling almost entirely at night. Oury had had the foresight to assign to some other conspirators the job of intercepting messengers from Tucson to Camp Grant; in fact, the departure of the mob had not gone unnoticed, and two soldiers were hurriedly dispatched to warn Whitman. They were, in Oury's words, "quietly detained at Canada del Oro and did not reach [Camp Grant] until it was too late to harm us."

Just before daybreak on April 30, after an all-night march, the volunteers came in sight of the Apache camp. Elias, in charge, divided his motley army into two wings and ordered an immediate charge. "The Papagoes bounded forward like deer," wrote Oury later, "and the skirmish [line] began and a better executed one I never witnessed even from veteran soldiers."

The Apaches were taken completely by surprise. Their only lookouts were a man and a woman playing cards beside a campfire; they "were clubbed to death before they could give the alarm." The attack lasted only half an hour, at the end of which "not an adult Indian was left to tell the tale." Between 125 and 144 Indians (their bodies were never definitively counted) were murdered as they slept inside their wickiups.

Later Oury gave speeches to his fellow pioneers, recounting that "glorious morning of April 30th 1871 when swift punishment was dealt out to these red handed butchers, and they were wiped from the face of the earth." What he did not readily acknowledge was that no more than eight, and perhaps as few as two, of the dead Apaches were men. On the fateful day, most of the Aravaipa men were off hunting in their beloved canyon; lulled into a sense of security by Whitman's benevolence, they had left a camp peopled almost entirely by women and children. Others, including Eskiminzin, had been able to flee at the onset of the dawn attack.

Nor did Oury dwell on the details of the carnage, which shocked and sickened the Camp Grant soldiers who, warned too late, came upon the massacre only hours afterward. The attackers had shot with guns and arrows and clubbed the sleeping Apaches. Some who were only wounded by gunfire then had their brains beaten out with stones. A number of women were raped before they were killed. According to the army surgeon from Camp Grant, nearly all the dead were mutilated, and "one infant of some ten months was shot twice and one leg hacked nearly off."

As they returned to Tucson "in the full satisfaction of a work well done" (as Oury put it), the vigilantes carried with them twenty-eight to thirty Apache "papooses." These infants were taken by the Papagos, who sold most of them into slavery in Sonora. Their surviving relatives later pleaded passionately with Whitman to do what he could to restore them to their tribe. Seven of these children were eventually returned; the rest never saw their people again.

Overcome by the catastrophe, Whitman offered each of his interpreters $100 to go into the hills and attempt to convey to the surviving Aravaipa that the soldiers had had nothing to do with the massacre. None of the interpreters was tempted, although $100 was a fortune. So Whitman did a brave thing: in daylight on the morning of May 1, vulnerable to the warriors he knew must be watching from the hills, he set about burying the mutilated corpses. This humanitarian act, he hoped, would persuade Eskiminzin's warriors that the army was not his enemy.

Whitman calculated well. That evening, the Aravaipa survivors began to straggle in. In his official report, the lieutenant left a vivid picture of their state:

> Many of the men, whose families had all been killed . . . were obliged to turn away, unable to speak, and too proud to show their grief. The women whose children had been killed or stolen were convulsed with grief, and looked to me appealingly, as though I was their last hope on earth. Children who two days before had been full of fun and frolic kept at a distance, expressing wondering horror.

Yet the Aravaipa believed Whitman, recognized that the perpetrators of the massacre were largely Mexicans and Papagos. One of the chiefs told the lieutenant, "I no longer want to live; my women and children have been killed before my face, and I have been unable to defend them."

White men in Arizona had performed atrocities against the Apaches before. But the Camp Grant massacre went beyond all previous bounds of wanton slaughter. Sixty-seven years later, a historian would call it "the blackest page in the Anglo-Saxon records of Arizona."

Not so the contemporary newspapers, even those published far from Arizona Territory. The San Francisco *Bulletin* argued that "such massacres are necessary in self-defense among the Apaches"; the Denver *News* gave "the citizens of Arizona most hearty and unqualified endorsement. We congratulate them on the fact that permanent peace arrangements have been made with so many, and we only regret that the number was not double."

But President Grant was outraged: calling the massacre "purely murder," he let the governor of Arizona know that if the perpetrators were not brought to trial, he would place the whole territory under martial law. In due course more than a hundred of the conspirators were indicted. A trial was held in Tucson that lasted five days. At the end of it, a jury of the vigilantes' peers deliberated for nineteen minutes before returning a verdict of not guilty. The celebration lasted for days.

In the May 1871 elections, Oury was voted into office as alderman; another conspirator was chosen mayor; and Juan Elias, the brother of Jesus and a leading figure in the assault, was elected town dog-catcher. Oury Park, within the city limits of Tucson, today commemorates the pioneer who spearheaded the massacre.

In December 1871, Lieutenant Whitman was put before a court-martial, on a series of trivial charges having to do with his alleged drinking and womanizing. In a Tucson saloon, for instance, he was charged with having called for drinks and then failed to pay for them. Local newspapers, unable to implicate him in the massacre, had assailed him on these more personal grounds. His softness toward the Apaches, for instance, was claimed to originate in an amorous propensity for "dusky maidens." The court, recognizing the absurdity of the charges, threw out the case, but Whitman's name was permanently blackened. He ended up in Washington, D. C., on early pension; for the rest of his life he brooded over the events at Camp Grant, insisting to all who would listen that he had taken the only possible course.

Perhaps the most tragic deed in the aftermath of the massacre came at the hands of Eskiminzin. Near the end of May 1871, he visited a rancher on the San Pedro who was his closest white friend. Many times Eskiminzin had stopped here for a meal, and now the rancher invited him once more to dinner. The Aravaipa chief ate his friend's dinner, drank his coffee, then pulled out a gun and shot him dead.

Years later, Eskiminzin explained his act to an army scout. "I did it," the chief said, "to teach my people that there must be no friendship between them and the white men. Anyone can kill an enemy, but it takes a strong man to kill a friend."

Six

■

The General on Muleback

*E*ven as he waited for the perpetrators of the Camp Grant massacre to be brought to trial, President Grant performed a deed that would be farther-reaching than any verdict. He relieved General George Stoneman, the Arizona commander who chose to direct his winter operations from the comfort of California, and installed in his place General George Crook.

The appointment was not a popular one within the army. As he accepted his post, Crook leapfrogged past a number of senior officers who were in line for the command. He was a general only by brevet rank, that largely honorific designation that brought with it no increase in salary and little in responsibility; Crook's promotion came as part of a wholesale handout of brevet laurels to Union officers who had performed well in the Civil War. In terms of "real" rank, Crook was no more than a lieutenant colonel. (He would become a brigadier general in 1873.) Crook, moreover, had done poorly at West Point, graduating thirty-eighth in a class of forty-three. Grant's own Secretary of War, as well as William Tecumseh Sherman, Commanding General of the Army, opposed Crook's promotion.

Yet before Crook's career was over, Sherman himself would call the man America's best Indian fighter. And Crazy Horse, whose warriors

Crook would fight at the battle of the Rosebud only eight days before the Custer massacre at Little Bighorn, would say that the officer was more to be "feared by the Sioux than any other white man."

When he arrived in Arizona in June 1871, Crook was forty-two years old. He was already a veteran not only of the Civil War but of relentless campaigns against the Shasta, Alagna, Pit River, Klamath, Tolana, Paiute, and other Indian tribes in the Northwest. By now, Crook was, in his own words, "tired of the Indian work," and he accepted his assignment to Arizona with considerable reluctance.

Crook stood just over six feet tall, with a stocky, powerful frame. The beard on his chin and his mustache were trim and short, but great bushy sideburns sprouted from either cheek. The gaze of his blue-gray eyes tended to assume an abstracted, melancholy cast.

A number of personal quirks had earned Crook a reputation for eccentricity. He hated to wear his uniform, preferring to go about in unostentatious civilian garb. He chose to ride a mule rather than a horse, thus presenting to his troops a figure more quixotic than chivalric. His great passion was hunting, and often, even in the midst of pursuing Indians across a difficult wilderness, he would take a few hours out to scare up and shoot deer or wild turkey.

As an officer, Crook was thoroughly unpretentious. He dealt plainly and honestly with the soldiers he commanded; according to his right-hand man, John Gregory Bourke, "No officer of the same rank, at least in our service, issued so few orders."

Everyone who met Crook found him aloof, stern, even gloomy. Bourke, who worshiped his general, called him "as retiring as a girl," but insisted, "Although taciturn, reticent, and secretive, moroseness formed no part of his nature, which was genial and sunny." But few of Crook's comrades ever glimpsed that sunny interior.

Crook's unfinished autobiography, written late in life, is an awkwardly phrased but forceful document. There is almost nothing of the private man in it. Crook sums up, for instance, what gossip claimed was a wonderfully romantic courtship of his wife in one bald sentence: "I was married on August 22, 1865." When Crook deals with his own exploits, the tone of the work is modest to an extreme, but it becomes blunt and aggrieved when he treats his rivals and superiors. By the end of his life Crook harbored few warm thoughts about the U. S. Army, and the narrative of his campaigns is full of fellow officers who were drunken cowards and pompous incompetents. "It was galling to have to serve under such people," he writes of his superior officers in the Civil War. Elsewhere he sums up his career: "I have had to do the rough work for others afterwards to get the benefits from it."

During the Civil War, Crook played a pivotal role in such major battles as the second Bull Run, Antietam, Fredericksburg, Lynchburg, and Appomattox. At Winchester, Virginia, in 1864, Crook devised and pulled off the crucial flanking maneuver that led to the capture of one thousand Confederate soldiers. His superior officer in this battle was Major General Philip H. Sheridan, who had been Crook's classmate at West Point. Almost two decades after the war, "Little Phil" would become General-in-Chief of the army, and thus Crook's commander in Washington during the last years of the Apache campaign. Sheridan, ironically, was the man who coined the phrase that has come down to us as "The only good Indian is a dead Indian."

Two years after the battle of Winchester, in his official report, Sheridan managed to take credit for the flanking maneuver that Crook had conceived and executed. The public was fooled, but not Crook's peers: Rutherford B. Hayes spoke for them in a letter to his uncle: "Intellectually, [Sheridan] is not Crook's equal, so that, as I said, General Crook is the brains of the army." Though Crook maintained a surface cordiality over the years toward his ex-classmate and commander, his private bitterness was deep. In a diary entry in 1889, he sardonically epitomized Sheridan's career: "The adulations heaped on him by a grateful nation for his supposed genius turned his head, which, added to his natural disposition, caused him to bloat his little carcass with debauchery and dissipation, which carried him off prematurely." (Crook, it may be pointed out, never smoked or swore or drank alcohol, tea, or coffee.)

Crook was also involved in one of the great Union fiascos, the battle of Chickamauga in 1863. Obeying orders he thought absurd, and against which he had protested in vain, Crook "lost a hundred men in about fifteen minutes," as he candidly admitted. His autobiography is venomous toward the commanding officer who glossed over the catastrophe of Chickamauga in his official report, even though that officer warmly commended Crook's actions.

Another Civil War fiasco, quite odd in its unfolding, must be laid to Crook's own carelessness. Near the end of the war, in February 1865, Crook was ensconced in his departmental headquarters at a hotel in Cumberland, Maryland. On the night of February 21, a daring gang of

Confederate guerrillas extorted the password from a sentry, then used it to slip brazenly behind the Union lines all the way to the hotel, where they captured Crook and General Benjamin F. Kelley without firing a shot.

The two officers were rushed on horseback to Richmond, Virginia, where they were held prisoner for a fortnight. General Grant managed to barter for their freedom as part of a large prisoner exchange, although Secretary of War William Stanton, in his vexation with Crook, opposed the trade. Crook himself minimizes the events in his autobiography, devoting two dry paragraphs to a résumé of the humiliating capture and exchange. Eighteen years after the Cumberland embarrassment, deep in the Sierra Madre of Mexico, Crook would be involved in an equally puzzling contretemps, this time with Geronimo and the Apaches as his adversaries rather than Confederate guerrillas.

By 1871, Crook had fought Indians for thirteen full years, eight before the Civil War and five after. In 1857, in the northeast corner of California, Crook killed his first Indian, a member of the Pit River tribe. A few days later, he received his first injury at their hands when an arrow lodged in his right hip; Crook pulled the shaft loose, leaving the head buried in his leg, where it remained the rest of his life.

Over the years, Crook formed his views of the Indians whose freedom it was his duty to eliminate. When he felt that a particular tribe had performed crimes against white settlers, he could be a righteous avenger. In 1867, for example, in an attack on a group of Paiutes in Idaho, Crook's company killed sixty men, women, and children and took twenty-seven women and children prisoner. A master psychologist, Crook knew how to deliver a speech that could demoralize a tribe as it pondered whether to fight on or to accept the white man's law. In 1868, when the Pit River Indians came in to Camp Harney, Oregon, to entreat for peace, Crook at first refused, addressing the chief through an interpreter:

I was in hopes that you would continue the war, and then, though I were to kill only one of your warriors while you killed a hundred of my men, you would have to wait for those little people [pointing to the Indian children] to grow to fill the place of your braves, while I can get any number of soldiers the next day to fill the place of my hundred men. In this way it would not be very long before we would have you all killed off, and then the government would have no more trouble with you.

Crook's vaunt, in the words of a witness, "took all the conceit out of" the chief; the Indians' surrender was as abject as the most heartless commander could have wished.

As he came to Arizona to take over the campaign against the Apaches, Crook initially sided with the Tucsonians who had perpetrated the Camp Grant massacre. But this reflective, private man differed from nearly all his fellow officers in the Indian wars in one vital respect. He was limitlessly curious about the Indian way of life, and out of his curiosity a measured sympathy had evolved.

In part, Crook's curiosity was merely strategic. The best way to fight an enemy was to know him through and through. In the opinion of his admiring lieutenant, John G. Bourke, "General Crook was admitted, even by the Indians, to be more of an Indian than the Indian himself." But the curiosity took on a life of its own. As he fought against the Alagna Indians in Washington, Crook learned their language, compiling vocabulary lists. Though he believed that "the salient points of Indian character" were that they were "filthy, odoriferous, treacherous, ungrateful, pitiless, cruel, and lazy," he saw a redeeming side. Fighting the Shasta Indians in California, he could not ignore the evidence that the tribe had been much wronged by whites, who had murdered and raped them for sport. As he quested after what he called the "secrets of the inner Indian," he came to admire the "cunning in all their little ways of capturing a livelihood."

Crook's ambivalence grew, and though he was committed to the army's goal of subjugating all the Indians in the West, the deeds that this mission required sometimes disturbed him. On the Columbia River in 1858, Crook captured five Indians who confessed to having murdered some prospectors. Crook felt he had no alternative but to execute them, but he did so with a heavy heart. "The whole business was exceedingly distasteful to me," he later wrote, "and as my 2nd Lt. Turner rather enjoyed that kind of thing, I detailed him" to carry out the executions.

In Arizona, Crook's first act was to interview every person he could who had experience against the Apaches; one by one, he drained his informants dry of their knowledge. In return, as was his taciturn manner, he gave no hint as to how he would proceed. His first interview was with the territorial governor, who insisted that the solution to the "Apache Problem" was to use Mexican scouts to trail and fight the Indians. "With a little pinole and dried beef," the governor told Crook,

Mexicans could "travel all over the country without pack mules . . . ; they could go inside an Apache and turn him wrong side out in no time at all." Crook hired fifty Mexican scouts and set off from Tucson toward Fort Bowie, hopeful of routing Cochise's Chiricahuas.

For a month, Crook's five companies of cavalry and fifty scouts crisscrossed southern Arizona, from Fort Bowie north to Mount Graham, through Aravaipa Canyon, at last to Fort Apache north of the Salt River. They saw a few Apaches, but managed to engage not a single one in combat. At Fort Apache Crook discharged the Mexicans. It had taken him only one scouting expedition to conclude that they were not the answer to the Apache Problem.

Although at first Crook had been optimistic about a quick conquest of the Chiricahuas, he soon realized that his Arizona foe was of a different mettle from the tribes he had forced into submission in the Northwest. The energetic campaigns of a decade of Arizona commanders, from Carleton to Stoneman, had hardly made a dent in the Chiricahua resistance. By 1871, there was a dawning recognition that in their wild and tenacious rebellion, the Apaches posed a unique threat to the settling of the Southwest. General Sherman himself grew so pessimistic that he recommended abandoning Arizona altogether to the Apaches.

Though tired to his very bones of "Indian work," Crook was not the sort of man to give up easily. Cautious, even conservative, by nature, he was at the same time an innovator. And within weeks of coming to Arizona, he had launched the two bold tactical strokes that, more than all other gambits combined, would lead to success against the Apaches.

The first had to do with style of travel. At Apache Pass in 1862, the two howitzers wheeled into action had turned the tide of that important battle, winning it for the White Eyes. Crook knew, however, that this was essentially a fluke, dependent on two circumstances: the Apaches had never before encountered mounted cannons, and at Apache Pass they were uncharacteristically entrenched in strategic positions from which it was their attackers' task to dislodge them.

Crook had never thought artillery efficacious in fighting Indians. His view was based in part on his bitter experience at Chickamauga in the Civil War. The argument Crook had lost with his commanding officer prior to that battle had to do with artillery, which he was forced to wheel into battle. Most of the hundred men who had gone down under Confederate fire during those terrible fifteen minutes had been trying to defend the useless cannons.

In Arizona, Crook realized that pursuit of the Apaches depended above all on mobility and speed. Not only the unwieldy artillery but the cumbersome wagons that typically accompanied troops on the move were, Crook decided, worthless against the Apache. His solution was a simple one: the perfection of the pack train of mules.

"He made the study of pack-trains the great study of his life," wrote Bourke. Crook's model was the Andean mule trains he had seen adapted to work in the mining towns of California. Packers of the day were a motley bunch, since their services were so little valued; many were alcoholic or barely competent. Likewise the mules varied greatly in health and strength. Crook weeded out the halt and the lazy among both mules and men, ensuring a minimum standard.

Before Crook, the army quartermaster issued a single size and design of *aparejo,* or pack-cushion, regardless of the size and shape of the mule. The government *aparejos,* wrote Bourke sardonically, "killed more mules than they helped in carrying their loads." Crook insisted that the pack-cushion be custom-made to the mule.

Crook's other innovation would turn out to be even more vital to his campaign. Having dismissed his feckless Mexican scouts at Fort Apache after his futile initial ride, the general began to enter into long parleys with the Coyotero and White Mountain Apaches who lingered in wary peacefulness near the fort. The keen student of Indian ways was in no danger of assuming all Apaches were alike. More than any officer before him, Crook grasped the ancient enmities that kept one band of Apaches at odds with another, and comprehended the absence of an overarching notion of an Apache people. He convinced himself, and then the Coyoteros and White Mountain men, that they might serve as scouts for the army in hunting down "hostile" Apaches of other bands.

It is hard today to recognize just how radical this idea seemed in 1871. In the thoughts of many white settlers, Crook's hiring Apache scouts bordered on the treasonous. If the only good Indian was a dead Indian, it was folly to pay Apaches to do soldiers' work. Lodged in the popular mind (and no doubt in the minds of many of Crook's nervous troops) was an apocalyptic fear that the army's Apache scouts might suddenly join with the renegades they pursued—their true, savage Apache nature coming to the fore as they slaughtered the whites who had come to civilize them.

But Crook had recognized what few Americans were willing to grant: that the average Apache was a far superior horseman, a far better conditioned athlete, a man far more attuned to the brutal landscape than the average American soldier. The notion was fixed in Crook's head long before it became a motto of the Southwest: it takes an Apache to catch an Apache.

Despite the old antagonisms between Coyoteros and White Mountain Apaches on the one hand and Chiricahuas on the other, it was not the easiest thing in the world to persuade the former to serve as scouts hunting down the latter. Crook paved the way with a masterly speech to the mistrustful Indians at Fort Apache. As he had to the Pit River people in 1868, Crook invoked the specter of a limitless tide of settlers from the east. In Bourke's paraphrase, Crook told the Apaches:

> The white people were crowding in all over the Western country, and soon it would be impossible for any one to live upon game; it would be driven away or killed off. Far better for every one to make up his mind to plant and to raise horses, cows, and sheep, and make his living in that way; his animals would thrive and increase while he slept, and in less than no time the Apache would be wealthier than the Mexican.

Crook promised to forgive the crimes of the past, to enforce the same laws for whites and Indians alike, and always to tell the truth. In a tone of gentle reason, he sold his listeners on the idea of Apache scouts:

> If every one came in without necessitating a resort to bloodshed he should be very glad; but, if any refused, then he should expect the good men to aid him in running down the bad ones. That was the way the white people did it; if there were bad men in a certain neighborhood, all the law-abiding citizens turned out to assist the officers of the law in arresting and punishing those who would not behave themselves.

The Apaches, recorded Burke, "listened with deep attention," and grunted *Inju* ("Good") at regular intervals.

From Fort Apache, Crook organized his first foray with Indians as scouts. His trail led north, into the deep forests of the Tonto Basin nestled under the high Mogollon Rim. His quarry was not Chiricahuas, but Tontos—the most northerly of all Apaches, a people, in Bourke's view, "wild and apparently incorrigible." Though the country was beautiful, well-watered, and teeming with late-summer wildflowers, Crook's party made painfully slow progress through the tangled woods, and for days at a time they were more or less lost.

At last, however, they fought a battle with fifteen or twenty Tontos, whose presence the soldiers divined when arrows began whizzing past their heads in the dense forest. They chased the Apaches toward the edge of a huge precipice, perhaps the Mogollon Rim itself. Two of the fleeing Indians were trapped by the cliff at their back. Crook fired and wounded one in the arm, and then the soldiers saw the fugitives leap off the cliff to an apparently certain death. But when they approached the cliff, the soldiers saw the two Tontos running down "the merest thread of a trail outlined in the vertical face of the basalt." No one even considered pursuing them.

Heartened by even so minimal a success, Crook arrived at Fort Verde, east of Prescott on the Verde River, where he planned a full-scale campaign against the Apaches. As he read his first newspapers in weeks, however, Crook realized, to his intense disgust, that he would have to put all his schemes on hold.

Four years earlier, a Board of Peace Commissioners had been established in Washington for the purpose of protecting Indians against the abuses of the frontier. Outraged by the Camp Grant massacre, the board now decided to send its secretary, Vincent Colyer, to Arizona to win over the Apaches by peace and kindness rather than by military terror. Approving the plan, President Grant gave Colyer the power to establish reservations. Crook understood that he must cease operations until Colyer's "interference" might run its course.

More than a hundred years later, it is hard to fix Vincent Colyer with a steady gaze. It is tempting to idealize him, for he seems to have been the first government official to treat the Apaches with the respect and humanity that we now, in the late twentieth century, believe was their due. Colyer was a Quaker from New York City and a successful artist. In the Civil War, as a staunch abolitionist, he had led a Negro regiment that he had mustered himself.

It was Colyer's view, both before and after his mission to the Southwest, that the Indians were innocent victims of American aggression. "The Apache Indians were the friends of the Americans when they first knew them; [and] they have always desired peace," he wrote in his official report, vastly oversimplifying the troubled history of Arizona. "The peaceable relations of the Apaches with the Americans continued until the latter adopted the Mexican theory of 'extermination,' and by acts of inhuman treachery and cruelty made them our implacable foes."

In the eyes of Crook and other veterans of the Indian wars, Colyer was a romantic fool. The historian Hubert Howe Bancroft called Colyer a "fanatic pacifist." Mild-spoken John G. Bourke referred to Colyer in his diary as "that spawn of hell." Crook could not contain his contempt, ridiculing Colyer's two-month ride through the Southwest in a memorable passage:

He harangued the Indians on his way, making peace as he went, and the Indians just immediately behind him left a trail of blood behind them from the murdered citizens. One Indian, Eskimi-yan [Eskiminzin, chief of the massacred Aravaipa], told Colyer that he was convinced that he, Colyer, could not come of mortal parents, for no man so good as he was could be so born. The discernment on the part of old "Skimmy" tickled Colyer's vanity to such an extent that he preached two sermons of which that was the text.

The territorial newspapers were even more savage. According to the *Arizona Miner,* Colyer was a "cold-blooded scoundrel [and] a red-handed assassin"; the citizens, the paper urged, ought to "dump the old devil into the shaft of some mine, and pile rocks upon him until he is dead."

Despite the brevity of Colyer's visit, its impact was profound. His first act in the Southwest was to establish a reservation for the Chihenne. Victorio's Apaches had long agreed that they would accept a reservation if it surrounded their sacred heartland at Ojo Caliente in New Mexico; but one bureaucrat after another had tried to push the Chihenne north onto the hated Tularosa River or far to the east with the Mescalero. Now Colyer repeated the mistake, insisting on Tularosa, in large part because of the valley's remoteness from white settlements. All the same, for the first time ever an official reservation for an Apache people had been created.

On September 2, 1871, Colyer arrived at Fort Apache. Within days he had established another sanctuary, this time for the White Mountain Apaches; it remains that people's reservation today. Colyer traveled on to Camp Grant, where he met the grieving Eskiminzin, who pleaded with the emissary from Washington to do what he could to restore the

Aravaipa children who had been sold into Mexican slavery. A week later, at Camp McDowell on the Verde River, Colyer listened to the plaint of a Tonto chief:

> We are tired of living in caves and on the tops of cold mountains. My women carry water two or three miles, from the little streams. They get water at night, because we are afraid of soldiers. Even rabbits are safer than my Tontos. We hide our children behind big rocks when we go to hunt the deer. But deer are not so many now. You say Tontos must not steal cattle, but *we must steal or starve.* White Americans have stolen our cornfields and our wheatfields. What are we to do?

It was a vivid evocation of what the American incursion meant to the lives of the Apaches, and it brought tears to Colyer's eyes.

Before Colyer left the territory in late October, he set up five more temporary reservations. Within weeks, more than four thousand Apaches had gathered on them. One "fanatic pacifist," it seemed, had done more in two months to advance relations between Indians and whites in Arizona than a decade of generals and governors. That Colyer's peace would not last was beyond his, or even President Grant's, control. In his report, Colyer sang the praises of the people he had mingled with so compassionately (if so briefly): "I have visited seven-eighths of all the Indians now under our flag, including Alaska, and I have not seen a more intelligent, cheerful, and grateful tribe of Indians than the roving Apaches of Arizona and New Mexico."

Biting his tongue, restraining all the military impulses that had become his second nature, Crook agreed to give the reservation system a fair trial. He sent Apache emissaries all through the wildernesses of Arizona and western New Mexico to spread news of his bargain. He would give the Apaches until February 16, 1872, to come in and settle on the reservations. After that date, any Indians still at large would be regarded as renegades, whom Crook would hunt down and kill or capture with all the rigor at his command.

Crook was not surprised when, only days after Colyer's return to Washington, the Apache depredations began anew. A particularly shocking attack was the ambush of a stagecoach near Wickenburg: seven of the eight passengers were killed, including three members of the government's Wheeler Surveying Expedition.

Though Colyer had left Arizona full of buoyant hopes about the results of his mission, his greatest disappointment was that, despite sending out word that he desired a conference, he had been unable to meet Cochise. No Arizona peace would ever be secure as long as the greatest Apache chief remained on the loose. Cochise's silence left Colyer uneasy.

The Quaker peacemaker had reason for his qualms. For Cochise and his Chokonen, the reservations Colyer had devised had little appeal. On September 4, at the very moment that Colyer was laying the groundwork for the White Mountain reservation at Fort Apache, Cochise led his warriors on a bold raid of Camp Crittenden, 130 miles to the south. In broad daylight, the Apaches drove off and captured the camp's entire herd of fifty-four horses and seven mules; the panic-stricken soldiers charged with guarding the herd failed to inflict a single injury.

Crook chafed at the reins that kept him in check. Like Cushing before him, he had formed something of an obsession. It was Cochise, above all other adversaries, whom he dreamed of conquering. In Crook's view, the Chokonen were "the worst of all the Apaches," and their famous leader was "an uncompromising enemy to all mankind."

Seven

■

This Is the Man

*C*ochise's parleys with white men near the Dragoons, at Cañada Alamosa, and at Fort Apache after 1869 marked his emergence from nearly a decade of furious secrecy. Between pledges of undying resistance, he had voiced the sorrows that beset him, giving his listeners an inkling of the attrition the White Eyes, for all their fumbling, had wrought among his Chokonen.

That Cochise was willing to talk at all was surprising. The Bascom affair had left him with an ineradicable distrust of white men. Now, as he conferred with representatives of the government, he kept a cadre of armed warriors around him as a bodyguard. He refused to enter any building or army tent, offering instead to spread blankets on the open ground. When he eventually accepted winter rations for his people, Cochise himself refused to eat agency beef, for fear it had been poisoned.

Sometime between 1867 and 1870, however, Cochise had met the man who would become the only friend among the White Eyes the great chief ever had. His name was Tom Jeffords, and his intercession had everything to do with the peace Cochise began to make in the 1870s.

Once the Apache wars were over, it was the generals who wrote the memoirs. No other white man ever gained a fraction of the understanding of Cochise's Apaches that Jeffords did. What we would not give for a detailed account of that knowledge, told in the man's own words!

But Jeffords never bothered to write a narrative of his remarkable journey into the heart of Chokonen culture, nor did he correct the errors and myths about his deeds that crept into print over the years. Although he lived until 1914, it was only in the last year of his life that a pair of historians sat down separately with Jeffords and wrung cursory résumés of his friendship with Cochise from the reclusive pioneer.

The legend of Jeffords and Cochise is one of the most powerful in the annals of the West. It serves the emotional needs of a nation of conquerors anxious to exorcise the guilt of conquest. The essence of the legend is that a lone civilian succeeded where whole armies had failed; that by walking unarmed into Cochise's camp, Jeffords astounded the chief with his bravery; that the two men became brothers, sealing the pact with a ritual commingling of their blood; and that shortly before Cochise died, he expressed his hope of seeing Jeffords again in the afterlife.

The legend was crystallized in Elliott Arnold's 1947 novel, *Blood Brother,* which three years later was made into a Jimmy Stewart movie called *Broken Arrow.* Both novel and film give Jeffords, who was never known to have romantic liaisons, not only a white woman but an Apache maiden as rival lovers.

Jeffords was a tall, slender man with a great red beard and whiskers. Late in life, he told one of his chroniclers that the name the Apaches gave him meant Red Whiskers. Around 1859, Jeffords had come to the Southwest as a prospector. By 1868 he was working for the Southern Overland mail service, which at great hazard sent stagecoaches on a regular run from Santa Fe to Tucson.

The discrepancy between the white and the Apache versions of Jeffords's first meeting with Cochise forms a lesson in the elusiveness of historical truth. Only weeks before he died, Jeffords told one of the historians that, as a supervisor for Southern Overland, he had lost fourteen drivers to Cochise in a short span of time. "I made up my mind that I wanted to see him," recalled Jeffords. Alone but armed, guided by an Indian of Cochise's band with whom he had made contact, Jeffords walked into the Chokonen camp. Surprised by this foolhardy act, Cochise let Jeffords, who spoke some Apache, talk. "I spent two or three days with him, discussing affairs, and sizing him up," Jeffords claimed. "This was the commencement of my friendship with Cochise. . . . He respected me and I respected him."

In the Apache version of the meeting, Jeffords was captured by Cochise's scouts. To their surprise, Red Whiskers showed no fear.

> The Apaches were so impressed by his courage that instead of killing him they took him to Cochise. . . . Cochise had shut himself off from White Eyes since the Bascom affair, and accepting a white man as his friend was a tribute to a brave man. No greater praise could be given Jeffords than to say that he won the friendship of Cochise.

According to the Apaches, the notion of blood brothers united by a ritual act was romantic bunk. The Chokonen had no such ritual. Nor, indeed, did Jeffords himself ever claim that he had mingled his blood with Cochise's, though he did insist that the chief's (as opposed to the tribe's) name for him was Chickasaw, or "Brother."

It was on account of Jeffords that Cochise came to Cañada Alamosa in late September 1871. The chief had avoided meeting Vincent Colyer there earlier in the month, but he grew curious about the reservation for the Chihenne that he heard Colyer had established. He sent a runner to Jeffords, telling his white friend that he wanted to come in to talk; then by cautious stages, guarded by well-armed warriors, he slowly approached Cañada Alamosa.

For the next six months, Cochise camped within fifteen miles of the temporary agency. He was not trustful enough to let his people erect their wickiups close by, as many of Victorio's Chihenne did. Instead he kept to the mountains, where he was safe from a surprise attack. But as winter approached, he allowed his people to draw rations from the agency. Again and again, Cochise turned over in his mind the White Eyes' insistence that the Apaches settle in the hated Tularosa valley. He had closed his eloquent September speech by enumerating his objections to the Tularosa. But the white men would not change their mind.

For the Chihenne, and even for Cochise, the appeal of a reservation centered around Cañada Alamosa lay above all in the fact that the sacred hot spring, Ojo Caliente, lay only a few miles upstream to the northwest. Long before the White Eyes came, however, Mexicans had built a small town at Cañada Alamosa. Over the years, the Apaches had developed a steady trading relationship with this village: it was a chief source for them not only of guns and ammunition but of whiskey. By 1871, the town, though part of New Mexico, was still peopled by Mexicans, still one of the only places north of the border where the Apaches could trade. (Called Monticello today, the town lies on a back-country dirt road, forgotten by history; it remains thoroughly Mexican in look and character.)

During his visit, Colyer had comprehended the appeal of Cañada Alamosa, but he was unwilling to displace the three-hundred-odd Mexican residents, a precaution that he believed establishing a reservation would require. Colyer had ridden up the beautiful canyon to Ojo Caliente, where he made a quick survey. Surprisingly for a man so sympathetic to Indians, he had concluded, without listening to any Apaches, that the land around the spring would never support the population of a reservation. This, despite the fact that for centuries the Chihenne had considered Ojo Caliente the best place to live on the surface of the earth.

Now, in order to reconcile the Apaches in Tularosa, the Indian agent and the army officers in charge in New Mexico hoped to persuade Cochise to travel along with prominent Chihenne to Washington to visit the Great Father, Ulysses Grant. In three or four separate meetings arranged by Jeffords, the Americans beseeched Cochise to make the journey. In subsequent years, a number of important Apaches would do so, including Cochise's eldest son, and those visits to Washington would have a powerful impact on all Apaches. But Cochise was not even tempted: he would rather talk to Grant on top of a mountain, he told one pair of officers.

From September 1871, when Colyer had set up the Tularosa reservation, through the end of March 1872, the situation at Cañada Alamosa withered into stalemate. Though at times Victorio and other Chihenne chiefs promised to send their people to the northern valley, whenever the actual removal loomed, they balked. When the Indian agent threatened to stop issuing rations, Victorio proudly told him to feed the government food to the wolves and bears. Their bluff having been called, the Americans moved their deadline back and back, until they declared that May 1, 1872, would be the date of the final removal.

During the months that Cochise camped near Cañada Alamosa, the whites were not always sure precisely where to find him. Thus when sporadic Chiricahua attacks on settlers flared up as far afield as Apache Pass, Cochise was routinely blamed: soldiers swore that the tactics the warriors had used were unmistakably Cochise's. The autonomy that lay at the heart of Apache life, dictating that each band had the right to seek its own battles, eluded the grasp of Americans who had just fought a great war to preserve their own nationhood. Among the Apache, even so great a chief as Cochise had no authority to order the humblest warrior into battle: the choice must be made of each man's free will each time. There was plenty of evidence of that autonomy close at hand. Although the Chihenne and the Chokonen were as close as any two Apache bands, in February a group of Chihenne under a chief named Loco, provoked perhaps by drink, had a nasty brawl with Cochise's men: two or three Apaches were killed and others were wounded.

The impasse over Tularosa was potentially explosive. Crook's counterpart in New Mexico, Colonel Gordon Granger, sensing the danger of further dithering, tried to force Cochise's hand. He called for a final parley with all the Chihenne and Chokonen to be held in March.

Cochise came. The meeting got off to a bad start. An officer presented the chief a personal letter from President Grant, bound with a red string. Cochise glowered, tore the string from the paper, and said, "The Red is not good." The startled officer tried to make light of the matter, unaware of the dangerous significance of red for the Chiricahua: it was a color that could attract lightning, and when someone died, it was a great insult to the bereaved if anyone wore red in their presence.

Granger addressed the chief, alternately blustering and pleading. He reiterated his demand that by May 1 all the Apaches must be settled at Tularosa. Cochise demurred and equivocated, but once more gave proof of his sorrowful eloquence. Thirty-five years later, an eyewitness recalled the chief's speech from memory. The exact words are thus suspect, but the phrasing and the meaning sound very much Cochise's:

> I have fought long and as best I could against you. I have destroyed many of your people, but where I have destroyed one white man many have come in his place; but where an Indian has been killed, there has been none to come in his place, so that the great people that welcomed you with acts of kindness to this land are now but a

feeble band that fly before your soldiers as the deer before the hunter.... I am the last of my family, a family that for very many years have been the leaders of this people, and on me depends their future, whether they shall utterly vanish from the land or that a small remnant remain for a few years to see the sun rise over these mountains, their home.

Cochise again pledged that if the government would set up its reservation here, near the sacred hot spring, rather than on the Tularosa, he would bring his people in. It was Granger's turn to equivocate. And when the colonel reiterated his plea that Cochise go to Washington, the chief turned contemptuous. He would not go to Washington, he said once more; he did not like white men's ways; "he did not care to eat little fishes out of tin boxes." (For Apaches, a strong taboo prohibited eating fish of any kind, for it was a creature close in nature to the dreaded snake; the white men's sardines seemed especially contemptible.)

Still Granger persisted. If Cochise would not go to Washington, would he authorize Loco and Victorio to make binding agreements for the Chokonen? Cochise did not even bother to answer.

"The great father in Washington wants you and Loco and Victorio to go to Washington," said Granger.

"I am not a child," Cochise rejoined sharply, "and would rather talk to you in this country."

The chief could not seem to convey to the stubborn colonel why he had no interest in going to Washington. "I would much rather live here in the mountains where the grass dies," he told Granger, "for when I [lie] down, if it gets in my hair and I can get it out, I know that all things are right here."

At the end of the talk, Granger tried to win Cochise's gratitude by inviting him to go with an escort of soldiers to Cañada Alamosa, where he would be showered with gifts. Jeffords himself urged the mission, vouching for the honesty of the soldiers. But Cochise turned upon his white friend, the bitter past blazing in his answer: "You believe these white men. I trusted them once; I went to their camp; my [brother and two nephews] were hung; no, I will not go."

The obtuse Granger seemed to think his grand parley had obtained the desired end. In the ultimate event, only 350 Apaches ever settled on the Tularosa, where they stayed for a mere four months. None of them were Cochise's Chokonen. Within ten days of his meeting with Granger, the chief had fled New Mexico. He had vanished in the night with all his people, leaving Granger to guess where he had gone.

Meanwhile, in Arizona, Crook had been impatiently biding his time, giving Colyer's honeyed dreams of peace the chance to prove their foolishness. As his deadline of February 16, 1872, for all Apaches to appear on the reservations neared, Crook prepared to go back into the field. He was all but certain that Cochise and others would refuse the reservation. Crook claimed he had planted spies—Apaches loyal to the government—among the Chokonen in the Dragoon Mountains. He stood ready to "iron all the wrinkles out of Cochise's band." His plan was to surround the Chokonen in the Dragoons with a huge force at night, and at daylight "give them such a clearing out that it would end him for all time."

Then, just before the deadline, to his chagrin, Crook was forestalled for the second time in half a year. The peace-lovers in Washington, Crook thought, ought to have learned from the futility of Colyer's mission that an aggressive military campaign was the only hope in Arizona. Instead, Grant and his Secretary of War concluded just the opposite: to try peace again. This time their missionary was Brigadier General Oliver Otis Howard, who outranked Crook.

Years later Crook complained that Howard's interference caused him to lose much face among "my Indians"—the White Mountain and Coyotero Apaches he had recruited as scouts. "They thought I was afraid of Cochise, because I left him unmolested. They said there was no justice or sense in not subjugating him, as he was the worst in the whole business."

Two years younger than Crook, Howard had performed as well at West Point as Crook had poorly, graduating fourth in his class of forty-six. In the Civil War he had served bravely, losing his right arm at the battle of Fair Oaks in 1862 but returning to the field for subsequent frays. Like Colyer, Howard was a fervent abolitionist: after the war he became commissioner of the Freedmen's Bureau, the agency set up to deal with the four million ex-slaves the war had liberated. Howard University, which he helped found in 1867, was named for him.

A fundamentalist Christian rather than a Quaker, Howard was famed for his honesty. The Apaches had never seen anyone like him. An eyewitness recorded the general's unintentional impact on one of the first groups of Indians he met at Camp Grant in 1872. No sooner had

Howard greeted the seated Apaches than he suddenly knelt and prayed out loud to God. "In two minutes there wasn't an Indian to be seen," claimed the witness. "They scattered just like partridges when they see a hawk." To the Apaches, the bearded one-armed man in the blue uniform must be conjuring up some sort of black medicine. Only reluctantly were they coaxed back to the conference ground.

Crook greeted Howard civilly, and was civilly greeted in return. The Arizona commander's private thoughts were less generous:

> General Howard was fond of public speaking. His themes generally were "How He was Converted" and "The Battle of Gettysburg." . . . I was very much amused at the General's opinion of himself. He told me that he thought the Creator had placed him on earth to be the Moses to the Negro. Having accomplished that mission, he felt satisfied his next mission was with the Indian.

In turn, Howard privately found Crook "peculiar":

> He was even more reticent than General Grant, carefully keeping all his plans and thoughts to himself. . . . The general had that art which some men possess of saying very little to you in conversation, being at the same time such an attentive listener that one was unconsciously drawn out in discourse.

Howard managed to make treaties with some of the more peaceful bands of Apaches. He established another reservation, headquartered at San Carlos, contiguous with the Fort Apache reserve to the south: it, too, has lasted till the present day. In June he returned to Washington, taking an entourage of Indians with him. Even as he headed east, he planned a second trip to Arizona, for, like Colyer before him, Howard had been frustrated in the chief goal of his mission: to meet with Cochise.

The party of Indians who had been talked into coming to Washington to meet the President included two Pimas, a Papago chief, two Yavapais, two Aravaipa Apaches, and two White Mountain Apaches. With wagons carrying their gear they rode on horseback to Santa Fe, where they boarded a stagecoach for Pueblo, Colorado.

It is likely that no Arizona Apache had ever before seen a railroad. Curious and fearful, the Indians sat on the tracks at Pueblo and fingered the cross-ties and spikes. When Howard bade them climb aboard a passenger car, their fear intensified. As the train began to move, the Indians hid on the floor and covered their faces with their hands.

Howard tried to reassure them, and soon they were sitting upright and staring out the window. The general noticed that as the train slid through the landscape, the Apaches assiduously counted the mountains. Finally Meguil, a White Mountain Apache who had lost an eye in combat, told Howard in a resigned voice that he could no longer count the mountains; he would have to rely on the general to lead him back to his homeland.

Back east, Howard took his charges on energetic sightseeing tours of New York, Philadelphia, and Washington. In New York, the Indians saw tall buildings, Central Park, and the shipyards. Nothing astonished them so much, however, as when Meguil returned from a brief absence with two eyes—a glass one having been inserted into his sightless socket by a specialist.

Perhaps the most frightening episode on the eastern tour was a visit to a Pennsylvania penitentiary. Howard observed the Indians' deep dismay and compassion for the inmates, without recognizing its source. For an Apache, to be locked in a cage was the most hideous of punishments, worse than the cruelest torture. Meguil knew: he had spent a year in a Santa Fe prison for a crime he said he had not committed.

In Washington the Indians met President Grant and exhanged speeches with the Great Father. They were far more impressed, however, with the students at the College of Deaf Mutes (today's Gallaudet College). Within minutes, the Indians had improvised a sign language with these students, pantomiming animals such as the horse, dog, and bear.

The theory behind the practice of taking prominent Indians back east, which had begun long before Howard's 1872 jaunt, was that these ambassadors would be overwhelmed by the sheer size and might of the United States and dazzled by its technological accomplishments. The Indians would thus lose the heart to fight on against impossible odds, and would also come to envy and then to emulate white ways. Once back home, their testimony to what they had seen would ripple through their people, multiplying the impact of the visit a hundredfold.

Howard witnessed gratifying instances of such "conversions." In a Presbyterian church in New York, Pedro, the other White Mountain Apache, spoke to the congregation through an interpreter.

You have schools, churches, places where clothes are made, houses filled with wealth; you have wagons, horses, [railroad] cars, and more than I can speak of. We have nothing. We are very poor. I have been thinking hard. We had long ago all the land; the Indians were once as one man. Now they are divided and the white men have all the land and all things. Now I am going to be a white man. I shall wear the white man's clothes. I shall cook and eat the white man's food, and I want my children to go to school and learn to be white men.

The churchgoers answered Pedro with "ringing applause."

But Howard was intelligent enough also to listen when a skeptical and experienced fellow officer who had heard Pedro's speech took him aside. "When a chief returns from Washington to his tribe his Indians do not follow him," the man whispered in Howard's ear. "They declare that he has been bewitched, or had 'bad medicine,' and they do not believe anything he tells them."

This gloomy prediction would come true again and again. Howard was never able to gauge the long-term effect of his foray east with his Indian friends, and he wanted badly to believe in the best outcome. Even his own testimony, however, sounds ambiguous today. Meguil's glass eye provoked the expected astonishment and wonder among his White Mountain people. The nonetheless one-eyed Apache said good-bye to the one-armed general. Several years later Howard learned that Meguil had been killed "in a petty Indian outbreak." Santo, an Aravaipa man who was Howard's favorite among the touring party, accepted the gift of a New Testament from the devout general. Decades later an officer told Howard that Santo always slept at night with the book under his head, though he had never learned to read.

During Howard's journey east and back, from April through August 1872, Cochise spent much of his time near Janos, in Chihuahua, where his people could still trade with Mexicans, and much in the Dragoon stronghold in Arizona. For five months he avoided all contact with Americans. During that time there were many Chiricahua raids on settlers in southern Arizona, though few if any of them were led by

Cochise himself. Crook fumed in his unwanted leisure, as he awaited Howard's return.

The all-consuming goal of Howard's second mission was to meet Cochise. From Fort Apache, the general sent out several Apache messengers to try to make contact with the Chokonen chief; they all came back empty-handed. Following a vague rumor, Howard decided to seek Cochise in New Mexico.

He had already planned to visit the new Tularosa reservation, where some 350 Apaches, mostly Chihenne, had grudgingly settled. From the moment he arrived, Howard was besieged by Apache complaints. The water at Tularosa was bad, they insisted; the climate was cold, with too short a growing season; the children were falling ill and dying. The Apaches pleaded once more for what they had always desired: to be allowed to live near Cañada Alamosa. Howard walked around the Tularosa camp, recognized the validity of the complaints, and on September 16 declared that he would abolish the ill-starred reservation.

While he was at Tularosa, Howard for the first time met "a singular character" of whom he had heard a great deal. Much of the gossip was slanderous: "Tom Jeffords! He's a bad egg; he trades with Indians, sells them whisky, powder and shot. They don't kill him 'cause he's bought 'em up." But an army officer told Howard about Jeffords's past success in finding Cochise. Howard arranged an interview.

As soon as he had entered the tent of the tall, red-whiskered frontiersman, Howard blurted out, "Can you take me to the camp of the Indian Cochise?"

Jeffords took a moment to answer, as he stared into Howard's eyes. "Will you go there with me, General, without soldiers?"

Howard knew the risk involved, knew that few officers would agree to such terms. But he was a brave man and a determined one, and he believed absolutely in God's benediction. "Yes, if necessary," he answered.

"Then I will take you to him," said Jeffords.

Thus began an extraordinary pilgrimage that was to have a profound result. Jeffords's first act was to locate two of Cochise's allies, Chie and Ponce, and persuade them to lead the praying general to the Chokonen chief. Chie was a nephew of Cochise. Ponce, a Chihenne, may have been Mangas Coloradas's son; he was related by marriage to Cochise. Without the skill and protection of these two Apaches, Howard's search would have ended either in a wild goose chase or a fatal ambush.

Near Silver City, New Mexico, the small party crossed paths with a group of prospectors, one of whom had lost a brother to Cochise's Apaches. Cursing vividly at the sight of Ponce and Chie, the man raised his rifle and prepared to shoot. Howard at once stepped between the prospector and the Apaches and said, "You will kill me first." The man relented, riding on as he flung back aspersions against the President's peace policy.

When they were still seventy miles from Cochise's stronghold, Howard witnessed an impressive display of Indian alertness. Chie abruptly stopped, built a fire, and sent a smoke signal into the air. Then, walking ahead of the rest of the party, he barked like a coyote. From high above, a coyote cry answered him. Chie ran up a mountain and soon returned with one of Cochise's scouts. The man informed Howard's entourage that he had been trailing them for two days and forty miles. Chie and Ponce might have been aware of his presence; Howard had no inkling.

The peace party consisted of Jeffords, an army captain, the two Apaches, and Howard. During the following days, as they rode west toward the Dragoons, the junior officer grew terrified and urged Howard to turn back. Firm in his resolve, the general tried to stiffen his captain's backbone, even as he privately deliberated whether to send the man back to Fort Bowie at Apache Pass.

Guided by Chie and Ponce, the party traversed the Dragoons by a low pass and came to a campsite on the range's western slope. Ponce maintained a day-long smoke signal: five fires in a circle, a semaphor for five riders coming on a journey of peace. There was no answer.

That morning, without explanation, Chie had bolted off up the mountain and disappeared. Many hours later, at dusk, two Apache boys approached on a single horse. They bore the message that Chie was in camp a few miles to the north, where the Apaches awaited the rest of the party. Without hesitation, Howard packed up and set off into the twilight. Well after dark, the party entered a cul-de-sac of granite boulders and cliffs, where Chie and a small group of Apaches greeted them.

The night must have been an anxious one, though Howard's account is staunch with retrospective equanimity. Their hosts appeared "curious and happy," and children nestled at the foot of Howard's bedroll; but a subchief who visited the general seemed "gloomy and reserved," and there was no word from Cochise.

"Will it be peace?" Howard asked Ponce.

The Apache shook his head and said softly, *"Quien sabe?"*—"Who knows?"

In the morning, as the party's anxiety grew, a sudden cry came from the distance; Ponce blurted out, "He is coming!" The Apaches hurried to rearrange their campfire circle and to lay a blanket on the ground for Cochise's seat. A fierce-looking solitary rider, lance in hand, galloped toward camp. It was not Cochise, however, but a "short and thick-set" man "painted in that ugly way where vermilion is combined with black."

The man dismounted and hurried up to Jeffords, whom he embraced in Apache fashion, first clasping him on one side and then the other. Jeffords whispered to Howard: "This is *his* brother." In Cochise's presence, no one dared utter his name. Jeffords so respected this ritual acknowledgment of the chief's authority that he could not violate it even in English.

Soon four Apaches approached on horseback. The "fine-looking Indian" who led them dismounted and embraced Jeffords, who turned to Howard, saying, "General, this is he; this is the man."

Cochise grasped Howard's hand and said, *"Buenos dias."* The general later recorded his first impression of the chief: "A man fully six feet in height, well proportioned, large, dark eye[s], face slightly painted with vermilion, unmistakably an Indian; hair straight and black, with a few silver threads, touching his coat-collar behind." As he stared into Cochise's eyes, Howard was seized with a Christian perplexity: "How strange it is," he said to himself, "that such a man can be the robber and murderer so much complained of."

With Jeffords interpreting from Apache directly to English, the two leaders began to talk.

"Will the General explain the object of his visit?" Cochise asked.

"The President sent me to make peace between you and the white people," Howard answered.

"Nobody wants peace more than I do."

Howard leapt in his eagerness: "Then as I have full power we can make peace."

The general explained that he wished to set up a single reservation for Chihenne and Chokonen near Cañada Alamosa. "I have been there," said Cochise evenly, "and I like the country." Then suddenly he made a counterproposal: "Why not give me Apache Pass? Give me that and I will protect all the roads. I will see that nobody's property is taken by Indians."

Caught off guard, Howard argued on for the Cañada, lecturing the Chokonen chief on the virtues of the Chihenne country in terms of hunting, planting, and grazing. Instead of answering, Cochise asked Howard if he was prepared to stay in the Dragoons for the ten days it would require to call in his subchiefs. Howard agreed.

Without warning, Cochise launched into a diatribe on the decade of American persecution he had endured. "The worst place of all is Apache Pass," he said angrily.

> There, five [actually six] Indians, one my brother, were murdered. Their bodies were hung up and kept there till they were skeletons. . . . Now Americans and Mexicans kill an Apache on sight. I have retaliated with all my might. My people have killed Americans and Mexicans and taken their property. Their losses have been greater than mine. I have killed ten white men for every Indian slain, but I know that the whites are many and the Indians are few. . . . Why shut me up on a reservation? We will make peace. We will keep it faithfully. But let us go around free as Americans do. Let us go wherever we please.

As Cochise had known, it took precisely ten days for all his subchiefs to come in. Ever distrustful, the Chokonen leader demanded at the outset that Howard return at once to Fort Bowie to declare a cease-fire, so that his people would not be attacked by soldiers as they streamed from afar to the Dragoon stronghold. Wearied by his journey and reluctant to leave, Howard offered to send his captain. No, said Cochise, only the general himself could command the obedience of American soldiers.

It was fifty miles to Fort Bowie, and Howard did not know the way, but he agreed to go if Cochise would furnish a guide. Cochise gave him his nephew.

With Chie guiding day and night, the two men made a lightning trek to Fort Bowie and back. Howard spoke only a little Spanish; Chie had but two phrases of English, "Yes, sir," and "Milky Way." As they approached Apache Pass, Howard noticed that a profound distress came over his young companion. Mistakenly thinking Chie to be a son of Mangas Coloradas, Howard attributed his sorrow to memories of his father's martyrdom, which the general thought—also mistakenly—had occurred at Apache Pass. In fact, Chie's sorrow had an equally direct source. He was most likely the son of Coyuntara, Cochise's gifted brother, whom Bascom's superior officer had hanged at Apache Pass in 1861.

At Fort Bowie Howard issued orders against any attack on Apaches heading toward the Dragoons, and he sent written notice of his doings to Washington. The next day he was back on the trail. That night was an unusually cold one. The two men bivouacked at Sulphur Springs, where Howard was given a chance to demonstrate his magnanimity. The general invited Chie to lay his bedroll next to his and to crawl under the great bearskin robe he used as a sleeping bag. Chie was horrified. *"Shosh toujudah Apache!"* he exclaimed, an oath that Howard managed to construe as "Bear bad for Apache."

He was right: the bear was a mystic, quasi-human creature for the Chiricahua. They never ate its flesh, or killed it except in self-defense; they believed that evil people sometimes returned after death in the bodies of bears. Howard accepted Chie's revulsion. "I told him to throw [the bearskin robe] aside and we would sleep without it. He was a warm bed-fellow."

Back in the stronghold, Howard whiled away the time as the various Chiricahua bands assembled. The Apaches held a dance of welcome and shared their venison and mescal. Howard made lively ethnographic notes on the customs and material culture of his hosts. And he bargained on with Cochise.

On October 10, the last subchief arrived. The next day Cochise called a conference of all his lieutenants. Howard impetuously started to join the gathering, until Jeffords told him to "stay where he was." Up to the very end, Howard held out for the Cañada Alamosa reservation, but he was no match for Cochise's stubbornness. At last the general granted the Chiricahua a large reservation around Apache Pass. Jeffords would become the Indian agent.

Cochise announced his agreement in a characteristic formula: "Hereafter," he said, "the white man and the Indian are to drink of the same water, eat of the same bread, and be at peace." Howard silently rejoiced as he thanked his God. "I felt," he later reported, "that the object of my mission was now accomplished."

There was no dearth of doubters both within and beyond Arizona as the Chokonen prepared to settle on a new reservation. George Crook felt sure that, sooner or later, Cochise would return to his rampages. The territory's newspapers castigated Howard for knuckling under to the chief's demand for land around Apache Pass: far better had the general forced the Chokonen to migrate to New Mexico.

In the eleven years during which he had waged all-out war against the White Eyes, Cochise's rage had slackened little. Yet he was not the same man in 1872 that he had been in 1861. A dark sense of doom burdened his spirit, as his people were reduced to building tiny fires at night for fear of discovery, as they hid in mountains that they had always owned without challenge. Cochise bitterly mourned the passing of every warrior whom American bullets hurled to an early death.

The great chief had himself been wounded in battle a number of times. He could accept these passing affronts, as his stoic pride drove him through quick convalescences. Not once in those eleven years had a personal injury slowed Cochise's charge on a saddleless horse.

Yet something else was wrong. Jeffords knew about it, but perhaps no other white man. Cochise was in constant physical agony. The pain centered in his stomach; it sharpened whenever he ate, and for days at a time he could swallow only water. Unlike the wounds the bullets had made, this havoc inside him responded to no medicine. Day after day, the pain grew worse, and the chief of the Chokonen grew weaker.

Eight

■

Geronimo Ascendant

By 1872 Geronimo was still virtually unknown to white Americans. If by that date Crook had even heard the name of the warrior who would become his most persistent antagonist, it would have conjured up little more than one of a hundred renegades loosely linked to Cochise's band. By his own testimony, Geronimo had already led war parties for both Cochise and Mangas Coloradas. He was, however, neither a Chokonen nor a Chihenne, but a Bedonkohe Apache.

The Bedonkohe were a small tribe whose territory lay north and west of that of the Chokonen. By 1905, there were only nine or ten full-blooded Bedonkohe still alive. As a people, they have a shadowy place in the works of American ethnographers. Morris Opler, the great student of the Chiricahua, does not even recognize the Bedonkohe as a separate group. Among themselves, however, the Bedonkohe zealously preserved their tribal identity. The name means "In Front at the End People," apparently a reference to their position on the western fringe of Chiricahua territory, bordering the homeland of the Pima.

Geronimo was born sometime around 1823, near where the Middle Fork of the Gila joins the West Fork, not far from the Gila cliff dwellings in southwestern New Mexico. As an infant, he bathed in the hot springs that made the Middle Fork such an appealing campsite for the Bedonkohe, just as it had been for the Mogollon who had built the cliff dwellings six centuries before them. The towering canyon walls, of ruddy andesite and conglomerate, sheltered Geronimo's people; huge sycamores and cottonwoods stood alongside the stream, whose thread ran clear and sweet throughout the year.

Like all Apaches, Geronimo attached a special significance to his birthplace: whenever in his wanderings he came again to the Middle Fork, he would roll on the ground to the four directions. Geronimo's mother taught him the legends of the tribe, while his father steeped him in the lore of famous battles. He was the fourth of eight children. Nearly eight decades later, Geronimo would recall cavorting with his siblings in the canyon that was home:

> Sometimes we played at hide-and-seek among the rocks and pines; sometimes we loitered in the shade of the cottonwood trees or sought the shudock [a kind of wild cherry] while our parents worked in the field. Sometimes we played that we were warriors. We would practice stealing upon some object that represented an enemy. . . . Sometimes we would hide away from our mother to see if she could find us, and often when thus concealed go to sleep and perhaps remain hidden for many hours.

Like all Apaches, Geronimo's family were nomadic; yet they tended small plots of corn and beans, of melons and pumpkins, in a two-acre valley-bottom field. Much of the harvest was stored away in caves, to be retrieved during the lean weeks of winter. There was tobacco growing wild in the valley, which the adults gathered, dried in the sun, and rolled in oak leaves to smoke. Tobacco was a rare, luxurious substance, and smoking was forbidden boys until adolescence, women until middle age. Adults also gathered medicinal herbs: cinque-foil ground to a powder for bodily aches, cudweed for diarrhea, oak root as an eyewash, crushed sage for colds, the osha root for coughs, and the like.

Apaches did not routinely name their babies at birth. Often two or three months passed before something in the child's behavior suggested a name; even then it was provisional, and might be changed as late as the child's tenth year. In a sense, an Apache had to earn his name. We do not know at what age the name Geronimo's people gave him stuck, nor what exactly they meant by it: Goyahkla, "One Who Yawns."

From childhood on, Geronimo practiced the arts of war and survival: even hiding from his mother was part of his schooling as a raider and warrior. A Chiricahua boyhood in fact amounted to a rigorous apprenticeship in hunting, gathering, fitness, and combat. To learn accuracy, a small boy would take a willow branch, affix a pellet of mud to the end, and whip it like a projectile at a bird sitting on a branch. He would construct a slingshot out of hide and thong, and a kind of popgun out of a cored stick of elderberry or ash. From an early age he owned a toy bow and arrows, which he shot for hours, practicing for distance and accuracy. In a typical game, one boy shot an arrow into an earthen bank; his opponent tried to plant his own arrow so that it touched or crossed the first one. If he succeeded, he won the arrow. A boy would also make a target of twisted grass, throw it into the air, and try to shoot it before it hit the ground.

The bow-and-arrow play evolved into real hunting. As young as six or seven, a Chiricahua boy would bring down squirrels, birds, rabbits, mice, and even badgers. Much of his training involved learning how to crawl close enough to his prey to shoot it. When he had made his first kill, the young hunter was supposed to swallow its heart whole and raw, to guarantee further plenty in the chase. Boys also built small fires at night to attract bats, then threw their moccasins at the flying creatures so adroitly as to bring them to earth, where they killed them.

Both boys and girls went out on gathering missions, seeking delicacies it would have been a waste of time for adults to collect: the fruits of certain cactuses, willow and cottonwood buds (chewed like gum), ground cherries. They learned how to catch a certain kind of bee, cut it open, and suck out its honey without getting stung.

A boy's fitness training began in earnest at age eight. He would be forced to get up before dawn to run to the top of a mountain and back before sunrise. He might run as far as four miles with a mouthful of water he was not allowed to swallow, or with his mouth full of pebbles. "Your legs are your friends," his mentors would tell the boy; after a meal, he was supposed to rub grease on them to "feed" his legs. To train for speed, a boy would chase butterflies and birds and try to catch them with his bare hands. In winter, he was required to push a ball of snow around until his elders let him stop, or to break through the ice on a stream or lake for a predawn plunge; if he refused, he was whipped. As a kind of graduation exam, a boy undertook a two-day cross-country run without food or sleep.

When still quite small, a Chiricahua boy would fight a tree with his hands, trying to break a limb as big around as his arm. At a later age, boys would practice war by fighting in groups of four against others their own age, with slingshots and stones or even bows and arrows. Occasionally serious harm was done in these training fights.

Another vital piece of warcraft was learning to "creep and freeze." Apaches became extraordinarily good at standing or crouching absolutely motionless for minutes at a time. Soldiers chasing Apaches into the mountains would report again and again that the Indians seemed to "melt" into the landscape. The Chiricahua themselves believed that certain men (including, in his adulthood, Geronimo) had the power to make themselves invisible. The Apache training in immobility no doubt helped account for both phenomena.

At age seven a boy began his novitiate in horsemanship. He learned to climb on a horse's back by planting a foot on its leg, clutching its mane, and crawling on top. The boy mastered everything there was to know about guarding and caring for horses. Once he could ride bareback, he learned to make the horse jump barriers, and he practiced riding down a steep slope while he hung off one side and snatched objects from the ground.

As early as age ten, the boy began a long ceremonial training as a raiding and war novice. He had to perform well on four actual, as opposed to training, expeditions (four being the Apaches' sacred number) to be elevated to the status of full warrior. Geronimo achieved this milestone—the most important in a Chiricahua's man's life—at seventeen.

One day during his adolescence, Geronimo's Bedonkohe were visited by a band of Nednhi from far to the south in the Sierra Madre of Mexico. One of the Bedonkohe was cousin to one of the Nednhi. It was thus that Geronimo met Juh, who would become his chief, his constant ally in war, and his brother-in-law. Himself a teenager, Juh befriended Geronimo during this visit in the Gila Mountains; a "mischievous" boy, he tormented the Bedonkohe girls by trailing them as they gathered acorns, then stealing their baskets when they were full. In this fashion, Juh got to know Ishton, Geronimo's tall, beautiful sister. Later Juh returned to the Gila to take Ishton as his bride.

Although Geronimo's people had been at war with the Mexicans, and with the Spanish before them, for centuries, the Bedonkohe led a peaceful and secure life in their sanctuary at the headwaters of the Gila. Not until he was an adult did Geronimo see his first white American.

While he was still a teenager, Geronimo fell in love with a "slender, delicate" Nednhi girl named Alope. As soon as the council of warriors admitted him, Geronimo went to Alope's father to ask for her hand. "Perhaps he wanted to keep Alope with him," Geronimo mused many years later, "for she was a dutiful daughter; at any rate he asked many ponies for her." The seventeen-year-old warrior departed without a word. A few days later, he returned with a herd of ponies, gave them to Alope's father, and took her as his bride. "That was all the marriage ceremony necessary in our tribe."

Geronimo built a new lodge near that of his mother and covered it with buffalo hides. Inside he hung mountain-lion hides as trophies of his hunting; Alope put up beadwork decorations that she had made, and drew pictures on the inner surfaces of the buffalo-hide walls. "She was a good wife, but she was never strong," Geronimo said later. "We followed the traditions of our fathers and were happy. Three children came to us—children that played, loitered, and worked as I had done."

Because of these new alliances with the Nednhi—his marriage to Alope, Juh's to Ishton—Geronimo began to spend much time south of the border, in the Nednhi heartland. Both northern Mexican states, Sonora in 1835 and Chihuahua in 1837, had enacted genocidal laws offering a bounty on every Apache scalp turned in, even those of women and children. As late as 1849, Chihuahua raised the price on an Apache man's scalp to 200 pesos (about $200), while the rate for a woman or child taken captive was set at 150 pesos. In that year alone, the Chihuahuan government paid out 17,896 pesos to bounty hunters. But instead of controlling the Apaches, the lucre created a bloody chaos. Cynical hunters soon learned that the government could not tell an Apache scalp from that of a Comanche or a Tarahumara; they even killed Mexicans and cashed in their scalps.

Despite the official bounty, the presidio (or fort) of Janos, in northwestern Chihuahua, maintained a tradition dating back to the eighteenth century of offering the Apaches a place where they could safely trade and camp. Recognizing that the bounty system was not working, Chihuahuan officials reluctantly canceled it in June 1850, signing a peace treaty at Janos with three Apache leaders. Unfortunately, the Sonorans made no such truce.

The most important event in Geronimo's life—one that shaped the course of his angry career—occurred on March 5, 1851. With Alope, his mother, and his three children, Geronimo and other Bedonkohes had camped just outside Janos. Mangas Coloradas himself was in charge of the Apache band. For several days running, the men went into town to trade, leaving a small guard with the women and children to take care of camp.

Fifty-four years later, Geronimo remembered the tragedy:

> Late one afternoon when returning from town we were met by a few women and children who told us that Mexican troops from some other town had attacked our camp, killed all the warriors of the guard, captured all our ponies, secured our arms, destroyed our supplies, and killed many of our women and children. Quickly we separated, concealing ourselves as best we could until nightfall, when we assembled at our appointed place of rendezvous—a thicket by the river. Silently we stole in one by one: sentinels were placed, and, when all were counted, I found that my aged mother, my young wife, and my three small children were among the slain.

The party that accomplished this massacre was an army of four hundred soldiers from Sonora, led by the newly appointed commander and inspector of the military colonies, Colonel Jose Maria Carrasco. One scholar characterizes Carrasco as "a highly controversial figure who thought himself omniscient." On the flimsy pretext of pursuing raiders who had stolen seven mules from Bacerac, a town just inside Sonora, Carrasco crossed the border into Chihuahua and marched toward Janos, where he knew a large band of Apaches was camped.

Carrasco sincerely believed that these Apaches under Mangas had been responsible for numerous recent depredations in Sonora. Even so, he lacked the authority to cross state lines and take military action. Chihuahuan officials were outraged at the slaughter, and complained bitterly to Mexico City. They insisted further that the Apaches camped near Janos had been living in peace and were innocent of the Sonoran raiding. In the end, the Mexican government exonerated Carrasco.

By his own account, Carrasco's surprise attack left twenty-one

Apaches dead in the field: sixteen men and five women. It seems likely that he vastly underreported the number of women and children killed. Sixty-two others, all but six of them women and children, were taken captive. They were transported hundreds of miles to the south, then distributed as "servants"—a euphemism for slaves—among many different haciendas. None of them ever rejoined their people.

Geronimo's grief left him mute. "There were no lights in camp, so without being noticed I silently turned away and stood by the river. How long I stood there I do not know."

That night Mangas called a council of his warriors. To the various measures proposed, Geronimo offered not a word of support or opposition. As fiercely as they longed to avenge their loss, the Apaches recognized the odds. They had eighty warriors left against Carrasco's four hundred, and they were without horses, arms, or supplies. Finally Mangas decreed that the survivors must walk north at once, in the middle of the night, and hope to cross the border into Arizona before the Mexicans could again attack. Most bitterly, they could not even retrieve and bury their dead. Geronimo had to leave his mother, his wife, and his three children to the vultures and coyotes.

"I stood until all had passed," he later reported, "hardly knowing what I would do—"

> I had no weapon, nor did I hardly wish to fight, neither did I contemplate recovering the bodies of my loved ones, for that was forbidden. I did not pray, nor did I resolve to do anything in particular, for I had no purpose left. I finally followed the tribe silently, keeping just within hearing distance of the soft noise of the feet of the retreating Apaches.

As the wretched band made its way north, Geronimo kept his silence; he could not eat for several days. Other Apaches respected his gloom, for no other warrior had lost so many members of his family. When he arrived at the headwaters of the Gila, he was smitten anew by the sight of his children's toys, of the beadwork and drawings Alope had hung inside their lodge. Geronimo burned everything, buffalo hides and all, and also burned his mother's lodge to the ground.

All the way north, he had brooded with an Apache intensity. For the rest of his life, as he testified in old age, "my heart would ache for revenge upon Mexico."

Geronimo would never become an Apache chief, in part because his Bedonkohe tribe grew so fragmented during his lifetime. His paramountcy would rest on two things: his brilliance as a war leader and his talent as a medicine man. An Apache could not deliberately seek what the people called Power: it came to him mysteriously, often in visions. Nor could he refuse to wield whatever Power Ussen, god of the Apaches, granted.

As far as we know, Geronimo's first inkling of his Power came to him as he was mourning his family after the Janos massacre. In the telling of an Apache who as a boy was close to Geronimo:

> He had gone out alone and was sitting with his head bowed weeping when he heard a voice calling his name, "Goyahkla!" Four times . . . it called. Then it spoke. "No gun can ever kill you. I will take the bullets from the guns of the Mexicans, so they will have nothing but powder. And I will guide your arrows."

According to Geronimo's account, once Mangas's men had reached safety in the north, they set about collecting arms. Mangas then called a council, in which every warrior declared his desire to wreak revenge on the Sonoran soldiers. Geronimo was sent as an emissary first to Cochise, then to Juh, to enlist the aid of the Chokonen and the Nednhi. In his address to the Chokonen, Geronimo spoke forcefully:

> We are men the same as the Mexicans are—we can do to them what they have done to us. Let us go forward and trail them—I will lead you to their city—we will attack them in their homes. I will fight in the front of the battle—I only ask you to follow me to avenge this wrong done by these Mexicans. . . .
>
> If I am killed no one need mourn for me. My people have all been killed in that country, and I, too, will die if need be.

Geronimo's pleas fell on receptive ears. Nearly a year after the massacre at Janos, a three-winged army under Mangas, Cochise, and Juh—one of the largest Chiricahua forces ever assembled—came together at the Mexican border. The warriors painted their faces, fastened their head bands, and started south on foot, eschewing horses for reasons of stealth. They traveled forty to forty-five miles a day, with Geronimo as guide.

Near Arizpe, one of the few important towns in northern Sonora, the party camped. Eight Mexicans rode out from town to parley: the Apaches seized and killed them on the spot. "This was to draw the troops from the city," recalled Geronimo, "and the next day they came." An all-day skirmish was inconclusive, but the Indians managed to capture the Mexican supply train, greatly augmenting their store of guns and ammunition.

The pitched battle—a rarity for Apaches—took place the following day: some two hundred Chiricahuas against one hundred Mexican soldiers representing two companies of cavalry and two of infantry. "I recognized the cavalry as the soldiers who had killed my people at [Janos]," insisted Geronimo. Since he had never seen the soldiers who perpetrated the massacre of his family, this claim may seem dubious. Yet keen-eyed survivors could have described the attackers to Geronimo in such detail that he could recognize their horses and uniforms when he saw them.

Because of the magnitude of his personal loss, Geronimo was allowed to direct the battle against the Mexican soldiers. He arranged the Apaches in a hollow circle among trees beside a river. The Mexicans advanced to within four hundred yards, cavalry ranged behind infantry. Armed with the vision that bullets could not kill him, Geronimo led a charge. "In all the battle I thought of my murdered mother, wife, and babies—of . . . my vow of vengeance, and I fought with fury. Many fell by my hand."

The battle lasted two hours. At its climax, Geronimo stood at the Apache vanguard, in a clearing with only three other warriors. They had no rifles; they had shot all their arrows and used up their spears killing Mexicans: "We had only our hands and knives with which to fight." Suddenly a new contingent of Mexicans arrived, guns blazing. Two of Geronimo's comrades fell; Geronimo and the other ran toward the Apache line. In step beside him, the other Apache was cut down by a Mexican sword.

Reaching the line of warriors, Geronimo seized a spear and whirled. The Mexican pursuing him fired and missed, just as Geronimo's spear pierced his body. In an instant Geronimo seized the dead soldier's sword and used it to hold off the Mexican who had killed his companion. The two grappled and fell to the earth; Geronimo raised his knife and struck home. Then he leapt to his feet, waving the dead soldier's sword in defiance, looking for more Mexicans to kill. The remainder had fled.

It was one of the greatest Apache victories of the nineteenth century. By the Mexicans' own count, they had lost twenty-six dead and forty-six wounded. The tattered survivors limped back to the town of Cumpas. A fresh force sent out to bury the dead and pursue the Apaches was so horrified by the battle scene that they refused to trail the Indians further.

According to Apache tradition, it was at this battle that the Mexicans spontaneously gave Geronimo the name that would become famous around the world. The only version passed down to Americans was recorded by an Indian agent decades later. In his telling, Geronimo

> was not content to fight according to Apache custom, from behind rocks and greasewood bushes. Instead, he rushed into the open many times, running zigzag and dodging so that bullets from the rurales' [soldiers'] rifles did not hit him. Each time he ran out this way, he killed a rurale with his hunting knife, took the rurale's rifle and cartridges, and ran zigzag back again to his people. [Geronimo] did not know how to use the rifles, so he gave them to other Apache warriors.

The soldiers, addled by the behavior of this berserker, began to cry out, *"Cuidado! Cuidado!* Geronimo!"—"Watch out! Geronimo!"

Geronimo's biographer, Angie Debo, speculates that the Mexicans were invoking St. Jerome—Geronimo, in Spanish. Yet it is hard to imagine why terrified young soldiers would appeal to the bookish Jerome, patron saint of librarians and scholars. Perhaps the battle took place on Jerome's feast day, September 30; but Geronimo's account locates it in summer, Mexican records in January.

In any event, according to the Indian agent who recorded the tale, the other Apache warriors had no idea what the Mexicans meant by the cry "Geronimo!"—they "thought it might be the name of some god who did not like the rurales." The Apaches themselves took up the cry. Eventually even his fellow warriors began to call him Geronimo. He had earned the name.

After this great battle of retribution near Arizpe, Geronimo would recall, "all the other Apaches were satisfied . . . , but I still desired more revenge." There is, however, a serious problem with Geronimo's version of events. Edwin R. Sweeney, the only scholar who has ransacked the obscure Mexican records of events on the northern frontier in 1850–1851, identifies the battle as one that took place at

Pozo Hediondo (Stinking Wells), about twenty miles east of Arizpe. His argument is based on similarities between the Mexican account and Geronimo's (both have the Mexicans initially lured into combat by a deceptively small Apache band), the size of the forces, the location near Arizpe, the identification of Mangas Coloradas as a leader, and—the apparent clincher—the fact that "no other fight comparable in size and significance is known to have occurred in the 1850s."

The problem is this: Mexican sources unmistakably date the battle at Pozo Hediondo as unfolding on January 19, 1851. This is six weeks *before* the massacre at Janos.

Geronimo claimed that, after the truce of June 1850, his people were "at peace with the Mexican towns as well as with all the neighboring Indian tribes." He swore that Carrasco's attack was wanton and unprovoked. The lifelong bitterness, the thirst for revenge that sprang from the loss of his family, seem like the passion of a man betrayed, not the reaction of a combatant who accepts the shifting vicissitudes of war.

Sweeney further documents that, far from the Apaches being at peace with Sonora, they had murdered 111 Mexican residents of that state in 1850 alone. The implication of his research is clear: Carrasco had ample justification for his attack on Janos; it was in fact *his* revenge for the catastrophe of Pozo Hediondo.

What are the possible ways of untying this Gordian knot of discrepancy? The explanation least favorable to Geronimo is that he lied about the sequence of events, casting the brilliant success of his frenzied assault at Pozo Hediondo as a just response to the murder of innocent Apaches, when in fact it was part of a long pattern of gratuitous depredations in Sonora. Alternatively, Geronimo's memory could have played tricks on him. By the time he dictated his account to an Oklahoma school superintendent in 1905, he was an old man of more than eighty years. The agony of his early tragedy, which without question sparked a lifelong hatred of Mexicans, could have caused his memory to transpose events into an emotionally more logical sequence. Some blend of these two scenarios—deliberate falsehood or a faulty memory—forms the explanation that Sweeney tacitly advances.

There are, however, other solutions. Pozo Hediondo—as well as the Sonoran depredations of 1850—might after all have been the

work of other Apaches than Mangas's. Geronimo may have been ignorant of these deeds. And the great battle he narrates may somehow
have slipped into the cracks of the Mexican record. Geronimo's is the
only firsthand Apache account of that battle that has come down to us,
but other Apaches agreed that the Janos massacre was unprovoked.

For all the similarities cited by Sweeney between the Mexican version of the fight near Arizpe and Geronimo's, there are glaring differences. The Mexican version has the soldiers pursuing a band of
mounted Apache raiders driving thirteen hundred stolen horses and
cattle north ahead of them—not Geronimo's three-pronged assault
from the north by warriors on foot. Pozo Hediondo is twenty miles
from Arizpe, much closer to Nacozari, a town equal in importance;
Geronimo insists that the warriors marched south past Nacozari and
camped "almost at Ari[z]pe." The Mexican account places the battle
on high ground, Geronimo's in heavy timber on a river bottom.

These ambiguities exemplify the difficulty of telling the Apache
story right. A chasm gapes between Mexican and American percep-
tions of what took place along their common border in the nineteenth
century. Hispanic accounts of the Mexican-American War, for instance,
are unrecognizable to Texans who would have us remember the
Alamo.

The difficulties magnify when one attempts to match the record
preserved in Apache memory with the scraps of paper stored in American or Mexican archives. Dates, place names, personal names, all
issue from incompatible universes. Colossal misunderstandings yawn
between languages, cultures, moralities.

All this, combined with the fact that he was almost unknown to the
White Eyes until the mid-1870s, makes Geronimo's path through the
Apache wars a shadowy trail, easily lost in the chronological underbrush. He remarried within months of the Janos debacle. His second
wife, a Bedonkohe, was, in the view of other Apaches, "a very handsome young woman." Geronimo would eventually marry nine wives,
keeping as many as three at once (which was not unusual for a prominent Chiricahua), but no woman seems to have been as close to his
heart as the lost Alope.

It was in 1851, perhaps only weeks after the Janos attack, that Geronimo saw his first white Americans. They were members of a government commission surveying the boundary between the United
States and Mexico. In his home in the Gila Mountains, Geronimo

heard about these interlopers, so with several other warriors he set out to visit them. The language barrier was insuperable, but the Apaches shook hands with the surveyors and camped near them. They traded buckskins and ponies for shirts and food; they hunted game for the surveyors, who paid them in American cash. "We did not know the value of this money," Geronimo reported, "but we kept it and later learned from the Navajo Indians that it was very valuable."

How innocent this first exchange with the White Eyes seems, in light of later history! Fascinated by the boundary commission's odd occupation, the Apaches watched by the hour. "Every day they measured land with curious instruments and put down marks which we could not understand. They were good men, and we were sorry when they had gone on into the west."

For ten straight years after Arizpe, Geronimo raided into Mexico. He was nearly always the instigator, for his lust for revenge upon the Mexicans was insatiable. He led parties of as few as three warriors, as many as thirty. The first such expedition came close to costing him his life.

With only two fellow warriors, Geronimo slipped into Sonora, traveled the length of a mountain range, and decided to attack a small town—a tactic that, for good reasons, Apaches almost never pursued. As they were about to seize five horses hitched outside the houses, townsmen opened fire from within. Geronimo's two companions were instantly killed. Then a horde of Mexicans, some on foot and some on horseback, appeared. "Three times that day I was surrounded," Geronimo drily recounted, "but I kept fighting, dodging, and hiding." With only bow and arrows against the Mexican rifles, Geronimo several times shot dead a Mexican who was stalking him. After a whole day of desperate dodging and hiding, he was able to make his getaway north. On horseback the Mexicans trailed him for two days, firing at him often. Geronimo had shot his last arrow, "so I depended on running and hiding, although I was very tired. I had not eaten since the chase began, nor had I dared to stop for rest."

On the second night, at last he shook his pursuers. It was a virtuosic piece of survival, but it won him only scorn among his fellow Bedonkohe. Half a century later, Geronimo recalled his shame: "Some of the Apaches blamed me for the evil result of the expedition, but I said nothing. Having failed, it was only proper that I should remain silent."

Emboldened to the point of recklessness by his vision that bullets

could not kill him and by his rage against the Mexicans, Geronimo
suffered other close calls. In one hand-to-hand battle, he charged a
Mexican soldier, spear against rifle. As he ran, his foot slipped in "a
pool of blood" and he fell at the feet of the soldier, who clubbed
Geronimo unconscious with the butt of his rifle. The soldier was
about to finish his work when one of Geronimo's allies thrust him
through with a spear. By the next day, Geronimo could walk un-
steadily north toward Arizona. It took months for him to recover, and
he bore a scar from the rifle butt for the rest of his life.

In an engagement a year later, Geronimo was struck near the left
eye by a glancing bullet and again knocked unconscious. Thinking
him dead, the Mexicans rushed past his body to attack other Apaches.
Geronimo came to, got to his feet, and ran for the woods; bullets
whizzed all around him, and one caught him in the side. In his laconic
way, he later described yet another amazing escape:

> I kept running, dodging, and fighting, until I got clear of my pur-
> suers. I climbed up a steep cañon, where the cavalry could not
> follow. The troopers saw me, but did not dismount and try to follow.
> I think they were wise not to come on.

During these years, Mexican troops sometimes defied international
law and hunted the Chiricahua well inside the United States. As Geronimo was recovering from his twin bullet wounds in the Gila Mountains, his people were surprised one day at dawn by three Mexican
companies. Many women and children were killed, and it was all the
others could do to flee.

> My left eye was still swollen shut, but with the other I saw well
> enough to hit one of the officers with an arrow, and then make good
> my escape among the rocks. The troopers burned our [wickiups]
> and took our arms, provisions, ponies, and blankets. Winter was at
> hand.

In these early battles against Mexicans, Geronimo fought with only
bow and arrows, spears (which the Apache made from a sotol stalk,
one end being sharpened and hardened in the fire), and knives. If by
1851, as the tale of his earning his Mexican name had it, Geronimo
did not know how to use a rifle, he quickly learned. Eventually he

became a superb shot. Well into his seventies, Geronimo would put on stunning exhibitions of his marksmanship.

The decade of raiding into Mexico served to turn Geronimo into a master warrior and a leader of men. The early fiascos were succeeded by glorious triumphs. One of his larger parties, thirty warriors on horseback, returned from Mexico, as he put it, with "all the horses, mules, and cattle we wanted. . . . During this raid we had killed about fifty Mexicans." On another expedition, with only three allies, Geronimo once again attacked a small town, this time a village in the Sierra Madre near the Chihuahua-Sonora border. They managed to kill one resident and chase all the others out of town. Dazzled by the variety of goods that were theirs for the picking, the four warriors looted houses and stores. As Geronimo remembered it,

> Many of the things we saw in the houses we could not understand, but in the stores we saw much that we wanted; so we drove in a herd of horses and mules, and packed as much provisions and supplies as we could on them. . . . This was perhaps the most successful raid ever made by us into Mexican territory. . . . [W]e had supplies enough to last our whole tribe for a year or more.

Apaches harbored a deep curiosity about the strange objects Americans and Mexicans furnished their lives with. For years after a raid, the Chiricahua would carry with them items—not only watch-chains and jewelry, but photographs and hand-written letters—that must have had only a fetishistic value for them.

Geronimo's numerous raids into Mexico also perfected his knowledge of its geography, particularly of the tortured canyons and rocky summits of the Sierra Madre. This store of memorized topography would serve him vitally in the 1880s. On one raid, Geronimo must have traveled all the way to the Gulf of California, for he described "a great lake extending beyond the limit of sight." Few Apaches had ever seen the ocean, and though rumors of its existence had filtered back to the heartland, they were generally discounted. Most Apaches were convinced there was no water in the world that one could not easily see across.

Returning from one of the Mexican raids in the 1850s, Geronimo had his first skirmish with a white man. In a canyon of the Santa Catalina Mountains near Tucson, nine Apache warriors surprised a solitary man on horseback leading a pack train. The man bolted away up the canyon, leaving the spoils to the finders. Opening the pack bags, Geronimo and his warriors were puzzled to find that the baggage was entirely cheese. For weeks therafter, Geronimo's people feasted on cheese and mule meat.

The quality of deep responsibility for his people that would characterize the mature Geronimo emerged in the 1850s. In one raid, his party seized a pack train laden with bottles of the potent alcohol the Mexicans called mescal. Most of the raiders proceeded to get blind drunk; as happened all too often in such binges, they began to fight each other. Geronimo, too, was drunk, but not out of control. The sole voice of reason among the intoxicated gang of twenty, he tried to stop the fighting and to post a guard against Mexican troops who were still in the area. These efforts failed. At last, when most of the warriors were too drunk to walk, Geronimo poured the rest of the mescal out on the ground, extinguished the campfires, and moved the pack mules far from camp. Then he operated on the two most badly injured warriors, cutting an arrowhead out of one man's leg, a spear point from another's shoulder. Finally he stayed up all night, the only sentinel guarding the drunken camp.

As he developed his skills as a warrior, Geronimo also came into a deeper awareness of his Power. It was not something he flaunted, or even spoke about. Many years later, Juh's son would testify,

> He was by nature already a brave person; but if one knows that he will never be killed, why be afraid? I don't know that Geronimo ever told his warriors that he had supernatural protection, but they were with him in many dangerous times and saw his miraculous escapes, his cures for wounds, and the results of his medicine; so his warriors knew that Geronimo was alive only because of Ussen's protection.

Geronimo's Power grew and diversified, until he became a famous healer. To cure an old man who, the Apaches believed, had been made sick by a coyote, he built a fire, laid the patient before it, and carried out an elaborate ceremony involving an eagle feather, an abalone shell, a bag of pollen, and an oak-leaf cigarette whose smoke he blew to the four directions. Geronimo sang many songs about the coyote while he beat a drum. The entire ceremony lasted four nights.

It was probably in the winter of 1869–1870 that Geronimo climbed the mountain and prayed for four days to save his sister Ishton, who lay near death from childbirth. On the mountaintop the voice speaking to him told Geronimo again that he would die a natural death, not a death by bullets.

Later Geronimo's Power would take on another aspect—the ability to divine events as they were taking place many miles away. Whatever the "rational" explanation of this talent, it would prove to have great strategic value for the bands Geronimo led.

The decade of Geronimo's raiding in Mexico after 1851 is documented only in his own memoir. If Mexican records of these raids exist, they have never been correlated with his account. It is odd, perhaps, that Geronimo's own narrative of the pivotal encounters with Americans after 1861 is so sketchy, compared to his rendering of the Mexican years. We know with reasonable certainty, for instance, that Geronimo fought in the crucial battle of Apache Pass in 1862, when the howitzers defeated the combined forces of Cochise and Mangas Coloradas; but Geronimo never mentioned it.

From piecemeal Apache testimony, we know that Geronimo may have helped torture to death the hostages Cochise had hoped to trade with Bascom for his relatives in 1861; that he was part of the council that begged Mangas not to go to his doom at Pinos Altos in 1863; that he camped with Victorio's Chihenne near Cañada Alamosa in 1871. He undoubtedly led many raids on the White Eyes for Mangas and Cochise, and he grew almost inseparable from his brother-in-law Juh. He might have been a member of Juh's party that led Cushing into the fatal trap in 1871, but we shall never know.

We do know that Geronimo was present at the peace conference between Howard and Cochise in the Dragoons in October 1872. On the march to Fort Bowie following the armistice, Geronimo rode double with Howard on the general's horse. He impressed Howard by mounting in a single spring, directly over the horse's tail. As the Chiricahua reservation came into being late in 1872, Geronimo was one of more than a thousand Apaches who prepared to settle down within its generous boundaries.

By the end of 1872, Geronimo was almost fifty years old. He had three wives and at least two living children, having lost another wife and child to Mexican soldiers sometime in the 1850s. A powerful man, verging on stockiness, he weighed about 170 pounds. At about five feet eight inches, he was shorter than Cochise, much shorter than the giant Mangas. Geronimo was nonetheless taller and heavier than the average Chiricahua warrior, who stood five feet six and a half inches and weighed 135 to 140 pounds.

The rigors of Geronimo's life, along with the scars of battle, had fixed his face into the mask of defiance that would haunt a continent. A livid crease, perhaps the scar of another bullet, crossed his right cheek, and his mouth drooped on the right, "so that even in repose he seemed to sneer," as one observer put it.

Like Cochise, Geronimo had experienced an ineradicable early betrayal, costing him the lives of family members, that determined the shape of the rest of his life. Geronimo's response to the betrayal, however, was as unlike Cochise's as the two men's temperaments were different.

In Cochise the will for revenge assumed the guise of an adamantine fury, a monolithic purposiveness that awed his own warriors. "I have killed ten white men for every Indian slain," he boasted to Howard, nailing that epigraph to his decade of terror.

Geronimo, on the other hand, was a fretful, moody man of quicksilver doubts and shifting whims. Crafty, highly intelligent, a born manipulator, he gained a reputation even among warriors devoted to him for not always telling the truth. Geronimo was a worrier, a man torn by dark internal debates; there was a steak of the paranoid in him even before the massacre at Janos. Despite the visionary mysticism that spoke in his Power, he was a pragmatic opportunist, a talker, a politician. His curiosity was as large as his distrust, and the two often warred for his soul. Had he been a white man in the twentieth century, we might call him a severe neurotic. Rather than Cochise's iron purposiveness, Geronimo's characteristic state was vacillation—no matter how sheer or sharp the flights his fickle will drove him to.

With the establishment of the Chiricahua reservation, Apaches and whites alike believed they were about to enter a lasting peace based on a workable coexistence. Like so many pools of hope that parched to arid earth under the Southwestern sun, this dream of peace would prove an illusion. At the end of 1872, Geronimo stood on the threshold of what would become the last Indian war in America, a war that would eventually be synonymous with his name.

Nine

■

The End of Cochise

*I*t was a bitter disappointment to Crook that Howard's peacemaking in the Dragoons robbed him of a chance to go after Cochise. Crook had little faith that Howard's truce with the fierce and independent Chiricahua would last; the one-armed general seemed only marginally less naive than the fanatic Quaker whom President Grant had sent west before him. As was Crook's wont, however, he kept his feelings to himself. Even decades later, after history had largely vindicated him, Crook confined his self-righteousness to a mild complaint in his autobiography: "I never could get to see the treaty stipulations, although I made official applications for them."

Forestalled in his wish to deal with the Chiricahua on his own terms, Crook turned his attention to the remaining Apaches in Arizona who had refused reservation life. The wildest of these "hostiles" were Tonto Apaches, who used the tangled wilderness north and west of the San Carlos and Fort Apache reservations as their refuge.

Crook declared a new deadline of November 15, 1872, for the onset of what he was confident would be the final campaign. By sending out as many friendly Indians as he could with news of this deadline, Crook convinced himself that any Apache still on the loose after November 15 was deliberately flouting his edict. This was in fact a dubious conclusion.

On paper, at least, the terms Crook set were strict but humane. When hostile Apaches were encountered, every effort should be made to convince them to surrender before the fighting began. Women and children were to be spared at all costs. Prisoners would be well treated. Almost as soon as they were subdued, adult male prisoners were to be converted into scouts, on the theory that "the wilder the Apache was, the more he was likely to know of the wiles and strategems of those still out in the mountains." But when warriors refused to surrender, then they were "to be hunted down until the last one in hostility had been killed or captured." In this way, Crook believed, the campaign should prove "short, sharp, and decisive."

Setting the deadline in mid-November was a canny stroke. Winter was always the hardest time for the Apaches, and the regimen they required to get through the cold months was incompatible with flight and secrecy. The Tonto Basin lies at altitudes up to 8,000 feet; winter temperatures there routinely plunge to the teens or below. Had it not been for the need to stay hidden, the Apaches would have resorted to much lower camps in the winter. In the years before they were hunted, the Indians could build campfires wherever they wanted, but now their smoke was a giveaway to Crook's patrols. Because winter hunting was so poor, the Apaches relied on food—nuts, berries, dried mescal hearts, jerked meat—harvested in the fall and cached in caves. Now, when a patrol attacked a winter encampment, the Apaches might flee without a single casualty, but with the loss of all their precious winter stores, which the army burned or confiscated.

The plan of Crook's final campaign was to divide all the troops at his disposal into nine separate commands, each with a different route through the wilderness. Crook himself would move from one command to another, keeping his eye on the overall scheme. Without perfect logistical execution, this plan could have been a recipe for chaos—nine patrols floundering more or less lost through the woods, duplicating efforts here and missing huge tracts of land there. Under Crook's superintendence, it succeeded, as he had hoped, in leaving "no nook or corner" of the wilderness unscoured.

Crook's success depended absolutely on the skill of the Apache scouts he had recruited: in the Tonto Basin, for the first time, the deadly efficacy of the general's bold experiment was demonstrated. As each patrol moved through the mountains, the scouts stayed from twelve to twenty-four hours ahead, trailing the holdouts. Soldiers alone would have lost the scent many times over.

In theory, the scouts were supposed to find the enemy's camp, then report back to the soldiers, who would "do the work of cleaning them out." However, the scouts were too impetuous and too fond of a good fight to act as mere messengers: often they attacked as soon as they located the enemy. When it turned out the Indians were as effective in these skirmishes as the soldiers were, the scouts were more or less given their head.

Initially, Crook experimented with scouts from other tribes, but the Apaches outperformed them. As Bourke later wrote, "The longer we knew the Apache scouts, the better we liked them. They were wilder and more suspicious than the Pimas and Maricopas, but far more reliable, and endowed with a greater amount of courage and daring."

As shrewd as Crook's use of Apache scouts was his choice of the men he appointed chiefs of scouts. In this sensitive role, well-educated army officers simply would not do: they lacked the necessary rapport with Apaches, as well as the wilderness skills it took to command respect from the best hunters and trackers Arizona had ever seen. As chiefs of scouts, Crook selected drifters, loners, men of mixed heritage who had been orphaned by their tribulations. Two generations earlier, these mavericks would have become trappers and mountain men. Some of them learned to speak Apache. So difficult was this complex language for European tongues that in a quarter century of conflict in the Southwest, only a handful of Americans ever achieved the most rudimentary command of it.

The deeds of these chiefs of scouts in the epic of the West have never been adequately sung. Like Tom Jeffords, none of them saw fit to write his own memoir. The passage of these plucky loners through the Indian wars is recorded only in the patchwork chronicle of newspaper interviews cadged from their old age by casual journalists.

Crook's own favorite chief of scouts was Archie McIntosh, who had first hooked up with him in the Northwest in the late 1860s. Born in Ontario of a Scot father and a Chippewa mother, McIntosh started trapping at age ten in the Canadian west. One day when Archie was still a boy, as he and his father paddled a canoe up the Fraser River, Indians fired from ambush, killing his father instantly. The boy managed to escape. McIntosh later worked for the Hudson Bay Company before hiring on as a guide for the U. S. Army in 1855.

By the time he came to Arizona, McIntosh had already saved Crook's life once, guiding the officer thirty miles across an Idaho plateau in a blinding snowstorm. Like other chiefs of scouts, McIntosh was a heroic drinker, who sometimes had to be propped on his horse or carried in a wagon after an all-night debauch. The abstemious Crook forgave him this bad habit: drunk or sober, McIntosh's judgment was razor-sharp. Although McIntosh "never advised anything, or expressed any protests in words," Crook learned to heed his guide's instincts without question.

The most famous chief of scouts was Al Sieber. Born in Germany, Sieber emigrated to Pennsylvania with his mother, fought in the Civil War, then wandered west, where he fetched up in Prescott, Arizona, flat broke from months of luckless prospecting. Here he befriended an army chief of scouts who later may have persuaded Crook to hire him. Sieber would become the man Crook depended on more than any other as a liaison with the Apaches. By the end of his long career, as Sieber's biographer claims, he had taken part "in more Indian fights than Daniel Boone, Jim Bridger, and Kit Carson together." Sieber would kill more than a hundred "hostiles" himself, in the course of suffering a reputed twenty-nine woundings in Indian battles.

Mickey Free, "the coyote whose kidnapping had brought war to the Chiricahuas," who as the boy Felix Ward had been seized by Apaches in 1861, precipitating the Bascom affair, resurfaced in the 1870s with his damaged eye and his sullen temper to become an army scout. Eventually he would serve as interpreter for Crook at crucial parleys with the Chiricahua.

Perhaps the most intriguing chief of scouts of all, as well as the most mysterious, was a man named Merejildo Grijalva. In 1891, an Arizona pioneer who interviewed him asserted that Grijalva "could tell more about [the Apache wars] than any American, Mexican, or Indian now living."

Born in northern Sonora around 1840, Grijalva was a Mexican. At age ten, he was captured by a band of Chiricahuas, who raised him for the next eight years as one of their own. This was a common practice; Apaches would lavish upon the captive all the love and instruction they gave their own children. Cases are recorded in which, when the captive had a chance to return to his people, he refused. But Grijalva escaped at age eighteen, fleeing to an American fort. By 1866, he was in Arizona, serving as a guide and interpreter for the American army.

Thanks to his eight years' training for the warpath as an Apache,

Grijalva possessed the most intimate knowledge of Chiricahua ways. He took part in raids and battles against Mexicans, and his abductors must have thought that he had "turned Apache" for good. Grijalva's band was closely allied to Cochise's. He recalled seeing Cochise once, furious with a warrior for stealing horses with a U. S. brand on them (army stock, whose loss would bring military wrath upon the Chiricahua), suddenly drive his lance through the warrior's heart.

Uniquely among Crook's chiefs of scouts, Grijalva could track as well as an Apache. He had a better understanding of Apache traps and ambushes than any Anglo scout. He knew Cochise's people so well that he once identified them from moccasins and beadwork that had been seized from a deserted camp. For Grijalva to take on the job of leading patrols against the Apache was a supremely perilous commitment. He knew that the Chiricahua regarded him as the ultimate traitor; should they ever capture him, they would save their cruelest and most prolonged torture for him. Sometimes as he chased Apaches, Grijalva could see that they recognized him and could read the full intensity of their hatred. He always kept an extra bullet in reserve, to kill himself if capture were imminent.

Grijalva retired from army service in 1880 and settled down as a rancher in the San Simon valley in southeastern Arizona. He lived at least into the 1890s, but no one recorded the story of his life. More than any other person in the nineteenth century, Grijalva had something like an equally deep firsthand understanding of Mexican, Apache, and American life. His matchless knowledge is lost to history.

The day after Crook's deadline of November 15 passed, his nine commands began to set out from various forts, each with its own itinerary for combing the Tonto wilderness. The going was often miserable, as deep snow and arctic winds hindered the soldiers' progress; sometimes the pines were so soaked with snow and rain the men had trouble starting campfires—a condition that is rare in Arizona.

The troops maintained a rigid discipline, according to Crook's design: no one sang, whistled, shouted, or even struck a match while on the march, and small campfires were allowed only when the officers felt sure they could not be seen by the "lynx-eyed enemy." On rocky ground, the soldiers changed their boots for moccasins, to ensure a quiet tread. The food was Spartan: mostly flour, beans, bacon, and coffee, with a small quantity of chocolate and dried peaches as occasional luxuries.

Although the snow made marching difficult, it helped the trackers immensely, and Crook's hunch that the Apaches would be most vulnerable in winter paid off. Again and again, the army patrols came across isolated rancherias—camps of a few dozen Apaches. Inevitably the Indians fled, abandoning their winter supplies. In a typical engagement, several Apaches would be killed, and several more (mostly women and children) captured, all with minimal casualties among the soldiers. This lopsided result was the credit of the Indian scouts, for it was they who usually first fired upon the renegades, they who bore the brunt of their best returning salvos.

Inexorably through the heart of winter, the commands pursued their "mop-up" of the basin. Crook himself, as he ranged from one patrol to another, set an inspiring example; often, when an exhausted patrol collapsed in camp, he would take his shotgun and go out into the dusk, returning with a packful of dead birds to cook for next day's breakfast. In the words of the admiring Bourke, "there was no private soldier, no packer, no teamster, who could 'down the old man' in any work, or outlast him on a march or a climb over the rugged peaks of Arizona; they knew that, and they also knew that in the hour of danger Crook would be found on the skirmish line, and not in the telegraph office."

Though they fought few decisive battles, the patrols exacted a terrible toll. Bourke calculated that the command of which he was a member traveled twelve hundred miles in 142 days, and took the lives of five hundred renegade Apaches. The Tonto Basin sweep has always been treated by historians as a brilliant military campaign. That it was: but the "overhauling" of the basin, to use Bourke's jaunty term, was also brutal in the extreme. Crook's pursuit of the renegades verged on the kind of genocidal persecution favored by Carleton and Baylor a decade before. In the anarchy of sudden attack precipitated by Indian scouts, there was little chance for the besieged Apaches to give up peacefully. Bourke records not a single fray during the winter campaign that resulted in surrender rather than bloodshed.

The climactic episode of the campaign came in late December. It was Crook's propensity—as it was that of most nineteenth-century observers—to distinguish between "good" and "bad" Indians. The refusal of certain bands to bend to white ways sprang, in this analysis, not from deep-seated cultural differences so much as from the influence of certain spectacularly bad leaders. (A synonym for "bad" was often "wild" or "savage.") Thus Cochise's band were, in Crook's words, "the worst of all the Apaches."

In the Tonto Basin campaign, it was a chief named Delche who won Crook's strongest enmity. Crook nicknamed him The Liar, swearing that Delche "had the worst reputation amongst all the Indians for villainry [*sic*] and devilment." To a boy who grew up close to his people, on the other hand, Delche was "a great chief," leader of the band of Western Apaches who "were most willing to fight the Chiricahuas who used to make raids upon them and capture their women."

As the winter campaign began, Crook made it known that the capture or killing of Delche was among his highest priorities. At this point, two pieces of Apache information dovetailed, with tragic consequences. An Indian told Crook that Delche's stronghold was a cave high in the Mazatzal mountains, north of the Salt River (west of today's Roosevelt Dam). And one of Crook's Apache scouts, a man named Nantaje, said he had been raised in that stronghold and offered to guide the soldiers there.

A hundred and twenty years later, we can see what came to be known as the Battle of Skeleton Cave more clearly than Crook could. Delche was probably a Tonto Apache chief. He had certainly spent time in the cave high in the Mazatzals, which was indeed a stronghold. Delche was not in the cave, however, in December 1872. The people who were camped there were not even Apaches.

They were Yavapais. Because they sometimes joined in raids with Western Apaches, they were often thought to be Apache themselves; the standard term for them in the nineteenth century was Apache-Mojaves. In reality, however, they spoke a language entirely different from any Apachean dialect. They were not even part of the same large family as the Apaches, being a Yuman people rather than an Athapaskan. These differences were beyond the understanding of Crook and his soldiers.

The Yavapai may have known of Crook's edict. Some of them had come in to Camp Grant earlier in the year to try to live in peace with the whites. But they had gotten sick from the beans and flour and beef the agents fed them, and many had contracted malaria. For all they knew, the white men had poisoned them. Most of the Yavapai fled Camp Grant and headed back to the Mazatzals, dying as they walked.

In late December, guided by Nantaje, a command of 220 soldiers and scouts (many of them Pima and Maricopa) closed in on the remote cave. Among their number was Bourke, who left a vivid account of the battle. On the morning of December 28, well before dawn, the attacking force slipped out of a bitterly cold camp and scrambled toward the cave. A detachment of twelve to fifteen sharpshooters led the way. Just as dawn began to break, these marksmen sneaked silently up an old path toward the cave, turned a corner, and suddenly beheld the stronghold. Inside the cave a fire was burning. Warriors danced before it, while women prepared food.

There was no discussion of surrender. In the morning gloom, each sharpshooter chose a warrior; at the whispered signal, all fired. Six of the Yavapai men fell dead. Hearing the gunfire, the rest of the army patrol came running up. A broken wall of boulders ranged across the front of the cave: at once the Yavapai warriors sprang to positions behind these rocks and started shooting at the soldiers, while the women, children, and old men cowered inside the cave. There was no hope of flight, for the soldiers had the cave surrounded.

The commander now, according to Bourke, "directed his interpreters to summon all to an unconditional surrender." Apache scouts yelled out the appeal. "The only answer was a shriek of hatred and defiance," reported Bourke, "threats of what we had to expect, yells of exultation at the thought that not one of us should ever see the light of another day, but should furnish a banquet for the crows and buzzards."

Perhaps. Who knows what meanings flew through the air that December day? To be sure, the Apaches and the Yavapais could communicate with each other, but between the shouted demands in an alien tongue and the unprovoked attack at dawn, what could the Yavapais think except that a vengeful horde had descended upon their stronghold to annihilate them? With six of their men already dead on the cave floor, they did what all Indians would do: fight back until they had no more arrows or bullets.

The battle might have turned into a prolonged standoff, but for two pieces of strategy the American commander devised. He sent a small contingent climbing to a ledge above the cave, from which the men were able to roll boulders down on its inhabitants. The rocks took their toll. When the survivors crept to the innermost recesses of the shelter, the American commander directed his troops to fire at the cave ceiling. The ricocheting bullets killed indiscriminately. In desperation, twenty Yavapai warriors, each armed with a rifle and a bow, mounted a suicidal charge. Six or seven were killed, the rest driven back into the cave.

When it was all over, the bodies lay in a heap inside the cavern. The death of a single Pima scout was the only army casualty. Seventy-six Yavapai men, women, and children lay dead; only twenty women and children, many wounded, were taken alive. According to a boy who survived the fight, the Pima and Maricopa scouts were even more ruthless than the soldiers; when they rushed the cave, they pounded the heads of the dying before the soldiers could stop them. "One woman who was badly wounded and could not sit on a horse was left behind," testified the Yavapai boy. "Some soldiers gave her food and water, but when they were out of sight, some Pimas went back and mashed her head to jelly."

Crook was gratified with the Battle of Skeleton Cave, though disappointed that Delche was not among the dead. "Battle" is hardly the word for this fight, however: in its wanton carnage, it was a massacre nearly as senseless as the slaughter of Aravaipa Apaches near Camp Grant twenty months before.

Sixty-one years later, a visitor to the remote site testified that "the bleached and crumbling bones of the slain" still lay in and around the cave. Eventually a party of Yavapai gathered up what remained of the bones and carried them to the Fort McDowell Indian Reservation, where they were buried. The bullet scars can still be seen on the ceiling of the cave.

By April 1873, the remaining holdouts had lost all will to fight. As the various patrols headed with their captives back to Camp Verde, an unprecedented thing began to happen. Each procession was joined by hundreds of "wild" Apaches; in twos and threes they quietly slipped among the marchers, uttering only the word *Siquisn*—"my brother"—to the scouts who had hunted them. When Crook counted all the hostiles who had come in, he found that he had twenty-three hundred prisoners of war—including the notorious Delche.

Crook spoke to the leaders in his firm, paternal way. If they would live at peace on the reservations, he promised, "he would be the best friend they ever had." One of the chiefs told Crook, "You see, we are nearly dead from want of food and exposure—the copper cartridge has done the business for us. I am glad of the opportunity to surrender, but I do it not because I love you, but because I am afraid of

General." Delche however told Crook that (in the general's paraphrase)

> he had one hundred and twenty-five warriors last fall, and if anybody had told him he couldn't whip the world, he would have laughed at them, but now he had only twenty left. He said they used to have no difficulty in eluding the troops, but now the very rocks had gotten soft, they couldn't put their foot anywhere without leaving an impression by which we could follow, that they could get no sleep at nights, for should a coyote or a fox start a rock rolling during the night, they would get up and dig out, thinking it was we who were after them.

As far as Crook knew, there were no Apaches left at large in Arizona or New Mexico. The Nednhi and some of the Chokonen might still be on the loose south of the border, but that was the Mexicans' problem. It was understandable that in April 1873, Crook believed he had solved the Apache problem and put an end to a war that had raged for twelve years. Six months later, Crook was rewarded for his "final" campaign with promotion to brigadier general.

Since reservations were still new to Arizona, everything about them had to be invented virtually from scratch. Crook devised the rules and routines by which "his" Apaches would live, in accordance with the orderly bent of his mind. Every Indian was issued a small brass tag with a number on it, which he was to wear on a string around his neck. At a daily head count, the Indians were checked off by number. The impulse behind this regimentation—to give peaceful Apaches proof of their innocence when depredations off the reservation were blamed on them—was not inhumane, but the tagging and numbering seem to foreshadow in a macabre way the treatment of inmates in our own century's most diabolical prison camps.

Crook put the Apaches to work on vast agricultural projects: digging a five-mile irrigation ditch at Camp Verde, planting acre after acre with vegetables and grains. The rationale was capitalist: once an Indian, as Bourke put it, "began to see the fruits of his industry rising above the ground, and knew that there was a ready cash market awaiting him for all he had to sell," he would lose all appetite for raiding and the warpath.

Many Apaches, like Geronimo's family, had raised small crops of beans and corn and pumpkins; but nomadism was bred into their very blood. With only a layman's grasp of the culture-bound ethnography of the nineteenth century, neither Crook nor any other American official could comprehend the violence it did to an Apache's identity to try to turn a warrior and a nomad into a sedentary farmer. Menial work, in Apache culture, was the business of women: a man only humiliated himself by stooping to it. Crook thought such scruples mere laziness, and forced his charges to dig the great ditch with pointed sticks hardened in campfires.

There were other cases of mutual incomprehension between the alien cultures. Apaches put the highest possible value on chastity in their women; for centuries, the accepted punishment for a wife who committed adultery was for her husband to cut off her nose. Horrified by this practice, Crook forbade it. When a man persisted in dealing out the time-honored penalty to his unfaithful wife, Crook sentenced him to a year's imprisonment.

The soldiers who enforced the reservation rules could not be bothered to master Apache names. With the arrogance of conquerors, they bestowed nicknames of their own coinage upon their wards. Nantaje, the scout who led the soldiers to the Yavapai cave, became "Joe." Nochedelklinne, who would later become a visionary prophesying a golden age when the White Eyes would vanish, was labeled "Bobby." A seven-year-old Yavapai boy who was captured by the troops found his name, Hoomoothyah ("Little Wet Nose"), converted to "Mike Burns," in honor of his captor, Captain James Burns: "We will make an Irish Indian," joked one of Burns's fellow officers.

In hindsight, one might argue that no one ought to have been surprised when tensions on the San Carlos reservation came to a boil. The immediate causes were various and obscure; the pattern would become a familiar one. Many Apaches resented their number tags and the head count, as well as Crook's interference in such private matters as how they dealt with their wives. Civilian agents hired to ration the Indians cheated them, pocketing the profit. At San Carlos, where tensions were the most volatile, Aravaipas and Tontos camped in mutual hostility. Even Crook lacked the nerve to try to disarm the reservation Indians, so violence could easily turn lethal.

Matters came to a head in late May. A petty quarrel over rations escalated to a showdown. Hoping to quell it, Lieutenant Jacob Almy, a Quaker like Vincent Colyer, strode unarmed into the crowd. Gunfire erupted: Almy staggered away, badly wounded, exclaiming, "Oh, my

God!" Another bullet caught him in the head, and he fell dead. At once hundreds of Apaches fled for the hills.

No army man ever knew which Apaches fired the shots that killed Almy. Most of the Indians who had scattered at the outburst soon returned. It was at this juncture that Crook demonstrated his justice at its most draconian. As the Apaches thronged back toward San Carlos, insisting on their innocence, Crook refused to accept them. He told them that "I would drive them all back into the mountains, where I could kill them all, that they had lied to me once, and I didn't know but what they were lying to me now."

Crook had identified three more bad Indians as the fatal provocateurs, leaders named Chunz, Cochinay, and Chandeisi ("John Daisy" in Crook's spelling). Now the general told the Apaches suing for peace that he would allow them to return only on the condition that they go into the hills and kill these three influential miscreants. As proof of their deeds, they must come back carrying the severed heads of the outlaws.

Army patrols hunted the renegades, managing to kill a number of followers of Chunz, Cochinay, and Chandeisi, but the principals escaped. Meanwhile, Delche had fled the reservation with forty followers. Since Delche's head was the one Crook most desired, he offered the Apache scouts a reward for it.

In the end, the maxim of the day proved true: it takes an Apache to catch an Apache. The four great outlaws managed to elude capture for a full year. Then one day in May 1874, a band of scouts rode into San Carlos; from a sack they took out the severed head of Cochinay. A month later Chandeisi's head was brought in. With fewer and fewer followers, Chunz was finally tracked down and killed in the Santa Catalina Mountains near Tucson at the end of July. The triumphant scouts rode up to Crook's tent, opened a bag, and dumped seven heads on the dusty ground: those of Chunz and the last six warriors who had been loyal to him. Crook had the heads arrayed on the parade ground, as a grisly reminder to the one thousand Apaches at San Carlos whose peace the decapitations had bought.

Only Delche was left. A few days later, two separate parties rode in, each claiming they had killed The Liar. As Crook later wrote without remorse, "Being satisfied that both parties were earnest in their beliefs, and the bringing in of an extra head was not amiss, I paid both parties."

"This about quieted them," Crook reported of the Apaches at San

Carlos. Ruling by iron edict and bloody reprisal, Crook had broken the spirit of the Tontos. Bourke echoed his general's sense of conclusion as he wrote, "The Apaches of Arizona were now a conquered tribe."

A single doubt, however, troubled Crook's sleep. It had to do with Cochise's Indians. The general was maddened to reflect that the Chiricahua, alone among Arizona Apaches, lay outside his jurisdiction. It was all very well for Howard to hasten back to Washington and the congratulations of the President, to preen himself on the illusion that in one jaunt into the Dragoon stronghold he had forged a lasting peace. Crook believed that until an Apache tribe had been soundly beaten in battle, it would never truly adapt to American life.

And to Crook's orderly mind, the state of affairs on the new Chiricahua Reservation was dangerous and chaotic. A single agent, Tom Jeffords—who didn't want the job in the first place—was in charge of more than a thousand Apaches. There were no troops to keep the law, and the Chiricahua were allowed to range wherever they wanted on the reservation. Crook was unable to learn the explicit terms of Howard's treaty with Cochise for the simple reason that nothing had ever been put in writing. In his cavalier way, the praying general had believed that Cochise's word was enough to bind his people for an eternity.

Anxious to learn exactly what Cochise thought he had agreed to (and to ferret out an excuse for intervention), Crook sent a small delegation in February 1873 to the Chokonen chief. Bourke was among their number. The observant lieutenant described Cochise as

> a fine looking Indian of about fifty winters [he was closer to sixty-five], straight as a rush—six feet in stature, deep chested, roman nosed, black eyes, firm mouth, a kindly and even somewhat melancholy expression tempering the determined look of his countenance. He seemed much more neat than the other wild Indians I have seen and his manners were very gentle. There was neither in speech or action any of the bluster characteristic of his race.

A crucial question for Crook was the extent to which the Chiricahua continued to raid in Mexico. Pressed on the matter, Cochise said that

the Mexicans "had not asked him for peace as the [Americans] had."
He admitted that some of his younger warriors "are liable to go down,
from time to time and do a little damage to the Mexicans. I don't want
to lie about this thing; they go but I don't send them." The meeting
was inconclusive, failing to offer Crook a pretext for interfering with
Jeffords's reservation.

Even before Bourke's visit, the territorial governor, Anson P. K.
Safford—a brave man who had led volunteers in action against the
Apaches—made his own trip to see Cochise. Safford's description of
the man complements Bourke's:

> His height is about six feet; shoulders slightly rounded by age; fea-
> tures quite regular, head large and well proportioned; countenance
> rather sad; hair long and black, with some gray ones intermixed;
> face smooth, the beard having been pulled out with pincers, as is
> the custom of Indians.

To Safford, Cochise recited his usual lament about the vanished
glory of his people, about his betrayal at the hands of Bascom. "I told
him," Safford wrote, "that the conduct of Lieutenant Bascom was disliked by our people, and if he had not gone to war, Bascom would
have been punished and many lives would have been saved."

Eight years after its conclusion, Cochise learned for the first time
the cause of the great American war between blue and gray. The
information came in an oddly roundabout way. Cochise complained
fervently to Safford that a Mexican boy he had taken captive and raised
for ten years as an Apache had escaped. At sixteen, the boy had made
his getaway to an Arizona settlement and had been sent to Safford for
protection; the governor managed to restore him to his uncle in Sonora. To the Apache way of thinking, the boy was Cochise's property,
and Safford ought to have turned him over to the chief. When Safford's
legalistic answer failed to satisfy Cochise, the governor resorted to an
oversimplified history lesson.

> I . . . inquired of him if he knew we had a war sometime ago among
> ourselves and why we fought with each other? He said he knew of
> the war but did not know the cause. I then explained to him that
> part of our people owned slaves and a part did not; that upon this
> question they became angry with each other and many men were

killed; that those opposed to holding slaves had conquered; that afterwards laws were made prohibiting any one from holding as a slave a negro, Indian, Mexican or any one else. He said he supposed it was all right and he would say no more about it.

After parting from Cochise, Safford made a prescient observation: "My impression is that he is now in good earnest, and that he desires peace, but he and his followers are wild men, and with the best of efforts on our part some real or imaginary cause may at any moment set them again upon the warpath."

The Chiricahua Reservation, which became official in December 1872, was a square tract fifty-five miles on a side occupying the southeast corner of Arizona. From the point of view of its Indian inhabitants, no more perfect reserve was ever created in the United States. Included in its boundaries were the Dragoon stronghold of Cochise, the convolutions of the sacred Chiricahua Mountains, Apache Pass with its important spring, and dozens of canyons full of antelope and deer. The only American dwellings inside the square were a trader's post at Sulphur Springs and the scattering of adobe buildings at Fort Bowie, which continued to be occupied by a skeleton force of soldiers with few duties. As late as 1872, no miners had laid claim to any part of this wilderness.

The Chiricahua Reservation ought to have worked, if any Apache reserve could. Thanks to the meddling of theoreticians in Washington, it was never given a real chance.

At first the Arizona press raised a hue and cry about Howard's giveaway of vital land, predicting endless bloodshed at the hands of savages coddled by Jeffords. But as the months passed, Cochise kept his word for all the Apaches: depredations in Arizona dwindled to almost nil. The papers grew guardedly optimistic, then grateful to Howard and Jeffords.

With his keen understanding of the Chiricahua, their new agent gave them a freedom no other Apaches enjoyed. They wore no brass tags, endured no daily head count; Jeffords let the bands camp wherever they pleased, and rather than calling them in to his agency to receive their rations, he often traveled to dispense the government food. Unlike Crook, Jeffords was reluctant to convert the Apaches to farming; in the face of official pressure, he argued that there was too little arable land within the reservation.

Cochise's people reveled in their freedom. According to Bourke, "some of the Chiricahuas called their brethren at the San Carlos 'squaws,' because they had to work; on their side, a great many of the Apaches at the San Carlos . . . , feeling that the Chiricahuas deserved a whipping fully as much as they did, were extremely rancorous towards them."

Despite the flimsiness of his grounds, Crook, exasperated by the loose regime on the Chiricahua reservation, tried to take over from Jeffords. Appealing to his own official order of a year previous, which required all reservation Apaches to camp within one mile of the agency and to submit to a daily head count, he argued that unless the Chiricahuas obeyed, he would take matters into his own hands. Jeffords called the leading Chiricahuas together to discuss this threat, then reported to Washington that they would bolt rather than submit to such rules. This may have been just what Crook wanted: he was itching to go after Cochise with his soldiers and scouts and give the Chiricahua the "whipping" he had given the Tontos. But in his ruminative way, the general relented, rather than force Jeffords's hand.

Meanwhile the beleaguered agent was finding it all he could do to keep the reservation going. The fault lay almost entirely in Washington. The Department of Interior, under whose aegis the Bureau of Indian Affairs operated, had launched a power struggle with the Department of War over control of the reservations; the feud would last a decade and a half and cause untold damage, bewildering the Apaches who were caught in the crossfire.

The new Commissioner of Indian Affairs, Francis A. Walker, was an incompetent bureaucrat obsessed with petty details. To Jeffords's impassioned pleas for financing and supplies, he responded with red tape, legalisms, or silence. In the words of the reservation's historian, "After twenty years of reports, memos, and letters emphasizing this point, the Indian Bureau could still neither arrange nor pay for the pound of beef and pound of flour per day per person" that had long been agreed upon as the standard ration. Sometimes Jeffords paid for rations out of his pocket; other times he had nothing to give the Chiricahua, who were then forced to raid into Mexico.

Even worse, Walker pressured Jeffords to turn the Chiricahua into agriculturalists. His motives might be regarded as sinister, had they betrayed any comprehension whatsoever of Indian life. The Apaches, Walker declared, must cease their nomadism, now that they were "pensioners upon the national bounty." Once they were pacified as farmers, their "limits of actual occupation" were to be narrowly fixed. In this way, the rest of the reservation could eventually be put up for sale.

Jeffords resisted gamely. He had had bad luck choosing a site for his agency, moving it three times within a year. Rather than force his charges into farming, he paid them to help erect the agency buildings. Yet he grew so discouraged that at the end of 1873, he tried to resign —an offer that, insultingly enough, Walker neither accepted, rejected, nor even acknowledged.

The issue that threatened to destroy the reservation was the raiding in Mexico. Though he privately tried to discourage the practice and never indulged in it himself, Cochise publicly affirmed that his agreement with Howard had nothing to do with leaving Mexicans alone. Jeffords, who was not fond of Mexicans, looked the other way; in a careless moment, he told a reporter that "he did not care how many Mexicans his people killed . . . , that for acts of treachery with those Indians, the Mexicans deserved the killings."

Meanwhile Crook, still looking for a wedge to pry open the reservation, corresponded with the governor of Sonora about putting a stop to the raids. South of the border newspapers feverishly claimed that Howard had armed the Chiricahua and sent them with his blessing into Mexico. A Sonoran source insisted that the Apaches had killed one hundred citizens of the state in the first six months of 1873 alone.

The controversy over the raids began to cause tensions among the Chiricahua. Of the more than one thousand Apaches now on the reservation, about 475 were Chokonen who followed Cochise without question. The aging chief also had some sway over the other six hundred, mostly Nednhi and Bedonkohe. But to warriors like Juh and Geronimo, raiding in Mexico was an immemorial right. It was not they who had made peace with Howard. They were willing to use the reservation as a handy refuge, but they were not about to make peace with the hated Mexicans.

In March 1873, Cochise made his first visit to Apache Pass in eleven years, since the great battle when he and Mangas had had to yield to the army's howitzers. Accompanied by twenty warriors, he rode in to Fort Bowie. Among the people greeting him was Merejildo Grijalva, the chief of scouts who had been captured at age ten by the Chiricahua. Cochise knew Grijalva well, and his odd behavior at this reunion says something about his feelings toward Mexicans. Before the chief had dismounted, Grijalva offered Cochise his hand; but, said a witness, "Cochise told him he would not shake hands with him until he whipped him; so he got down off from his horse, and struck him two or three times with his whip and then they had a friendly embrace, and commenced to talk over old times."

About a year later, a trader from Sonora, guarded by twenty Mexican soldiers, came to Fort Bowie. The trader said he would like to meet Cochise and make a pact to establish the right to sell goods to the fort's employees. Cochise came in a fury. With Grijalva interpreting, he lashed out at the trader:

> You come in here and ask to make a treaty with me and to cross my reservation with your wagons and goods. You forget what the Mexicans did to my people long ago when we were at peace with the Americans, and you would get my people down into your country, get them drunk on mescal and furnish them with powder and lead and tell them to come up and get the big mules from the Americans. And when they would commit a depredation and steal mules and bring them back to your country, your people would get them drunk on mescal and cheat them out of their mules.

Cochise told the terrified trader that he was never again to cross the line with soldiers in his company. "You've got twenty soldiers, and what do they amount to!" the chief spat. "I can take five of my men and wipe them off the earth." According to a witness, one of Cochise's men was so stirred by this tirade that he raised his rifle and was about to shoot the trader. When Cochise, with a gesture of his hand, forestalled the warrior, he wept from sheer frustration.

Perhaps the oddest business to take place on the reservation was a pursuit so carefully concealed that its traces have escaped American records, lingering only in the oral tradition of the Chiricahua. In his years as a prospector, Jeffords had developed a keen eye for gold. It seems that in his rambles across the reservation, he spotted a number of deposits. Jeffords knew well the Apache abhorrence of digging gold out of the earth, which was so strong that one chief prophesied, "It is this stuff that will bring our people to ruin and cause us to lose first our land and then our lives."

Yet Cochise apparently did not share his people's sense of the taboo. In a clandestine agreement with Jeffords, he approved a limited gold-mining operating; his own son became one of the miners. If word of Jeffords's finds got out, the agent knew, it would mean the end of the reservation, for Indian rights carried little weight in the face of gold fever. The Chiricahuas took the precious metal to Janos, in Chihuahua, where they traded it for the kinds of goods the Bureau of Indian Affairs was so slow to provide, telling the Mexicans they had found the gold in Sonora.

By the spring of 1874, Cochise's ailment gave him no relief. It was excruciating for him to eat solid food. Dispirited, he resorted more and more to tizwin, the weak corn beer the Apaches made, or binged on whiskey the officers at Fort Bowie shared with him. Drunk or not, he never spent a night in Apache Pass, with its terrible personal memories, but always mounted his horse before sunset and rode back to his camp, insisting that his followers do likewise.

Late in May a government official paid Cochise one of the last visits any white man would make to the Chokonen chief. He found Cochise "exhausted," "suffering intensely," and "failing rapidly." Yet when the official gave him a photograph of General Howard, the chief held it in his hand, looked at it again and again, and declared his affection for the man who had ridden into the Dragoons to offer an American truce.

Some contemporary reports call Cochise's complaint dyspepsia, but it seems more likely that he suffered from stomach or colon cancer. World-weary and melancholic, he accepted his fate. As he felt his strength waning, he gathered his leading men and told them that he was appointing his eldest son, Taza, to lead the people after his death. Strictly speaking, a chief could not choose his successor; the new chief had to be elected by the men of the tribe. But Cochise's authority was still sovereign: at once his leaders vowed to follow Taza.

As the chief lay in his agony, some of his supporters concluded that he had been bewitched. Indeed, for the Chiricahua, most illness was attributable to sorcery. The culprit was identified: he was either a Chihenne or a White Mountain Apache, an old, crippled man who had recently visited Jeffords's agency. Taza led a small band of warriors in pursuit of the witch; if they could burn him to death, they believed, Cochise might still recover. Warned of their mission, the old man fled into the mountains, but Taza's band hunted him down, captured him, and started back to the stronghold. Jeffords interceded, and managed with "an extraordinary amount of talk and persuasion" to convince Taza to let the old man go.

On June 7, 1874, Jeffords met Cochise for the last time. The agent had hoped to stay at the chief's deathbed in the stronghold, but he needed to cross the Sulphur Springs Valley to issue rations. Many years later, Jeffords recalled his last conversation with the chief. As he said goodbye, Cochise asked, "Do you think you will ever see me again?"

A startled Jeffords answered honestly, "I do not know; I don't think I will, for you have been failing very rapidly in the last three days, and I think that by tomorrow night you will be dead."

Cochise agreed: "I think so too, about tomorrow morning, at ten o'clock, I will pass out, but do you think we will ever meet again?"

"I don't know. What do you think about it?"

"Well," said Cochise, "I have been giving it a good deal of thought since I have been sick here, and I think we will."

"Where?"

"I don't know, somewhere up there." Cochise pointed to the sky.

True to his prediction, the great chief died on the morning of June 8. Many stories have been passed down about Cochise's burial, some fanciful, some grounded in fact. Since no white men were present at the chief's death or funeral, whatever truth there is in the stories ultimately depends on what the Chiricahua told Jeffords.

Cochise was dressed in his war garments, according to some, painted for war, and wrapped in a blanket with his name woven into it, the gift of an army colonel. Propped on his favorite horse, with a warrior holding him upright, he was carried to a secret crevice in the Dragoons. Only a few warriors were allowed to make this last ride. Next to the crevice, Cochise's horse and favorite dog were shot. His gun—a combination rifle-shotgun, some say, with gold and silver inlaid—was thrown into the abyss. First the horse, then the dog, then Cochise himself was lowered with ropes into the deep fissure in the granite outcrop.

Some say the warriors rode their horses back and forth across the ground near the burial site, to obliterate the trail leading to it. Others insist that as the warriors rode out of the stronghold, they shot two more horses and buried them at one-mile intervals, as mounts for the chief to ride in the afterlife.

The ceremonial mourning lasted four days, a span of lamentation granted only the greatest leaders and shamans. The mourning swept across the reservation. Jeffords's assistant saw it seize the Chiricahua who were camped near the agency. When the news of Cochise's death came, "the howl that went up from these people was fearful to listen to. They were scattered around in the nooks and ravines in parties, and as the howling from one rancheria would lag, it would be renewed with vigor in another. This was kept up through the night and until daylight next morning."

Only a few Chiricahuas—and Jeffords—knew the location of Cochise's grave. Jeffords never told anyone else.

Thus passed the greatest Apache of the nineteenth century. Never again would a chief so command the hearts and wills of the Chiricahua, or so unify them in war and peace. Yet, in the deceptive calm of the new reservations, as they talked at night in their wickiups, the Apaches were poised to set out on one of the most heroic—albeit tragic—quests the continent had ever seen. That quest had a goal with which the white settlers swarming into the Chiricahua heartland might well have sympathized: freedom.

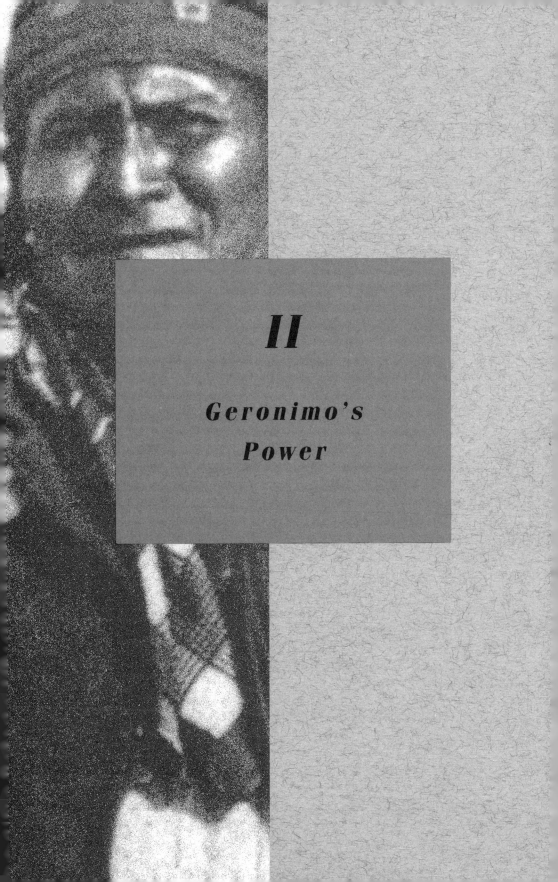

II

Geronimo's Power

Ten

■

Turkey Gobbler

*A*pache: the name itself is of uncertain origin. Some scholars explain it as a Spanish pronunciation of the Zuni word *apachu,* or "enemy." The Apaches both traded with the Zuni, who lived (as they live today) in pueblo villages in northwestern New Mexico, and raided against them. Others believe that the name comes from a Yuman language, via a Spanish pronunciation of the word *e-patch* ("man"), or from the Ute name for Apaches, *Awa'tehe.* It has even been suggested that *Apache* derives from the Spanish verb *apachurar,* "to crush," in homage to the alleged Apache practice of turning captives over to women and children who pounded them to death with stones.

The Apaches call themselves *N'de* (the apostrophe indicating a glottal stop) or *Déné,* a word that means simply "the People." They are Athapaskans, linked ethnically, linguistically, and physiologically to tribes that still inhabit subarctic Canada and Alaska, peoples such as the Koyukon, the Tanana, the Dogrib, the Yellowknife, and the Chipewyan Indians.

No one knows when the Apaches entered the Southwest: scholars place the intrusion as early as the thirteenth century or as late as the beginning of the seventeenth. Even these wide parameters are based on the most conjectural kinds of evidence. The early date postulates that the turn toward defensive architecture among the Anasazi and Mogollon cliff dwellers in the thirteenth century was a response to the invasion of warrior bands. The case for the seventeenth century depends on the absence of mention of Apache-like Indians in the accounts of the first Spanish explorers of the Southwest. When Coronado rode through southeast Arizona in 1540–1541, bisecting the Chiricahua heartland, he described the region as uninhabited. This does not mean, of course, that the Apaches were not there: they may well have watched the Spaniards' every step from their well-hidden lookouts.

Nomads such as the Apaches slide through the sifting screens of archaeology. At Mesa Verde, seven centuries old, the ruins of four-story towers, of great ceremonial kivas, of elaborate room-blocks, tell a vivid tale of the daily life of the sedentary Anasazi. The Apaches who came later left behind only the odd ring of stones, the scattering of flint flakes; it is a rare site indeed that can be carbon-dated to freeze an Apache moment in the stream of time.

Before their first contact with the Spaniards, the Apaches had a remarkably different culture from the one Anglo-Americans would discover in the 1850s. Their only domesticated animal was the dog, which they used to transport their belongings, strapping packs to the animals' backs or harnessing them to travois like those used by the Plains Indians. What may have been the first contact between Europeans and Apaches occurred in the spring of 1541, when Coronado's party met a band of nomads somewhere near the Texas panhandle. Coronado reported that these people were called Querechos. Their identification as Apaches depends crucially on the fact that the Indians who live today at Jemez Pueblo in New Mexico (and whose ancestors the Querechos may have attacked) call Navajos and Apaches *Kearitsa'a* —which Coronado may have rendered as Querecho.

Fascinated by these nomads, whom they nonetheless regarded as "coarse, vile, and wicked," the Spaniards carefully observed their way of life. The Querechos, who traveled "like gypsies, wandering about from place to place, following the natural sources of their food supply," were entirely dependent on the buffalo. They drank its blood, said the Spaniards, ate its meat raw, and sun-dried the meat for carrying; they dressed in buffalo skins, and slept in tepees covered with buffalo hides. They were ignorant of how to raise corn or make flour, supplementing their diet instead with prickly pears and dates.

All this sounds so different from nineteenth-century Apache life that one wonders whether the Querechos ought not to be identified as Plains Indians. Yet the Spanish descriptions bear many similarities to the way of life of the Lipan Apaches, easternmost of the several Apache bands, who still live in western Texas and eastern New Mexico.

At the time of contact in the sixteenth century, the distinctions among various bands of Southern Athapaskans (as anthropologists call them) may already have been well formed. These included the Jicarilla and Lipan Apaches in the northeast and east, the Navajos in the north, as well as the many bands of western Apaches, among them the Tonto, Coyotero, Mescalero, Aravaipa, and Chiricahua.

During the first century of Spanish contact, nothing changed the way of life of the Apaches so profoundly as their acquisition of the horse. It seems likely that for decades, Apaches stole horses only to kill and eat them, for they considered horsemeat a great delicacy. It may have been Pueblo Indians, sometime between 1600 and 1638, who taught the Apaches to ride. But as they mastered horseback travel —an art of which they would become perhaps the finest practitioners ever seen in North America—the Apaches discovered an immense new power. Suddenly they could move twice as fast as a man on foot, could travel many times as far in a day as their wretched dogs could go. They could carry far more belongings and hunt buffalo and deer and antelope far more efficiently.

A hallmark of the Southern Athapaskans has always been their skill at adapting to their own culture what they took from others. With the Spanish entrada, the Navajos and Apaches, once so close as to be cousin tribes, diverged fundamentally. The Navajos seized upon another beast the Spanish introduced, becoming once and for all sheepherders. The Apaches felt only contempt for this new practice of their neighbors to the north; even as food, the sheep interested them little. They were, in fact, so unwilling to compromise their nomadism with husbandry of any kind, that for all the importance of the horse to their culture, the Apaches never learned to breed them. To the end of their freedom in the Southwest, they were content to steal horses from Mexicans and Americans, ride them until they were played out, then kill and eat them.

To what extent the Apaches were raiders and warriors in precontact times remains an unsolved problem. One Spaniard in 1581 found the Querechos "well formed, lively, warlike, and brave, and feared by those in the neighboring districts." Yet Coronado's own historian had described the same Indians as "gentle people, not cruel." Many anthropologists believe the Apaches were forced westward around the time of contact by fierce conflicts with the Comanches on the plains.

In any event, by the time the Spaniards really began to know them in the seventeenth century, the Apaches had established a stable round of life. They hunted deer, antelope, mountain lion, and porcupine, and relied more regularly on the fruit of the prickly pear, yucca, cholla, and saguaro (the Apache favorite), and on berries, acorns, piñon nuts, and mesquite beans. Their most important food of all was mescal—the heart of certain kinds of agaves, including the century plant, desert spoon, and soapweed. In May or June, the women would dig up these plants, cut off the spiky leaves, then bake the hearts for a full day and night in a four-foot-deep pit covered with dirt. Sun-dried, baked mescal became a vital foodstuff carried about through the rest of the year.

The Apaches named the seasons after the rounds of harvest and hunting. Among the Chiricahua, there were six two-month periods, called by such names as "Many Leaves" (late spring), "Large Fruit" (early autumn), and "Ghost Face" (the barren winter). Each staple food had its time of year for gathering. Acorns and mesquite beans were collected in July and August, piñon nuts and juniper berries in October and November. All four were vital for getting through the winter, and the Apaches were so assiduous in gathering them that a single family might store up five hundred pounds of the tiny nuts and berries in a single harvest.

Hunting was best in the late fall. Two animals, however, were forbidden to eat: the bear, because he was quasi-human ("If you meet a bear," testified one Chiricahua, "and he stands on his hind feet and holds his hands up, he is trying to tell you that he is your friend"); and the fish, regarded as a relative of the snake, that creature of evil. Later, when the Apaches had grown accustomed to the animals the Spaniards introduced, they developed a hearty appetite for horsemeat and beef, even for mule and goat, but they would never eat pigs— "because hogs ate animals that lived around water." Apaches ingeniously made a canteen for carrying water out of the horse's intestine, a flexible tube as long as thirty feet.

By the eighteenth century, Apache men dressed in shirts and loincloths made of deer and antelope skins, with high-topped moccasins whose toes were turned up. They wore earrings made of seashell, turquoise, feathers, or mouse skins; painted their faces with chalk and ocher; wore their hair long but plucked their beards and whiskers. Women's garb was similar to men's, with a buckskin shirt pulled over the head and a medium-length buckskin skirt. Women often made necklaces of shells, fragrant roots, or deer and antelope hooves.

Before the Apaches learned to use Spanish firearms, a warrior relied on the standard five weapons. The bow, about five feet long, was usually made of mulberry, the bowstring of deer sinew; the arrows were three-foot shafts of cane, stabilized with hawk or eagle feathers, tipped with flint or obsidian heads. Sometimes the arrowheads were poisoned. To supply the venom, men would catch poisonous insects, or cut the heads off snakes and extract the deadly substance from the fangs, or bury a deer's stomach underground and cause it to ferment. Apaches were so skillful with bow and arrow that in battle some warriors could put seven arrows in the air before the first came to earth. Their range was easily one hundred fifty yards.

The lance—the weapon of which Cochise was the peerless master —was an agave stalk about fifteen feet long, sometimes reinforced with the skin of a stag's leg. Spears for close combat amounted to little more than sharpened sticks, often decorated for luck and power. Many fighters carried war clubs, and nearly every one had a flint knife.

By the eighteenth century, the Apaches had acquired firearms from the Spanish; according to a chronicler in 1799, they had already become good marksmen. Yet half a century later, when Geronimo began to wreak havoc among the Mexicans, it was still the exception for an Apache to wield a rifle. Only in the late 1870s did the rifle become de rigueur for the well-armed Apache.

Among the Apachean peoples in the Southwest, none had a stronger cultural identity than the Chiricahua. The name is a corruption of *Chihuicahui,* as the people referred to themselves; in the strict sense the designation applied only to the Chokonen, but so intertwined were their destinies with those of the Chihenne, Bedonkohe, and Nednhi, that all four peoples are commonly referred to as Chiricahua. Some say the name means "People of the Rising Sun"; others, "Mountain People"—an appropriate interpretation, for the twisted canyons and craggy summits of the Dragoons, the Chiricahuas, and the Sierra Madre were the ultimate sanctuaries for these Apaches. When threatened by Spaniards or Mexicans, the Chiricahua lived and traveled almost entirely in the mountains, crossing the level basins between ranges hastily and at night. After contact with Americans, the Chiricahua adopted a saying, "The Indian follows the mountains and the white man the streams."

The Chiricahua have their own migration legend, which gives the lie to the theories of the anthropologists. According to their own tradition, the people came south along the eastern edge of the Rocky Mountains, entering the Southwest from what is today Colorado. By reckoning generations, they date this entry to the late twelfth or early thirteenth century—earlier than any anthropologists place them in the Southwest. The Chiricahua were the vanguard of all Apaches; other tribes came later. Ensconced in their heartland, the Chiricahuas fought Comanches on the east, Pimas on the west, Tarahumaras and even Aztecs on the south. From Aztec traders, says the tradition, they learned of the apocalyptic advent of the Spaniards in the New World; they even heard about Cortés's conquest of Tenochtitlán. When the Spaniards began to explore their heartland in 1540, the Chiricahua stayed hidden and observed them for "the lifetime of one man."

The religion of the Chiricahua, as of all Apaches, was polytheistic and animistic. Ussen, who is usually referred to by whites as the supreme Apache god, was really a supernatural power whose existence predated the creation of the universe. The most important intermediaries, created by Ussen, were White Painted Woman and Child of the Water: in variant tellings, one or the other was responsible for creating the earth, and all agree that Child of the Water created the Apaches. His brother, Killer of Enemies, though an important aide to the Chiricahua (he freed the game animals from an underground home), was also the creator of the white man.

The most important ceremony in Chiricahua life was the girl's puberty ritual, which lasted through four days and nights of dancing. During the ceremony, men wearing masks represented the *G'an*—the Mountain Gods, benevolent deities who protected the Chiricahua from harm. In practical terms, the paramount religious concern of the people was Power. Unlike other Indian tribes, the Apaches did not believe that a few exceptional individuals—shamans, or medicine men—possessed all the Power. Almost any man or woman could have Power of one kind or another, even though, on the whole, Power could not be sought, but came unbidden, often in a dream or a vision. As one Chiricahua put it, "There are so many enemies that if you don't have Power, you can't do anything." Because of the ubiquity of these supernatural gifts among the people, Indians from other tribes concluded that all the Chiricahua were witches.

Cochise himself had possessed a strong Power, of the kind his people called "enemy-against": this was, they believed, a prime source of his success in battle. His son Taza, to whom on his deathbed he had bequeathed the chieftainship of the Chokonen, also had Power, which lent him considerable authority to balance the drawback of his youth. Taza's younger brother, Naiche, Cochise's only other son, had no Power of his own. This fact would prove to have profound consequences, not least for Geronimo.

Despite the death of Cochise, in the summer of 1874 the Chiricahua enjoyed an enviable freedom. Like no other Apaches, they could come and go as they pleased on their reservation, a generous tract that covered the heart of the land that—so their own traditions told them —they had made their own more than six centuries before. No general told them where to camp, or made them stand in line and show brass tags. For all the grumbling on the part of American officials, none had seriously tried to rescind the Chiricahua privilege of raiding into Mexico.

As they drank the clear streams in the ancestral mountains, hunted the deer, drew rations of beef and flour from Tom Jeffords, and told the old stories around the campfire, the Chiricahua gloated in their superiority to the "squaws" at San Carlos. Theirs would prove to be a fragile exultation. In the dry soil of the Chiricahua Reservation, the seeds of loss and betrayal were already sprouting.

The trouble began, as it would so often during the Apache wars, in Washington. Crook's defeat of the last renegade Tontos, along with Howard's treaty with Cochise, had created a mood of gilded optimism concerning Arizona. Even the canny Governor Safford, who had talked to Cochise face-to-face, was fooled by the calm. At the beginning of 1875, he told his legislature, "Comparative peace now reigns throughout the Territory, with almost a certainty that no general Indian war will ever occur again."

Since the establishment of the reservations, the Departments of War and the Interior had feuded over which should be in charge of them. The overlapping jurisdiction, with all its ambiguities, worked a hardship on the Indians, who were caught in a crossfire of quibbling and posturing between civilian agents and military officers. Now President Grant acted to simplify the situation, decreeing that the reservations were to be run and supervised by Interior. Yet because a military presence was still required to enforce orders and safeguard the whites, what one officer called "the ancient curse of dual control" persisted in Arizona.

An even more consequential act on the President's part came in the spring of 1875, when he transferred General Crook to the Department of the Platte. With matters so well in hand in Arizona, America's best Indian fighter was needed on a more volatile front. A gold rush in the Black Hills of South Dakota had launched an illegal invasion of the Sioux reservation, resulting in a mass flight to the hills by the outraged Indians. Not only Sioux, but Cheyenne as well, led by such charismatic chiefs as Crazy Horse and Sitting Bull, were refusing to return to their reservations. Washington was confident that the outbreak could be squelched by the flamboyant General George Armstrong Custer, but it would not hurt to send Crook out for backup.

Crook had fought side by side with the golden-locked Custer in the Civil War, and was not impressed. In April 1865, in Virginia, Crook had masterminded an attack that broke the spirit of a Confederate brigade, while Custer's men made a half-hearted and ineffectual charge on Crook's right. In his sardonic fashion, Crook later wrote, "As soon as the enemy hoisted the white flag, Gen. Custer's division rushed up the hill and turned in more prisoners and battle flags than any of the cavalry, and probably had less to do with their surrender than any of the rest of us." Custer's record at West Point had been even poorer than Crook's: he graduated thirty-fourth in his class of thirty-four.

In Arizona, Crook was replaced by General August V. Kautz, a competent officer, but a man with only a fraction of Crook's understanding of Apaches. Kautz was hamstrung, moreover, by the transfer of jurisdiction over the reservation to the Department of Interior.

To the crucial post of agent for the San Carlos reservation, Interior appointed a twenty-two-year-old named John Clum. His only qualification for the job was that he was a member of the Dutch Reformed Church. The Bureau of Indian Affairs (under the Interior Department) had decided that Indian agents were best chosen from the ranks of the devoutly religious: whence the mission of Vincent Colyer, the passionate Quaker, in 1871. Clum's parents had wanted him to study for the ministry; instead, he had gone to Rutgers, where he had the distinction of taking the field against Princeton in the first intercollegiate football game ever played in America.

Clum's youthful inexperience daunted him not at all as he took on his difficult new assignment. He possessed certain admirable qualities: a rigid honesty, great courage, and the energy of a dynamo, in which respects he far surpassed the five agents who had preceded him at San Carlos. The flip side of Clum's character, however, was a cocksure vanity issuing in bombastic pronouncements and grandiose resolves. With tongue only slightly in cheek, he described the Arizona in which he alighted on August 8, 1874, as "that notorious nation of red men which I was supposed to subdue and Christianize, single-handed, at a salary of sixteen hundred dollars per annum." Clum had the mind of a reductionist, turning everything complex and shadowy to black-and-white, with himself always standing boldly in the right as he opposed the forces of error and pusillanimity. He could never admit he was wrong; worse, he could not perceive when a phenomenon lay beyond his ken. Some Apaches at San Carlos liked him. The Chiricahua would come to have another view.

Clum had a pair of passions—for military drill and for amateur theatricals. Both would have a major impact on the history of the Southwest. Far more of a demon for order than even the orderly Crook, he set out at once to regularize life at San Carlos. With a Christian fervor for cleanliness, he insisted that the reservation Apaches live up to high standards of neatness and sanitation even inside their own wickiups. The tizwin, or corn beer, which Apaches had always made was strictly prohibited: Clum personally led midnight raids on back-country stills, dumping the kettles of tizwin on the ground and seizing the "moonshiners," who served fifteen days in jail for each infraction. Apaches had always held that it was beneath the dignity of a warrior to engage in common labor, a belief that won no sympathy from Clum. "Red devils find just as much for idle hands to do, as white devils, or black devils," he theorized, as he set up a six-day work week for the Apache men, paying them fifty cents a day to build new quarters for himself and his assistant. In his spare time, the agent practiced marksmanship with his new Colt .45 by shooting at saguaros—a pastime that would become an enduring sport in Arizona.

Clum trained a special force of twenty-five "policemen" to serve, as he jauntily put it, as "my personal body-guard and freelance army." For days at a time, he drilled these Apaches in the showy maneuvers of the manual of arms he had learned at sixteen as a cadet in a military academy in upstate New York. When his policemen were ready to perform, Clum staged a demonstration for Governor Safford, barking out commands in English—"Carry arms! Rear open order! About face! . . . Close order! Present arms!"—and beaming as he saluted the governor. The establishment of this "freelance army" also allowed Clum airily to decline whenever General Kautz offered the assistance of his soldiers.

The police were charged with the invidious task of arresting Apache lawbreakers on the reservation. Clum also created an Apache court, so that the criminals could be judged and sentenced by their peers. That turning a people against itself in this way might have a demoralizing effect never crossed Clum's mind; the "novel proposition" of Apache police and court, he wrote, "appealed to them strongly, for they were able, crudely, to detect in it the idea of self-determination." Had his reforms been copied by subsequent administrators, Clum would later claim in rueful retrospect, "our American red men would have developed quickly and securely into good and useful citizens."

Clum energetically furthered the renaming of Apaches that had begun under Crook's regime. "Eskiminzin's name was shortened to 'Skimmy,' and he enjoyed it. Sneezer's real name was unpronounceable. . . . Eskinospas became 'Nosey.' " Even the peerless scout and interpreter Merejildo Grijalva was saddled with the mocking nickname "Mary." Clum insisted that the title the Apaches gave him in turn, which he rendered as "Nantan-betunny-kahyeh," translated as "Boss-with-the-high-forehead." Perhaps some Apaches told him that. The Chiricahua, once they came to know Clum, gave him another name: "Turkey Gobbler," in observation of his strutting. Often, as the agent approached, one Apache would say to another—in Apache, of course—"Look out; he's dragging his wings."

Far more pernicious than any of Clum's reforms, however, was a decision made by the incompetent Commissioner of Indian Affairs, Francis Walker. The bureaucratic mind has always been drawn to the tidy notion of consolidating "savages" in a single place under a uniform regimen. Ignorant of tribal differences, Walker envisioned an ultimate concentration of all the Apaches into two reservations, San

Carlos in Arizona and Mescalero in New Mexico. Even before Clum's appointment, the process was set in motion, with the removal of fourteen hundred Indians—many of them Yavapais—from Camp Verde to San Carlos. In 1875, at Fort Apache, the twin reservation north of San Carlos, a quarrel between the civilian agent in charge and the army captain whose troops were quartered there escalated until the captain marched on the agency and took it over by force. This debacle gave Commissioner Walker an excuse to put Clum in charge of the northern reservation as well, with orders to remove its Apaches (mostly Coyoteros) to San Carlos. By the end of July, the eighteen hundred Indians who had lived in relative contentment at Fort Apache were driven south and forced to cohabit with Aravaipas, Tontos, and Yavapais.

Though at first he was unhappy with the concentration policy, for it threatened to overwhelm him, Clum soon gloried in the self-importance it conferred upon him. By August 1875 he had, according to his own count, forty-two hundred Indians at San Carlos, including the largest gathering of Apaches yet assembled in Arizona. All that remained to accomplish Walker's consolidation was a pretext for forcing the Chiricahuas to abandon their own reservation. Sniffing for smoke, the bureaucrats discovered fire.

As Crook had left Arizona, he had uttered an eloquent protest against the concentration policy. That keen student of Apache ways realized as few Americans did the folly of forcing tribes away from their homelands, into tense proximity with other peoples who had at times been their enemies. Crook's warning fell on deaf ears.

Even with Cochise alive, there had been dangerous tensions on the new Chiricahua reservation, between the Chokonen loyal to their chief and the other Chiricahuas, mostly Nednhi, who only accepted the truce Howard had forged as an artful convenience. Mexican officials increasingly complained about raids in Sonora launched from the reservation. Taza found it impossible to hold the allegiance of all the Apaches as his father had. He was opposed by a pair of willful Chokonens, brothers named Skinya and Pionsenay, and to some extent by those emerging leaders, Juh of the Nednhi and Geronimo of the Bedonkohe. In the face of the bitter conflict that was brewing, Tom Jeffords was helpless to assert any real authority.

In March 1876, matters came to a nasty head. At Sulphur Springs on the reservation lived a trader named Nick Rodgers. Returning from a lucrative raid into Mexico, Pionsenay and Skinya's band traded gold and silver for Rodgers's whiskey. An all-out drunk ensued, during which Pionsenay shot to death two of his own sisters. Perhaps still drunk, the Chokonen warrior rode back to Rodgers's post and demanded more whiskey. When the trader refused, Pionsenay's men shot and killed him and his cook as well.

Taza had taken his father's deathbed injunction to cooperate with Jeffords to heart; now he set out with the agent to hunt Pionsenay down. Two months of trailing and parrying ensued, until finally, in a blazing gun battle, Naiche, Taza's younger brother, fatally shot Skinya, and Taza badly wounded Pionsenay in the shoulder.

Here was the pretext Washington needed. Clum received a telegram instructing him to proceed to Apache Pass, take over from Jeffords (who was to be summarily dismissed), and IF PRACTICABLE, REMOVE CHIRICAHUA INDIANS TO SAN CARLOS.

Clum set out from San Carlos with a bodyguard of fifty-six Aravaipa and Coyotero Apaches, declining once more General Kautz's offer of an escort. At Fort Bowie in Apache Pass, the agent met with Taza and Naiche. Surprisingly, they agreed to give up the Chiricahua Reservation and go to San Carlos. Within a few days, Clum led a procession of some three hundred twenty-five Chokonen, Nednhi, and Bedonkohe Apaches as they headed northwest toward the reservation they had never wanted. Among them was Pionsenay, who, crippled by Taza's bullet, had hoped for mercy. Clum turned the fugitive over to a pair of deputy sheriffs, but Pionsenay, sensing the rigor of American justice, escaped. He was later killed in Mexico.

Even as he was relieved of duty, Jeffords protested in writing to Commissioner Walker, not against his own firing but against the betrayal of Howard's treaty. The killing of the trader and his cook, Jeffords argued, was not the result of a general outbreak by the Chiricahua, but of the drunken folly of three warriors. Breaking the treaty now would only lead to further bloodshed in Arizona. But Commissioner Walker was bent on consolidation. Jeffords went back to his mining, and eventually retired to a lonely ranch thirty-five miles north of Tucson, where he lived out his days in reclusive contentment. When he died in 1914, his great understanding of Cochise's Chiricahuas died with him.

As Clum had parleyed with Taza, Jeffords had informed the agent of the divisions within the Chiricahua. A few days later, Clum met with

Geronimo and Juh. Geronimo did the speaking for his brother-in-law the stutterer. According to Clum, Geronimo agreed to go to San Carlos with all his people, but pleaded that he needed time to gather them up from just south of the Mexican border. In the night, the whole party—as many as seven hundred Apaches—slipped away. "Every bit of superfluous camp equipment was cast aside," Clum reported; "feeble and disabled horses were killed. Dogs were strangled, lest their bark betray the route taken by the fleeing renegades."

The Chiricahua version differs somewhat. According to Juh's son, the Apaches held a talk to discuss Clum's ultimatum. Fully two-thirds of the warriors opposed going to San Carlos—"What right had this arrogant young man to tell them what to do?"—and at that moment they broke with Taza, elected Juh as their chief, and fled south into Mexico.

Clum put the best face possible on the fact that he had transported only a third of the Chiricahuas to San Carlos, implying that the renegades were few and relatively unimportant. Privately, Geronimo's outwitting him rankled the agent deeply. The event gave birth to a preoccupation with Geronimo that would grow to be a personal obsession.

Geronimo's duplicity bothered other whites, who had the model of Cochise's stoic honesty before their eyes. Years later, after Geronimo had become the most famous Apache, a pioneer spoke for many Arizonans when he derided the Bedonkohe warrior: "When he loafed around the agency at Sulphur Springs . . . in the years 1874–75, he was simply a hanger-on, a recipient of weekly rations, with no standing other than that of an ordinary, shiftless buck, roaming here and there, looting and raiding under the leadership of other men."

Clum's mission of removal spelled the end of the Chiricahua reservation. What had seemed the ideal reserve had lasted barely three and a half years. President Grant rubber-stamped the demise in an executive order on October 30, 1876, returning the land to the public domain.

With Clum's partial success, his sense of his role as guardian of the Apaches became truly grandiose. As he strutted around San Carlos, he nursed the fantasy that he had created a "happy family," that he was the Indians' "one sympathetic friend." On his arrival two years earlier, Clum's own first impression of San Carlos—a makeshift camp erected on the salt flats where the Gila and San Carlos rivers come together—

had been a gloomy one: "Of all the desolate, isolated, human habitations!" he wrote. "Wickiups, covered with brush and grass, old blankets, or deerskins, smoky, smelly. Lean dogs, mangy, inert." In his 1875 report, he had duly noted the high rate of disease on the reservation, including 123 cases of gonorrhea and 289 of "quotidian intermittent fever." But now, distracted by his own improvements, Clum saw San Carlos through rose-tinted glasses. Now it became "that wonderful reservation where all was peace, plenty, and happiness."

Many years later, Juh's son Daklugie remembered San Carlos from the Chiricahua perspective.

> San Carlos! That was the worst place in all the great territory stolen from the Apaches. If anybody ever lived there permanently, no Apache knew of it. Where there is no grass there is no game. Nearly all of the vegetation was cacti; and though in season a little cactus fruit was produced, the rest of the year the food was lacking. The heat was terrible. The insects were terrible. The water was terrible. What there was in the sluggish river was brackish and warm.

That brackish water spawned millions of mosquitoes. "At San Carlos, for the five time within memory of any of my people," recalled Daklugie, "the Apaches experienced the shaking sickness." Clum's "quotidian intermittent fever" was malaria. The death rate was high, especially among infants. Bewildered by the disease, the Apaches assumed it was a deliberate punishment inflicted by the Americans. "It is because of the sickness that we must be put there—," one Chiricahua said of San Carlos: "they wanted us to die." "White Eyes accuse us of cruelty," said another, "but never have we done anything so bad."

In the midst of this gathering horror, Clum concocted a harebrained scheme. The agent had a sweetheart in Ohio whom he wanted to marry. To finance his trip back east to claim her hand, he created a touring theatrical company, choosing some of his most prominent Apaches as his "thespians." They would attend the Centennial Exposition in Philadelphia, visit the Great White Father in Washington, and pay their expenses with the gate receipts from what Clum called his "Wild Apache show." The trip would also serve a didactic purpose: "I wanted my Indians to see the greatness of our United States and become impressed by the progress of their white brothers."

At the end of July 1876, twenty Apaches and two Yavapais parted from San Carlos with Clum. They included Eskiminzin, the aging chief of the Aravaipa, who had lost so many of his people in the Camp Grant massacre, and Taza, Cochise's son. "A great throng of excited Apaches," Clum reported, "had assembled to wave and shout a sincere *bon voyage.*" Clum understood only a few words of Apache, and his preconceptions kept him from perceiving the true nature of the farewell. In the testimony of a Chiricahua, "When their people saw their young chief and his men depart they mourned for them as dead, for their experiences had caused them to feel that they were being taken away to be executed."

As they boarded a railroad train for the first time, the Indians, like the group Howard had taken east four years before, grew frightened. Mile after mile, the sprawling country drifted by the windows, an endless succession of farms and towns. As they sat on a hotel balcony in Cincinnati, Clum asked the Apaches what they thought about America. "Eskiminzin protested that he was unable to express his feelings, and, waving his hand about his head, he said that all the very wonderful sights made him 'dizzy.' " Taza, who a few days earlier had boasted about his father's decimation of the White Eyes, now maintained a morose silence.

In St. Louis, the troupe made its theatrical debut. With Clum introducing each scene, the Apaches appeared in war paint, naked from the waist up; sang what a reviewer called a "peculiar and monotonous song" around the campfire; were suddenly attacked by white men, who routed them in battle; simulated a council of war; and danced a scalp-dance—even though Clum knew the Apaches almost never scalped their victims. Clum's production was an early example of the kind of spectacle that would culminate in Buffalo Bill's Wild West Show. At a remarkably short remove from the time when they still rode in freedom as enemies of the United States (in St. Louis Taza was less than three months from his gunfight with Pionsenay), the Apaches were packaged and trivialized, their culture turned into bathetic tableaux for the amusement of gentlemen and ladies in evening dress.

Clum thought the acting fine indeed, but the tour flopped and the debts mounted. The agent blamed Custer's annihilation at Little Bighorn, which had occurred only two months before, and which had left the American public in a sour mood about Indians. At the St. Louis performance, observed a reviewer, "when the knife of the white man gleamed in the face of the Indian, who was held in his strong embrace, the applause, especially from the galleries, was deafening."

In Washington, the Indians visited President Grant, who had only a

few months left to serve. While he was there, Taza fell ill with pneumonia. "Although the best medical skill available was called to attend
him," as Clum put it, the young chief's condition worsened; after a
short time, Taza died. Rather than being carried back to his people in
Arizona, he was buried with some ceremony in the Congressional
Cemetery; General Howard came to the funeral service.

Clum left "his" Indians to go back to San Carlos without him, while
he traveled to Ohio to get married. A honeymoon to San Francisco
and San Diego delayed his return to the reservation until December.
Thus he did not witness the shock among the Chiricahua when the
Indian delegation came home without Taza.

There had been many Apaches who were not happy with Taza's
leadership, but he was in the end the undisputed chief of the Chokonen, as well as Cochise's son. Now the Chiricahua believed that Taza
had been poisoned in Washington—that that had in fact been the
main object of the journey. When Clum returned, Naiche went to the
agent's office to find out what had happened to his brother. "For three
days," remembered a Chiricahua, "he stood at the door and Mr. Clum
refused to see him. That insolence was never forgotten."

The Turkey Gobbler managed to find a silver lining even in this
unmistakable tragedy. "The illness and death of [Taza]," he later wrote,
"were not devoid of beneficial results, for the reason that they af-
forded the Indians with our party an opportunity to observe the civi-
lized methods and customs of caring for the sick and preparing the
dead for burial."

Cochise Stronghold, in the Dragoon Mountains of Arizona. In 1874 his warriors buried the Chiricahua Apache chief in a secret grave here in Cochise's range. (BRUCE DALE. © 1992 NATIONAL GEOGRAPHIC SOCIETY)

Mickey Free, "the coyote whose kidnapping had brought war to the Chiricahuas," resurfaced in adulthood as a scout and interpreter for the U.S. Army. (ARIZONA HISTORICAL SOCIETY)

An early winter snow dusts the headwaters of the Gila River in New Mexico, near the birthplace of Geronimo. (BRUCE DALE. © 1992 NATIONAL GEOGRAPHIC SOCIETY)

Near this spot in Skeleton Canyon in the southeast corner of Arizona, Geronimo surrendered to Miles in September 1886, ending the last Indian war in America. (BRUCE DALE, © 1992 NATIONAL GEOGRAPHIC SOCIETY)

An extraordinary photograph of the final band, as they paused beside the train that took them east in 1886 as prisoners of war. Left foreground, Naiche; center foreground, Geronimo; third from right in the back row, the only known image of Lozen, the woman warrior. (FORT BOWIE NATIONAL HISTORIC SITE. DETAIL BY BRUCE DALE, © 1992 NATIONAL GEOGRAPHIC SOCIETY)

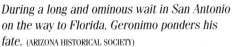

During a long and ominous wait in San Antonio on the way to Florida, Geronimo ponders his fate. (ARIZONA HISTORICAL SOCIETY)

Right: *Geronimo in Oklahoma, dressed up in motley regalia to suit the fantasies of tourists, who paid for his autograph.* (ARIZONA HISTORICAL SOCIETY)

The graves of Geronimo (pyramid of stones), his wife Ziyeh, and three of his children, at Fort Sill in Oklahoma. (BRUCE DALE, © 1992 NATIONAL GEOGRAPHIC SOCIETY)

Eleven

■

Geronimo in Irons

With his new bride, Clum returned to San Carlos on New Year's Day, 1877. To verify that the forty-five hundred Indians under his charge were as contented as he imagined them to be, he made a goodwill tour of the reservation: "We called on all the tribes, had big smokes and big talks." Only the Chiricahua, still bitter over the disappearance of Taza, refused to flatter his illusion.

Meanwhile a new spate of raids was plaguing southeastern Arizona. In only a few weeks nine men had been killed and more than a hundred horses and mules stolen. Eleven troops of cavalry set out to intercept the raiders; all came back empty-handed. The Apache bands responsible for these depredations have never been identified: they might have been led by Juh, by Geronimo, by the vengeful Pionsenay, or indeed by warriors whose names were yet unknown to Arizonans. With the demise of the Chiricahua Reservation, all bets were off: Cochise's treaty had been annulled by the White Eyes themselves.

Since the previous summer, Clum had brooded upon Geronimo. Now he believed that the fresh troubles in the territory could all be laid to the Bedonkohe's hand. In his reductionist way, Clum convinced himself that Geronimo alone stood in the way of a quick and lasting peace. Many years later, nursing the grievances of hindsight, Clum would argue that if he had only been allowed to pursue his conquest of Geronimo to its logical conclusion, the Southwest would have been spared a final decade of bloodshed.

Clum's great opportunity came in March. A lieutenant under General Kautz, on a visit to the Ojo Caliente reservation in New Mexico, saw and recognized Geronimo at the agency headquarters; the warrior had one hundred stolen horses with him. The lieutenant notified Kautz, who appealed to Governor Safford, who in turn telegraphed Washington. In place of the myopic Francis Walker, a new Commissioner of Indian Affairs had been installed—an official, unfortunately, every bit as wedded to the grand plan of consolidation. On March 20, the new commissioner telegraphed Clum: IF PRACTICABLE, TAKE YOUR INDIAN POLICE AND ARREST RENEGADE INDIANS AT OJO CALIENTE, NEW MEXICO. SEIZE STOLEN HORSES IN THEIR POSSESSION; RESTORE PROPERTY TO RIGHTFUL OWNERS. REMOVE RENEGADES TO SAN CARLOS AND HOLD THEM IN CONFINEMENT FOR MURDER AND ROBBERY.

The ambitious agent sprang into motion. He recruited an additional forty Indian police to augment the force of sixty he had paraded before the governor. But Clum sensed he was up against a formidable adversary; Governor Safford himself had estimated that the raiding party that had killed the nine civilians in southeastern Arizona must have numbered at least a hundred warriors. Though it galled him to do so, Clum appealed to General Kautz for military support.

For his part, Kautz could not abide the cocky young agent. A month earlier, behind his back, Kautz had written the Adjutant General in Washington accusing Clum of "reputed criminality," of starving Indians until they had no recourse but to flee the reservation, and "of such lax management he was unaware of their absence." When he later learned of these charges, Clum flew into a tantrum, telegraphing the commissioner, I WILL PROVE GENL. KAUTZ GUILTY OF CRIMINAL INACTIVITY. Now Kautz replied to Clum's request with a bureaucratic demurral, insisting that as Ojo Caliente was in New Mexico, it lay beyond his jursidiction; Clum ought to appeal instead to the general in charge of the Department of New Mexico. Once again, "the ancient curse of dual control" fell heavily on Indian affairs.

Clum stormed eastward toward New Mexico with his Indian police. One of their leaders was Eskiminzin, chief of the martyred Aravaipa: the Camp Grant massacre had cured him of the passion for war against the White Eyes, and he had grown deeply loyal to Clum after the agent, arriving at Camp Grant in 1874 to find Eskiminzin in chains, had set him free.

Another of the policemen, it is almost shocking to learn, was Naiche, Cochise's sole surviving son. Between New Year's Day and mid-March, something had happened to assuage Naiche's fury against the agent who had taken his brother, Taza, to Washington to die. In his memoirs, Clum renders this reconciliation in a mawkish scene in which Naiche threateningly confronts Clum, only to be won over by Eskiminzin's sage oration. The Aravaipa chief is made to describe the majestic pomp of Taza's funeral; to say, among other honeyed things, "A good man, a great chief, is no longer with us. We are sad, and yet to any family it is an honor to have had one of their members cared for in the grand city of the Great White Father, as [Taza] was while ill, and then buried among graves of paleface heroes."

Perhaps some such confrontation took place; perhaps Eskiminzin mollified the wrathful Naiche. Clum can hardly have known what the Aravaipa said to the Chokonen, for he still understood only a few words of Apache. The sentiments he puts in Eskiminzin's mouth come straight from Clum's own fantasies, and the agent was always slow to notice when reality diverged from his dreams. In any event, there is a plangent irony in the fact that Naiche rode out in March 1877 as part of a police force to attempt the arrest of Geronimo. For Naiche would live to be the last free chief the Chiricahua ever had, would ride to the very end side by side with Geronimo, as both warriors took their toll among White Eyes and Mexicans alike.

It was some four hundred miles from San Carlos to Ojo Caliente. Clum's force took more than three weeks to cover the distance. The Indians pleaded for a rate of forty miles a day, but Clum had trouble maintaining twenty-five. Along the way, he reported, "Many bets were made as to where and when we would find Geronimo; whether or not we would have to kill him in order to capture him; the number of renegades in his band. Not a single Indian in my cavalcade had the least doubt we would get Geronimo."

At Fort Bayard, near Silver City, Clum received a message from the New Mexico general promising that eight companies of troops were on their way. In his reports, Clum later insisted that the soldiers arrived too late to help. As he had marched east with his confident Apaches, however, Clum had realized that no feather would ever crown his cap more gaudily than if he could pull off the capture of

Geronimo without the aid of the army. A scout had returned from Ojo Caliente, reporting that Geronimo was camped about three miles from the agency, with eighty to one hundred followers. The troops were only a day away from arrival, but Clum forged ahead on his own.

The sacred spring at Ojo Caliente lies in a sheltered glade, up a side-valley of the Cañada Alamosa. The spring itself forms a crystalline pool of warm water, across whose surface dragonflies dance and skim. Gnarled alders shade the pool. Its waters, so the Apache believed, were curative, particularly in winter. Downstream the trickling creek carves a sharp gulch in the rust-red mud of the banks—the clay with which the Chihenne, the Red-Paint People, daubed their faces. A quarter mile south, the side-creek joins the main stream, which plunges abruptly eastward through a V-notched gateway. The tall crags that wall this notch are loud with swifts and swallows. Before the white men came, Ojo Caliente flocked with deer and antelope; and there were always berries, nuts, and fruit in abundance.

On a flat shelf south of the main stream, about half a mile from the spring, the Americans had built their reservation agency out of adobe and a few planks of lumber. Six buildings ranged along two sides of a square, the other two sides of which were guarded by an arroyo and by the bank where the shelf plunged to the streambed. The center of the square made a classic parade ground. (The ruins of the agency, a few forlorn walls of crumbling adobe, stand today, proclaiming still the army's rectangular sense of order.)

On arriving at the agency, Clum made a careful inspection of its strategic possibilities. The only account that has come down to us of what happened on April 21, 1877, is Clum's own. Only three other white men witnessed the events, and none of them left a record. In the long life of John Clum—he would live to be eighty-one—the momentous confrontation that he engineered at age twenty-five would turn out to be the giddiest, the proudest day. By the time he narrated it for posterity, half a century later, the episode had shaped itself into a dramatic scene straight out of one of the amateur theatricals of which he was so fond. The scene realizes, in fact, the perfect fusion of his twin passions, for melodrama and for manual-of-arms drill.

According to Clum, as he approached Ojo Caliente from the south, he was warned of an aggregation of "from 250 to 400 well armed, desperate Indians, and that these rude and ruthless redskins were impatiently awaiting for an opportunity to greet us in the most enthusiastic fashion." Such numbers would have comprised not only Geronimo's band, but Victorio's Chihenne, who had settled hopefully on the reservation established in 1874.

Now Clum—if his account can be believed—hatched his plan. On the evening of April 20, he rode ahead with a select band of twenty-two mounted Apache policemen. (We do not know if Naiche was among them.) The idea was to lull the observant "renegades" into believing Clum's force was too small to be a threat. The advance guard took possession of the agency at sunset. In the middle of the night, the remaining eighty-odd Apaches, under Clum's second-in-command, marched silently to the agency, where Clum hid them inside the commissary building. This structure lay about fifty yards south of the main building, in which Clum's smaller force was ensconced: the two buildings formed the west side of the agency square.

At sunrise Clum sent a messenger to Geronimo, requesting a talk. "They came quickly—," Clum reported, "a motley clan, painted and equipped for a fight." Clum's twenty-two policemen, each with a rifle and thirty rounds of ammunition, formed a pair of flanking lines on either side of the main building's porch, where Clum greeted Geronimo. The warrior stood about ten feet away, his back to the parade ground, flanked by his staunchest allies.

Clum opened with a speech, scolding Geronimo for violating General Howard's peace treaty, for killing whites and stealing cattle and horses, and for lying to Clum when he had fled after their talk at Fort Bowie the previous summer. According to Clum, Geronimo addressed him as "Nantan-betunny-kahyeh" ("Boss-with-the-high-forehead"), and rejoined: "You talk very brave, but we do not like that kind of talk. We are not going to San Carlos with you, and unless you are very careful, you and your Apache police will not go back to San Carlos, either. Your bodies will stay here at Ojo Caliente to make food for the coyotes."

Another version of this rejoinder has come down to us, via a circuitous and unreliable route. But as it claims to spring directly from the interpreter's recollections in old age, and as it sounds like the true Geronimo, it bears hearing. In this version, Geronimo spat at Clum,

Your words shout false bravery! You are the false White-Eyes who came to the Chiricahua Reservation a year ago and broke the peace treaty made by the Great Chief and Taglito [Tom Jeffords] and the one-arm general. Do not talk to me about breaking treaties . . . you and your sick brain! You sent the evil-eyed snake [the messenger] to my rancheria last night to beguile me into accepting a truce that you have proven false. I would not accept your word for it if you now said the sun is shining!

We are not going to San Carlos with you. If you make any more mistakes you and your two-faced Apaches will not go back to San Carlos, either! Your bodies will remain to stink here at Ojo Caliente for the zopilotes and lobos [buzzards and wolves]. Observe! You have 120 men; I have but 90. Are such odds ever effective against true Apache men?

One of the implications of this version is to undermine Clum's claim that he baited his trap by hiding eighty of his men inside the commissary.

When Geronimo had finished speaking, according to Clum's account, the agent raised his left hand to touch his hat. At the prearranged signal, the commissary doors flew open, and eighty armed Apaches came running out in an orderly line. They circled behind Geronimo's band on the east and north until they had surrounded it. "I was watching Geronimo's face," Clum later recalled,

and particularly the thumb of his right hand, which was about an inch back of the hammer of his fifty-caliber United States Army Springfield rifle. . . . When five or six of my Apache reserves had emerged through the commissary doors, I noticed Geronimo's thumb creeping slowly toward the hammer of his rifle. My right hand was resting on my right hip, akimbo fashion, and not more than an inch away from the handle of my Colt forty-five.

Clum touched the handle of his revolver. It was the second signal.

Up came the rifles of Beauford [Clum's second-in-command] and my twenty-two police, each one aimed point-blank at Geronimo or his most notorious followers. My eye was still on Geronimo's thumb. I saw it hesitate, just before it touched the hammer of his rifle. Intuitively I knew that Geronimo had reconsidered; that he was my prisoner; that there would be no blood shed, unless we spilled it.

Now Clum insisted on disarming the Chiricahuas. This too forced a moment fraught with danger. Clum strode forward and clasped the rifle in Geronimo's hands. "I have seen many looks of hate in my long life," he wrote half a century later, "but never one so vicious, so vengeful."

Disarmed, at Clum's mercy, Geronimo agreed to talk. With his leading warriors, he squatted on the porch, while Clum sat enthroned in a chair. Throughout the parley, Clum's policemen kept their guns trained on the Chiricahuas. Clum berated Geronimo for his escape from Fort Bowie, for his supposed depredations in the months since. Geronimo glared back.

"This time," Clum hammered, "you are not going to get away. You are my prisoner, and must go with my police to the guard-house, you and your six sub-chiefs. And you must go *now.*"

> Geronimo leaped to his feet; another picture one could never forget. Forty-five years old [actually about 55], erect as a lodge-pole pine, every outline of his symmetrical form indicating strength, endurance, arrogance. Abundant black hair draping his shoulders, stern, paint-smeared features, those vindictive eyes, the livid scar [on his cheek]. Geronimo, the renegade, strategist, trickster, killer of pale-faces—now under arrest, but still defiant, still looking for a way out. His right hand moved slowly toward his knife, his only remaining weapon. Should he draw it, cut right and left, die fighting or surrender? He was thinking hard. His moving hand hesitated only an instant.

In that instant, one of Clum's Apaches "sprang forward and deftly snatched the knife from Geronimo's belt."

Still agitated, Clum ordered his police to take Geronimo and his six "sub-chiefs" to the blacksmith shop. There he addressed the Bedonkohe once more. "I am so fond of you," Clum taunted Geronimo, "that I want to be sure you will not run away. We are going to rivet ankle-irons on you and your chiefs." Geronimo bore the operation in stoic silence.

"Thus was accomplished," Clum would crow for the rest of his life, "the first and only *bonafide capture* of GERONIMO THE RENEGADE."

The Chiricahua have always dismissed Clum's account of things. Juh's son Daklugie later said, "And that scene that [Clum] described with the police filing out of the old fort that had also served as the agency—well it just didn't happen; especially the part about Clum's taking the rifle from Geronimo." In the words of a Chihenne who was an infant at the time, "If the melodramatic scene described as Mr. Clum's 'capture of Geronimo' occurred no Apache knew of it, and about five hundred witnessed the event."

Geronimo himself was vague about the event. Late in life he denied that he had ever been captured. In his autobiography, alluding to his flight from Clum at Fort Bowie in 1876, he said, "I do not think I ever belonged to those soldiers at Apache Pass, or that I should have asked them where I might go." Yet both Geronimo and other Chiricahuas admitted that somehow he had been tricked into imprisonment, and that he was carried to San Carlos in leg-irons—"which might," as he realized, "easily have been the death of me."

Perhaps Clum's account is essentially truthful after all. To be grandiose is one thing, dishonest another, and few men ever called Clum dishonest. Among the records of his great deed, he left a manuscript map of the agency, with the positions of forces and the vectors of action drawn as one might chart the course of a Civil War battle.

Soon after the capture, Clum met with the Chihenne. Remarkably, Victorio agreed to take his people to San Carlos, leaving behind the reservation that he had fought so hard to keep. The only explanation is that he sought peace at almost any cost. But San Carlos would prove too great a price.

On May 1, Clum set out for the reservation. In his entourage he counted 343 Chihenne and 110 followers of Geronimo. The shackled leaders were carried in wagons. The promised troops, who had showed up a day late for the pivotal action, now escorted the procession of captives. Protocol demanded that Arizona troops take over for them at the border, but Clum poured fuel on his feud with General Kautz, haughtily telegraphing Fort Bowie, I WISH TO SAY, NO ESCORT HAS BEEN ASKED FROM ARIZONA, NOR WILL ANY BE ACCEPTED. For this impudence, Clum was officially censured by Secretary of War Sherman.

Another tragedy besides removal from their heartland attended the procession of 453 Apaches. Among them, a smallpox epidemic broke out. Clum tried to keep the infected in a separate wagon, but the virulent disease spread. Eight Apaches died en route; no one ever calculated how many at San Carlos ultimately succumbed.

Oblivious as ever to anything that contradicted his illusions, Clum saw in the desolate forced march only a "momentous western hegira to the promised land"; he observed "no regretful tears in this Apache exodus, just a silent hopeful migration of a weary and bewildered people to Utopia."

Clum's pilgrimage reached San Carlos on May 20. He confined nineteen of his prisoners to the guardhouse, including Geronimo and his six warriors, still in leg-irons. At once, following his cabled orders to hold the prisoners "in confinement for murder and robbery," he notified the civil authorities in Tucson of his captives, wrote the sheriff promising to furnish evidence "to convict each of the seven chiefs on many counts of murder," and offered to deliver his prisoners to Tucson for trial.

It seemed to Clum an inevitability that Geronimo would be swiftly tried, convicted, and hanged. Such was the obvious, the just course. But it was not to be, and for the rest of his life, Clum told all who would listen what might have been. As his son, Woodworth Clum, wrote in 1936, echoing the moral of the tale as his father had told it countless times, "The inescapable fact is . . . that had Geronimo been hanged in July, 1877 . . . ; if John P. Clum had been kept on his job at old San Carlos, the Apache wars would have been over in 1877, instead of 1886."

Twelve

■

Victorio

Geronimo languished in the San Carlos guardhouse, still shackled at the ankles, for two months. Clum later claimed that the Tucson authorities failed to respond to his offer to deliver his seven "murderers." Back on his reservation, the short-fused agent threw himself into a new round of telegraphic squabbles with his superiors in Washington. For all his good work, he complained, he had received no increase in salary; and once more the military was trying to interfere with his regime. "I felt that my success had actually been *penalized,*" he wrote.

Behind his back, indeed, General Kautz had been working to undermine the reputation and authority of the agent whose arrogance he could not bear. Clum had bragged about the huge numbers of Indians he had concentrated at San Carlos, but Kautz, in his official report for 1877, pointed to the Apaches who had escaped Clum's net. Before the two reservations were forcibly broken up, Kautz claimed, the Chiricahua reserve had harbored twenty-one hundred Indians (a generous estimate), the Ojo Caliente 965. In his two grand removals, Clum had brought only 779 Apaches to San Carlos. "There are thus 2,286 Indians unaccounted for since 1875," wrote Kautz drily.

Meanwhile he appointed a lieutenant to carry out military inspection at San Carlos. Clum flew into a fury and refused to allow the lieutenant to do his job. Then he fired off to the Commissioner of Indian Affairs his most grandiose telegram yet: IF YOUR DEPARTMENT WILL INCREASE MY SALARY SUFFICIENTLY AND EQUIP TWO MORE COMPANIES OF INDIAN POLICE FOR ME, I WILL VOLUNTEER TO TAKE CARE OF ALL APACHES IN ARIZONA— AND THE TROOPS CAN BE REMOVED. The commissioner, fed up with Clum's runaway autonomy, leaked the cable to the press. Even the Arizona papers were alarmed at Clum's pretensions. "The brass and impudence of this young bombast," editorialized one, "is perfectly ridiculous."

Clum had already twice offered his resignation; now, when he offered it a third time, the commissioner accepted it. "Therefore, at high noon on July 1, 1877," the agent later wrote, "I mounted my favorite horse and hit the trail for Tucson." In subsequent years, Clum became the first mayor of Tombstone, Arizona, where he cofounded and edited the famous newspaper, the *Epitaph*. Eventually he found his way back to New York State, where he worked as a Post Office inspector. He died in Los Angeles in 1932.

Obsessed as he had become with Geronimo, Clum gnawed for decades on the bone of his disappointment that the authorities had failed to hang the "renegade" in 1877. "Who cut the rivets that held his shackles and released him from the guard-house at San Carlos I do not know," he claimed fifty years later. In 1936, summing up his father's view of the matter, Woodworth Clum wrote, "Upon whose orders this murderer of at least a hundred men, women, and children, was turned loose, has been a mystery for more than half a century."

In his peevish self-righteousness, Clum himself came to regret his impetuous resignation. Mulling it over in 1928, he ventured,

> Had I remained in authority at San Carlos there is not the least doubt in my mind that [Geronimo] would have been speedily brought to trial in the United States courts, and that his career would have ended abruptly then and there. What a vast amount of expense, tribulation, distress and bloodshed would have been avoided if this arrest had been followed swiftly by prosecution, conviction and execution—thus dropping the name GERONIMO into oblivion before it had become generally notorious outside of territorial frontier limits.

There is one other explanation of Geronimo's survival in June 1877, but it appears only in the Apache record. According to Daklugie, his father, Juh, hearing about the removal from Ojo Caliente, rode to San Carlos before Clum's procession arrived; there he won over Eskiminzin (supposedly Clum's most fervent champion among the Indian police) to his cause. As the smallpox-ridden train of captives neared the reservation, Juh lay in hiding along the road. He saw Geronimo in his wagon, and Geronimo saw him, but neither man gave any sign of recognition.

One day Juh and Eskiminzin confronted Clum in his headquarters. Eskimizin spoke for the stutterer.

"We have come," he said, "to demand that you turn the prisoners loose. We won't stand for this any longer." Clum sputtered and strutted about, dragging his wings while attempting to put them off. But Eskiminzin said, "You will do it, and you'll do it right now or we'll have every Apache on this reservation on your back."

Clum led the way to the guardhouse and ordered the door to be unlocked and the prisoners released. Within a short time their shackles were removed and Geronimo and the others were free.

No white source corroborates any part of this story. Geronimo's most careful biographer, Angie Debo, claims that the agent who succeeded Clum struck the shackles off the warrior's ankles. Geronimo's own laconic account of his captivity could conceivably jibe with either theory: "I was kept a prisoner for four months. . . . Then I think I had another trial, although I was not present. In fact I do not know that I had another trial, but I was told that I had, and at any rate I was released."

Despite Clum's illusion that he led a happy band to San Carlos, the Chihenne under Victorio marched westward from their homeland with bitter hearts. Some of them blamed Geronimo for their misfortune, for if Clum had not come to Ojo Caliente to arrest the notorious Bedonkohe warrior, the Chihenne might well have been left in peace. Eighty years later, the last survivors of that march still nursed their sense of betrayal. "We were innocent," said one, "and should not have been driven from our homes. We were not to blame for what Geronimo did. The United States didn't give this land to us. It was ours."

To blame Geronimo, however, is to overlook the fact that the root of the Apache misery lay not in the malarial barrens of San Carlos, but in Washington, where theorists dreamed of consolidation. For his own part, Geronimo considered himself guiltless of attacks on Americans —the Mexicans whom he so despised were another matter—and it seems likely that the Arizona depredations attributed to him were carried out by other Apaches.

There is evidence that the Chihenne had no intention of staying long at San Carlos, for they cached their best weapons in the vicinity of the sacred spring before leaving New Mexico. Why was it so hard for the White Eyes to comprehend the people's love of Ojo Caliente? In 1909, a Chihenne remembered the lost paradise from his exile in Oklahoma:

> That is a good country. There are mountains on this side and on that side, and on the other side. In the middle there is a wide valley. There are springs in that valley, fine grass, and plenty of timber around. Dig a well and get water in forty feet. . . . Horses and cattle will not freeze there. It is a healthy place for man and beast. Women nor children get sick there. Neither do animals. . . . For years I have been on other people's ground and trouble has always come of it.

The Chihenne settled on a particular tract at San Carlos that Clum had assigned them. At once things began to go wrong. The hunting was wretched; the valley of the Gila was as malarial here as it was a few miles downstream, beside the agency; the rations Clum issued were irregular and often insufficient. And conflicts developed at once between the Chihenne and the White Mountain Apaches. The White Mountain people feared the arrival of these Indians from the east, in particular because they had learned about the smallpox they carried. Then a White Mountain man killed a Chihenne; Victorio hunted down the offender and killed him along with his family. Clum and his successor seem to have been unaware of these bloody tensions.

On September 2, 1877, 310 men, women, and children, led by Victorio, stole a herd of White Mountain horses and bolted en masse from the reservation. They were at once pursued by troops under both Arizona and New Mexico commands, by citizen volunteers from San Carlos, and by the Indian police whom Clum had organized. A few Chihenne were killed; more—mostly women and children— were captured. In turn, the fugitives, desperate for stock animals to aid their flight, killed as many as a dozen white settlers.

A splinter group, led by the unregenerate Pionsenay, fled into the

Sierra Madre of Mexico. The main body under Victorio managed not only to avoid all pitched battles for a month but to edge by secret trails back toward the beloved homeland around Ojo Caliente. On September 29, to test the waters, Victorio, still not committed to all-out war, sent two subchiefs to Fort Wingate, well to the northwest of the sacred hot spring, in Navajo country. The upshot of their negotiations was that the relatively enlightened colonel in charge at Ojo Caliente—an abolitionist from Maine who led a cavalry of black soldiers—agreed to receive almost two hundred Chihenne there, and to feed them indefinitely. He warned his superiors that to force the Apaches to mingle with the Navajo at Wingate was asking for trouble. As for returning them to San Carlos—to a man, the Chihenne swore that they would die first.

For most of a year, the Chihenne stayed at Ojo Caliente. Swelled by more cautious warriors who gradually came in, their numbers reached 260. They felt relatively secure in their homeland, with their best weapons hidden near at hand; all along the rims of the surrounding cliffs, they had propped boulders for rolling upon an enemy, ready to be released by an easy touch. Some 143 of their relatives, however, were still confined at San Carlos, and this was a sore grievance for the Chihenne.

Meanwhile the government, befuddled as usual by the feud between the Departments of War and Interior, pondered what to do ultimately with the Chihenne. There was no valid reason for not leaving them in the land they valued above all other, no reason not to reunite them there with their relatives at San Carlos: but this option was never seriously considered. High officials argued the merits of sending the Chihenne to Fort Stanton, with the Mescaleros; to Fort Wingate, with the Navajos; back to San Carlos, with the White Mountain Apaches; even to Fort Sill in the Indian Territory of Oklahoma.

Although aware of the uncertainty swirling about their fate, the Chihenne were so content at Ojo Caliente that they told an army officer to tell Washington "that they are happier than they ever have been were it not that they feared removal and that if the Government would permit them to remain where they now are they would gladly accept only one-half of their present ration."

The myopic obstinacy of the government almost defies credibility. After eleven months of feeble deliberation, the Department of Interior ordered the Chihenne returned to San Carlos. On October 8, 1878,

Victorio's people were informed of the decision. According to an eyewitness, Victorio told the captain in charge of the removal "that his home was here, that his people had been born here, that they loved their home, and, further, that not a buck of his band would go to San Carlos."

The captain insisted that he had to obey orders. Suddenly Victorio uttered a piercing yell and ran for the mountains. More than ninety of his people, mostly warriors, followed him at once. Troops mustered to pursue the fleeing Apaches were thwarted by autumn storms.

The momentum of removal, however, was relentless. In late October, the army loaded 169 Chihenne on wagons and shipped them west once more, through mud and early snow, to the hated reservation. At San Carlos, these demoralized people were guarded with especial zeal, for fear Victorio might arrive in the night to try to set them free.

Through the winter of 1878–1879, the free Chihenne raided and killed along the Rio Grande and in southwestern New Mexico. In true Apache fashion, despite the universal allegiance the Chihenne felt toward their chief, the roving band fragmented into smaller units. As government officials had mulled and fussed through the previous year, the Apaches had learned that Fort Stanton, in eastern New Mexico, was one of the possible destinations the White Eyes were considering for them. To be forced to dwell on uneasy terms among the Mescalero Apaches was far from an ideal prospect. But it was so much preferable to San Carlos that, in piecemeal surrenders from December through June, gradually the Chihenne came in to Fort Stanton. Victorio, with twelve warriors, was the last. By July 1879, there were 145 Chihenne living on the Mescalero reservation. The agent in charge was optimistic about lasting peace. The government mulled on.

The two years during which officials in Washington had toyed with the fate of his people had turned Victorio steadily more distrustful of whites. As summer waned among the Ponderosa pines of the high Mescalero reservation, the chief's guard grew ever more vigilant. And new insults added to his dissatisfaction. When Victorio presented himself at the ration window, the Mescalero agent said that he could not issue the Chihenne chief any food unless he presented an official ration card. Victorio asked what he had to do to get a card. The agent replied—apparently with no sense of irony—that it would take at least a month for one to be issued in Washington and sent to New Mexico.

Through the interpreter, Victorio observed, "A month is a long time to be without food." The agent turned back to his papers.

An explosion was waiting to happen: that Victorio's fuse would catch fire was all but inevitable. Yet the pivotal deed was an absurd misunderstanding. As a result of Chihenne raiding near Silver City the year before, officials there had indicted Victorio on charges of murder and stealing horses. Although Grant County lay one hundred fifty miles as the crow flies from the Mescalero reservation, somehow the chief learned that "a paper was out against him."

On August 21, several white men on a hunting and fishing trip rode close to the Mescalero reservation. One of them was a judge, another a prosecuting attorney. Some of the Chihenne, including Victorio, recognized these men, and assumed the party was bent on arresting the chief. In a wild fury, Victorio confronted the Mescalero agent, and pulled his beard violently. The frightened agent sent to Fort Stanton for troops. The chief heard the bugle of an approaching column, and fled at once.

Never again would Victorio attempt peace with the White Eyes. The chance meeting of the judge and attorney on their fishing trip with the chief whose nerves were stretched to the snapping point served to launch an all-out war. The fourteen months of that final Chihenne campaign would turn into one of the darkest of all Apache tragedies.

By the summer of 1879, Victorio had wreaked little vengeance on Americans, and had no record of settlers sent to their graves to compare to that of Cochise or Mangas Coloradas after the White Eyes had stirred those chiefs to fury. It is possible that Victorio had killed not a single Anglo-American: the citizens slain during his spells at large from September 1877 to June 1879 may well have died at the hands of other Chiricahuas.

Nonetheless, among his own people, Victorio commanded an unflinching loyalty that rivaled that of Cochise among the Chokonen. One Chihenne, a boy in 1879, remembered his awe seventy years later: "Victorio was not as tall as Naiche [Cochise's surviving son], but I think he was the most nearly perfect human being I have ever seen." His people called him by an Apache name whose nearest translation is "The Conqueror."

By the time of his breakout from the Mescalero reservation, Victorio was some fifty-five years old, about the same age as Geronimo. John Clum, who was almost as proud of bagging the Chihenne chief in 1877 as he was of his "capture" of Geronimo, left a close description of Victorio as he appeared that April day at Ojo Caliente:

> His long black hair, tinged with gray, glistened in the morning sun. He carried his rifle resting easily in the crook of his left arm, its muzzle protruding from under the light blanket thrown carelessly over his shoulder. His serious, intelligent face was unmarred by war paint, and as he walked, his head turned slowly while he surveyed the unusual picture in front of him.

Only a single photograph of Victorio was ever taken. (Of Cochise, none exists.) In it, the Chihenne looks startled and angry. Though the photographer remains unknown, the legend has come down that Victorio was unwilling to pose, that he was seized and held by whites while the image was shot, and that in the struggle Victorio's headband came off. In the photo, his long, wavy hair lies disordered on Victorio's shoulders. Strong creases stretch from the corners of his nose to the corners of his mouth, emphasizing his will. The eyes stare straight and clear, as if they never blinked. Held for the camera or not, Victorio looks supremely powerful, a man not to be trifled with.

In character, Victorio was as different from Geronimo as two Apache leaders could be. Atypically for a great chief, Victorio took only one wife (versus Geronimo's nine) during a life that was long by Indian standards. He was never known to be drunk: "Drunkards are the white man's scourge," he told his warriors. Fearing the treachery of Mexicans, Victorio forbade his men to drink the proffered mescal when they were trading in a town in Chihuahua or Sonora.

Like Cochise, but unlike Geronimo, Victorio was a man of stern and unvacillating determination. He carried himself with a controlled dignity, yet could burst, like Cochise, into sudden violence. He was as fearless under fire as the bravest of his warriors.

With Victorio in his final campaign rode a number of remarkable Chihenne, some of whom, more than a century later, escape the gray blur of anonymity to which the Anglo record consigns all "enemy" Indians. One was Victorio's sister, Lozen. As a young girl, she was considered a great beauty, and many men wooed her. She refused them all, and Victorio would not intercede to force her to marry.

Lozen chose as her destiny to become a warrior, riding, as a certain number of Apache women did, beside the male warriors, expected to perform all the deeds of combat they themselves undertook.

James Kaywaykla, the young Chihenne in the last free band, remembered his first sight of Lozen, at a crossing of the Rio Grande when the river was in flood. The Chihenne were hesitant to plunge into the dangerous current.

> There was a commotion and the long line parted to let a rider through. I saw a magnificent woman on a beautiful black horse— Lozen, sister of Victorio. Lozen, the woman warrior! High above her head she held her rifle. There was a glitter as her right foot lifted and struck the shoulder of her horse. He reared, then plunged into the torrent. She turned his head upstream, and he began swimming.

The rest of the band followed Lozen across the river.

This extraordinary woman was an expert at roping, and thus at stealing horses. As a girl, she had outrun all the men she had competed against in footraces. She often took upon herself the hazardous role of covering the band's rear guard as it fled from pursuers. She was as good a shot with a rifle as any man among the Chihenne. She was also an expert at dressing wounds so they did not become infected. Like Victorio, she distrusted the Mexicans, and was opposed to trading and drinking mescal in their villages. In respect for her deeds and her wisdom, she was made a full-fledged member of the council of warriors. "Lozen is as my right hand," Victorio told his subchiefs. "Strong as a man, braver than most, and cunning in strategy, Lozen is a shield to her people."

What distinguished Lozen above all from the other Chihenne—and what made her invaluable in the final campaign—was her Power. The people believed that she alone among the band had the capacity to locate the enemy. To do so, she would stand with her arms outstretched and turn slowly in a circle as she chanted a prayer to Ussen. When her hands began to tingle and her palms changed color, she knew she was facing the enemy. She could even divine how far away they were. James Kaywaykla, who later underwent decades of skeptical education in white society, swore near the end of his life that he had seen Lozen thus locate the pursuing troops "time after time."

Another stalwart was old Nana, himself a chief only slightly subordinate to Victorio. He looked anything but a chief, and the white soldiers who later suffered his vengeance had a hard time taking him seriously when they met him. Seventy years old, or even older, by 1879 (Nana himself had no reckoning of his age), he walked with a pronounced limp from an old injury. In camp, he would rub the stiff ankle surreptitiously with tallow. Behind his back, the Chihenne called him Broken Foot. He had the odd habit of wearing a gold watch chain —taken from some white victim—in each ear.

In a surviving photograph, a seated Nana gazes imperturbably at the camera. His round face looks placid rather than fierce. A Mexican sombrero sits absurdly high on his oversized head, as if the slightest breeze would knock it off. In his right hand, Nana holds a curved walking stick, like a shepherd's crook.

Yet Nana, according to Kaywaykla, was "the fiercest and most implacable of all Apaches . . . , the shrewdest in military strategy, surpassing Victorio himself." His endurance was legendary: he could go many days without food, and on a raid he could easily ride seventy miles a day, sleeping in the saddle part of the time. "No young man in the tribe," testified Kaywaykla, "could spend more hours in the saddle without rest than he."

Nana was a tracker par excellence, who could find prints on the stoniest ground. He had a Power for locating ammunition trains among the White Eyes and Mexicans, and also a Power against rattlesnakes, one of the creatures most feared by Apaches. (The Apache reluctance to fight at night came in part from this taboo, in observance of the rattlesnake's fiendish propensity to hide by day and hunt by night.) Finally, Nana was a great warrior and leader. Victorio often deferred to the wisdom of the older man, as he did to none of the other Chihenne.

When Victorio's band bolted from the Mescalero reservation in August 1879, they headed straight for Ojo Caliente. Gone, however, was any hope that the Chihenne could live in peace in their sacred homeland. Victorio needed horses, and he knew that the army kept a big herd near the Ojo Caliente agency. In a bold and unexpected attack, within minutes the Chihenne slew the eight men guarding the herd and made off with sixty-eight horses and mules.

Newly aroused, army troops from both New Mexico and Arizona, as well as gangs of citizen volunteers, set out to hound Victorio into submission. For two months he led them on an exhausting chase, zigzagging among the Black Range and the Mogollon Mountains of southwestern New Mexico. Time and again the soldiers, having crept close in the night, would charge at daybreak upon Victorio's camp, only to find it abandoned hours or even days before. At one point the Chihenne succeeded in circling completely around the army company that was on its heels. In several pitched battles, the Chihenne lost a few men and women, but in each case they inflicted more damage than they suffered.

On the families of Mexican ranchers scattered across this empty country, Victorio's warriors exacted a pitiless toll. A pioneer who helped bury nine Mexicans killed at McEvers Ranch (near today's hamlet of Nutt, New Mexico) insisted that the Chihenne had "brained the children, outraged the women and mutilated their bodies."

A new rigor governed the lives of the fugitives, for Victorio knew that his campaign of vengeance meant a fight to the death. Water was the key to staying alive in this parched land, and now all the training every Apache boy and girl underwent paid its dividends in survival. Sometimes the Chihenne came to a seep with only a limited supply of water: in such cases the horses drank while the people went thirsty. Once, after many hours without water, the Chihenne came to an abundant spring; but Nana tasted the strange-smelling water and declared it unpotable.

The Apaches could turn their knowledge of water against their pursuers. Sometimes they drank a spring dry, leaving only mud for the soldiers. They could, moreover, find water where white men went thirsty. In Kaywaykla's sardonic words, "One thing White Eyes never learned—to detect the presence of water underground. Many perished, when by digging two or three feet they could have obtained water." One day, frantic with thirst, a New Mexico command on Victorio's trail came upon a beautiful "tank," or pool of water. But as they knelt to drink, they discovered to their horror that the Chihenne had disemboweled a coyote in the water, poisoning it.

At the time of his breakout, Victorio had no more than forty warriors with him. During the following months, his band was swelled by other free Chiricahuas, even by some Mescalero and Lipan Apaches, and by a single Comanche. There is reason to believe that in certain battles, Chiricahua bands led by Juh and Geronimo reinforced Victorio. It says much about the Indian knowledge of the land that at a time when it was all the army could do to trail Victorio's people, rarely closing to a fight with them, large numbers of other Apaches had no trouble joining up with the Chihenne and yet avoiding detection as they sought their brethren.

At its largest, Victorio's band numbered 450 people, of whom not more than 110, and more often not more than 75, were warriors. Eventually four thousand soldiers, both American and Mexican, would join in the fatal hunt.

Constant flight required from the Chihenne an astounding discipline. Sometimes women and children were left for weeks at a time in caves known only to Apaches, which had been stocked with food. More often, the women and children camped and ran with the warriors. Small children were tied to horses or to adults during the most headlong rides. Seventy years later, James Kaywaykla recalled the fugitive days with dry understatement: "It was a hard life, but we liked it better than the hopeless stagnation of the reservation. . . . I think we subsisted where White Eyes would have died."

General Crook's great innovation, using Apache scouts to trail Apache "renegades," was employed by his successors. In the hunt for Victorio, what success the army did have could be largely attributed to the scouts. In turn, Victorio's men saved their bitterest contempt for these Apache traitors (so they regarded them). It was an easy task to hide from white soldiers, but it took all the skill the Chihenne had to hide from Apache scouts. According to one American officer, in the midst of his flight Victorio somehow got word to San Carlos promising that he would come to the reservation and murder the families of the scouts who were on his trail.

Sometimes in the middle of a battle the Chihenne would taunt the scouts, inviting them mockingly to come to dinner or waving their breechcloths in insult. In October 1879, during an intense fray fought by moonlight, a reliable officer claimed that during one lull,

> the only noise was the tum-tum beaten by Victorio himself all during the fight, accompanied by his high keyed, quavering voice in a song of "good medicine." He was at this juncture holding forth to our scouts, trying to persuade them to desert and join his men, and together they would kill the last white and black soldier present.

At the end of October, having gained the edge in every fight he had made with the army, Victorio led his band across the border into Mexico, where he knew the Americans could not legally follow. The major in charge of the exhausted troops who pursued him to the boundary line tried to put the best face on things, insisting his men had driven Victorio out of the country. But Kaywaykla and the other Chihenne knew Victorio's move for the virtuosic ruse it really was: "Like the quail that pretends to be wounded in order to lure pursuers away from his hidden family, the chief crossed the border into Mexico. . . . Victorio's object in going was to draw the cavalry from our old haunts." Unbeknownst to the army, many Chihenne, especially women and children, were still in New Mexico. Victorio bought them the time they needed to reunite with the warriors south of the border.

Victorio's military tactics varied brilliantly from one combat to the next, but they hinged around a logic common to all Chiricahua. Surprise attack, ambush, and sudden flight were its chief components. American officers, accustomed to the pitched battles of the Civil War —to the battles, in fact, of all the wars they had studied at West Point —managed to believe that time after time they drove Apaches from their craggy positions and "routed" them. The Apaches, however, were not Confederates: retreat was no ignominy, but an essential gambit of war.

Kaywaykla summarized the Chihenne tactics he learned as a boy:

We were essentially a mountain people, moving from one chain to another, following the ridges as best we could. . . . I think we may have invented trench warfare, and we infinitely preferred a mountain at our backs. I doubt that any people ever excelled us as mountain climbers. Scaling walls was taken for granted. When closely pursued we killed our horses and scaled cliffs no enemy could climb. Men tied ropes to women and children and lifted them from ledge to ledge until they could take cover or escape. . . . We moved at night only when forced to do so and never fought in the darkness unless attacked. There was a believe that he who kills at night must walk in darkness through the Place of the Dead.

Only a week after entering Mexico, Victorio's warriors pulled off one of their most thorough victories. Their success depended on the daring of a Chihenne named Sánchez. As a young man, Sánchez had been captured by Mexicans in Chihuahua. Instead of killing him, they made him a slave. For years, Sánchez guarded the herd of cattle belonging to the man who had captured him; before he escaped, he became a vaquero (cowboy) in the true Mexican style.

Now, in November 1879, as the Chihenne camped on the side of a mountain in the Candelaría Mountains, Victorio grew curious about unusual activity his scouts had detected in the nearby town of Carrizal. Sánchez volunteered to undertake an extraordinary mission. He dressed himself in the clothes of a vaquero he had slain, chose a horse with the brand of a well-known rancher from Chihuahua City, and rode alone into Carrizal. There he drank in the cantina and chatted with townspeople; with his perfect Spanish, he passed himself off as a Mexican. In so doing, Sánchez learned that Carrizal was planning the usual Mexican trap: to lure the Chihenne into town, flatter them with liquor, then kill them as they slept off their drunk.

When an emissary came to Victorio's camp with the invitation, the chief feigned friendliness; he also hid most of his warriors. Lulled into overconfidence, a posse of eighteen vaqueros from Carrizal rode out to the camp. Victorio had set up a three-pronged ambush. Not until the last of the eighteen had entered the trap did Victorio signal for the first shot. All eighteen died within a few minutes. One Mexican managed to wedge himself inside a rock crevice where he could be fired on from none of the three vantage points; but his legs protruded from the crevice, and the Apaches shot them to pieces below the knees.

Alarmed at the disappearance of their townsmen, a larger group set out from Carrizal a few days later. Victorio caught them in the identical trap, killing fifteen of their thirty-five horsemen. Not a single Apache was wounded.

Like Geronimo, Victorio and his Chihennes felt a special loathing for Mexicans, mainly because Apache conflicts with them had lasted centuries, and a long history of gruesome encounters had accumulated. Even Kaywaykla—so accustomed to war that he could say many decades later, "Until I was about ten years old I did not know that people died except by violence"—was shocked deeply by the treatment of one group of luckless Mexican prisoners, two men, a woman, and a small boy whose coach the Apaches intercepted. The men were led into a nearby arroyo and shot.

The woman stood motionless until she heard [the shots]. In the manner of her people she fell to her knees and with hands uplifted cried, *"Dios! Dios!"* over and over. Her little son ran to her; she drew him close and bent protectingly over him. I did not realize what was to happen until a stone struck her forehead and blood dripped upon the child. She fell forward, still shielding him. I ran into the mesquite thicket until Grandmother overtook me. She knelt, even as the woman had done, and took me in her arms.

She, too, was shaking.

The major in charge of the troops who had chased Victorio the previous autumn was sure it was only a matter of time before Victorio crossed the border north again. In the interim, he put in an order for two mountain howitzers—"like requesting baseball bats for a flea hunt," in the pithy words of historian Dan L. Thrapp.

In January 1880, the Chihenne indeed crossed the line and headed north. For months Victorio led the troops on a chase every bit as frustrating as the previous year's. The arduous forced marches left the New Mexican patrols, in the words of one of their officers, with "horses worn to mere shadows, men nearly without boots, shoes and clothing." Victorio's command of the country was so confident that even as he was being pursued by the army, he succeeded in passing within a day's march first of Ojo Caliente and then of the Mescalero reservation, to both of which he sent emissaries inquiring whether there were still any chance of peaceful surrender. But his own wariness precluded negotiating.

Victorio even made good his boast of sending a punitive expedition to San Carlos to try to wipe out the families of the turncoat Apache scouts. For this reckless mission he chose his son, a brave young man whom whites knew by the curious name of Washington. With fourteen warriors, Washington was ordered to make his way to the reservation undetected, then "kill and destroy as many and as much as possible." But twenty miles short of the San Carlos agency, Washington's band accidentally crossed paths with a group of hunters from the reservation. After a brief fight, Washington proceeded to attack a band of Apaches camped on another part of the reservation. These were not White Mountain or Coyotero Apaches, however, but members of Juh's and Geronimo's band—until recently, close allies of the Chihenne. The reason Washington attacked them is lost to history. Washington survived this encounter and rejoined Victorio.

All through the Black Range and the Mogollons, Victorio struck through the spring of 1880, killing settlers and soldiers at a steady pace. Some of the deftest victories were old Nana's, who with eight picked warriors rode through the territory devastating all about him. In one skirmish, Nana's party killed twenty settlers beside the Rio

Grande in a matter of minutes. Thomas Cruse, one of the more observant army officers in the Victorio campaign, was among the party who
discovered the carnage: scores of cartridge shells, dead animals, half-
burned corpses on a pyre of charred wagons. "I dreamed of it for
weeks afterwards," Cruse later wrote.

After the campaign was over, Cruse calculated that in fourteen
months of crisscrossing New Mexico and Chihuahua, Victorio's warriors, seldom more than seventy-five strong, had taken the lives of
more than one thousand whites and Mexicans while eluding three
American cavalry regiments, two American infantry regiments, a huge
number of Mexican troops, and a contingent of Texas Rangers. The
death toll is probably exaggerated, but not wildly so.

Yet even as they struck terror through the countryside, Victorio's
Chihenne were suffering the attritions of a hopeless war. In May 1880,
they met their first real setback, which came, significantly, not at the
hands of an army patrol, but of an autonomous party of Apache scouts
under a single white chief of scouts. This skillful guerrilla band found
Victorio's camp on the Palomas River in the Black Range, circled it in
the night undetected, and struck at dawn. Some thirty Chihenne men,
women, and children were killed, and Victorio was wounded. In the
midst of this battle, the scouts called out to the Chihenne women,
entreating them to surrender unharmed. The women shrieked defiantly back that "if Victorio died, they would eat him, so that no white
man should see his body!" A few days later, an army regiment chasing
a small band of Chihenne toward the border fired on its rear, killing
ten, including Washington.

Dan L. Thrapp, Victorio's biographer, sums up the chief's dilemma
in June 1880:

> From his breakout in 1879 until now Victorio had never been
> trapped, never clearly defeated. But from this time forward his star
> was in decline. Although he would win his other engagements, until
> the final one, they would more and more resemble rear-guard ac-
> tions of a force growing gradually weaker. Victorio was discovering
> what Cochise had learned before him: you could whip the soldiers
> time and again, but they were too many and so well supplied and
> reinforced that they would wear you out.

Some of the army officers harbored a sympathy for Victorio.
Thomas Cruse later admitted, "The Government ignored Victorio's

just grievances and forced him to the warpath." And Charles B. Gatewood, who would play the pivotal role in the final hunt for Geronimo, told Cruse "that any man of discretion, empowered to adjust Victorio's well-founded claims, could have prevented the bloody and disastrous outbreaks of 1879."

Each Chihenne warrior who died was an irreplaceable loss. It was during these grim days that the young Kaywaykla learned of a terrible event. After one raid, a weary Victorio sought out Kaywaykla's mother. Beside the campfire, he told her quietly, "Meet this thing bravely as your husband would wish you to do. He is dead. Let his name be unspoken henceforth." A good Apache, Kaywaykla observed the old taboo: never again did he speak his father's name.

In June, having separated to forestall pursuit, the various bands of Chihenne crossed the border and rendezvoused in Chihuahua. The people were shocked to find that Lozen was not among the warriors. Assuming her dead, the Chihenne avoiding speaking her name. Later they would conclude that the disaster that befell them would never have happened had Lozen, with her Power for detecting the enemy, rejoined her people.

During the next weeks, Victorio led his people east into the cactus-thick hills of west Texas, country beyond his familiar domain. It was a measure of the group's desperation. Indian scouts who trailed the Chihenne into Mexico reported that Victorio's people were "in a very crippled & demoralized condition, having their wounded with them & their stock played out." At this juncture the leader of the contingent of Mescalero Apaches with Victorio announced that they had had enough and planned to return to their reservation. Victorio refused: in the subsequent fight he killed the Mescalero leader. Fearing the chief's wrath, the other Mescaleros stayed with the Chihenne.

The governor of Chihuahua chose his cousin, Joaquín Terrazas, to organize a body of Mexican troops and volunteers to hunt Victorio down. He also offered a reward for every Apache scalp, and a bounty of 2,000 pesos—a fortune, at the time—for Victorio, dead or alive. It has often been the fashion to denigrate Mexican military efforts—not only Anglo historians, but the Apaches themselves made withering remarks about the supposed cowardice and incompetence of soldiers south of the border. But Mexico had its great Indian fighters, and Joaquín Terrazas was one of the best.

After a month spent ransacking the towns of Chihuahua to recruit fighters, Terrazas had gathered 350 men under his command; he later sent home the ninety least committed among them, honing his army into a disciplined band of 260. Among them were a number of Tara-humara Indians, superb athletes who were traditional enemies of the Apaches to their north. Unlike the American troops whom Victorio had run ragged, the Mexicans were fresh, well fed, and well armed.

In September, Victorio led his people far to the southeast, out into a barren desert crawling with rattlesnakes and gila monsters, at the very limit of Chiricahua territory. His biographer wonders why Victorio did not head instead for the sanctuary of the high Sierra Madre:

> He led an exodus from the land and places he knew into the blazing wilderness. Toward a promised land? He could not have believed that. . . . He was getting old. Perhaps he was tired. He had whipped his pursuers, his tormentors, time without number, but their hordes were inexhaustible, and his warriors were few and becoming weary. His was an exodus to nowhere, from the land of broken hopes to the land of no hope whatever.

Kaywaykla offers some insight. Victorio's greatest problem by September 1880 was lack of ammunition. At a council of warriors, he chose Blanco and Kaytennae, two of his most dependable men, to go on a foraging expedition for bullets. Meanwhile he hoped to camp briefly at a lake near the Tres Castillos, three spiky hills protruding from the desert. "For a short time we may be comparatively safe here," he told the council. "The cavalry will look for us in the mountains, not on this plain. We need rest badly. We need food."

Victorio turned to Nana for advice, but the old man deferred in turn. "I have fought with three great chiefs of my people, Mangas Coloradas, Cochise, and Victorio," said Nana. "The problems confronting you are more difficult than either of the others had to meet. To the future of our people your decisions are of great importance. Your wisdom has never failed us. Command and we obey."

Victorio's plan was to recuperate at Tres Castillos, then move west into the Sierra Madre—the Blue Mountains, as the Apaches called them. Though Kaywaykla had never been there, he had absorbed the idyllic descriptions of the elders.

> Grandmother was talking of the tall pines, mountain meadows, and clear, cool water in the land of Juh. A few more camps, a few more

plains to cross, a few more days of attempting to avoid discovery, and we would find a refuge from White Eyes and their attack. We would dwell in a land such as our fathers had enjoyed, untouched by greed and cruelty. It would be like the Happy Place with no suffering, no injustice, no hunger.

For once, Victorio miscalculated. Terrazas's army had been trailing the Chihenne steadily. On October 15, the Mexican leader climbed a hill, scanned the horizon with his binoculars, and saw two puffs of dust near the Tres Castillos.

Terrazas's attack, which came at sunset, relied on no particular subtleties. When the oncoming column was still a thousand yards away, the Chihenne spotted it, with the Tarahumaras in the vanguard, and the shooting began. The landscape itself was a trap for the Apaches. Instead of a mountain at their back, they had a barren hill scarcely a hundred feet tall.

The shortage of ammunition paid its tragic dividends. The Chihenne threw up hasty breastworks of rock, from behind which they fired when they could. The fighting continued into the moonlit night. At midnight, claimed Terrazas, the Apaches burst into a death song, which they chanted for two hours.

At daybreak the fighting resumed with new frenzy. According to Terrazas, much of the struggle was hand to hand, "the combatants wrestling with each other and getting hold of each other's heads." This seems unlikely, for an Apache warrior was matchless at close combat with a knife. It was rather the huge discrepancy in bullets that took its toll, overwhelming the defenders.

By 10 A.M. on the sixteenth, the battle was over. In Terrazas's official summary, he claimed seventy-eight Apaches killed, of whom sixty-two were warriors, and sixty-eight women and children taken prisoner. His own losses were slight: three dead, ten wounded. The dead Chihenne were scalped for the bounty. Apaches who later returned to bury the victims claimed that most of the corpses had been burned in a bonfire.

Terrazas himself did not know which Apache was Victorio, and was assured that the chief was among the slain only by the testimony of captives. Mauricio Corredor, leader among the Tarahumara Indians, was credited with firing the shot that killed Victorio. The government of Chihuahua paid him the two thousand-peso bounty and also gave him a nickel-plated rifle. But the Chihenne themselves swore that Victorio fought until he was out of ammunition, then took his own life with his knife. Their descendants swear this today.

A month after Tres Castillos, some Apaches—probably not even Chihenne—ambushed a Mexican column near Carrizal. One of the soldiers was a sergeant mounted on Victorio's saddle, which the Apaches recognized. The attackers cut his corpse into tiny pieces.

Some Chihenne escaped from Tres Castillos, crawling away in the night, chief among them Nana. The young Kaywaykla managed to get away with his mother, after an ordeal of creeping and hiding; at one point they lay in a shallow crevice only a few feet from a Mexican soldier who rolled a cigarette, smoked it, tossed the butt to the ground and crushed it with his heel before walking on. "Had I not been in the way," Kaywaykla later wrote, "[my mother] could have killed him with her knife, while he smoked." In the flight, Kaywaykla was separated from his baby sister and his beloved grandmother. Four years would pass before he learned their fate; meanwhile he speculated that his grandmother had been killed, his sister sold into slavery.

Days after the massacre, the dazed survivors—seventeen in all—met in their prearranged rendezvous in a deep, hidden arroyo. Nana spoke of Victorio. Seventy years later, Kaywaykla remembered the substance of his words.

> The chief had died as he would have wished—in the defense of his people. He was the greatest of all Apache chiefs, yes, of all Indian chiefs. He had died as he had lived, free and unconquerable. We knew well the fate of Mangas Coloradas and of Cochise. They, too, would have preferred death in battle; they would have envied Victorio. So—we were not to mourn for him. He had been spared the ignominy of imprisonment and slavery, and for that he would have been thankful to Ussen.

That night, Blanco and Kaytennae returned from their expedition in quest of ammunition, only to learn of the massacre. They carried hundreds of cartridges. "Too late," said Kaytennae bitterly.

"It is not too late," answered Nana, "so long as one Apache lives."

Thirteen

■

The Dreamer

*O*ne might imagine that in the summer of 1877, the first act Geronimo should perform after the shackles were struck from his ankles would be to flee the San Carlos reservation. He knew that the consequence of his imprisonment by Clum "might easily have been death to me." Yet instead of fleeing, Geronimo stayed on, camping with other Chiricahuas on the reservation for another seven months. In September he resisted the temptation to break out with Victorio.

In his autobiography, Geronimo explains his passiveness in one bland sentence: "After this we had no more trouble with the soldiers, but I never felt at ease any longer at the Post [the San Carlos agency]." Twenty-five miles upstream on the Gila, however, the Bedonkohe warrior lived in relative contentment among the reservation Chihenne. It may well be that with Clum gone, Geronimo felt safe from the worst the White Eyes could do. Clum's successor held a conference with Geronimo in late September at which he appointed the warrior "captain" of the Chihenne who had stayed put—even though Geronimo was no Chihenne.

Geronimo's lingering on near San Carlos bespeaks also his usual ambivalence. The advantages of reservation life—and by 1877 these were not insignificant—were balanced in his soul against the longing for freedom that would later tip the scales.

It was not until April 4, 1878, that Geronimo bolted. The precipitating event had nothing to do with white authority. Geronimo and others got drunk one day on bootlegged liquor; according to a young Chiricahua who was present, the inebriated warrior began "scolding his nephew, for no reason at all." Taking the criticism hard, the nephew committed suicide. An agonized Geronimo fled south to Mexico with his old ally, Juh. Along with him each man took a small group of loyal family.

For the next year and a half, Geronimo and Juh operated out of Juh's stronghold deep in the Sierra Madre. In Geronimo's life after the middle 1870s, when he became well known to white Americans, this period is the most obscure. His own memoir glosses over these months without a word. In all likelihood, both Juh and Geronimo joined Victorio in certain battles against the White Eyes during the last fourteen months of the Chihenne chief's struggle. It seems likely too that the Chiricahua leaders fell out with Victorio, for not only did Victorio's son Washington attack Juh and Geronimo's people at San Carlos in May 1880, but a trader on the reservation swore at the time that "instead of being in sympathy with Victorio's band, [Juh and Geronimo's people] exhibit hostile feelings toward them."

At the end of their year and a half on the loose, in December 1879, Juh and Geronimo voluntarily came in to live once more on the San Carlos reservation. Watching from Tombstone, Clum was cynical: "What [Geronimo] wanted was government blankets, government firewood, government beef, beans, flour, and a good rest from the rigors of the trail. . . . He was the hero of the reservation for twenty months, ample time to develop plans for future deviltry." Juh and Geronimo stayed at San Carlos while the Chihenne fought and fled their painful way toward Tres Castillos.

In the wake of the massacre that had all but wiped out the free Chihenne, Nana gathered together the survivors. Both Mexican and American cavalry were still abroad, searching for the few who had gotten away. The tattered remnant of the band hid by day and rode at night. "No warrior," remembered Kaywaykla of those terrible days, "knew whether his wife lay dead or was a slave in the hands of the Mexicans. No one but Nana seemed to care whether he lived or died."

In the midst of these tribulations, Nana somehow managed to send messengers to the Black Range in New Mexico, where other Chihenne had been left in hiding; they were summoned to join the survivors. And Nana recruited Apaches from other tribes. Slowly he rebuilt the devastated band into a respectable force—"though in comparison with Victorio's it was but a handful," Kaywaykla admitted. Nana even sent the remarkable Sánchez on another perilous mission—to trail Terrazas's victorious army in hopes of ascertaining the fate of the captives. Sánchez returned with the gloomy news that about one hundred women and children (some thirty more than Terrazas acknowledged) had been marched to Chihuahua City, where they would surely be sold into slavery.

One obvious course for the survivors would have been to throw themselves on the mercy of the U.S. Army and beg to surrender at the Mescalero or San Carlos agency. The latter reservation, hated though it was, still harbored about one hundred forty Chihenne. Juh and Geronimo were there as well. Bad blood there may have been between these Chiricahuas and Victorio, but Nana had married a sister of Geronimo. Within the coming year, the old man would once again ride side by side with his Bedonkohe brother-in-law. But now, Nana scorned the idea of surrender: he was after revenge.

One day a solitary rider approached the fugitives' camp. It was Lozen, who had been missing for weeks. She had an extraordinary story to tell. Her separation from the Chihenne had come about less than two months before Tres Castillos, as her band was being hotly pursued by American troops near the banks of the Rio Grande in Texas. Lozen was riding with a young, pregnant Mescalero woman who abruptly went into labor. Without hesitation, Lozen gave the woman's horse and her own to another fleeing Chihenne and slipped on foot into the brush to hide with the soon-to-be-mother. (Had the women retained their horses, the cavalry would have found them.)

Even as the soldiers rode by within earshot, Lozen delivered the baby in the underbrush. There followed a long ordeal of survival, as Lozen guided the woman and her infant back to the Mescalero reservation. During their weeks of hiding and furtive movement, Lozen performed one virtuosic feat after another. Twice she stole Mexican horses from under the noses of their owners, fleeing in a hail of bullets. She killed a longhorn steer with only a knife, so the women could eat, then turned the animal's stomach into a water jug. Finally she managed to kill a cavalryman and helped herself to his rifle, ammunition, and canteen.

At the reservation, from Mescaleros who had straggled home, she learned about the massacre that had ended her brother's life. Eluding the soldiers who still patrolled the country, Lozen traveled alone many miles south once again into Mexico, where she found Nana and the survivors. Now she was eager to ride with the old man on his mission of revenge.

Nana was now about seventy-five years old. Less than ever did he look the great warrior. A journalist who would meet him a few years later would describe Nana as "a short, fat, wrinkled old man of four-score years, leisurely in his movements, but active upon occasion as a kitten. His face, far from attractive, was the most impassive and undecipherable one of all [the Chiricahua leaders]—and that is saying a great deal." The savvy Lieutenant Charles B. Gatewood found Nana even less impressive: he looked to Gatewood like a "palsied, aged and decrepit chief, who was barely able to accompany the squaws and children in their forays."

For the Chiricahua, as for all Apaches, revenge was not primarily a matter of personal spite. It was a means of redressing an imbalance in the state of things. To kill members of the enemy after they had killed one's own was almost a sacred duty—though a leader such as Nana had no right to order any warrior to fight. The Apache ideal of revenge bears a kinship with the Greek notion of Nemesis. As Kaywaykla put it, "Ussen had not commanded that we love our enemies. Nana did not love his; and he was not content with an eye for an eye, nor a life for a life. For every Apache killed he took many lives."

For seven months after Tres Castillos, Nana nursed his band back to power. The aged chief sought meaning in his people's tragedy. "It is not good for people to have an easy life," he told Kaywaykla. "They become weak and inefficient when they cease to struggle." The Chihenne went out on the occasional raid or ambush, killing Mexicans, but they suffered setbacks of their own when two of their best warriors were slain in firefights. Employing his Power, Nana concentrated on gathering arms and ammunition. Once the Apaches seized a mule train laden with heavy bags. To Nana's disgust, the booty turned out to be not ammunition but bars of silver. Sánchez, with his knowledge of his former captives, hefted a bar and ventured, "If we could get this to Casas Grandes we could trade it to the Mexicans for things of value to us. . . . if each man took two or three bars to trade for bullets—"

"Instead of ammunition," Nana interrupted, "he would get mescal and be killed."

Early in 1881 Nana led his people to a high sanctuary on the west side of the Sierra Madre. At last the young Kaywaykla saw the storied land of Juh.

> In that place we lived a few weeks as those who have gone to the Happy Place must. Again we hunted, feasted, and danced about fires. Again fathers spent time with their families—those who had fathers left to them. . . . For the first time within my memory we lived as Apaches had before the coming of White Eyes.

From this sanctuary Nana's band made long forays. One of the boldest was all the way north to Ojo Caliente, which had been deserted by the army now that it no longer had Apaches to guard there. Posting a sentry, the Chihenne bathed for two days in their sacred spring. "How good it was to lie in that water!" Kaywaykla remembered. "On the desert where even drinking water was difficult to obtain we had rubbed our skin with fine sand. We lay in the cleansing pool and enjoyed its beneficent water for hours."

At the end of June 1881, the chief launched what has ever since been known as Nana's Raid. Of all the extraordinary deeds of war ever performed by the Chiricahuas, this was arguably the most brilliant. The summary statistics only hint at the intensity and perfection of Nana's wild campaign. In two months, the chief and some fifteen warriors rode three thousand miles—an *average* of fifty miles a day. They fought seven serious battles with cavalry, winning every one, and attacked more than a dozen towns and ranches. With one thousand soldiers and another three hundred to four hundred civilians chasing them, the warriors escaped every trap. During those two months they killed at least thirty-five of their enemy, wounded many more, and captured more than two hundred horses and mules. Their own casualties are uncertain, but not a single dead or wounded Apache was found by any of the pursuing horde. All this, with a relative handful of warriors under the leadership of a lame-footed chief some seventy-five years old!

The full story of Nana's Raid will never be told: only the Apaches knew it from the inside, and Kaywaykla was too young to ride with the warriors. From the point of view of white settlers and soldiers in New Mexico, it was a two-month ordeal of frustration and fear. The confident colonel in charge of the chase believed he could use the new railroad and telegraph lines to box Nana in; instead the warriors blithely outmaneuvered the troops at every step. The Chihenne rode their horses until they were nearly dead; then they shot them (sometimes for food) and stole others. With their matchless knowledge of the New Mexico mountains, they could hide whenever they chose to. Victorio's larger band had always been hindered by the numbers of women and children among them; Nana's party was all warriors.

The lightning mobility of the raiders dumbfounded New Mexicans, who could not believe that the same Apaches who burned a ranch in one part of the territory could ambush a wagon train seventy miles away less than two days later. At one point, Nana rode up to the Mescalero reservation, where he recruited some thirty to forty Mescalero who proceeded to wage part of the long raid with his Chihenne. Knowing Nana was coming, the army proved powerless to thwart his coup. The panic of the territory was reflected in its newspapers: the entire Mescalero tribe, some claimed, had stampeded off the reservation.

Nana's ravages were not indiscriminate. Among a trio of ranches in southwestern New Mexico, for instance, the Chihenne spared the one that belonged to a Mexican who had traded with Nana's people. Yet the rampage left its grisly scenes. Civilians and soldiers who came upon the dead bodies reported men "mutilated," women "outraged."

By the end of August 1881, the raid was over. Nana retreated effortlessly into Sonora. The American army heaved a sigh of relief as it declared the chase officially abandoned. From a white point of view, the wild ride seemed senseless—a fusillade of destruction wrought by Indians who had no strategic aim save terror, no land or rights to win. But Nana, nursing his thoughts in the Sierra Madre, knew that he had paid back some of the debt the White Eyes had laid upon Victorio.

Meanwhile, far to the north on the White Mountain reservation in Arizona, one of the most confused and sorry chapters in the Apache wars was beginning to unfold. It centered around a medicine man named Nochedelklinne. White men knew little about him in 1881, and whites know little today. About thirty-six years old, Nochedelklinne was physically slight and unimpressive, standing roughly five foot six and weighing no more than 125 pounds. According to Lieutenant Thomas Cruse, who met with the medicine man during the crisis that was about to unfold, "His face—very light in color for an Apache—was drawn and ascetic-looking. It was an interesting face in every way."

Cruse insisted that Nochedelklinne had been part of the Indian delegation that visited President Grant in 1871 (though he does not appear in the record under that name), and that he also attended school in Santa Fe, where he "picked up the merest smattering of Christianity." Added Cruse, "He was a Dreamer, then, tending to mysticism and possessed (I have always believed) of certain crude powers of hypnotism."

In June 1881, Nochedelklinne began preaching a vision and teaching a dance to all Apaches who were interested. In the dance, men and women were arrayed in columns leading outward from a common center, like spokes of a wheel. As they performed a slow, solemn step, the medicine man sprinkled them with hoddentin—the powder of the tule (a cat-tailed bulrush), one of the most magical substances the Apaches owned. The dance often lasted all night.

The substance of Nochedelklinne's vision was that the whites would soon vanish from the Apache country, and that great chiefs who were dead would come back to life. In this respect, the movement the Dreamer launched was one of a number of what would come to be called ghost dances—the first arising among the Paiutes in Nevada in the 1870s, the last and most famous among the Sioux in 1890. Cruse thought the "smattering of Christianity" that had most vividly seized Nochedelklinne was the account of the Resurrection.

Though many Apaches were at first skeptical, the Dreamer's power won them over. Juh and Geronimo attended meetings, declined to dance, but were so impressed that in time they came to accept Nochedelklinne's vision. At some point, Nana came all the way up from Mexico to look into the phenomenon. According to Juh's son Daklugie, who was a boy on the reservation at the time,

> After performing until almost morning, Nochedelklinne had terminated the rite, and, accompanied by a few dancers, he started up an incline in the misty light. Before he reached the crest, he stopped and lifted his arms in prayer. Dimly those with him saw the bodies of three great chiefs—Mangas Coloradas, Cochise, and Victorio—rise slowly from the earth. When they had emerged and were visible to their knees, they slowly sank back. Nana said that he had seen this and the word of Nana was not to be questioned.

As the word spread of the new "religion" and Nochedelklinne's dances attracted more adherents, the white authorities on the reservation grew alarmed. The new San Carlos agent, a man already infamous for his corrupt practices (the effects of which contributed to Apache misery), requested additional troops from the colonel in charge, warning darkly of "trouble with White Mountain Indians, Tontos and San Carlos Indians, growing out of the evil advice of a bad medicine man." Cruse sent his trusted chief of scouts, who was part Choctaw Indian, to investigate, and was shocked when the man came back offering his resignation, full of dire predictions of a mass outbreak.

Yet according to Daklugie, "Of all the encounters Apaches had with their enemies I believe that [the Nochedelklinne affair] is least understood by white people." The nervous Anglos saw in the Dreamer's meetings only the groundwork of revolt. The colonel in charge, Eugene A. Carr, muttered anxious telegraphic omens:

> [The] Indians think that this doctor will be the head of all Indians . . . ;
> he says the ground will turn over, the dead will rise and the Indians
> will be above the whites; that they will have possession of this Post;
> that the soldiers will have to give up their horses to them, etc.

Cruse was similarly baffled by the "revival meetings," as he called them: "They began to appear much like the negro camp meetings of our own South, where the darkies 'get religion' with enthusiastic shouting and acrobatics."

From the Apache point of view, however, the medicine man's vision was in an important sense a call *not* to revolt. Near the end of his life, Geronimo told Daklugie "that he had never understood why he and Juh could have been so easily influenced by that Medicine Man; but he had convinced them that the Apaches should leave revenge to Ussen."

With tensions on the reservation building daily, with officials in charge who had little or no grasp of what was going on, the inevitable happened. On Cibecue Creek, forty-six miles north of the San Carlos agency, Nochedelklinne held a series of dances. Wiring Colonel Carr, the San Carlos agent revealed his hidden agenda: IT WOULD BE WELL TO ARREST [NOCHEDELKLINNE] AND SEND HIM OFF OR HAVE HIM KILLED WITHOUT ARRESTING. Carr sent two Apache scouts to Cibecue to order Nochedelklinne to come in to Fort Apache. When six days passed with no answer, Carr marched toward Cibecue with seventy-nine soldiers, six officers, and twenty-three Apache scouts. They reached the Medicine Man's camp on August 30.

As to what happened next on Cibecue Creek, there are as many versions as there were eyewitnesses. Carr claimed that he found No-chedelklinne standing outside his wickiup, surrounded by fifteen to twenty warriors. Through an interpreter, he arrested the medicine man, while promising that if the "charges" were proved untrue, he would be released. But Carr also promised "that if he tried to escape he would be killed," and "if there was an attempt at rescue he would be killed." Nochedelklinne merely smiled, according to the colonel, "and said he did not want to escape—he was perfectly willing to go."

Carr admitted indirectly that he had trouble communicating his thoughts to the gentle shaman. Their colloquy seems to have been yet another of those fateful turns in the Apache wars where language difficulties wreaked havoc. Al Sieber, the canniest of all the white chiefs of scouts in the Apache campaign, later claimed that the whole catastrophe hinged on "the interpreter not knowing enough of the Indian language" and making in consequence "a fatal blunder" of translation—though Sieber did not specify what the blunder was.

Carr prepared to move out with his prisoner, but Nochedelklinne insisted on eating a meal first. Daklugie corroborates this detail: "I watched from the hillside. We could see Nochedelklinne eating and we could hear the scouts urging him to hurry." The situation grew more tense by the moment.

Finally Carr started toward Fort Apache with his prisoner. In high brush, he allowed his command to separate into two groups. Yet now the colonel relaxed, telling one of his captains "that I was rather ashamed to come out with all this force to arrest one poor little Indian." The party moved down Cibecue Creek, with the uneasy Apaches riding parallel to make sure no harm came to the Dreamer. It was late, so Carr called for a camp.

According to the colonel, Nochedelklinne's supporters now crowded close to the camp. A captain stepped toward them, waving his hands and uttering a single word in Apache that meant "Go away." Still the Indians crowded in. Daklugie claimed later that all the Apaches wanted to do was watch; the suspicion was growing among them that harm was about to come to their prophet.

The tension had wound too tight. A shot rang out, and at once a furious gun battle began. The captain who had tried to disperse the

Apaches was killed instantly, as was a private beside him. A lieutenant later testified that at this moment, Carr approached the soldier guarding Nochedelklinne and spoke firmly: "Kill the Medicine Man!" Nochedelklinne was shot through the thighs, but crawled away when the man who shot him was in turn felled. Another soldier reached Nochedelklinne, stuck his pistol in the medicine man's mouth, and fired. Still the Dreamer did not die. At last a civilian guide finished off Nochedelklinne by smashing his forehead with an axe.

The Apache story differs. According to one witness, the soldiers tried to disperse the crowding Indians by drawing their guns and thrice driving them off. According to another, Nochedelklinne was shot before the first Apache fired.

The battle lasted until dark. Daklugie said that his father, Juh, as well as Geronimo and Lozen, took part in the fighting. Lozen rode boldly into Carr's camp and drove off a large portion of the herd of army horses. But the most remarkable fact about the battle was that, from the first shot, nearly all the Apache scouts who had ridden out with Carr deserted and fought against the bluecoats. It would be the only occasion during the Apache wars when scouts mutinied against the army, but it confirmed the worst fears of the Arizonans who had never trusted General Crook's experiment with Apache scouts.

By the end of the battle, six American soldiers and one officer lay dead. Carr had lost fifty-five horses and mules, along with three thousand rounds of ammunition. Cruse estimated eighteen Apaches dead, including six turncoat scouts.

Carr's shellshocked command limped back to Fort Apache, where rumors preceded him that nearly his whole army had been wiped out. During the next few days, six whites were killed in several attacks in the vicinity of the fort. Then, on September 1, Apaches attacked the fort from two sides—an almost unprecedented action from warriors who preferred the quicksilver tactics of guerrilla combat. A lieutenant was badly wounded, Carr had his horse shot out from under him, and the Apaches set fire to several buildings.

The death of Nochedelklinne was to reverberate among the Apache far more deeply than the most pessimistic officers imagined. Americans might have learned from John Brown and Harpers Ferry that the martyrdom of a visionary could ignite a passionate cause. Official dismay, however, took the form of a court of inquiry into the actions of Carr and Cruse, which focused not on the wisdom of the effort to squelch the Dreamer but on military decisions. Carr was censured, for instance, for letting his command drift into two groups among the head-high rushes of Cibecue Creek.

Even the usually sensitive John G. Bourke—who would later write a book about Apache medicine men—failed to comprehend the profound betrayal the Apaches experienced in the loss of their visionary prophet. In his diary, he wrote sardonically,

> I have never been quite able to divest myself of the notion that it would have been wiser and cheaper to offer this prophet fifty cents a head for all the ghosts he could resuscitate, and thus expose the absurdity of his pretensions, than to shed so much blood and incur so much expense to prove to the savages that the boasts of their charlatans ruffled our serenity so deeply.

In the aftermath of the Cibecue battle, the Apaches discovered a new American horror. The scouts who had deserted in the battle stayed at large for weeks, eventually surrendering in the face of a huge military buildup on the two reservations. Five of their supposed "ringleaders" were court-martialed. Two were sent to Alcatraz for long sentences; the other three were condemned to death.

After an imprisonment lasting almost four months, the luckless trio was marched to the gallows at Fort Grant on March 3, 1882. To this day, no one has proved they were guilty of the killings the court claimed they inflicted. A last-minute appeal to the President was advanced on their behalf. Grant, with his sympathy for Indians who had been unjustly dealt with, might have reprieved them; but now the President was Chester A. Arthur, who "declined to interfere."

Even as the nooses swung above their heads, the scouts were consigned to the pseudonymity of the nicknames whites had laid on them. The Arizona public knew them only as Dead Shot, Dandy Jim, and Skippy (his real name was Skitashe). For fear of another Cibecue, the government had buttressed the execution with an overkill of military preparation. Six thousand rounds of ammunition were delivered to the guards who watched over the gallows.

The festive atmosphere of a lynching prevailed. Under the headline, "By the Rope Process Dandy Jim, Dead Shot, and Skippy Become Good Indians," a reporter for the Arizona *Star* described the scouts' last hours. The day before, they had peered from their cells at the newly built gallows.

After seeing it Dandy Jim declined to partake of any food, but Dead Shot and Skippy made light of it by laughing and mimic[k]ing at the manner at which they should die by the rope. They have no fears of the hereafter and say their hands are clean, meaning innocence, and if nothing can be done for them in this life they are prepared to die.

The next day, according to the reporter, "They mounted the scaffold laughing and showed no signs of fear; said they were happy and would soon meet their friends."

Another eyewitness painted a darker picture.

The day of the hanging Skitashe was so weak he could not stand. The Indian scouts were lined up, facing the scaffold. Dead Shot and Dandy Jim walked up unassisted, but Skitashe had to be carried up on the platform. Here he said to the sergeant of the guard: "No veno; commandanta give Indian clean clothes one day; hang him next day; what for?"

On the same day, sixty miles away at San Carlos, Dead Shot's wife committed suicide by hanging herself from a tree. According to Daklugie, "Because she loved her husband very much she wished to go through eternity with him, even though it might have meant a deformed (elongated) neck."

Fourteen

■

In the Stronghold

On September 30, 1881, a month after Nochedelklinne's martyr-dom, Juh and Geronimo fled the reservation in the night. With them went seventy-two men, women, and children, including Naiche, Coch-ise's son, who until this point had declined to join the "hostiles." The immediate spur was the sudden appearance on ration day of three companies of cavalry, part of the military overreaction to the hostilities at Cibecue. But according to Geronimo, it was the killing of the prophet that launched the outbreak by the Chiricahuas. "They had heard, too," Geronimo told an interpreter many years later, "that the soldiers from Camp Thomas were coming to round them all up and make them prisoners, so were badly frightened. There was a rumor, too, that they were to be sent off somewhere. . . . The Indians were badly scared up and Juh counciled going." The government had in fact toyed with the idea of a mass hanging of all Apaches who had fought against Carr on Cibecue Creek.

Juh, the Nednhi chief, was the leader of the group that fled south toward Mexico. On Taza's death in Washington in 1876, Naiche had become chief of the Chokonen. Yet it was Geronimo, neither now nor ever a chief, who assumed intellectual and spiritual ascendancy among the free Chiricahuas. As Jason Betzinez, a young Chihenne who would soon join the fugitives, remembered, "Geronimo was pretty much the main leader although he was not the born chief of any band. . . . [He] seemed to be the most intelligent and resourceful as well as the most vigorous and farsighted. In times of danger he was the man to be relied on."

The 1881 breakout was pivotal in Geronimo's life: it formed the fulcrum against which he drove the last five years of the Chiricahua resistance, which would become the last Indian war ever fought in the United States. Though Geronimo would vacillate and reverse his course during those five years, his iron temper acquired a new rigor after Cibecue; his awareness of injustice hardened into a rage that lay always just beneath his implacable surface. It was during those last five years of battle that Geronimo earned the reputation among white Americans that would follow him to his grave in Oklahoma in 1909— "the worst Indian who ever lived."

Long before 1881, Geronimo found his detractors among whites who got to know him on the reservation. The census taker at San Carlos in 1880 thought Geronimo a "lazy, indolent creature, who spent his time in gambling, with an occasional 'tiswin' drunk. . . . Daily he could be seen loafing around the little adobe that served as a shelter for the sub-agent and telegraph operator." Whatever Geronimo was, he was not a loafer: if he loitered about the buildings of the White Eyes, it was to indulge his quenchless curiosity about their alien ways. Geronimo studied his enemy.

Looking back after the Apache wars were over, the same census taker commemorated Geronimo in a purple passage oddly mixing contempt and horror:

> Among those ungrateful, restless fiends [of the 1881 breakout], who only awaited a plausible excuse to flee, was Geronimo, not a chieftain, but an adviser; not a leader in war, but an exhorter; not a captain who exposed himself in battle, but the sly and vicious inciter of rebellion and bloodshed. A schemer, whose villainous suggestions caused the wrecking of countless homes; the pillage and plunder of ranches; the making of widows and orphans; the cause of carnage and torture; the mutilation of surprised victims.

A new severity attended the flight toward the Sierra Madre. As Geronimo's biographer puts it, "On their way to the border the fugitives

killed everybody they encountered." It was horses, guns, and ammunition that Juh and Geronimo needed, but Cibecue was on their
minds, and the dark joy of vengeance inflamed their flight. Several
companies of troops chased the Chiricahua, but managed only a pair
of ineffectual sniping actions.

On their run south, the fugitives passed close to Tombstone. As
word of their killings filtered into town, the "news made business
men turn pale. Men could hardly talk for some time." But John Clum
was delighted at the chance to settle scores with his old adversary. At
once he formed a posse, which counted among its members three of
the five Earp brothers—Wyatt, Virgil, and Morgan. "Remember, men,"
exhorted Clum as the posse mounted up, "no quarter, no prisoners. I
delivered Geronimo to the army once, in irons. They turned him
loose. If we get him this time, we will send him back to the army,
nailed up in a long, narrow box, with a paper lily on his chest."

Thirty-five strong, the posse set out full of cocksure vaunts, which
heavy rain, mud, and saddle sores soon muted. For two days the
"hardy pioneers" trailed the fleeing Chiricahua men, women, and
children, to the Mexican border and illegally beyond. They never saw
a single Apache.

Virtually all the northern part of the Sierra Madre was a sanctuary
for the Chiricahua. It was the homeland of the Nednhi, who would
still boast seventy years later that they were the bravest and cruelest
of the Chiricahua. One high enclave in particular was the sanctum
sanctorum: Apaches knew it as Juh's Stronghold. (Scholars of the Indian wars argue passionately today over the precise location of the
Stronghold. Daklugie placed it "just west of the Chihuahua–Sonora
line in the Sierra Madre, about a three-day walk from Casas Grandes,
Mexico"—a formula open to considerable ambiguity.)

Now, in the autumn of 1881, the followers of Juh and Geronimo
assembled in the Stronghold, and Nana brought his rehabilitated band
there. The Chihenne camped for the night on the streambed beneath
the Stronghold. In the morning, Nana pointed to a summit a mile
above camp, and said, "Tall pines on the flat top of the mountain. Juh's
stronghold. His lookout has seen us and men are coming down the
Zigzag Trail. If you watch that white spot near the top you may see
them cross it."

The Stronghold seemed to the Chiricahua the ultimate refuge, the
perfect natural fortress. The zigzag trail was the only route of access,

whose vertiginous bends the Apaches had boobytrapped with boulders "poised so that even a boy could send them crashing down." Mexican troops had once tried to attack the Stronghold, but the Chiricahua had unleashed their stones. Insisted Sánchez, "There are still bits of metal and bones at the foot." On top of the huge, level mountain there was an abundance of game, tall grasses, edible plants, and perennial streams. The Stronghold had a near-mystical significance for the Chiricahua. According to Nana, "[The Mexicans] can never reach the mountain upon which Juh lives, and we could live [there] as our fathers did in the old days before the coming of the White Eyes."

The few white men who had met Juh described him as fat—an unusual characteristic for an Apache. Thomas Cruse insisted that the Nednhi chief weighed at least 225 pounds. Kaywaykla, who met Juh now for the first time, remembered him more particularly:

> He rode toward us, a powerful figure on a sturdy war horse much larger than the Spanish ponies we used.... I think Nana must have been close to six feet in height, but Juh towered above him. He was very large, not fat, but stockily built. His body was twice as thick as [Nana's]. His heavy hair was braided and the ends fell almost to his knees.

Although he stuttered when he spoke, Juh was able to sing at a war or victory dance without impediment. "He had a soft, deep voice," recalled Kaywaykla, "and was skillful in improvising rhythmic accounts of the exploits of his band." Juh had several Powers, including the gift of prophecy: his name meant "he sees ahead." But his strongest Power was the ability to handle his men.

With the union of Nana, Juh, and Geronimo, the Chiricahua had assembled their strongest force since the glory days of Cochise. At the dance in the Stronghold that celebrated their coming together, one by one the chiefs and warriors stood before the fire and were hailed by the cheers of the people. When Geronimo was saluted, he answered with a speech full of arrogance. The young Kaywaykla whispered his surprise to his mother. "All Apaches are arrogant," she replied. "They have a right to be."

The last introduced was Lozen. Nana praised her: "She whom we had mourned as dead has returned to her people. Though she is a woman there is no warrior more worthy than the sister of Victorio."

Of a temperament opposite Geronimo's, Lozen stood with her eyes cast down and wept at the cheers. Nana asked her to use her Power.

Lozen lifted her arms, palms up, and turned in a slow circle as she sang:

> Over all in this world
> Ussen has Power.
> Sometimes He shares it
> With those of this earth.
> This Power he has given me
> For the benefit of my people.
> This Power is good.
> It is good, as He is good.
> This Power I may use
> For the good of my people.

Lozen completed her circle; no tingling had come to her hands, and the palms had not reddened. "No enemy is near," she said.

Nana spoke: "For that we thank Ussen."

The bond between Juh and Geronimo was of long standing, born in their youthful play together and cemented with Juh's marriage to Ishton, Geronimo's favorite sister. Now Nana skillfully blended his Chihenne in with the other Chiricahua. Geronimo took charge of the training of boys to become warriors. Daklugie never forgot one ordeal: Geronimo made a group of boys build a fire, then line up beside a stream (sometimes covered with ice) and jump in at his command. They were allowed to huddle for a few minutes beside the fire, then ordered to jump into the icy water again. Geronimo stood with a switch in hand to enforce his drill.

Despite the rigors of the fugitive life, there was joy in the Stronghold. "The young men were happy," Kaywaykla observed, "for war was their life." One day Juh and Nana played a joke on Geronimo. As the Bedonkohe rode in from a raid, a number of warriors hid along the canyon that approached the Stronghold. Geronimo was off his guard. After he had ridden past all the concealed men, he dismounted.

Nana called out, "Welcome to my trap!"

"I knew all the time you were there," grumbled Geronimo lamely. Had the hidden men been enemy, he could have been cut down easily.

"You did not," Nana teased. "And you the sly fox of the Apaches!"

Geronimo's chagrin at being made fun of was a recurrent fault. "He was extremely credulous and completely lacked any sense of humor," says the Chiricahua anthropologist, Morris Opler. "His tribesmen were well aware of these weaknesses and used to play pranks at his expense." Another time, Geronimo was told that the most pacifistic warrior in his band had vowed to kill him on sight. The Bedonkohe's credulity merged with his tendency toward paranoia: he avoided the warrior for weeks until the man himself reassured Geronimo that he bore him no malice.

In the Stronghold, the Chiricahua felt their dignity heal as they luxuriated in their freedom. Within the alliance of Nana, Juh, and Geronimo, it was Juh who retained paramount status. Yet along with his implacable hatred for the enemy, Juh possessed a streak of dark fatalism, which he did not hide from his people. As long ago as 1876, when he had fled from the Chiricahua reservation rather than march with John Clum to San Carlos, Juh had been seized with a sense of doom. Even as he recruited his warriors, he told them time and again "that he could offer them nothing but hardship and death." He reminded them that "they would be hunted like wild animals by the troops of both the United States and Mexico."

One day in the Cañon del Cobre, far to the south of the Stronghold, Juh received a vision. Out of a thin cloud of blue smoke seen across a chasm, thousands of soldiers in blue uniforms marched into an evanescent cave. Juh's warriors saw the vision, too. A medicine man explained it: "Ussen sent the vision to warn us that we will be defeated, and perhaps all killed by the government. Their strength in numbers, with their more powerful weapons, will make us indeed *Indeh*, the Dead. Eventually they will exterminate us."

Yet there was no alternative in Juh's pessimistic soul but to fight on toward that inevitable end. As powerful as the people felt in their united strength in the Stronghold, their numbers still seemed insufficient. It was Geronimo, the worrier, who came up with a plan that at first must have seemed utterly farfetched. Still ensconced on the San Carlos reservation were a large number of Chihenne, including some seventy-five warriors. Their leader was Loco, the chief who, with Nana, had succeeded to command after the death of Victorio. Geronimo called a council, at which he unveiled his plan. It was to ride north, slip stealthily onto the reservation, and compel Loco and his people

—at gunpoint, if necessary—to break out and join the fugitives in the Sierra Madre.

A long debate ensued. Nana defended the right of his fellow Chihenne chief to choose peace or war for himself. Geronimo argued that as many Apaches would die from "bad water" and "the terrible sickness that causes people to shake like leaves in the wind" at San Carlos as might be killed in an outbreak. Besides, "Loco belongs with his people." One of Geronimo's warriors sneered, "Loco is a woman!" Geronimo silenced the man with a sharp word.

As the warrior's outburst had indicated, feelings toward Loco among the free Chiricahua were mixed. The Chihenne chief was a generation younger than Nana, coeval with Juh and Geronimo. Like Nana, he walked with a limp, the legacy of a desperate battle with a grizzly bear many years before. Before he killed the bear with his knife, its claws had deeply scarred his face. Loco had a bad eye; some said the bear had put it out, others that he could see with it dimly through a clouded cataract.

Some Apaches said that Loco's Spanish name came from the Chiricahua verdict that he was crazy to trust the White Eyes. Like Juh, Loco had reacted to the tide of Anglo-American immigrants with grim fatalism. But while the sense of doom only stiffened Juh's will to fight, in Loco it emerged as a resignation to the white man's rule.

At last the council agreed to Geronimo's improbable plan. Nana stayed in the Stronghold to guard the women and children left behind; Juh and Geronimo rode north with Lozen and many other warriors. In contrast to their flight south six months before, the raiders now moved secretively, killing no one and stealing no horses. When the telegraph had first come to Arizona in 1873, army officers had delighted in dazzling the Indians with its technological magic. As a result, the Chiricahua knew the importance of the thin metal wire to the White Eyes' tactics. As they approached Loco's camp on the Gila River, they cut the telegraph line to the San Carlos agency three miles away.

On the morning of April 19, 1882, Loco's Chihenne woke to shouts. As they ran out of their wickiups, they saw Apaches riding toward them with guns raised; some were swimming their horses across the river. One of their leaders (most likely Geronimo) shouted, "Take them all! No one is to be left in the camp. Shoot down anyone who refuses to go with us!"

Within minutes, the Chihenne were on the move. The twenty-one-year-old Jason Betzinez echoed his people's dismay:

> We did everything they told us to do. We were given no time to look for our horses and round them up but were driven from our village on foot. We weren't allowed to snatch up anything but a handful of clothing and other belongings. There was no chance to eat breakfast.

Despite the severed telephone wire, the white chief of police at San Carlos learned of the disturbance and rode out with a single Apache policeman. The two men ran into the rear guard of the Chiricahuas and were shot dead. This deed convinced the unarmed Chihenne that the blood of a white officer would be laid to their hands. Like it or not, Loco's people were now outlaws. "We were filled with gloom and despair," remembered Betzinez. "What had we done to be treated so cruelly by members of our own race?"

The flight to Mexico would cost the Chihenne dearly. Their situation was in one sense even worse than Victorio's as he had fled two armies in 1880, for Loco's people had just as many women and children and virtually no weapons. Geronimo supplied some Chihenne with guns he had cached, but the band remained seriously underarmed. The sheer logistics of the flight were staggering. Knowing the army would block the path south, Geronimo and Juh led the renegades on a circuitous trail east. At one point, to feed the runaways, Geronimo attacked a rancher's camp and stole several hundred sheep. The Chihenne rested in hiding for two days while they gorged on fresh mutton.

This attack, on Ash Flat near the town of Safford, remains one of the best-documented of Geronimo's "depredations." The various accounts differ considerably, but all reveal the cruelty Geronimo was capable of when vexed. The ranch belonged to a white man who, though sheriff of Graham County, had married an Apache woman. When Geronimo surprised the ranch hands at their range camp, he found a White Mountain Apache named Bylas (a close relative of the rancher's wife) with his family, three other Apaches, a Mexican foreman named Mestas, Mestas's wife and three sons, two other Mexican women, and nine Mexican herders.

Geronimo pretended friendship, professing an interest only in taking livestock. His band, at least sixty strong, started killing sheep. Since he disliked mutton, Geronimo shot a favorite pony of the rancher's son. The Mexican women were ordered to cook a meal for the Chiricahua. Bylas and Mestas knew Geronimo well. According to one account, when he saw Geronimo coming, Bylas quickly drank down most of a bottle of whiskey. When they met, Geronimo said, "I know you. You always have some whiskey around. Give me a bottle." Bylas insisted he had no whiskey, adding to Geronimo's pique.

According to another version, Geronimo suddenly took Mestas to task for the hangings of the Cibecue scouts Dead Shot, Dandy Jim, and Skitashe, which had taken place just a month before at nearby Fort Grant. Mestas said he knew nothing about the executions. The Mexican was wearing a fancy embroidered shirt. "Mestas," Geronimo railed, "you have never given me anything. Why don't you give me that white shirt?" The terrified Mexican pulled off his shirt and gave it to the Bedonkohe.

Geronimo's warriors read his mood; several, including Naiche, tried to intercede. "Geronimo," one said, "you promised Mestas you would not injure any of them, and now you are going to kill them." Bylas pleaded, "If you are going to kill the Mexicans, let Mestas and family go."

Geronimo said nothing. Perhaps he thought of the massacre near Janos three decades in his past, when Mexicans had killed his wife, his mother, and his three children. At his order, the warriors bound the hands of the herders, Mestas, his wife, two of his sons, even the women who had cooked the meal; then all were tied together with a long rope. Geronimo led them stumbling up a nearby hill, where they were shot and stabbed to death one by one.

The third of Mestas's sons, a nine-year-old boy, had hidden himself under the skirts of Bylas's wife. When Geronimo discovered the boy, he wanted to put him to death; some versions say that in his fury he would have killed Bylas's whole family and the other White Mountain Apaches too. But Naiche stood firm, "telling Geronimo they were Indians, relatives and friends, and not to harm a hair of their heads." When Geronimo showed signs of balking, Naiche called to his nephews and told them to shoot Geronimo if he argued. The White Mountain Apaches and the Mexican boy were spared.

According to an unreliable newspaper account, Mestas was tortured to death ("When they were tired of torturing him one of them split his head with an axe"), while his wife and two sons had their brains beaten out with stones. The accounts of white men who came upon the Apaches' victims often lapsed into hysterical exaggeration; but Geronimo's path in April 1882 seems to have been strewn with atrocities. Near the border, claimed a Tombstone volunteer, Geronimo attacked a ranch, killed three adults and took a sixteen-year-old girl captive; a small child "was grabbed up by the legs and its brains battered out against the house."

In the midst of the fugitives' unwieldy fight, a Chihenne girl began her first menses. Of all the rituals that regulated Apache life, the most important was the girls' puberty ceremony. Normally it stretched across the sacred number of four days and nights, with elaborate dancing, singing, feasting, and gift giving. It says much about the importance of this rite to the Chiricahua that now, despite the pursuit of the U. S. Army, the fleeing Apaches stopped and held a puberty ceremony for the girl—much curtailed from its normal four days, but nonetheless fully observed.

Before they could reach the border, the fugitives were caught in a pitched battle with army troops near the New Mexico border. They won the fight, killing three soldiers and four Apache scouts while losing at most two of their own. Another command chased the Chihenne into Mexico, then (in contravention of the border agreement) kept up the pursuit until they forced a second battle, fought on a barren hill twenty miles inside Chihuahua.

Caught by surprise, the Apaches were dancing and celebrating their escape into Mexico. In the daylong battle, a number of Chihenne were killed, mostly women and children (the army estimated seventeen); Loco himself was shot in the leg, though not badly injured. The troops also succeeded in separating the fugitives from their belongings, including horses and mules. In Betzinez's view,

> This was the worst thing that had happened to us since we left the agency at San Carlos. While it is true we hadn't been able to take much with us when we were forced to leave the agency, we did have a few blankets and utensils. Now we had nothing except our bare hands and the clothes on our backs.

The depleted band staggered on foot toward the Sierra Madre, heartened only by their last sight of the American soldiers retreating northward. Once more they began to relax, assuming that they had fought their last battle with the troops that had hounded them since their escape from the reservation. On the very next day, they walked into a trap.

The ambush, from a wayside ravine, was laid by soldiers under Colonel Lorenzo Garcia, who with Joaquín Terrazas was one of Mexico's finest Indian fighters. The skirmishes with American troops had been waged with long-range gunfire from behind breastworks; the Garcia battle was a chaos of soldiers running through the panicked Apaches, shooting women and children point-blank. The action was desperate on both sides, and accounts of it vary so greatly that it is hard to know what really happened.

A man named Fun—Geronimo's cousin and most trusted warrior —was singled out by the Apaches as the bravest fighter. According to Kaywaykla, who had the story second-hand, Fun dashed alone out of an arroyo to meet the Mexican advance, his belt full of bullets, carrying cartridges between the fingers of his left hand. Dodging the enemy's shots, he felled so many Mexicans that he singlehandedly turned away their charge.

The Apaches' most grievous problem was lack of ammunition. At one point an unarmed Chihenne woman sprang from the arroyo, ran to a Mexican horse, cut loose a bag full of cartridges, and dragged it back to her people. Lozen covered her brave dash, firing calmly, "dropp[ing] a man with every shot."

It is Geronimo's role in this battle that remains controversial and problematic. The Mexicans recognized the great warrior on sight, for an officer yelled, "Geronimo is in that ditch! Go in and get him!" Other soldiers cried out, "Geronimo, this is your last day!" According to Betzinez, who was in the battle, Geronimo and another man rallied thirty-two warriors to make a stand, saving the lives of many women and children. Yet Kaywaykla insists that a Chihenne who was in the battle told him that at the turning point, Geronimo called to his men, "If we leave the women and children we can escape."

The Chihenne could not believe his ears: such a deed would represent the ultimate betrayal of the Apache ideal of courage, and all his life, Geronimo had been conspicuous for his responsibility to his people. The Chihenne swore that Fun turned toward Geronimo and said, "What did you say? Repeat that."

"Come on!" Geronimo urged. "Let's go!"

Fun raised his rifle, pointed it at his ally, and spoke, "Say that again and I'll shoot."

In response, Geronimo climbed out of the arroyo and disappeared.

If this strange vignette is true, it marks the only case in either the white or Apache record in which Geronimo was accused of a cowardly act. It may well be a suspect tale: for the rest of his life, the Chihenne warrior who told Kaywaykla the story harbored a bitter grudge against Geronimo for forcing his people off the reservation.

The savage fight between Garcia and the Apaches took its toll on both sides. By Garcia's own admission, he lost twenty-one soldiers, including three officers. He claimed seventy-five Apache dead, with twenty-two wounded women captured. Without giving any numbers, Betzinez lamented, "We lost nearly half our families in this tragedy." On top of the massacre of Victorio's people at Tres Castillos, here was a second devastation for the Chihenne within a year and a half.

With Geronimo in charge, the fugitives limped on toward the Sierra Madre, carrying their wounded with them. At last they joined the rest of the free Chiricahua. To the young Chihenne in Loco's band, who had spent much of their lives on the reservation, the wild Nednhi whose homeland they now entered seemed an alien people. "When they couldn't find anyone else to mistreat," claimed Betzinez, "they fought among themselves. They were hard to deal with on friendly terms."

Yet there was joy for the Chihenne in greeting friends and relatives from whom they had been separated for years. "These people attempted to make up for our recent sorrow," recalled Betzinez. "They gave us food and blankets and by talking to us cheerfully tried to take our minds off our losses." Though with his people he had in effect been kidnapped by Geronimo, Loco now accepted his outlaw status; in the coming months, he would fight Mexicans alongside his abductor. Yet some vital spark had seemed to go out of him. Juh's son Daklugie, who had little respect for Loco and the "servile things" who followed him, later moralized, "Loco had been a brave and fearless warrior; perhaps his spirit was broken. When that happens, a man is finished."

If Geronimo ever felt remorse for the great loss of Chihenne lives their abduction from San Carlos had brought about, he never expressed it. In a sense, despite the debacle with Garcia, he had achieved his aim. The greatest Apache force in a decade—more than six hundred men, women, and children, including all the best warriors —was gathered in the Stronghold, where Juh and Geronimo believed they could never be attacked. Perhaps Arizona was lost forever; but the Chiricahua could live in the Sierra Madre indefinitely. The Americans would leave them alone, and as for the Mexicans—well, there were plenty of boulders lying ready to be rolled upon foolhardy soldiers who ventured near the sanctuary.

For the next year, the Apaches moved from camp to camp within the Sierra Madre, raiding at will on the outlying villages and creating a reign of terror that seized two Mexican states. Of the Chiricahua skill at horse stealing, Kaywaykla wryly observed, "We took care to leave enough horses so that the Mexicans would raise more for us."

Lozen led many raids at the behest of Geronimo. Perhaps the most daring mission was prosecuted almost single-handed by Fun. A group of Chiricahua women and children out baking mescal hearts had been attacked by Mexicans; the older boys were slain and scalped, the women and the rest of the children taken captive. Fun trailed the victors to their hometown, then brazenly approached the prison after dark, slipped inside, and found the captives without arousing the attention of the guard who paced nearby.

One of the women told Fun that all the villagers would assemble in the church on the fourth day following. Fun slipped away, sent word to Juh and Geronimo, and watched the village. On Sunday, during the service, the Apaches crept silently up to the church and barricaded the doors with stones and logs. Fun climbed to the roof, dug a hole in the adobe, and dropped a lighted chili bomb made of peppers and inflammable wood inside the church. The Mexicans burned and suffocated while the Chiricahua freed their prisoners, plundered the town, and rode away with their spoils.

Flushed with overconfidence, the Chiricahua made one bad mistake. Betzinez blamed it on Geronimo's love of whiskey. The Apache leaders had established trade relations with the town of Casas Grandes. Now the townspeople pulled the old Mexican trick. For two days they gave the Apaches the run of the town, professing good will, wiping the record of past grievances. On the third morning, as the Chiricahua slept off their drunk, the Mexicans attacked their camp. Some ten to twelve warriors were killed, with twenty-five to thirty women captured. Geronimo escaped, but among the captives was his second wife, Cheehashkish, whom he had married thirty years before, while still in mourning for his beloved Alope. Geronimo never saw Cheehashkish again.

During this year, Juh also suffered personal losses. In an attack on a Chiricahua camp, Mexican cavalry shot and killed Ishton, Juh's wife and Geronimo's sister, whom the Bedonkohe had saved with his healing Power when she nearly died in childbirth. In the same attack, Ishton's daughter was shot in the knee and badly wounded. Daklugie and his two older brothers carried their sister by improvised stretcher to safety. Although she would walk hundreds of miles with her people, her leg never healed properly, and a year later it was amputated by a surgeon at San Carlos.

In November 1882, the Nednhi chief pulled off perhaps the finest triumph of his military career. This brilliant coup, which Juh almost surely masterminded, may have come in response to the treachery at Casas Grandes. It would mark the last joint effort of the triumvirate of leaders of the free Chiricahua—Juh, Geronimo, and Nana.

The Apaches sent a small group of raiders along the main road to Galeana, a town twenty miles south of Casas Grandes, where they knew a patrol of Mexican cavalry was stationed. These warriors rode boldly to the edge of town, seized some Mexican horses, and started north. The decoy worked: at their heels charged some twenty-three cavalry, led by the renowned Juan Mata Ortiz, who had been Terrazas's second-in-command at Tres Castillos. The Apaches let the Mexicans almost catch up.

Suddenly, from the ravine beside the road, the main force of the Chiricahua under their three leaders rose into view. Mata Ortiz's men were caught in a trap. They retreated at once to the only defensible ground, a small conical hill, on top of which they threw up paltry breastworks with an energy born of terror. The Apaches surrounded the hill. Lying on their stomachs, each with a stone to roll in front of him as a shield, a number of warriors crept up the hill, while the leaders and best marksmen kept up a covering fire from a big cedar tree nearby. The addled Mexicans shot wildly until they were almost out of ammunition. At last, from only a few feet away, the warriors leapt to their feet and took the Mexicans in hand-to-hand combat. All but one was killed, including Mata Ortiz.

As the sole survivor fled, some Apaches prepared to ride after him; but Geronimo cried, "Let him go! He will tell the rest of the soldiers in town what has happened whereupon more Mexicans will come out to the rescue. In that way we can destroy other soldiers." In the event, the remaining soldiers in Galeana were too frightened to ride out to the fatal hill. Yet in his cavalier insolence, Geronimo had paraded before his warriors the contempt for Mexicans that burned in his soul.

In the sleepy courtyard of Galeana, 104 years to the day after the massacre of the cavalry, the citizens built a stone pyramid and raised a plaque. It commemorates the twenty-two Mexican dead name by name, then ends with the curt notation: *"Jefe Indio 'Ju.' Geronimo."* The conical hill, bare, studded with cactus, stands not far from the highway to Casas Grandes, visited today only by the odd rancher out looking for stray sheep. Near its summit the rearranged stones, pathetic vestiges of seven or eight of the hasty Mexican breastworks, still speak the hopelessness of men about to die.

In 1871, with his ambush of Cushing, Juh had brought about the death of the finest American officer ever to fall to the Apaches. Eleven years later, with his trap of Mata Ortiz, Juh wiped out the preeminent Mexican Indian fighter ever to die in Apache battle.

Sometime in 1883, Juh and Geronimo separated. Daklugie remembered no breach between the men; it was merely the old Apache independence coming to the fore. Geronimo wanted to head north, while Juh was content to stay in the Sierra Madre.

One day, as the band rode peacefully up the Rio Aros, Juh's horse shied without warning, fell off a steep bank, and dumped its rider face down in the current. Later the gossip filtered back to the States that Juh had gotten drunk on mescal in Casas Grandes, fallen off his horse, and drowned. But Daklugie and one of his brothers were there. They plunged into the river and tried to pull their heavy father to safety. They could not drag Juh out of the current, so Daklugie held his face out of the water while his brother ran for help.

His father was not drunk, Daklugie later insisted. The sudden fall, he thought, had either caused or been caused by a stroke or a heart attack. "Two or three times I thought Juh was trying to speak," Daklugie remembered. "I know that he moved and that his lips moved; but there was no sound." By the time help came, the chief had expired. His people scraped a grave out of the west bank of the Aros, wrapped Juh in his blanket, and buried him.

The greatest living Apache chief had died, gone with Mangas and Cochise and Victorio and so many others to the Happy Place. From now on, the free Chiricahua would be led not by any chief, but by a warrior and medicine man.

Fifteen

■

The Tan Wolf Charges

*A*larmed by the deterioration of Indian affairs in Arizona, President Chester A. Arthur brought back the only general who had ever shown much ability at dealing with Apaches. George Crook had not changed his habits during his seven years' absence from the Southwest. Returning in September 1882, "he 'slid' into [Fort] Apache with his usual Indianlike quiet," said Thomas Cruse. With the general came his perpetual aide, John G. Bourke—"as friendly as Crook was taciturn."

Crook pitched his tent a mile from the fort. All the officers paid him courtesy calls, not one of which he returned. He still rode his favorite mule, Apache, rather than any horse, and wore his uniform as seldom as possible, preferring his khaki civilian clothes. It was these that gave him his name among the Chiricahua—Nantan Lupan, or "Chief Tan Wolf."

When Crook had left Arizona in 1875, it was to plunge into the Sioux war that was flaring in the Black Hills of South Dakota. Now the opprobrium that attached to anyone who had had anything to do with the disaster at Little Bighorn stuck to the general's reputation. Crook had commanded the troops who fought Crazy Horse at the battle of the Rosebud, the first great confrontation between the soldiers and the Sioux, which occurred only eight days before Custer's army was annihilated a few miles to the northwest. At the Rosebud the Indians outnumbered the soldiers by three to one. Yet Crazy Horse also outsmarted Crook, using hit-and-run tactics that befuddled and separated the columns of bluecoats.

Crook could not admit that he had lost the Rosebud—the only Indian battle in which he would ever be defeated. In his official report, he obstinately maintained, "My troops beat these Indians on a field of their own choosing, and drove them in utter rout from it." The Sioux withdrawal, of course, was a characteristic Indian tactic: they had another battle to fight a week hence. In the words of the general's biographer, "The defeat rankled in Crook's memory all his life, and he steadfastly insisted that had the battle progressed according to his orders, it would have ended in real triumph." It is telling that Crook's unfinished autobiography breaks off in midparagraph the day after the Rosebud, leaving the last fourteen years of his life unexplained.

The defeat on the Rosebud prevented the union of army commands that might have turned Little Bighorn into a standoff instead of a massacre. When Custer went down, Crook was wandering around the Montana wilderness looking for him.

The great passion of Crook's life was hunting and fishing. An uncritical Bourke saw his general as a kind of Audubon of the West:

> Ducks, geese, turkeys, sage hens, prairie chickens; pike, pickerel, catfish, trout, salmon-trout, and whitefish; elk, deer, moose, antelope, mountain sheep; bears, wolverines, badgers, coyotes, mountain wolves—all yielded to his rod or rifle. He kept adding to his collection of stuffed birds and eggs until there was no man in the country who possessed a more intimate practical knowledge of the habits of fauna and flora of the vast region beyond the Mississippi.

But the obsession may well have gotten in the way of the general's soldiering. Immediately after the Rosebud, Crook camped on Goose Creek and indulged with his men in an orgy of fishing, landing seventy trout by himself in a single afternoon. Only a week after the Custer massacre, Crook led a party into the Bighorn Mountains, ostensibly to look for officers missing from the Rosebud fight; the search turned, however, into a four-day big-game hunt. Crook's passion would figure crucially in the upcoming Apache campaign.

The general had served on through the remainder of the Sioux war, chasing Crazy Horse and other "renegades," performing well if not spectacularly. After that he had helped suppress uprisings among the Bannocks and Cheyennes. During the two years prior to his reassignment to Arizona, however, Crook had been largely idle—so much so that he had plunged into a gold-mining scheme that turned into a fiasco.

When he had first risen to command Arizona in 1871, Crook had alienated many of his fellow West Pointers by leapfrogging past them in rank. His reassignment in 1882 elicited an even stronger protest. Eighty-six army officers anonymously petitioned the President, decrying Crook's "imbecility" in the Sioux campaign, closing with a sneer: "It is disgraceful that he should belong to the Army at all! But it would be insulting, should his imbecility and dishonesty be rewarded by promotion." The President ignored the petition.

If Crook's dress and habits had not changed since 1875, his soul had undergone some tempering. In his years of dealing with the northern tribes, he had gradually become convinced that most Indian conflicts sprang from legitimate grievances that the government failed to redress. In particular, he felt that ninety-nine percent of the trouble was caused by corrupt agents and traders.

As soon as he arrived in Arizona, Crook dug into the dark machinations that had led to the Cibecue fight. He did so in a manner that seems rarely to have occurred to his predecessors: ask the Apaches themselves. Thus he uncovered the widespread graft by traders and the reservation agent that had turned San Carlos into a powderkeg in 1881. Crook learned that government rations issued for the Apaches had been sold to nearby towns and mining camps; that the beef cows the Indians were issued had "not enough fat on the animals to fry a jackrabbit, many of them being mere skin and bones"; that the traders' scales were crooked; that "the weekly issue of flour . . . would hardly suffice a family for one day." Between ration days, Apaches begged for food from one another, or hunted rats and rabbits to supplement the paltry diet.

Crook also discovered that to a man the Apaches believed the killing of Nochedelklinne had been premeditated. Far from unleashing their bloodiest havoc, however, the Apaches who attacked Carr at Cibecue had actually shown restraint. "If the Indians had been in earnest," Crook observed, "not one of our soldiers could have gotten away from there alive."

Britton Davis, a perceptive lieutenant at San Carlos, remembered the mood of the reservation in 1882:

> Everywhere the naked, hungry, frightened little Indian children, darting behind bush or into wikiup at sight of you. Everywhere the sullen, stolid, hopeless, suspicious faces of the older Indians challenging you. You felt the challenge in your very marrow—that unspoken challenge to prove yourself anything else than one more liar and thief.

Davis peered through no such rose-colored spectacles as John Clum had worn about the grounds:

> Scrawny, dejected lines of scattered cottonwoods, shrunken, almost leafless, marked the course of the streams. Rain was so infrequent that it took on the semblance of a phenomenon when it came at all. Almost continuously dry, hot, dust- and gravel-laden winds swept the plain, denuding it of every vestige of vegetation. In summer a temperature of 110° in the shade was cool weather. At all other times of the year flies, gnats, unnam[e]able bugs . . . swarmed in millions.

Yet while Crook harbored a new sympathy for the Apaches as victims of white mismanagement, he persisted in his old predilection of distinguishing between good and bad Indians. Six weeks after arriving in Arizona, he called a conference of more than four hundred Apaches at San Carlos, where he announced his new rules: brass identification tags and a daily head count once more; official papers without which the Indians could not travel off the reservation; the banning of the manufacture of tizwin. In his old vein of deadpan irony, he told the throng that "If any of the Indians at the council felt disposed to break out, he thought it best for them to break out now and bring the question of supremacy to a test without more delay."

Along with his new rules, Crook set out to reform the abuses that were rampant on the reservation. He paid the Apaches one cent a pound for all the hay they could gather. According to Davis, with fair treatment, "the rancor of the Indians quickly faded away. Little children no longer fled from us."

Only two months before Crook's arrival, Arizona troops had fought what would turn out to be the last Apache battle waged on American soil. It was also the last hostile action by any Apaches other than

Chiricahuas. In a revolt linked to the Cibecue affair, a band of White Mountain Apaches under a leader named Natiotish killed eight Indian police and headed north for the mountains. But Natiotish was no Geronimo, and the White Mountain Apaches were no Chiricahuas. The fugitives committed a number of strategic errors; the army drove them to cover high on the Mogollon Rim, then systematically wiped them out. According to Britton Davis, who fought in the battle, of fifty-four renegades, twenty-six were killed, the rest wounded. For years after the battle of Big Dry Wash, the skeletons of Apaches who had crawled wounded from the fight to die lay exposed in shallow limestone caves.

By the time of Crook's advent, some fifty-five hundred Apaches lived on the San Carlos and Fort Apache reservations. Only the six hundred-plus Chiricahuas in the Sierra Madre roamed at large. There was no doubt in Crook's mind that these were bad Indians. "They are an incorrigible lot," he wrote to the Secretary of Interior; "the worst band of Indians in America." Crook insisted that he "should be glad to learn that the last of the Chiricahuas was under ground."

Having launched his reservation reforms, the general now focused his attention on the Apaches south of the border. He did not underestimate the prowess of the Chiricahua. In a manifesto detailing "The Apache Problem," he lauded the individual warrior's "acuteness of sense, perfect physical condition, absolute knowledge of locality, almost absolute ability to preserve [him]self from danger," arriving at a pithy apotheosis: "We have before us the tiger of the human species."

Meanwhile, deep in the Sierra Madre, the Chiricahua lived a wary life. For years, leery of false security, Geronimo had organized the caching of secret stores of food—dried deer meat, cactus fruit, baked mescal, acorns and piñon nuts and mesquite beans. In caves from New Mexico to Sonora, his men had deposited tanned hides, clothing, moccasins, cooking pots, and guns. A kind of fanaticism spurred his efforts, as he rode from one band to another, exhorting young men to prepare for all-out war against the White Eyes.

There were warriors Geronimo knew he could count on in extremis: Fun, above all, and Lozen. There was Kaytennae, the young Chihenne whom Victorio had sent on the ammunition raid just before Tres Castillos. Among his people, he was unsurpassed as a warrior; he could load and fire a rifle faster than any other man Kaywaykla ever saw. Kaytennae had never been on a reservation. Nana was grooming the young man to become chief of the Chihenne when he himself died.

But there were other warriors who should have led and failed to do so. Geronimo was disappointed in Naiche, the young Chokonen chief, and in Mangus, son of the great Mangas Coloradas. "Naiche and Mangus have seen what happened to their fathers," Geronimo spat out on one recruiting mission, "and they do nothing!"

Although he would fight valiantly to the end, Naiche was widely regarded as weak. For one thing, he was that rarity among the Chiricahua, a chief who had no kind of Power. (This was not Naiche's fault; Power had simply never come to him, through a vision or in any other form.) Apaches told Britton Davis that Naiche "was a good warrior with no peace scruples; but he was fond of the ladies, liked dancing and a good time generally, and was not serious enough for the responsibilities of leadership."

The attacks on Mexican villages, ranches, and pack trains continued apace. When warriors went out on a raid, even the language they spoke was different from everyday Apache. A kind of circumlocutory dialect took over: the word for "heart" became "that by means of which I live," for "pollen," "that which is becoming life."

Geronimo lorded the ease of his victories over the Mexican peasants. As they laid waste to one walled village in Sonora, he and his warriors jeered and gesticulated at the inhabitants, who had retreated to the rooftops where they cowered in fear. But some of the raids proved costly. Newly orphaned by the death of their father, Juh's two oldest sons tried to wage war when they were still adolescents. The younger of the two was captured by Mexicans, and in a reckless attempt to free him, the elder son was captured as well. With only his crippled sister left among the free band, Daklugie, the youngest of Juh's children, was virtually alone in the world. Decades later, at Fort Sill in Oklahoma, he finally learned the fate of his brothers, from an old man who had been captive with them. The Mexicans could torture as well as Apaches: Juh's sons were bound, sharpened sticks were imbedded in their jaws so that they could not close their mouths, and they were marched as part of a chain of future slaves to the city of Chihuahua. Languishing in prison, the brothers succumbed to smallpox.

Disheartened by the occasional setback, stung by the loss of the sovereign freedom they had enjoyed in the past, even some of the Nednhi began to regard the reservation as inevitable, resistance as a dead end. Loco, Naiche, and Mangus counseled as much. But Geronimo and old Nana scorned their pessimism. Death, both leaders asserted, was preferable to captivity.

Through the remarkable verbal pipeline by which the Chiricahua stayed in touch with the reservation, Nana learned of the Tan Wolf's return to Arizona. Despite his own respect for Crook's skills as a general, Nana heard the news as positive: "He was an enemy, yes, but he was an honorable enemy. His promise was good; his understanding of Apaches was fair."

Crook set out to establish his own pipeline. He and Bourke covertly interviewed one of the White Mountain Apaches whom Geronimo had wanted to put to death at the Ash Flat sheepherders' camp the previous spring. This man gave the officers a great deal of information, much of which was reliable: somehow he knew of the quarrels going on among the Chiricahua in the Sierra Madre, and he calculated that they had a total of only 103 fighting men left.

Crook recruited what he called "secret scouts" (two of them women) on the San Carlos and Fort Apache reservations; they were internal spies, charged with sniffing out any hints of rebellion or outbreak among the pacified Apaches. When a spy had something to report to an officer, he or she tapped on the window pane late at night. Crook also sent Indian spies into Mexico, hoping to glean news of Chiricahua doings.

All the while, the general was hatching a wildly audacious plan for dealing with the Apaches south of the border. In July 1882, the governments of the United States and Mexico had signed a new border agreement that allowed the troops of one to cross into the country of the other if "in close pursuit of a band of savage Indians." The treaty was designed merely to allow actions such as the (then illegal) fight a few months earlier in which the American army had attacked Loco's band twenty miles inside Chihuahua. The treaty stipulated that encroaching troops must leave the foreign country as soon as they had either fought the Indians they pursued or lost their trail.

But Crook wanted to use the new border agreement to permit a massive and concerted thrust into the heart of the Chiricahua sanctuary. Unwilling to do this by subterfuge (which of course could have caused an international incident), he traveled by rail, first to Guaymas in Sonora, then to the city of Chihuahua, to confer with Mexican generals and state officials and win their sanction for his bold scheme.

What Crook needed also was a pretext for crossing the border "in close pursuit." He got one in March 1883. A raiding party of Chiricahuas came north, slipped into New Mexico, and terrorized the countryside. In style and savagery, this sortie was reminiscent of Nana's Raid two years before. In less than a week, riding as far as a hundred miles a day, twenty-six warriors killed twenty-six whites and stole scores of horses, with the loss of but a single man of their own.

Though Apache descendants argue to this day over who was in charge of the raid, it is most often credited to Chatto. If, in the words of Kaywaykla's mother, "All Apaches are arrogant," Chatto took the prize. Geronimo, his mentor, often had to silence the obstreperous young man or remind him of his place in the council of warriors. Kaywaykla remembered the young raider in a telling sentence: "Nobody questioned Chat[t]o's bravery, but nobody could be sure of his loyalty." Neither Nana nor Kaytennae trusted Chatto, whom they saw as ambitious and dangerous. Later, after he turned on his people and became an army scout, the Chiricahuas reviled Chatto as "the arch traitor."

In a posed photo shot after the Apache wars, Chatto's shoulders are hunched, his face dark with suspicion, as he stares at something to the photographer's right and clutches the barrel of a long rifle planted on the ground. He was said to be short though thick-chested, with a nose that had been flattened by the errant kick of a mule.

The panic Chatto's raid inspired in southern New Mexico spread to Arizona. At San Carlos, Britton Davis could not sleep because of rumors that the hostiles would next strike the reservation to steal ammunition and recruit more dissidents. In Tombstone, John Clum deduced that Geronimo was in charge of the raid. (Obsessed as always with his nemesis, Clum argued also that it was Geronimo who had put Nochedelklinne up to his visionary dances the year before.)

The newspapers, with their usual hysteria, blamed Crook and his reservation—"the breeding pen and fattening fold of the blood-thirsty savages who prey upon honest industry and civilization." Clum's own Tombstone *Epitaph* editorialized bluntly, "Those fellows with passes [to leave San Carlos] should be killed." From as far away as San Francisco, journalists shrieked over the remorseless savages, fattened and caressed by the government . . . , barbarians with whom war is a pastime and slaughter a delight. Desperate diseases require desperate remedies—and San Carlos is a disease. The surgeon in dealing with a dreadful ulcer which threatens the life of his patient does not hesitate to apply the knife.

The feeling against the reservation reached such a pitch that a group of volunteers calling themselves the Tombstone Rangers organized to ride to San Carlos and, in Britton Davis's words, "massacre all the Indians on the reservation." Fueled by booze, they got as far as the southern edge of San Carlos, where they found an old Apache gathering mescal plants. "They fired at him, but fortunately missed," Davis reported. "He fled north and they fled south. That ended the massacre."

Although Chatto and his raiders killed many in New Mexico, one attack in particular galvanized the imagination of the whole nation. On the road between Lordsburg and Silver City, the Apaches seized a wagon containing three members of a frontier family. They shot and killed the parents, then took the six-year-old boy captive. The victims happened to be a federal judge, H. C. McComas, and his wife. The newspapers reported the bodies of both stripped naked, with their skulls crushed. Chiricahuas later maintained that Chatto's men did not mutilate the bodies, "because [Judge McComas] exhibited great bravery by jumping from the buckboard with his rifle in order to hold the warriors off so that his wife and child could escape."

The six-year-old, Charley McComas, became an instant symbol of the Apache menace. A photograph of the boy, bow-tied and dressed for church, blond hair neatly brushed, an appealingly dopey look on his face, circulated all across the United States, creating a powerful sentimental icon of Anglo-Saxon virtue outraged by savages. "Little Charley McComas," as he was inevitably called, became the most famous Apache victim of all.

His fate remained unknown to all but a few white Americans for seventy-seven years after his kidnapping. In that vacuum, a hundred theories proliferated. Newspapers at the time reported, on the one hand, that Charley had walked to the railroad, been picked up by a train, and tearfully reunited with relatives in Silver City; on the other, that his body had been found six miles away from his parents' corpses, "with his head beaten off against a rock. This is a picture for fathers and mothers to look at, and then imagine he was their darling."

As late as 1938, a Norwegian explorer of Mexico thought he had found proof that the abducted boy had wandered with a "lost tribe" of fugitive Apaches for fifty years, until he was "mysteriously slain." The explorer claimed to have found traces of hair in an Apache comb that might have come from Charley McComas's head.

In reality, Chatto's band had seized the six-year-old to raise as a captive. Apaches had often done this with Mexican boys and girls, whom they treated with all the love and care they did their own children. It was the Chiricahuas' intention to train the white boy to become a full-fledged warrior. The fate that intervened instead came as an odd corollary to Crook's thrust into the Sierra Madre.

With Chatto's raid, the general had his pretext for invading Mexico. "Close pursuit" in Crook's mind, however, need not mean immediate or even timely response. With his characteristic diligence, Crook bided his time while he prepared his thrust. He still knew too little about the Chiricahuas and their hideouts.

At this point, good fortune fell into Crook's lap. In the middle of the night at San Carlos, Britton Davis was awakened by one of his scouts, who slipped into the officer's bedroom and whispered, "Chiricahua come." Davis dressed and rode with his scouts through the dark night to a camp twelve miles away. There they charged and "captured" a lone Indian. About twenty-three years old, he was not a Chiricahua but a White Mountain Apache. His name was Tzoe; the soldiers soon called him Peaches, on account of his boyish complexion and light skin. (In a photograph, Tzoe indeed looks baby-faced and ingenuous by Apache standards.)

Miffed at being disarmed, Tzoe had come in to the reservation of his own volition. A year before, he had left San Carlos under duress as part of Loco's band, in large part because he had married two Chiricahua women. Both were killed in the battle with Lorenzo Garcia, where Tzoe was severely wounded. An ambivalence that sprang from his very identity dogged Tzoe's year at large. He fought with the Chiricahua, but he was not of their people. He had been one of the twenty-five picked men who had raided across New Mexico with Chatto; he had helped kill Judge McComas and his wife. But now Tzoe had had enough; he missed his relatives on the reservation, especially his mother. By nightfall he had slipped away from Chatto's band and ridden to San Carlos.

Tzoe would become the ace up Crook's sleeve. Among the free Chiricahua, he would be renamed Yellow Wolf, for his treachery. Yet at the time, Tzoe's story seemed so implausible, his advent so fortuitous, that many men at San Carlos hypothesized that he had actually been sent "as an emissary of the hostiles, who desired to have a peace talk," but who did not want their vacillation known. This was a theory born of Anglocentric vanity, in ignorance of the force of Geronimo's will.

As soon as he could get his hands on Tzoe, Crook interviewed him. The White Mountain Apache told the general that Chatto's raid had been a quest for ammunition, but its rigor had been steeled by resentment "of that agent with the Big Stomach"—the same San Carlos bureaucrat whose graft Crook had uncovered. "He used to kick them with his feet," Tzoe explained, "and cuff and beat them and all his employees got to doing the same. . . . He threatened to have them removed from the San Carlos to a far-distant country; so the Chiricahuas broke out and went on the warpath."

After Tzoe's wives had been killed in the Garcia battle, the Chiricahuas carefully watched the White Mountain man. "I was never allowed to go off anywhere by myself:—some one was always with me. They made me work for them; I had to cook their food and do things of that kind." One night Tzoe seized his chance; slipping off his moccasins, he fled in the dark, walking only on rocks so as to leave no trail.

Tzoe described Juh's Stronghold, which he said the Apaches called Pahgotzinkay. The plan had been for all the fugitives to rendezvous there soon, "but I don't think the Chiricahuas will do that now. They know I've run away and they may be afraid that I'll tell about them."

The young warrior detailed the plight of the fugitives. "Food is very scarce in the stronghold," he said; "there is no mescal—nothing. The Chiricahuas have been living on meat alone, taken from cattle, stolen or killed." Every other day or so, the band moved to a new camp. Loco wanted to return to the reservation, but was afraid of both American troops and his fellow Chiricahua. There were only seventy fighting men left and fifty "great big boys"—the Chiricahua were burdened by their large numbers of women and children. To Crook's jubilation, Tzoe agreed to guide the army into the Sierra Madre.

On May 1, 1883—a full six weeks after Chatto's raid—Crook crossed the border, heading south on what historian Dan L. Thrapp calls "the most important and dangerous United States Army operation against hostile Indians in the history of the American frontier." His expedition was large and potentially cumbersome: 42 soldiers, 11 officers, 3 chiefs of scouts, 2 interpreters, 1 journalist, 266 mules, 76 mule packers, and—most important of all—193 Apache scouts, including Tzoe. So that the Mexicans would not confuse these Apaches with the hostile Chiricahua, Crook gave his scouts red headbands to wear. This mark became the badge of their courage through the rest of the Apache war. The party carried food for sixty days, and each man had 150 rounds of ammunition.

Crook had studied his enemy with his usual thoroughness. He later analyzed the task that lay before him:

> An Indian in his mode of warfare is more than the equal of the white man, and it would be practically impossible with white soldiers to subdue the Chiricahuas in their own haunts. The country they inhabit is larger than New England, and the roughest on the continent, and though affording no food upon which the soldier can subsist, provides the Indian with everything necessary for sustaining his life indefinitely.

Crook went on to eulogize Apache hardiness, eyesight, tracking and fighting skills. Now more than ever he believed in the efficacy of Indian scouts: "In operating against [the Apache] the only hope of success lies in using their own methods, and their own people with a mixed command."

Crook's entourage included some remarkable men. Captain Emmet Crawford and Lieutenant Charles B. Gatewood, the officers in charge of the Apache scouts, would play vital roles in the last three years of the war. Al Sieber, the shrewd mountain man, was principal chief of scouts. One of the interpreters was the mysterious Mickey Free—the resurfaced Felix Ward, the boy whose kidnapping in 1861 had triggered the Bascom affair and twenty-two years of war between the White Eyes and Apaches. Crook's aide, John G. Bourke, was such an indefatigable diarist that an Apache had nicknamed him "paper medicine man," for he was always "writing, writing, writing." The journalist, on assignment for the New York *Herald,* was Frank Randall, who was also a good photographer. A year later, he would take the first and finest of all photos of Geronimo: glaring fiercely at the camera as he kneels on his right knee, a rifle gripped defiantly in his hands, he looks as if he might let fly at the nearest aggravation. Randall's photo remains the best-known image of any American Indian. The newsman took photos all through the Sierra Madre—priceless documents that were lost to posterity when a mule rolled off a cliff and smashed his glass plates and camera.

In charge of this extraordinary expedition was the man who, whatever his faults and failures, had become the most effective Indian fighter the United States ever had. George Crook was fifty-four years old now; there was more gray in his beard, and a weariness in his gaze that had not been there in 1875. But he was still as fit as his junior officers and as unpretentious as the humblest mule packer.

As soon as they crossed the border into Sonora, Crook's party came upon eloquent signs of the Apache terror. For three days, the expedition met not a single human being, as the men trudged past one abandoned ranch after another, the wheat and barley fields run wild to canebrake. On May 4, they struck the Bavispe River near its great northern bend, and came the next day to their first Mexican town. Bavispe was, Bourke wrote, a "feeble, broken-down" village. Every man, woman, and child came out into the streets or gathered on the rooftops to greet the Americans: "They looked like a grand national convention of scarecrows and ragpickers." The men were so shell-shocked from Apache raids that they dared not go into barley fields only a quarter mile away.

Bacerac, population 876, where the party camped late the same day, seemed to Bourke, "if possible, more dilapidated and down at the heels than was Bavispe. . . . The mass of the people are living in a condition of squalor and penury beyond description." It was Saturday night, however, and the villagers, overjoyed at the prospect of an end to Apache depredations, put on a grand *baile,* or dance, for the Americans. The mule packers bought every last drop of mescal in town, the drums pounded and horns blared until long past midnight, and in the morning the men struggled through their hangovers to get off at the early hour decreed by their abstemious general.

At Huachinera (population 300), "a squalid hole, with a squalid church," Tzoe recounted how Chatto, on his way north for his raid, had brazenly ridden with fifteen warriors into the main plaza in broad daylight and bought tobacco from a startled vendor. On May 8, the expedition left the Bavispe River and headed into the mountains.

By the standards of Colorado or even New Mexico, the peaks of the Sierra Madre are not high, seldom topping 9,000 feet. The range, however, is a maze of jagged crests and gloomy ravines as deep as 5,000 feet. On its margins, the mountains crumble into desert, spiky badlands of cactus and mesquite. Even in the heart of the Sierra Madre, clothed in forests of pine and oak, there are few natural passes and a surprising scarcity of running streams.

At once, the trackers found signs of the Chiricahua; they led Crook to camps abandoned only about a week before, where dead and played-out horses and the carcasses of slaughtered cattle lay on the ground. The army started marching at night, so as to be less conspicuous. Before the expedition had left Arizona, a skeptical scout had told Crook his mission would fail because the Chiricahuas "could hide like coyotes and smell danger a long way like wild animals." But the remarkable fact is that a party of 328 men and more than three hundred animals (mules plus horses) moved for a week through the Sierra Madre with such skill and stealth that the Chiricahua never suspected their presence.

The going was arduous in the extreme. "To look at the country is grand," wrote Bourke; "to travel in it, is Hell." A number of mules fell to their deaths. The men had constantly to dodge stones knocked loose by their comrades. Rocks lacerated the soldiers' boots, and shrubs and cactus tore their clothes to shreds. The scouts, however, were in their element, hiking along "without a complaint, and with many a laugh and jest."

Bourke, fast becoming a self-taught ethnographer, made many notes on Apache customs and beliefs. On their first night in the mountains, he persuaded the scouts to let him join them in a sweat lodge ceremony. When it came his turn to chant, he offered his hosts a full-lunged rendition of "Our captain's name is Murphy." One day Frank Randall, the *Herald* reporter, trapped a young owl, which he tied to the pommel of his saddle. In doing so, he unwittingly violated a solemn Apache taboo. The owl was the most dreaded of all animals, the embodiment of a ghost; parents scared their unruly children with owl threats. Merely to be in the presence of an owl, or even to talk about one, was to invite the "darkness sickness" that could bring death. Now the horrified scouts complained to Crook, who ordered Randall to free the bird.

One day a medicine man among the scouts worked a spell to divine the whereabouts of the Chiricahua. He thumped his breast, pointed to the east and north, and, Bourke wrote, "soon had worked himself into a hysterical condition." Another scout translated the invocation for Bourke, in the reservation English he had been taught:

> I can't see the Chiricahuas yet; Bimeby, me see him; me catch him me kill him; me no catch him me no kill him. Mebbe so six days, me catch him, mebbe so two days. To-mollow, me send 25 men hunt him trail; mebbe so to-mollow catch him squaw. *Chilicahui* see *me,* me no get him; no see me me catch him.

By May 10, the scouts were on a trail they knew to be only a few days old. They passed two ridge-crest camps, one with the remains of forty wickiups still standing, the next of thirty. The following night, the scouts called a conference, during which they urged Crook that, for speed and efficiency, they be allowed to go ahead of the main party. Crook agreed, appointing Crawford to lead an advance band of 150 scouts. Messengers would keep Crook apprised of their discoveries.

The scouts were full of brave boasts. They told Crook that "if they had a fight and the Chiricahuas refused to submit, they would kill the last one, and if they did submit they thought that some of the bad ones, like Ju[h] and Hieronymo[,] ought to be put to death anyhow, as they would be all the time raising trouble." Privately, they lived in fear of the wild Chiricahua. As they advanced, each carrying a hundred rounds of ammunition, the scouts jockeyed with each other to avoid being at the head of the force.

On May 12, Tzoe found the huge natural amphitheater where he had last camped with the Chiricahua. It lay atop a ridge beside the upper Bavispe River, which the expedition had joined again after five days of crossing rugged divides. The amphitheater was, Crook observed, "a formidable place, impregnable to attack." Evidently the Chiricahua had vacated the place only days before. They had left all kinds of belongings behind: cow- and horsehides, meat drying in the trees, bolts of calico, even a pair of Apache baby dolls. Ninety-eight wickiups stood ready for use.

Two days later, during a lunch break, some scouts with field glasses saw their first Chiricahua, in a ridge camp only one mile away. Crawford brought all his scouts together that night as he planned to surround the Chiricahua camp in the morning. To his gratification, the enemy was still unaware of the presence of invaders. According to John Rope, a White Mountain Apache in the vanguard, "Some of the scouts were afraid. . . . That night we could not sleep but sat and talked in whispers."

In the morning, the scouts stripped off their trousers and shirts, leaving on only their loincloths, as they prepared for battle. Then they went down to the river and dipped their hands to drink. "Some of the scouts," Rope reported, "started to say their knees hurt them as an excuse to keep in the rear." Before Crawford could deploy his encircling maneuver, a scout who had wandered off to urinate bumped into two Chiricahuas on mules. An overeager companion cocked his rifle, which went off by accident. The Chiricahua jumped off their mules and ran for cover.

The accidental shot set off a ragged and spontaneous charge by the scouts. Though they imagined they were about to clash with the well-aimed rifles of Juh and Geronimo and their scores of warriors, the scouts had in fact found only a small and harmless band. The "battle" was quickly over. The attackers killed nine, mostly old men and women, and took five children captive. Several Chiricahua warriors escaped. As John Rope guarded one of the captives, the boy "saw all the scouts in a line shooting with their red headbands. 'What kind of people are these?' he asked. 'These are scouts,' I told him, 'and they are after your people.' Then he started to cry."

It happened that nearly all the Chiricahua were off raiding villages in Sonora and Chihuahua at the time. Crawford's scouts had seized an important camp; they found so much booty it took forty-seven horses and mules to load it all up. A captive revealed that the camp was that of Chatto and another leader. But as a military triumph, the attack was insignificant. As soon as he came up to the battleground, Crook realized that his work had only begun.

At the moment, Geronimo and thirty-six warriors were far to the east, on the plains of Chihuahua. They were raiding not for ammunition, but to seize captives whom they hoped to trade for the prisoners the Mexicans had taken at Casas Grandes. At about the time Crawford's scouts attacked Chatto's camp, Geronimo was sitting beside a fire eating a piece of roasted beef; he held the meat in one hand, his knife in the other. Suddenly his Power spoke to him. He dropped his knife and blurted out, "Men, our people whom we left at our base camp are now in the hands of U.S. troops! What shall we do?"

Jason Betzinez, who was sitting next to Geronimo, told this story after decades of living in white America, during which he had lost much of his Apache belief. But he swore to this instance of Geronimo's clairvoyance. "I cannot explain it to this day," Betzinez wrote in 1959. "But I was there and saw it. No, he didn't get the word by some messenger. And no smoke signals had been made."

His warriors doubted Geronimo's Power not at all. At once they packed up and headed for the Sierra Madre, though Chatto's camp lay 120 miles away.

It was Betzinez in 1959 who finally revealed to the world the fate of "little" Charley McComas. The six-year-old was in fact in the camp when Crawford's scouts attacked. Enraged when his mother was killed by scouts, a Chiricahua seized the boy and beat him to death with a rock in revenge. For fear of retribution, the captives hid the body and told the invaders that Charley had run off into the brush. Among the booty found by the scouts was a family photograph album that Bourke thought belonged to Judge McComas: "Nearly all the faces were decidedly intellectual." Crook, who persistently questioned the Chiricahua about Charley, believed for weeks that he was on the verge of recovering the orphan. Five months later, two American emissaries into Mexico announced that Charley was alive and well and would soon be traded by his captors for cartridges.

Oddly, though speculation would linger for more than seven decades about the boy's fate, an Arizona historian found out about Charley's murder in 1905, when he corresponded with Geronimo's interpreter at Fort Sill. But the historian's unpublished account languished unnoticed in a Tucson archive.

Crook's first act after the battle was shrewdly calculated. Through an interpreter, he had a long talk with the oldest of the captives, the daughter of a Chiricahua leader. She revealed the profound dismay her people had felt at the instant of realizing that their stronghold had been invaded by American soldiers. And she swore that many of the Chiricahua were tired of their fugitive life and wanted to live on the reservation.

Crook gave this girl and the older of the two boy captives food for a short journey. Then, as an earnest of his good will, he let the girl choose the best of the horses that the scouts had recaptured. The two youngsters rode off to contact their people and tell them that the Tan Wolf had "only come to take [them] back to San Carlos and not to make war."

Crook later analyzed his predicament:

The Indians were so thoroughly alarmed that to attempt further pursuit would be fruitless. We could never hope to catch them in the rugged peaks, and the effort would surely cost the lives of many men, each rock being a fortress from behind which the Chiricahuas could fight to the death with their breech-loading guns.

The men camped on a broad bend of the Bavispe and settled in to wait. Bourke observed a pair of captives: "The younger girl sobbed convulsively, but her little brother, a handsome brat, gazed stolidly at the world through eyes as big as oysters and as black as jet."

Even in the midst of a military campaign, the soldiers were aware of the beauty of their surroundings. "A more charming spot it would be hard to discover," Bourke wrote in his diary; and an account later delivered by a courier from Crook's party echoed the sentiment: "The troops stated that the place where the capture occurred is the prettiest spot on earth, and the road leading to it as rough as mortal man ever trod." The blue thread of the Bavispe wound around the camp, lined with stately cottonwoods. Tributary streams dwindled off behind labyrinths of hidden cliffs. The hills were covered with swaying grama grass. Near camp, scattered oaks and junipers offered shade; on the slopes rising at either hand, these trees gave way to Ponderosa pine. The days were hot and cloudless, the nights cool.

Two days after the attack, eight women came warily in, waving white rags of peace. One was a sister of a leader named Chihuahua; she said that her brother was weary of fighting, wanted to come in, and was gathering up his band. He was angry, however, for one of the women killed in the attack had been his aunt. The next morning, Chihuahua rode in with all the arrogance of a Chiricahua warrior. His horse was adorned with strips of red cloth; he wore two pistols and carried a lance. As John Rope recalled,

> He rode right up to where we were sitting under some oak trees. We all jumped up, not knowing what he intended to do. He asked where the head officer was, and we told him. Then he ran his horse right through us to General Crook's tent. He rode right through soldiers and scouts alike and they had to get out of his way.

With Mickey Free interpreting, Chihuahua berated Crook for killing his aunt. Then his mood changed. "He was tired of fighting," Bourke paraphrased. "His village had been destroyed and all his property was in our hands. He wished to surrender his band just as soon as he could gather it together." Then Chihuahua rode out of camp as insolently as he had ridden in.

Hour by hour, Chiricahua men, women, and children wandered in from the hills. By May 19, there were one hundred Chiricahua—though none of the chiefs—camped with Crook. One woman warned that "there was going to be more trouble" when Geronimo found out what had happened. The Chiricahua women tore up flour sacks to make white flags, which they hung all over camp, to warn their own warriors not to shoot.

On May 20, Geronimo arrived. Rather than come into camp, however, he lurked with his warriors on a ridge overlooking the camp. The chiefs, including Nana, Naiche, and Loco, and all the leading warriors—Kaytennae, Chatto, Fun, Lozen, Chihuahua, and the like—also kept their distance on adjoining ridges. The warriors and scouts shouted questions and taunts back and forth.

An acutely volatile situation had developed. It might take little more than a careless gunshot to unleash the bloodiest battle in all the Apache wars. If the Apache scouts switched allegiances, as they had at Cibecue, the potential for a massacre of American soldiers rivaling the one at Little Bighorn lay close at hand. The impasse that had seized the Chiricahua sanctuary offered no hope of an easy solution.

There is a great irony in the fact that what happened next—at a juncture that can fairly be regarded as the pivotal point in a quarter century of war between Apaches and Americans—should remain one of the most poorly documented, as well as one of the most richly ambiguous, of all the deeds in that war.

It began innocuously enough. On May 20, General Crook went out bird hunting with his shotgun. He wandered alone away from camp into a field of tall yellow grass. Suddenly Geronimo and "all the Chiricahua chiefs" sprang out of hiding and seized the general. They took his gun away from him, "and took the birds he had shot also."

Most historians, following the lead of Dan L. Thrapp and Angie Debo, have credited Crook with deliberately letting himself be captured as a bold gambit to break the impasse. Thrapp calls the maneuver "as daring as any recorded in the annals of Indian war." Debo hails it as "the most supremely courageous act of his adventurous career."

Such an explanation stretches the facts to meet an a priori notion—that Crook always knew what he was doing. The more obvious analysis is that Crook simply made a bad blunder. Hunting for him was no mere hobby; it was a virtual compulsion. In the days after his Rosebud fight and just before Little Bighorn, Crook had gone hunting and fishing when he ought to have been soldiering. On previous days during the thrust into the Sierra Madre, despite the grueling pace of the expedition and the absolute need for stealth, Crook had gone off bird hunting in his spare time. In the past, the general's hunting had sometimes gotten him in trouble. Once he was caught in a blizzard on a tributary of the Platte River and nearly drowned when he fell into a hole in the ice (two companions saved his life); another time he was charged by a bear that finally fell to his bullets only ten feet away.

It is significant that neither Crook nor Bourke ever mentioned the hunting misadventure in their accounts of the Sierra Madre jaunt. Bourke's narrative of the expedition, recording the meeting between Crook and Geronimo's warriors, avers, "Gradually their fears wore off, and in parties of two and three, by various trails, they made their way to General Crook's fire." Crook's own official report says baldly, "All the chiefs surrendered, gave themselves up."

We know about the Chiricahuas' seizure of Crook thanks to the narrative of John Rope, the White Mountain Apache scout, which was not published until 1936. A garbled version of the story trickled back to the States, however, to appear full-blown in newspapers all over the country under the headline, "The Capture of Crook." This rendition became valuable ammunition for Crook's detractors.

Geronimo certainly believed he had captured Crook, as he would insist for the rest of his life. The Chiricahua descendants living today are certain of the fact.

That said, an obvious question arises: why did Geronimo, having seized the general, not put him to death, or at least keep him prisoner? According to Rope, as soon as they had disarmed Crook, the Chiricahuas demanded an interpreter. Mickey Free was sent for, then "They all sat on the ground and talked." After two hours, the Chiricahuas came with Crook to the army camp.

The explanation is multifaceted. By May 1883, the Chiricahuas themselves were seriously divided on the issue of whether to give up the fugitive life, with Loco's people, who had not wanted to break out in the first place, the hungriest for San Carlos. Juh, with Geronimo the strongest proponent of resistance, had died on the Aros River. From talking to Mexican women Geronimo had seized in Chihuahua, Bourke later learned that "The Chiricahuas are almost destitute of ammunition." Even as he had listened to the gunfire from afar on May 15, hearing round after round shot by the scouts with only desultory answering fire, Bourke had mused in his diary, "I could not help indulging the fancy that the Chiricahuas were fighting without energy simply because they had no ammunition to throw away."

Most important, the successful thrust by American troops into the heart of the Sierra Madre, guided by the turncoat Tzoe, had dealt the Chiricahua a devastating psychological blow. No place, not even Juh's Stronghold, the soldiers had proved, was invulnerable. Bourke could see the dismay written on the faces of the Chiricahua.

If Geronimo killed Crook, or even held him captive too long, it would touch off the ultimate battle. The fifty-odd soldiers were not a prohibitive threat, and the seventy-six mule packers were militarily negligible. It was the Apache scouts that Geronimo worried about. One hundred ninety-three strong, their number was nearly twice that of the Chiricahua warriors. A battle would cost many lives on both sides, and it was not the Apache way to fight when great losses were inevitable.

Geronimo's own eternal ambivalence, moreover, played a part. He had tried twice before to live on a reservation, and he would try again. The hardships of the fugitive life had taken their toll even on the stern Bedonkohe fighter.

Finally, Geronimo had another plan. Where brute force could lead only to massive losses, subterfuge and deceit might win out.

So Geronimo and the chiefs came in to talk. Reading the unhappiness in his adversaries' looks, Crook drove home the significance of his penetration of their land. "I told them," he later wrote, "that the Mexican troops were moving in from both sides, and it was only a matter of a few days until the last of them should be under the ground." His official report plays up Crook's steely disdain as he dared them to fight on:

> The best thing for them to do [Crook claimed he told the Chirica-huas] was to fight their way out if they thought they could do it. I kept them waiting for several days, and each day they became more and more importunate. Hieronymo and all the chiefs at last fairly begged me to be taken back to San Carlos.

This was not the Chiricahua understanding of what transpired in the talks, which went on for several days. It has never been clear just what

Geronimo and Crook promised each other in the Sierra Madre. It may have been unclear at the time. Mickey Free did much of the interpreting, and already the Chiricahuas distrusted this dark-spirited loner. Later they would accuse him of deliberately altering what they said—for what purposes, only he knew. Mickey translated through the Spanish, his command of which, according to one who knew him, "did not include any use of tenses, so that it was extremely difficult to tell whether he meant the present, future, or past."

On May 22 or 23, the Chiricahuas announced they were going to hold a dance. As a token of their new friendship, they invited the White Mountain scouts to dance with their women. Normally a man had to offer a woman some token payment to partner her, but this time, said the Chiricahua, the dance would be free.

Here was Geronimo's trap. His hatred for Mexicans scarcely exceeded his revulsion for the scouts with red headbands. The plan, John Rope later learned, was to get the scouts dancing with the Chiricahua women, surround them with Chiricahua men, and shoot them all. "It didn't matter if they, the Chiricahuas, got killed, but they would get us scouts anyway." But Al Sieber, the chief of scouts, refused to let the White Mountain men join the dance. Whether he sniffed a trap or simply opposed the commingling on principle, he never made clear.

Finally, on May 30, Crook started for home. With him marched an entourage of 384 Chiricahua men, women, and children. Only Nana and Loco among the principal leaders were in the exodus; but all the chiefs and warriors had promised to gather up their bands and come to San Carlos in the near future. Crook would be much castigated for not bringing in Geronimo and other leading "hostiles." The fact remained that, through a combination of brilliant logistics, the tribulations of the Chiricahuas themselves, and a dash or two of dumb luck, he had turned the tide of the Apache war.

The Chiricahua rode and walked north toward the border. Bourke watched as little boys played a game of war: three "Mexicans" ran, hid, and were tracked to cover, where the "Apaches" killed one and captured two. Their parents walked with a heavier tread. By late June, the Chiricahua were settled at San Carlos. Most of them would never leave the reservation again.

Sixteen

■

Turkey Creek

When Crook resurfaced in Arizona in June 1883, he had been absent almost two months, during which no word of his progress had sifted back to the States. In the minds of worried citizens, even of officers left behind, his mission into the unknown had spurred fantasies of catastrophe. Custer's Last Stand was still imprinted on the American mind, and Crook's 328-man party had seemed to vanish altogether. "No word yet from Crook," the headlines ominously tolled.

Now the nation hailed the general's "brilliant success" in the Sierra Madre. Tucson hosted a banquet in his honor, "one of the grandest affairs ever witnessed" in the frontier town. Crook gave a dry résumé of his exploit; the crowd responded with cheers, toasts, and a pioneer's panegyric:

> All hail to the chief who accepts this ovation
> To honor the grandest achievement of arms,
> Ere long he may be the chief of the nation,
> The people will then be free of all harms.

But almost at once the grumbling began. Journalists took Crook to task for claiming, on the one hand, that he had obtained an unconditional surrender from the Chiricahua while, on the other, promising them amnesty for past crimes. Indeed, something like such a contradiction breathes in Crook's own official report. In his parleys with Geronimo and the chiefs beside the Bavispe, he had told them "that they had been bad Indians, and that I was unwilling to return without punishing them as they deserved"; that "I could not close my eyes to the atrocities of which they had been guilty." Yet the report concluded that it was "unjust to punish [the Chiricahua] for violations of a code of war he has never learned, and which he can with difficulty understand. . . . [T]o attempt to punish *all* after they had surrendered in good faith" would not only be "perfidious," but would start the war all over again.

Crook was not a duplicitous man: his honesty with the Apaches was the quality in him they most admired. The bind he had got himself into sprang from the fact that in the Sierra Madre, he was bluffing desperately, pretending a disinterested omnipotence that he knew he could not back up. When the Chiricahua weakened and agreed to come in, he was all but compelled to promise them amnesty. And he believed in amnesty: peace was more important than an eye for an eye.

The Arizona newspapers saw it otherwise. Trotting out shrill clichés of "ravished" women and "mutilated" men, they argued, as the *Star* succinctly put it, that "If the government fails now to hang these wretches by the wholesale, then Crook's campaign has been a failure."

As weeks went by and the chiefs and leaders who had promised to bring in their bands failed to appear, the public outcry in Arizona grew more rancorous. Crook noted defensively in his official report, "the fact that the Indians left behind have not come in is a matter of no significance. Indians have no idea of the value of time."

One of Crook's chief dilemmas was where to settle the Chiricahua. The mutual distrust and animosity between these people and the other reservation tribes had never been sharper, especially with the Chiricahuas' discovery of the horde of scouts in red headbands hunting them down. Crook's immediate solution was to encamp the newcomers as close as possible to army headquarters. "Feared and hated by the other Indians of the Reservation," wrote Britton Davis, a bit smugly, "they seemed to turn to us for reassurance and comforting." Davis, however, was notable among army men for his open-mindedness.

In fact we began to find them decidedly human. Much to my surprise I found that they had a keen sense of humor and were not averse to telling jokes on themselves as well as on others. The tales of their adventures in their years of warfare against whites and Mexicans would fill volumes.

Meanwhile Geronimo roamed as he always had. He was still determined to trade hostages to the Mexicans for the Apaches captured at Casas Grandes, his wife among them. The Mexican women he had seized in Chihuahua, and whom Crook had liberated, were full of dire stories about the Bedonkohe's cruelty. The women told Bourke "that the greatest terror prevailed in Chihuahua at the mere mention of the name of 'Hieronymo,' whom the peasantry believed to be the devil, sent to punish them for their sins."

The women also swore that on May 14, they had watched as Geronimo mutilated a hapless American he had seized near Casas Grandes before inflicting "final death by impaling." Under Geronimo's direction, his men slashed victims with lances or "crushed them to a jelly with heavy rocks"; one had his "privates" smashed between two flat rocks before the warriors' lances "darted through his body."

These instances of torture sound gratuitously sadistic. But Geronimo was obsessed with wringing information about Mexican and American military operations from his captives, and when they protested ignorance, his paranoid bent turned him blind with rage. Always before his mind was the image of his people sold into slavery—and slavery was worse by far to an Apache than torture. Nor had the Sonorans and Chihuahuans abated their practice: many of the captives who refused to work on local haciendas were sent to Yucatan, where most died of tropical diseases.

Three months passed with no sign of the bands still at large. Increasingly anxious, Crook sent Britton Davis and a company of Apache scouts—including a new complement of Chiricahua—to the Mexican border to try to make contact with the remaining fugitives. Davis camped at San Bernardino Springs, where Crook had crossed the border in May on his way into the Sierra Madre. There was no pretext now for entering Mexico, no "close pursuit" of "savage Indians." Davis sent three Chiricahua scouts across the line, with orders to go as far as they could without encountering Mexican soldiers. They came back empty-handed.

After weeks of waiting, Davis was rewarded when Naiche appeared with a dozen warriors and two dozen women and children. Davis escorted them to San Carlos, then returned to the border to wait. In November, Chihuahua arrived with ninety of his people. Other bands came in, until by the end of November the count of Chiricahua at San Carlos had reached 423. There was still no sign of Geronimo or Fun or Lozen.

As he had ridden with Naiche's band to the reservation, Davis had marveled at the Chiricahua physique: they were, he thought, "proportioned like deer," "perfect specimens of the racing type of athlete," their legs "sinewed as though with steel cords." (With their gift for ironic nicknames, the Chiricahua called the lieutenant Fat Boy in turn.) "The thought of attempting to catch one of them in the mountains," Davis mused, "gave me a queer feeling of helplessness, but I enjoyed a sensation of the beautiful in watching them."

Two months earlier, in September, a pair of New Mexico frontiersmen named Wilson and Leroy had claimed to have made contact with Geronimo near Casas Grandes in Chihuahua. Their shadowy adventure, which has all but escaped the historical record, may be half-apocryphal, yet certain details ring true.

A Mexican merchant had arrived in Deming, New Mexico, with news that Juh wanted to trade a captive white boy. Juh was dead by now, but Americans did not know this. On their own initiative, Wilson (who spoke good Spanish) and Leroy set off into Chihuahua, hoping to rescue Charley McComas. After preliminary negotiations with Chiricahua couriers, the two white men met with Geronimo about five miles from Casas Grandes on September 27. Theirs was a courageous deed (if it in fact took place), for Geronimo had twenty warriors with him.

They described the Bedonkohe as about thirty-seven years old (Geronimo was actually near sixty, but whites always underestimated his age), five feet ten, broad-shouldered, weighing about 190 pounds.

> He has a scar from a bullet wound across his forehead, has a bullet still in his left thigh and the third finger of the right hand is bent backward, also from a bullet wound. His face is a vicious one and made more repulsive by the scars upon it.

Geronimo was in a nasty, wary mood. In Spanish, through an Apache interpreter, he demanded of Wilson, "I want to ask you a question and I don't want you to lie. Are there any American troops or Crook's Coyoteros [scouts] in this country or on our trail?" Wilson said he knew of none, then inquired if Geronimo had a captive American boy. "What kind of boy do you look for?" Geronimo parried.

Yet when pressed, Geronimo went on to describe a white captive boy with blond hair and blue or gray eyes. He would sell the boy, but only for cartridges. The Chiricahua, Wilson discerned, were desperate for bullets. Geronimo offered to trade a horse for ten cartridges; later he offered $1,000 in coin for a thousand cartridges.

Geronimo knew, of course, that Charley McComas was dead. His offer of the boy sounds like a bluff. Perhaps he hoped to foist off a Mexican captive on the Americans, or trick them into supplying cartridges without keeping his end of the bargain. Perhaps the usual confusion in translating from Apache through Spanish to English reigned.

Geronimo further revealed that he had recently entered into a "treaty," or trading agreement, with Casas Grandes, but he was, as always, deeply distrustful of the Mexicans. The white men and the Chiricahuas agreed to meet the following morning. Geronimo promised to take the men to a camp where Charley was kept, then trade him for cartridges. Wilson and Leroy were in a tight spot. It was illegal by both Mexican and American law to furnish cartridges to "renegade" Indians. The Mexicans were already growing suspicious of the presence of the two men from north of the border. And Geronimo's plan could well be a trap, from which they might not emerge alive.

Yet (if they told the truth upon their return to New Mexico), Wilson and Leroy met Geronimo the next morning, intending to fulfill the bargain. As they waited for the interpreter to arrive, a Mexican guide rode up, mounted on a horse that Geronimo recognized as belonging to Joaquín Terrazas, the man who had led the massacre of Victorio's people at Tres Castillos. "His face grew ugly in its hideousness," the white men reported, "and his eyes flashed as he said, 'If the horse is here Terra[z]as is here, and if Terra[z]as is here the treaty is no good!' " All deals were off. Geronimo shook hands with the frontiersmen and rode away into the hills. Wilson and Leroy headed home.

There is just enough of the authentic in this wild tale to make it plausible that something like the exchange took place. If so, it seems to indicate that three months after his parley with Crook on the Bavispe, Geronimo had little intention of coming in to San Carlos. But his band's shortage of ammunition had made their very survival perilous.

Saluting the frontiersmen's brave errand, a Deming reporter wrote, with unconscious humor, "Too much credit cannot be given Messrs. Wilson and Leroy, though they were unsuccessful in getting the boy. They risked their lives and lived upon Mexican food, principally beans, and had a very hard time of it."

Chatto finally came in in February 1884, with nineteen other Chiricahuas. There was still no word from Geronimo, however. Davis waited patiently at the border; his scouts, now almost all Chiricahua men, less patiently. The latter put a medicine man to the task of "locating" Geronimo. After an all-day, all-night ritual, complete with sweat lodge, the burning of a "pungent powder," and nonstop incantations, the shaman announced that Geronimo was three days away, riding a white mule, and bringing many horses.

Four or five days later, Geronimo in fact arrived, riding a white pony. Like Betzinez at the campfire in Chihuahua, Davis was at a loss to explain the successful divination.

As the lieutenant watched from the border, he saw Geronimo's band approaching, some ninety strong with fifteen or sixteen warriors. Behind them by two miles trailed a huge cloud of dust. Davis thought at first it signified Mexican troops chasing the Chiricahua. The truth was more bizarre.

Geronimo was in his usual bad mood. He rode hard up to Davis and deliberately bumped the officer's mule with his pony's shoulder. In an angry voice, he demanded to know what Davis was doing there. He had made peace with the Americans, he told Davis; so why did he need an escort?

Davis pointed at the enigmatic cloud of dust. *"Ganado,"* Geronimo answered: "cattle," in Spanish. The ultimate provider, Geronimo had rustled 350 Mexican cows and calves and was driving them leisurely north. They were to sustain his people at San Carlos.

Davis was in a quandary. As he had escorted the previous bands to San Carlos, he had avoided all settlements and traveled forty to fifty miles a day, for Arizona was full of miners and ranchers who, with a little booze in their bellies, might waylay the Chiricahua rather than see them coddled on the reservation. Nor could he condone the theft without risking a deep offense to the Mexican government.

For the moment, the lieutenant had no choice but to proceed on

Geronimo's terms. With the huge herd, the Apaches moved only eighteen to twenty miles a day, and Geronimo complained that even this pace was too fast; Davis was "running all the fat off the cattle and they would not be fit for trading when we reached the Reservation."

The lieutenant played what he hoped would be his trump card. He told Geronimo that the entourage had to move fast, for there was a great chance that Mexican troops, using the border agreement of 1882, were already in close pursuit.

"Mexicans!" Geronimo spat. "Mexicans! My squaws can whip all the Mexicans in Chihuahua."

"But the Mexicans have plenty of cartridges," Davis argued, "and you have practically none."

"We don't fight Mexicans with cartridges," the warrior boasted. "Cartridges cost too much. We keep them to fight your white soldiers. We fight Mexicans with rocks."

The slow march was as harrowing as Davis feared. A debacle was narrowly averted at a ranch near Sulphur Springs, when a U. S. Marshal and a Customs official appeared. The cattle were contraband, they announced, and Geronimo and his Apaches were wanted for murder in Arizona. The whole band was under arrest, and if Davis did not cooperate, the pair would ride to the town of Willcox and mobilize a posse.

Failing to talk these officials out of their hare-brained mission, Davis slyly got them drunk on a bottle of "good Scotch whiskey." As soon as they passed out, Davis found Geronimo, told him the truth, and urged moving out the whole party, cattle and all, under cover of night. Outraged, Geronimo at first refused; he seemed to Davis bent on facing down the officials in the morning and, if need be, shooting them.

Davis appealed to the warrior's pride. He "suggested that probably he was afraid his people were not smart enough to get away without the men at the ranch knowing it." Geronimo took the bait. By morning the whole train—men, women, children, and cattle—had such a lead on the hungover officials that the latter gave up the chase.

As soon as Geronimo's band reached San Carlos, their livestock were confiscated. The cattle were slaughtered for agency beef and their Mexican owners duly compensated in dollars. This was really Crook's only course of action, if he wished to keep the good will of the Mexican government. It is surprising that Geronimo, with his reservation experience, did not anticipate as much. Side by side with his craftiness and habitual mistrust, the great warrior possessed a broad streak of naiveté. The credulity that led his fellow warriors to play practical jokes on Geronimo allowed him to play this unwitting joke on himself.

The confiscation rankled Geronimo for the rest of his life. As he dictated his autobiography in 1905, he dwelt bitterly on the event:

> Soon after we arrived at San Carlos the officer in charge, General Crook, took the horses and cattle away from us. I told him that these were not white men's cattle, but belonged to us, for we had taken them from the Mexicans during our wars. I also told him that we did not intend to kill these animals, but that we wished to keep them and raise stock on our range. He would not listen to me, but took the stock.

The very last band of fugitives came in to San Carlos in May 1884. A handful of Chiricahua might still be running loose in the Sierra Madre, although Crook doubted it. In any event, the general could be forgiven for thinking that he had put an end to the Apache war—to the last Indian war in the United States.

Like most thinkers in America at the time, Crook believed that the Apaches, along with all other Indians, must assimilate to white society. He was optimistic that they could do so. In "The Apache Problem," he expressed his gratification at the early strides the reservation dwellers were making as farmers, as capitalists (a cent for every pound of hay), even as scholars. "He is changing both inside and out," Crook wrote of the Chiricahua. As early as 1885, Crook would argue for extending the right to vote to the Apaches.

To the end of assimilation, like General Howard and John Clum before him, Crook gathered a group of Apaches to send east and impress with the might of the white man's civilization. Crook had trouble finding volunteers; most of the Chiricahua still believed that Taza had been poisoned in Washington in 1876. Finally some ten Apaches traveled with an officer to New York City and Washington.

The visit was dismaying to Indians and White Eyes alike. One chief told his host that he had decided to count all the white people he saw; before the train had even left Arizona he had given up. Crook's hope that the Apaches would "bring back tales of the white man's power and the futility of the Indian's efforts to oppose it" was fully realized. The shock of the Apaches was crystallized in a tragicomic episode. Lodged on an upper floor of the Fifth Avenue Hotel in Manhattan, the Indians gawked out the window at the passersby. After a while, they asked their host why the people on the street kept walking around and around the hotel. When the officer "explained that they were not the same people, but different ones passing by, [the Apaches] told him he was lying to have some fun with them."

On their return to San Carlos, the emissaries were treated just as Howard's had been in 1872. "The delegates were denounced as liars who had been corrupted by the white man, and for a time they were avoided as though they had the plague," Davis observed. "One of them went insane and several were long in recovering from a sort of daze, refusing to discuss what they had seen."

Crook had no illusions that the Chiricahua would easily mix with the other Apaches at San Carlos, but it was too late to think of establishing a separate reservation for them. With wisdom and magnanimity, he made a surprising decision, asking the Chiricahua to choose their own land anywhere on either of the two contiguous reservations. It was one of the rare instances in Southwestern history when an official bothered to ask the Apaches where they wished to live.

The Chiricahua unhesitatingly chose Turkey Creek, a tributary of the Black River on the Fort Apache reservation. The creek lay forty miles northeast of San Carlos, but Crook was confident that, under the stewardship of Britton Davis, Geronimo's people might dwell peacefully and productively there.

By the end of June 1884, the 512 Chiricahua were settled in their new home. Davis let them build their wickiups where they pleased. The lieutenant himself was delighted with the beauty of Turkey Creek. A perennial stream of cool, clear water wound across a plateau covered with tall grasses, indenting a shallow valley. Tall pines punctuated the clearings. Sometime before the fourteenth century, the Mogollon had built pueblos along the creek; the outlines of their walls, the scatter of their potsherds were still visible in abundance half a millennium later. The valley was cool in summer, mild and open to the southern sun in winter.

And the Chiricahua went at their new life with a zest and humor that won Davis's heart. With rare acumen, the lieutenant sensed the violence it would do to the Apaches' culture to try to turn them overnight from nomads into farmers. He urged an experiment in pastoralism instead, pleading that his charges be given sheep and cattle to raise. The Navajo, Davis knew, had quickly adapted to sheep-herding. But the Bureau of Indian Affairs in Washington overruled him: the Chiricahua must be farmers.

Even before leaving San Carlos, the men had made a few attempts at plowing land. Davis had witnessed the comic results.

> The ponies, unaccustomed to a slow gait, preferred to trot or gallop, and the plowpoints were oftener above ground than in it. Now and then a point would strike a hidden root or stump; then the plowman would execute a somersault over the plow handles, to the great delight of his friends.

Davis was amazed at certain Apache skills. There were big, fat frogs in pools near his own tent, whose croaking kept him awake at night and whose meat would make a welcome addition to his diet. Unable to catch any himself, he offered two small boys a nickel apiece for all they could bag, thinking they might get a dozen at most. "In two or three hours my contractors appeared," Davis wrote, "with more frogs than both [Sam] Bowman [Davis's chief of scouts] and I could have eaten in a week, and Bowman did not care for frogs." The boys had shot them with bow and arrow.

One day a sixty-year-old woman appeared with a wild turkey in her arms. She had run it down and caught it—a routine Apache deed, but one that almost no white man ever learned to perform. The woman told Davis that, as Apaches never ate turkeys (because turkeys ate snakes), they caught them merely for sport. Davis accepted the bird and broiled it for dinner.

Gradually the lieutenant came to know individual Chiricahuas—not the chiefs so much as the ordinary men and women. He listened for hours to their accounts of their own history, with Mickey Free or Sam Bowman translating for him; he heard tales of Mangas Coloradas and Cochise and Victorio that differed greatly from the white man's versions. Davis soon began to sympathize with the Chiricahua view. With surprising openness, he concluded that

> In treachery, broken pledges on the part of high officials, lies, thievery, slaughter of defenseless women and children, and every crime

in the catalogue of man's inhumanity to man the Indian was a mere amateur compared to the "noble white man." His crimes were retail, ours wholesale.

On the whole, Davis thought, the Chiricahuas were happy on Turkey Creek. In September, a delegate from the Indian Rights Association in Philadelphia, one of those eastern do-gooders whom even the most liberal officer in Arizona despised, made a tour of the reservation. Expecting to find abuses, he filed instead a favorable report. The Chiricahuas needed clothing, he said, but they had seventy-five acres under cultivation, and even such chiefs as Nana and Naiche claimed to be pleased with the army's treatment. "They said," the delegate wrote, "they wanted to turn their faces the same way as the whites, to work and make money." Even Geronimo, as he came to Turkey Creek, had told Crook, "I am hunting for a new world. I think that the world is mother of us all, and that God wants us all to be brothers."

One day an astounding thing happened. A wagon driven by soldiers came up to Davis's tent. Inside were five Chiricahua women, including Kaywaykla's grandmother (whom he thought dead) and his sister (who he assumed was in Mexican slavery). The five had vanished in the massacre at Tres Castillos, almost four years ago.

Davis thought the five women had been exchanged by the Mexican government in return for the captives Crook had saved from Geronimo. The Chiricahua on Turkey Creek soon learned the true story. The women had been taken all the way south to Mexico City, where they were sold into slavery and put to work on a big hacienda. They had bided their time, developed secret signals with each other, and finally slipped off in the night. Moving furtively on foot, they headed north through unfamiliar country. The women had waited until the prickly pear came into fruit, which happened in winter so far south. Living mainly on the fruit, suffering from the cold with one blanket among the five, separating and reuniting at times, they had walked and walked until at last they recognized the mountains of southern Chihuahua. At one point they found goods in a cave Victorio had stocked six years before. Finally they had crossed the border and come in to a town on the Cañada Alamosa; the soldiers carried them to Turkey Creek.

The distance was a thousand miles as the crow flies, much longer as the women had walked.

Despite the outward calm on Turkey Creek, there were undercurrents of dissatisfaction, to some of which Davis was oblivious. The lieutenant had enlisted a number of Chiricahua, including Chatto and Chihuahua, as scouts; others, among them Geronimo, Naiche, and Nana, had haughtily refused. Now Davis, who had taken a liking to Chatto, promoted him to "first sergeant," intensifying the distrust other warriors such as Kaytennae and Geronimo felt for the brash young man.

From the moment he had first stepped on the reservation at San Carlos, Kaytennae had been full of gloom. "We would find him standing silent and alone near an open window, or at a corner of the building, or near a doorway," Davis remembered; "watchful, but surly and unresponsive when spoken to." Crook's "secret scouts," or spies, reported that Kaytennae regretted having come in and was waiting for a chance to break out.

Davis came to like most of the Chiricahua, but he could never warm to Geronimo. In part this was a response to Geronimo's own wary and aloof manner: with his previous experience at San Carlos, shackled and under a death sentence, the Bedonkohe knew better than to lower his guard. With Mangus, Chihuahua, and a few others, he pitched his camp at the greatest distance from Davis's, miles up Turkey Creek. "Geronimo never came to my tent unless he wanted something," Davis claimed, "and this in four months was not more than eight or ten times."

Davis ridiculed Geronimo's efforts as a farmer. One day the warrior asked the lieutenant to visit his little plot, showing Davis a blister on his palm as token of a monumental effort. When Davis made the visit the next day, he found Geronimo sitting on a rail in the shade "with one of his wives fanning him. The other two were hoeing a quarter-acre patch of partially cleared ground, in which a few sickly looking sprouts of corn were struggling for life." Yet Davis himself acknowledged that Turkey Creek was poor soil for farming.

Later Davis would come to revile Geronimo, and a retrospective antipathy colors his account of life on Turkey Creek. Geronimo, Davis insisted, was "a thoroughly vicious, intractable, and treacherous man" whose "word, no matter how earnestly pledged, was worthless. . . . His only redeeming traits were courage and determination."

Something like this view became the stereotype of Geronimo among whites after 1883. Thomas Cruse swore that "even the Apaches thoroughly disliked and distrusted Geronimo." It became the fashion to read his nature in his remarkable face, as one pioneer who met him at San Carlos did in 1884:

> Geronimo's appearance was not prepossessing; his face was wrinkled, eyes keen and cruel. He was cool and calculating, the narrow forehead and firm lines indicating a superior degree of craftiness, and giving forth the idea of his cold, sneering character.

On Turkey Creek, Davis had retained his own spies, one of them a woman. Instead of a tap on the window pane, a pebble tossed against Davis's tent in the night alerted him to a messenger with secret intelligence. One night, Chihuahua, suspicious, hid in the dark near Davis's tent. He heard a pebble bounce off canvas three different times, and watched as Mickey Free, Chatto, and the woman informer crawled into the lieutenant's tent. So Chatto was a spy! Chihuahua eavesdropped as the secret agents warned Davis of an uprising that was brewing in the souls of Kaytennae and Geronimo.

In the morning, Chihuahua angrily confronted Davis with his discovery. Then he took off his scout's headband, rifle, and ammunition belt and threw them contemptuously in the corner, spitting out, through Sam Bowman's translation, "Take this stuff and give it to your spies."

"You can't quit," said Davis. "You've just reenlisted."

"I am quit," answered Chihuahua, and walked out of the tent.

The discovery of this treachery (which Davis's own memoir neglects to mention) badly damaged the Chiricahuas' friendship with the lieutenant; but it served to confirm their distrust of Chatto. Mickey Free, they thought, was also a thoroughly unreliable character. Whenever they needed to communicate with Davis, the Apaches sought Sam Bowman to translate; but Bowman, as a part-Choctaw, spoke only rudimentary Apache, while Free, thanks to his years of youthful captivity, was fluent.

Thus the Chihuahua sometimes had to resort to the bent translations of this "coyote" whom they hated. As Kaywaykla said many years later, "It is a terrible thing for the fate of an inarticulate people [i. e., in English] to depend upon the spoken word of a renegade with no whit of integrity." Though Davis had befriended him, no one ever knew Mickey Free well. With his damaged eye, his unkempt hair, his shabby clothing, he was, a pioneer recalled, "an indolent creature[,] and a more repulsive object could not be imagined." John G. Bourke held Mickey at arm's length, finding him "the most curious & interesting combination of good humor and sullenness, generosity, craft, and bloodthirsty cruelty to be found in America."

The simmering trouble boiled over in August. Crook had forbade two Apache practices of long standing: the making of tizwin, and the right for men to beat their wives. The Chiricahua protested that in the Sierra Madre, when they had agreed to come in, they had made no promises to the Tan Wolf concerning these practices, which were their own business. The white men had their whiskey—Davis himself was fond of the bottle—so what was wrong with their drinking tizwin? And a man whose wife was disobedient and who failed to discipline her would be ridiculed by his friends. Davis, Crook, and other officers had been appalled to see several women on the reservation with noses severed on account of adultery; their abhorrence overwhelmed any glimmerings of cultural relativism they might have entertained.

Kaytennae in particular continued to drink tizwin, in defiance of Davis. According to the lieutenant's account of the August showdown, his spies had told him that Kaytennae was castigating the other warriors as fools for having come in to the reservation. One day Mickey Free and the woman spy informed Davis that as he had hunted turkey the day before, Kaytennae, in the midst of a tizwin spree, had lain in ambush for Davis. Only the chance meander of a turkey had turned Davis's path out of the ravine and away from the fatal trap.

The Chiricahua version denies this scenario. Chatto had always been jealous of Kaytennae, since Nana had groomed him to be next chief of the Chihenne; now Chatto and Mickey Free made up the ambush story out of thin air.

Davis came to Kaytennae's wickiup and arrested him. Both white and Chiricahua versions agree that a tense and angry confrontation narrowly escaped turning to gunfire and bloodshed. Kaytennae demanded again and again that basic American right: to be confronted by his accuser. Davis told him he would learn the identity of his accuser at San Carlos.

Under armed guard, the young warrior rode to the army headquarters forty miles away. There he was tried, in absentia, by a jury of White Mountain Apaches, and convicted of vague charges. Emmet Crawford, the captain in charge of the trial, sentenced Kaytennae to five years' imprisonment, and Crook determined that his time should be spent at Alcatraz. In the end, Kaytennae spent eighteen months on "the Rock"; imprisonment broke his spirit, and he came back to the reservation a reduced and docile man.

The shock at Kaytennae's disappearance added to the troubles on Turkey Creek. When he learned of the warrior's arrest, the young Kaywaykla, whom Kaytennae had adopted after the boy's natural father had been killed, buried himself under a blanket and sobbed convulsively, while old Nana tried to console him. Chatto, now openly hostile, took pleasure in telling Kaywaykla that his stepfather "was chained on a rock so far from land that no man can swim across that water."

"You know well that he is a liar," Nana sneered. "There is no water so wide but that Kaytennae can swim across it. I have traveled far and seen all the rivers in the land."

Through the winter of 1884–1885 the Chiricahua kept a jittery peace on Turkey Creek. The appearance of calm fooled most observers, including a captain who, sent out by Crook to investigate Davis's warnings of trouble, concluded that the lieutenant's "fears were groundless; those Indians could hardly be *driven* out on the war trail."

It was not until May that the lighted fuse burned down to the powder keg. At San Carlos, new frictions between the civilian agent and the army officers were catching the Apaches in the usual squeeze; once more, "the ancient curse of dual control," Interior Department versus War, played havoc on the reservation. Later Davis would try to blame the San Carlos mess for the disruption on Turkey Creek, on the grounds that "The seed of divided authority sprouts and bears its natural fruit—defiance of all authority."

But the problem lay closer at hand. When a Chiricahua woman came to Davis with her arm broken in two places, he arrested and jailed the husband, then gave him a two-year sentence on his own authority. Soon thereafter he jailed a man who had organized a tizwin drunk.

On May 15, 1885, Davis awoke to find all the chiefs and leading warriors gathered outside his tent, demanding a talk. Chihuahua and Nana acted as spokesmen, while Geronimo sat silent; but Davis was sure the Bedonkohe's malevolence was at the heart of the confrontation. Chihuahua repeated the old arguments that his men had the right to brew all the tizwin they wanted and to beat their misbehaving wives. When he tried to explain these practices from the Chiricahua point of view, Davis interrupted with a condescending lecture.

Suddenly Nana stood up, blurted out in Apache to Mickey Free,

"Tell the Fat Boy that I had killed many men before he was out of baby grass," and stalked out of the tent. Mickey was afraid to translate, until Davis ordered him to.

"We all drank tizwin last night," bragged Chihuahua. "What are you going to do about it? Are you going to put us all in jail? You have no jail big enough."

The frightened lieutenant tried to buy time, replying that the decision was too big for him to make alone. He would wire General Crook at once.

Davis was already too late. The two-year peace had shattered.

Seventeen

■

Canyon of the Funnels

Britton Davis fired off a telegram to San Carlos, detailing the showdown that had just taken place and beseeching Crook's instructions. Unfortunately the general was absent from post headquarters; the wire fell into the hands of a captain who had been in Arizona only two months. He showed it to Al Sieber, the veteran chief of scouts.

Sieber, sleeping off his own whiskey drunk, was not happy at being wakened. Groggily he read the telegram, muttered, "It's nothing but a tizwin drunk. Don't pay any attention to it. Davis will handle it," and fell back to sleep. The captain filed away the message, which Crook read four months later. The general would insist that if he had received the telegram, the outbreak would never have occurred; or, if it *had* occurred, the renegades would have "been taught a lesson they would never have forgotten" before they could reach Mexico.

This was wishful thinking. The disgruntled Chiricahua on Turkey Creek were bound to flee, and no telegram could stop them. Davis was right in one respect, however: Geronimo was the architect of the breakout.

Ten months later, when he next talked to Crook, Geronimo would explain his reasons.

I was living quietly and contented [on Turkey Creek], doing and thinking of no harm. . . . I was living peaceably and satisfied when people began to speak bad of me. . . . I was behaving well. I hadn't killed a horse or man, American or Indian. I don't know what was the matter with the people in charge of us. They knew this to be so, and yet they said I was a bad man and the worst man there; but what harm had I done? . . .

Some time before I left an Indian named Wodiskay had a talk with me. He said, "they are going to arrest you," but I paid no attention to him, knowing that I had done no wrong; and the wife of Mangus, "Huera," told me that they were going to seize me and put me and Mangus in the guard-house, and I learned from the American and Apache soldiers, from Chat[t]o and Mickey Free, that the Americans were going to arrest me and hang me, and so I left.

There is no reason to doubt Geronimo's explanation, even granting his hypersensitivity to persecution. The Chiricahua had seen Kaytennae whisked from their midst on a flimsy excuse, to be carried away and locked up at unimaginable Alcatraz. Mickey Free and Chatto had been overheard filling Davis's ear late at night with tales of Geronimo's dark plots. Chatto had adopted the unpleasant white man's habit of walking about Turkey Creek and, whenever he met a chief, drawing his finger across his throat, a mocking prophecy of beheading.

In the middle of the night of May 17, 1885, some 42 warriors and between 90 and 103 women and children fled Turkey Creek. The leaders of the exodus were Geronimo, Nana, Naiche, Chihuahua, Mangus, and the woman warrior, Lozen. The only chief among the nearly four hundred Chiricahua who stayed on the reservation was Loco. In the pursuit that ensued, as many as one hundred Chiricahua scouts, led by Chatto, would hunt down the warriors with whom only two years before they had stood shoulder to shoulder in the Sierra Madre.

Geronimo and Naiche guarded the rear of the fleeing band. Old Nana directed a crucial tactic. In the past, Apaches had cut the telegraph wires to impede the communication of the White Eyes, but the line-breaks were quickly found and repaired. Now Nana sent young boys up the trees that held the wire, where they cut the metal line and spliced each break with a buckskin thong. It would take weeks to restore the line to service.

By the time Davis could rally pursuit, the Chiricahua had a twenty-mile head start. At dawn the lieutenant gazed across a broad valley at the distant cloud of dust the renegades were raising, and knew at once "that further pursuit by troops was useless and that we were in for a long campaign in Mexico."

Although by now, to war-weary army officers, such a recognition as Davis's was all but automatic, it bears noting that a twenty-mile head start on horseback meant only two hours of hard riding, and that more than two-thirds of the fugitives were women and children, chased by a force made up entirely of army men and Indian scouts. It was not only their skill at traveling fast, but their knack of scattering and hiding in a bare landscape that made Apaches so elusive a quarry.

In the Mogollon Mountains, the various bands separated to confound pursuit; some went directly south toward Mexico, but others circled back north, where the White Eyes would least expect them. In due time they, too, found their way south of the border.

There may have been another reason for the bands' separating. Davis later claimed that Apaches who stayed on the reservation told him that Geronimo and Mangus had worked a ruse to induce their allies to flee; they had come to Chihuahua, Naiche, and Nana and told them that Chatto and Davis had already been killed and that all the scouts had deserted. According to this telling, Chihuahua was so incensed when he discovered the deception, he set out with two friends to kill Geronimo; but the Bedonkohe, warned in time, fled south. Chihuahua's and Naiche's bands then hid out in Arizona for a while, intending to return to the reservation, but when they spotted Davis's troops hard on their trail, they themselves headed for Mexico.

There may be some truth to this account, which nearly all historians have taken at face value. Such a ruse would not be out of character for Geronimo, who had masterminded the forced removal of Loco's people from San Carlos three years before. As a manipulator, he was without peer among the Chiricahua. Yet no Apache source confirms even a hint of such deception. Chihuahua's own son, who was in the fleeing band, later said simply,

> After my father quit as a scout for the army, he knew that he would have to leave the reservation. He and Geronimo left at the same time. . . .
> When we got almost to the ridge we saw a cloud of dust and knew that the cavalry was after us. That is when Geronimo and Chihuahua separated, he and Naiche to go south and my father northeast.

The strongest argument against Davis's theory is that Chihuahua, Nana, and Naiche would soon reunite with Geronimo and fight together against Mexicans and Americans alike, Naiche to the very end of Geronimo's campaign.

Davis, of course, had a vested interest in minimizing the disaffection at Turkey Creek, which the story of Geronimo's ruse would accomplish. The lieutenant was an honest and self-critical man, but he had much to fear from Crook's wrath. It may be that Davis was misinformed by Chiricahuas who stayed at Turkey Creek; there was no shortage of men there, starting with Chatto and Mickey Free, who would tell him what he wanted to hear.

Using the network of telegraph wires that now spidered across southern Arizona, Crook launched twenty troops of cavalry and as many as two hundred Indian scouts out of five different forts; soon there were two thousand men pursuing the fugitives. With the scouts leading them, the troops had no trouble finding trails but were all but incapable of closing for a fight. The rigors of the Chiricahua escape had to be indirectly deciphered, as when pursuers found two dead infants—born to women as they fled and discarded of necessity.

Before they reached Mexico, the fleeing bands killed at least seventeen settlers and stole about one hundred fifty horses, losing not a single man, woman, or child of their own. Even as they ran for the border, the fugitive leaders seemed to have an uncanny knowledge of their pursuers' movements. In Guadalupe Canyon, near the border, Chihuahua's band hid near the camp of a cavalry troop on their trail, waited till the officers were off scouting, then attacked the camp, slaying five of the seven privates left to guard it.

When they attacked an isolated ranch, the Chiricahua killed every White Eye they found. Near Silver City, New Mexico, shocked civilians came upon the carnage of a raid they attributed to Geronimo, but which was probably perpetrated by Chihuahua. The Apaches had killed the rancher, his wife, and their three-year-old daughter. A five-year-old girl was discovered, still alive, hanging from a meat hook that entered the back of her head: she died a few hours later.

The panic of the citizens and the rhetoric of the newspapers reached an unprecedented pitch. Lieutenant Charles B. Gatewood, camped in southwestern New Mexico, wrote his wife: "We are still aimlessly wandering around these mountains hunting for Indians that are not. . . . Some of the settlers are wild with alarm & raise all kinds of stories to induce us to camp near their places." Prospectors fled to town at the sight of tracks left by Gatewood's scouts. Geronimo's warriors seemed to lurk behind every tree.

The outcry against Crook and the army raged like a brushfire across the Southwest. Headlines ridiculed the military effort: "BRAVE CAPTAIN CHAFFEE, And How he Didn't Fight the Apaches." Citizens sent their protests straight to President Grover Cleveland. The people of Pima County, Arizona (Tucson), proclaimed to Cleveland that "we, as American citizens, look with unutterable horror on the management of Indian affairs as conducted in Arizona and New Mexico." In the righteousness of their indignation, Arizonans did not bother to distinguish one Apache tribe from another. As a newspaper editorialized:

> The truth is, there is no more room in this territory for the Apache. For him THE RESERVATION SYSTEM IS NONSENSE. The people are taxed to maintain a horde of murderous banditti, in whose hands the government has placed arms and ammunition. When the lazy life of the reservation wearies these braves they sally forth, massacre, rob, torture, burn, pillage.

Settlers wrote personal letters to the White House, such as the heartfelt missive pleading for what would amount to a personal bodyguard, from a rancher in Locline, Arizona:

> Dont throw this away unread. I am a pioneer—living on the Mexican line, in South-Eastern Arizona. We are surrounded by the Apaches. We have many small children and women with us. We are poorly armed, there is not a soldier in hundreds of miles of us. . . .
> We are expecting a descent upon us at any moment. In the house in which I live are eight children—five of whom are girls. In the event of an attack upon us every one of them would be cruelly butchered or led away into a captivity worse than death. . . .
> I am writing on the only paper in the house, and hastily. . . . So for the sake of humanity send us some of the soldiers who are idle and who could be the means of saving many a life if sent here.

"Surrounded by the Apaches"—it was the primal terror of every citizen, and it is an image that lives on in Western movies. At the time, there were only forty-two Chiricahua warriors on the loose, scattered across a land as large as New England. But southern Arizona and New

Mexico had succumbed to something like mass hysteria, a state that would persist for another fifteen months.

The depth of that hysteria begs analysis. From May 1883 through May 1885, Crook could brag that not a single Apache depredation had occurred in Arizona or New Mexico. Not only the citizens of the Southwest, but those all over the country sighed their relief. More than two centuries of warfare against the Indians had come to a denouement at San Carlos. Manifest Destiny had proved its inexorable truth. The Indian, if he were to survive at all, must take on the white man's ways.

The passion of this near-universal belief can be seen in the aftermath of Little Bighorn. In 1876, the fury of the Sioux and Cheyenne who wiped out Custer's men was so intense that the warriors beat the dead soldiers' faces to a pulp, while the women cut off their genitals. The rage for American revenge was equally bloody. But once the Sioux and Cheyenne were conquered, with surprising celerity white America turned the "savage" into a sideshow curiosity, a trivialized totem of conquest. By 1883, when Geronimo was roaming the Sierra Madre, Sitting Bull had joined Buffalo Bill's Wild West Show, where he kissed little girls and sold his autograph for a dollar. In 1886, bizarre though it seems, army veterans held a ten-year reunion at the Little Bighorn battlefield—to which they invited the surviving Sioux and Cheyenne chiefs, who camped beside them, shook their hands, and drank their whiskey.

In the summer of 1885, however, Geronimo was still the archfiend, "the wickedest Indian that ever lived."

Once he was sure all the renegades were in Mexico, Crook tried to seal the border against their return. He moved his own headquarters to Fort Bowie, to be closer to the action. From the Rio Grande almost to the mouth of the Colorado River, he deployed small groups of soldiers to guard every known water hole, each troop with five Apache scouts who rode out daily searching for signs of the fugitives. Behind this front line he strung another net of cavalry, to intercept any Chiricahua who might break through the border patrol. In the end, even this, the most thorough attempt to that date in American history to guard a border against "outlaws," failed to thwart the fugitives, who crossed back into the United States more or less at will.

In an unguarded moment, Crook confessed his grudging admiration for his adversary's tenacity to a Tombstone reporter:

> When Geronimo left the reservation [said Crook], he was suffering
> from an incurable disease; he was severely wounded in an engage-
> ment with Lieut. Davis' command in the side and arm, he bled
> profusely, and yet this fellow and his band traveled over 700 miles
> in twenty days immediately after the fight.

Geronimo's incurable disease must have gone into miraculous remis-
sion, for he would live another twenty-four years. Davis himself never
claimed to have shot Geronimo during his flight; but there is no doubt
the warrior had often been wounded.

After sealing the border, Crook sent two strong companies of sol-
diers and scouts, led by Emmet Crawford and Britton Davis, into
Mexico. Through the summer of 1885, they doggedly pursued the
Chiricahua. Unlike Crook's well-planned jaunt two years before, Davis
and Crawford's thrusts had the ragtag character of guerrilla warfare.
Near Oputo, just west of the Sierra Madre in Sonora, a Mexican farmer,
ignorant of the significance of the red headbands, waylaid two of
Davis's scouts and shot them, killing one and badly wounding another.
The infuriated scouts in camp at once set out to ride to Oputo and
massacre the populace. Only with great difficulty did Chatto and Davis
dissuade them.

In the blazing heat of summer, travel alone was an ordeal. Davis's
surgeon recorded 128° in the shade one afternoon. A packer remembered the fatigue and futility of the constant march: "The Indians lured
us more deeply into the mountains. Our maps were worthless. The
cavalry horses and the men were worn out, and the clothing of all was
in tatters."

The observant Davis was struck by the squalor of the small Mexican
towns—"the poorest communities I have ever seen." The Apache
terror, which the villagers had begun to hope was over, had reawak-
ened. In Nacori, a town of 313 souls, there were only fifteen adult
males: "Every family had lost one or more male members at the hands
of the Apache."

Davis and Crawford occasionally crossed paths with Mexican troops
also out hunting the fugitives. In Davis's eyes, the Mexicans were a
sorry lot, most of them ex-convicts pressed into service, subsisting on
wretchedly meager rations of parched corn, dried beef, and sugar.
The two-pronged attack ought to have harried the Chiricahuas into a
corner. In the end, it would cause more harm than good.

The determination of Crawford and Davis paid off, however, in small dividends. In June, scouts under Chatto struck Chihuahua's camp, killing one woman and capturing fifteen women and children, including all of Chihuahua's family. One month later, a splinter group managed to locate Geronimo's camp, which they attacked, killing a boy and a woman and capturing another fifteen, among them a wife and son of Geronimo. Nana was at first reported slain, as he had been at least half a dozen times in previous years, but the lame old chief escaped once more. These skirmishes, though unimportant as military achievements, took a heavy psychological toll on the Chiricahua, especially in the capture of family members.

Having found Geronimo's trail, Crawford was dead set on keeping it. He sent the strongest party he could muster in pursuit, under Davis's command: they included Chatto, Al Sieber, Mickey Free, and forty of the best scouts.

It was now, in August–September 1885, that Geronimo performed one of the most virtuosic feats in all the Apache wars. Encumbered by women and children, he led his band for twenty-four days over a distance of more than five hundred miles, with Davis at his heels. The trail led south along the eastern edge of the Sierra Madre, deep into Chihuahua, then back north again. To befuddle the pursuers, Geronimo would change directions four times within a short span, or make a diametric turn on rocky ground where even the mules failed to leave prints. Not only did the handpicked band of soldiers never catch up to Geronimo's people; by the end they had hopelessly lost the trail. Worn out and fed up, Davis resigned his commission and settled down to manage a ranch in Chihuahua.

Geronimo was not finished. With only four companions, he slipped effortlessly through Crook's double line of border guards and headed north within Arizona. After the breakout from Turkey Creek, the remaining Chiricahua had been moved to Fort Apache, where they camped under the noses of the post command. Somehow Geronimo knew this. In the middle of the night of September 22, the five Chiricahuas sneaked past a patrol of White Mountain scouts, found the wickiup of Geronimo's family, recaptured Geronimo's wife and a three-year-old daughter, and got away in the dark.

To throw off the pursuers even further, Geronimo's party now rode far east into New Mexico, where they kidnapped some Mescalero women; Geronimo took the youngest as another wife. (She came to love her husband deeply.) To complete his cavalier adventure, Geronimo led the band, women and children and all, back into Mexico. No army man had seen them even from a distance.

One of the kidnapped Mescaleros was a young boy who later left a record of his captivity. Through the winter of 1885–1886, Geronimo trained him for the warpath, just as he had Kaywaykla's group of boys in the Stronghold in the Sierra Madre. He fashioned a toy bow and arrow for the boy to practice with. Miserable at first, the boy learned to revere his mentor. And he came to understand why Geronimo's depredations were so ruthless. It was the need for ammunition that motivated the Chiricahua raids into the United States—Mexican cartridges could not always be used with the Winchester and Springfield rifles the Apaches coveted. Many years later, the former captive would say:

> I do not think that [Geronimo] wanted to kill, but there were cases when he had no choice. If he were seen by a civilian, it meant that he would be reported to the military and they'd be after us. So there was nothing to do but kill the civilian and his entire family. It was terrible to see little children killed. I do not like to talk of it. I do not like to think of it. But the soldiers killed our women and children, too. Don't forget that.

By November, the fugitives were once again woefully short of cartridges. Chihuahua's older brother, a first-rate warrior named Ulzana, volunteered to lead an ammunition raid into Arizona. Like his brother, Ulzana had been an army scout; he had served, in fact, among the soldiers hunting down Nana in 1881. In the words of one historian, "Ulzana learned much about the arts and tactics of raiding from Nana, the old past-master, by following him with the troops and observing his methods and stratagems."

The sheer statistics of Ulzana's raid, the last of its kind, argue that it was the most skillful of all the Chiricahua lightning strokes. With only ten to twelve men—fewer even than Nana had in 1881—Ulzana rode 1200 miles in two months, killed thirty-eight, stole two hundred fifty horses and mules, and lost but a single warrior. The most daring of Ulzana's deeds came at the beginning of his wild foray, when he attacked Fort Apache itself, taking it completely by surprise. Driven more by the thirst for revenge than by the quest for bullets, attacking uncharacteristically at night, Ulzana's Chiricahuas killed twelve White Mountain Apaches within sight of the army buildings.

Ulzana's raid reduced Crook to exasperation. His response was, for the times, a radical one. Recognizing that white soldiers so impeded the Apache scouts as to make pursuit futile, he sent Crawford out with only three other officers, a pack train, and one hundred Indian scouts. The model for this high-speed party had been presented to Crook two years before in the Sierra Madre, when the scouts themselves had begged to be allowed to go ahead of the main expedition. Emmet Crawford had led that force; he was the obvious choice to lead the new hunt for Geronimo.

Davis, who had soldiered much with him, admired the captain without stint:

> Crawford was born a thousand years too late. *Sans peur et sans reproche* would have been sung of him in ballads of the Middle Ages. Mentally, morally, and physically he would have been an ideal knight of King Arthur's Court. Six feet one, gray-eyed, untiring, he was an ideal cavalryman and devoted to his troop, as were the men of it to him.

Crawford had a good sense of humor, Davis added, "but something had saddened his early life and I never knew him to laugh out loud."

On December 11, the streamlined command crossed the Mexican border once more. They moved steadily south in Sonora for three weeks, finding nothing. In Nacori, on the western edge of the mountains, Crawford set up a base camp and sent out scouting parties. At last, in early January, one of them came across a Chiricahua trail near the Aros River. The scouts reported that it led to Geronimo's band, holed up in a range known as the Devil's Backbone, reputed to be "the roughest region in all Mexico."

Crawford drove his scouts through a forty-eight-hour march without sleep. His party was more than one hundred fifty miles from the border, farther south in Mexico than any U.S. command had ever chased Apaches. On the evening of January 9, the scouts, still undetected, reached a point only twelve miles from Geronimo's camp. They pushed through the night and attacked at dawn.

The charge was not a total surprise to Geronimo's band. The braying of pack mules may have alerted the Chiricahua; the scouts were so worn out from the forced march that their usual hardihood may have failed them. Geronimo's people were able to flee into the surrounding mountains, but Crawford seized all the booty in camp— food, supplies, and horses.

Later that day, as Crawford rested his scouts in the captured camp, Lozen approached with a message from Geronimo and Naiche. The Chiricahuas wished to have a conference with Crawford the next day. The captain was overjoyed: the message seemed tantamount to an offer of surrender.

Shortly after dawn on January 11, however, Crawford's scouts reported a large party approaching. The captain assumed it was reinforcements from Crook, but suddenly bullets whizzed all through the camp. A 150-man troop of Mexican *nacionales* that had been hunting the Chiricahuas had attacked Crawford, apparently thinking the scouts were hostile Apaches.

Crawford ordered his own scouts to hold their fire, while he and other officers shouted out in Spanish, identifying themselves as American soldiers, and waved handkerchiefs. After some fifteen minutes, there was a lull in the gunfire. Crawford advanced toward the Mexican line, hoping to talk with its commander. He climbed atop a prominent rock, waved his handkerchief, and shouted, *"Soldados Americanos!"*

A shot rang out. Lieutenant Marion P. Maus, second in command, had just started back toward the scouts. He turned to see Crawford "lying on the rocks with a wound in his head & some of his brains upon the rocks." At once the scouts unleashed a furious fire upon the Mexicans. The battle raged for an hour. Four on the American side were wounded, while the scouts killed four of the Mexicans and wounded five others. Finally the Mexicans raised their own white flag.

Crawford was carried unconscious from the battlefield. He lingered in a coma for an excruciating seven days, as the scouts rigged a stretcher, one end fixed to a mule, the other carried by six men. Thus hindered, the party could travel only six or seven miles a day. Crawford died on January 18, and was buried in Nacori.

The causes, and even the details, of this fiasco remain murky more than a century later. Maus and others insisted that the Mexicans knew perfectly well whom they were firing on. A mule packer swore that Maus himself lost his nerve during the battle and hid under some rocks. The man who shot Crawford was reported to be Mauricio Corredor, the Tarahumara scout credited with killing Victorio five years earlier; the firearm he used was supposed to be the same nickel-plated rifle that the Chihuahua government had given him as a reward for that deed. Corredor was one of the Mexicans slain.

The debacle on the Aros River caused a serious diplomatic rift between the United States and Mexico. Both governments conducted official investigations. Crook regarded Crawford's death as "an assassination"; the Secretary of War called it "utterly unjustifiable." Congressional protests led the Secretary of State to demand reparations from the Mexican government.

The Mexican side of the story was slow in coming, and when it did, it boggled American minds. President Porfirio Díaz charged that Crawford's party had violated the border-crossing agreement of 1882. On their way south through Sonora, the scouts had killed two Mexicans and stolen and killed many horses and cattle, some of which were found with Maus. On the Aros, the Mexicans had indeed mistaken the scouts for hostiles, but had fired only after the Apaches did. And it was not a Mexican bullet that killed Crawford; he had been shot by one of his own scouts. Díaz demanded reparations of his own.

There was more truth to this telling than Americans wanted to believe. In correspondence with the governor of Sonora as early as January 11, Crook had privately acknowledged and regretted depredations by Apache scouts in Mexico. Many years later, a mule packer in Crawford's party published an account of the battle on the Aros. He had been left in a rear camp, so did not witness the gunfire; but he claimed to have his account straight from Lieutenant Maus.

Just before climbing atop the rock (claimed the packer), Crawford had handed his rifle to his most trusted scout, an Apache nicknamed Dutchy for his supposedly Germanic features. It was Dutchy who ran to Maus with the news that the captain had been shot. A large sum of money known to be on Crawford's person was missing. "Dutchy had robbed his commanding officer," concluded the packer. "No one else could have done it and I have always believed that Dutchy and not the Mexicans killed Captain Crawford." If this tale is not pure poppycock, it may implicate Maus (who was later decorated for valor) in a cover-up.

As the fighting had broken out, the Chiricahua sat on a hillside across the Aros River. "Geronimo watched it and laughed," a member of the band told biographer Angie Debo seventy years later—"with an emphasis," Debo added, "impossible to convey in print."

Nevertheless, a few days later, the leaders of the Chiricahua met with Maus. Geronimo would eventually admit that Crawford's appearance had dealt the fugitives another heavy blow, convincing them that no refuge, no matter how deeply hidden in the Sierra Madre, was safe. Now Nana, tired of flight, agreed to come in; a warrior and seven women, including a wife of Naiche and a wife of Geronimo, also joined the train of scouts that straggled north toward the border. Geronimo and the others agreed to meet with Crook "in two moons," but only on the condition that they choose the site and that the general come without soldiers. Maus had no option but to agree.

During the next two months, no officer, Mexican or American, had any idea where Geronimo was. Crook assumed the warrior had stayed in Mexico. Ranchers and miners in the Black Range of New Mexico, however, went through a new Apache scare in the early months of 1886, when a number of isolated families were wiped out. The locals assumed it was Geronimo who led these raids, and they may have been right.

The morale of the remaining free Chiricahua was at a low ebb. As the parley with Lieutenant Maus had revealed, they were divided among themselves as to whether continued resistance was futile. Mangus had separated from the other Chiricahua months before, with a small band of thirteen, six of them warriors. He would never rejoin Chihuahua and Naiche and Geronimo. Now Nana, with his fierce will, his ancient pride, had given up. Maus had tried to persuade Chihuahua to come in also, but that warrior had answered that unless he had proof that his captured family was alive at Fort Bowie, he would fight on.

Geronimo himself brooded over the dismal future. Freedom was as vital to him as the mountain air, and whenever he thought of the reservation, his thoughts darkened with the perfidies of John Clum, of Mickey Free, of Chatto. But the painful separation from his relatives gnawed at him as it did any other warrior. And there was no ignoring the fact that the Sierra Madre had ceased to be inviolable. Crook's 1883 thrust had depended on the luck of finding one man, the turncoat Tzoe, who knew the mysteries of the Blue Mountains. Now there were scores of Tzoes, starting with Chatto: Chiricahuas who had turned army scouts, every one of whom knew the range's secrets. The Mescalero boy Geronimo had captured five months before came to know his thoughts. "Geronimo knew that it was hopeless," he would say decades later. "But that did not stop him."

The Bedonkohe kept his two-month promise. In March 1886, using smoke signals, he contacted Maus, who had camped near the border. Geronimo would meet with Crook at Cañon de los Embudos, about twenty miles south of the boundary line.

The meeting place was well known to the Apaches. The "funnels" of its Spanish name are a series of gateway chutes carved out of the bedrock lava by a clear perennial stream. Long before the Apaches camped here, ancient agriculturalists made the canyon their home, leaving scores of grinding holes bored in the stone. A series of brushy terraces, separated by sharp ravines, gave Geronimo the security he craved. The Chiricahua camped two or three ravines east of Crook's party, on higher ground, with mountains at their back.

Crook came, as he had agreed, without a troop of soldiers. Among his party were his aide, John G. Bourke, who made a verbatim transcript of the conference, some seven men who could serve as interpreters (though not Mickey Free, whom Crook knew Geronimo despised), and his new model of a good Apache—Kaytennae, fresh from Alcatraz. The warrior had lost all his fierceness and independence: he was, Crook purred, "thoroughly reconstructed.... His stay at Alcatraz has worked a complete reformation in his character."

In prison, Kaytennae had learned to write English after a fashion. Bourke copied two of his pathetic sentences, written in schoolboy capitals: "MY WIFE HIM NAME KOWTENNAYS WIFE." "ONE YEAR HAB TREE HUNNERD SIXY-FIBE DAYS." In Bourke's view, "It wasn't in writing alone that [Kaytennae] was changed, but in everything: he had become a white man, and was an apostle of peace." The jaunty tone obscures the fact that Kaytennae had been effectively brainwashed. His first twelve months at Alcatraz had been served at hard labor and in solitary confinement; after that, he had been "liberated and taken to every place of note or interest around the Golden Gate ... to impress him with the power of the American people and the advantages of civilization."

Geronimo was glad to see his former warrior, who, for all he knew, had been put to death. During the conference, he asked Kaytennae to say something for the record. Kaytennae demurred, mumbling, "I have a sore throat," and kept his silence.

On the afternoon of March 25, the Chiricahua leaders sat on the bank of the stream with Crook's party, just west of the largest "funnel." "The whole ravine," Bourke noted, "was romantically beautiful: shading the rippling water were smooth, white-trunked, long, and slender sycamores, dark gnarly ash, rough-barked cottonwoods, pliant willows." Twenty-four heavily armed warriors sat just beyond the circle, within earshot. A nervy Tombstone photographer named Camillus Fly had talked his way into Crook's party. Now, with no hint of deference, he ordered the Apaches around like schoolboys as he posed them for his camera. Fly's startling images are some of the finest ever made of the Chiricahua. They also remain, as a scholar points out, "the only known photographs of American Indians as enemy in the field."

Geronimo began the conference by choosing his interpreter among the ones Crook had furnished. Then he launched into a long-winded recital of his grievances, justifying his flight from Turkey Creek ten months before. Yet he seemed in a conciliatory, even a defeatist mood. He strained to impress the dour general with his sincerity and honesty: "I think I am a good man, but in the papers all over the world they say I am a bad man; but it is a bad thing to say about me. I never do wrong without a cause."

Crook listened stolidly, his poker face betraying no reaction. Throughout Geronimo's speech, he stared at the ground, refusing even to glance at his adversary. This so nettled the warrior that he interrupted his harangue to ask the general, "Why don't you look at me and smile at me?" Bourke was surprised to see how nervous Geronimo seemed. As he spoke, "perspiration, in great beads, rolled down his temples and over his hands; and he clutched from time to time at a buckskin thong which he held tightly in one hand."

Now Geronimo summoned up the Apache rhetoric that whites always heard as flowery and vain, but which sprang from their deep animism:

> There is one God looking down on us all. We are all children of the one God. God is listening to me. The sun, the darkness, the winds, are all listening to what we now say.

Wearily Geronimo pled the case for his fugitives: "There are very few of my men left now. They have done some bad things but I want them all rubbed out now and let us never speak of them again."

Crook kept up his show of aloof intransigence. As he and Geronimo bickered over the causes of the breakout from Turkey Creek, he let sarcasm creep into his tone. Finally he delivered his ultimatum:

There is no use for you to try and talk nonsense. I am no child. You must make up your own mind whether you will stay out on the warpath or surrender unconditionally. If you stay out, I'll keep after you and kill the last one, if it takes fifty years.

With their exchange going nowhere, Crook and Geronimo agreed to adjourn the conference till two days hence. The Apaches retreated to their camp, where they talked among themselves. All the rest of that day and the next, Kaytennae mingled freely with them. He found them, as Crook later reported, "so excited and wild that they could not reason"; had Kaytennae urged surrender at first, the nervous warriors would have shot him. Before the conference, Geronimo had given his watching men orders to shoot all the White Eyes at the first hint of an attempt to seize the Chiricahua leaders. But now, among the fugitives, Kaytennae carried out Crook's instructions well, which were "to disintegrate them, and get them divided as much as possible."

In his own camp, Crook's thoughts roiled. The new Commanding General of the Army, his old West Point classmate "Little Phil" Sheridan, had ordered Crook to demand unconditional surrender from the "hostiles." But Sheridan was out of touch with Apache reality, and Crook knew that Geronimo would never give up without favorable terms. The Chiricahuas wanted amnesty for past crimes and the chance to return to Turkey Creek. This would not do; but Crook felt he had some room to negotiate within the letter of his mandate.

On the morning of March 27, Chihuahua sent Crook a secret message offering to surrender his own band, regardless of what Geronimo did. But Crook wanted to bring in every last Chiricahua, and he felt Chihuahua's submission could be used to demoralize Geronimo's followers.

At last the conference resumed. Chihuahua spoke first. His white listeners saw a man six feet tall, weighing some 200 pounds, with "not an ounce of fat surplus flesh"; he had "as pleasant a face as one would care to meet, strikingly good natured and very intelligent." The once-indomitable warrior was in a mood of abject submission. During a rambling speech, he shook hands with Crook three times, while he praised the general in words that sounded almost fawning:

It seems to me that I have seen the One who makes the rain and sends the winds; or He must have sent you to this place. I surrender myself to you because I believe in you and you do not deceive us. You must be our God. . . . You must be the one who makes the green pastures, who sends the rain, who commands the winds. You must be the one who sends the fresh fruits that appear on the trees every year.

Next Naiche took his turn. He was even taller than Chihuahua, about six feet one. He seemed to the whites "a tall, loose-jointed, graceful Indian, a dandy in his dress, with a handsome, almost effeminate face, and slender, elegant hands." Naiche, too, spoke abjectly.

What Chihuahua says I say. I surrender just the same as he did. . . . I throw myself at your feet. You now order and I obey. What you tell me to do I do. . . . I think now it is best for us to surrender and not remain out in the mountains like fools, as we have been doing. I have nothing further to say.

Their speeches sounded unconditional, but Crook had bought the Chiricahua surrender only at the price of a pledge he prayed his government would keep. He told the fugitives that all of them except Nana (thought to be too old and decrepit to bear exile) would be sent east for a period not to exceed two years, after which they could return to their homeland. It was this stipulation that won the resignation of Geronimo, who spoke last.

The Bedonkohe warrior had taken his place on the streambank under a mulberry tree. His face was blackened with a powder made from crushed galena. As Geronimo sat with his legs crossed, forearms on knees, the white men stared at the extraordinary face and waited for the crucial words. A journalist who would meet Geronimo five months hence left the most vivid description of that countenance ever penned:

Crueller features were never cut. The nose is broad and heavy, the forehead low and wrinkled, the chin full and strong, the eyes like two bits of obsidian with a light behind them. The mouth is the most noticeable feature—a sharp, straight, thin-lipped gash of generous length and without one softening curve.

Geronimo was much subdued from his mood of the conference two days before. Again he reminded Crook that he had kept his promise. "I was very far from here," he said. "Almost nobody could go to that place. But I sent you word I wanted to come in here, and here I am."

Crook, for his part, responded more gently than he had two days before. A huge burden seemed to be lifting from his shoulders. Geronimo shook the general's hand, then said, "I give myself up to you. Do with me what you please. I surrender. Once I moved about like the wind. Now I surrender to you and that is all."

Eighteen

■

Canyon of the Skeletons

*B*ut that was not all.

That night the Chiricahua went on a drunken spree. From the army camp two ravines away, Crook's men heard gunshots throughout the night. In the morning, Kaytennae came to Crook's tent to tell the general that Naiche was so drunk he could not stand up. Later Bourke found Geronimo and four other warriors riding aimlessly, five men on a pair of mules, "all drunk as lords."

Anxious to telegraph Sheridan with the terms of surrender, Crook moved out for Fort Bowie in advance of the main party, leaving Lieutenant Maus to bring in the fugitives. In their inebriated state, the Apaches made only a few miles of progress toward the border. That night they drank again. A cold rain had drizzled all day, and now the Apaches argued among themselves.

In the muffling darkness, with the rain coming down harder, thirty-nine of the Chiricahua bolted out of camp. Their number comprised eighteen warriors led by Geronimo and Naiche, thirteen women, and six children. It was not until morning that Maus realized the band had fled. He set out at once on their trail, hopeful of catching the rebels, for they had taken with them only two horses and one mule, while Maus's scouts were mounted.

The whiskey that the Chiricahuas had drunk was sold them by a nefarious figure named Tribolet (first name uncertain), a Swiss-American bootlegger who operated a makeshift saloon out of a tent four hundred yards south of the border. When he was later criticized for selling thirty dollars' worth of mescal to the Apaches in one hour, the unrepentant Tribolet bragged that he could have sold a hundred dollars' worth, at ten dollars a gallon. After the Apaches were good and drunk, Tribolet was supposed to have told them that as soon as they crossed the border, they would be seized and hanged.

Crook forever blamed Tribolet for the last outbreak, which nearly shattered his spirit. "If it had not been for his whisky . . . ," the general mused, "the whole thing would now be settled." Tribolet had been arrested before, and now Crook suggested that it would have been better had some army officer "shot him down like a coyote, as he deserved to be."

To blame Tribolet, his whiskey, and the warnings he may have whispered in the drunken Chiricahuas' ears, however, is like blaming the pigeonholed telegram for the breakout from Turkey Creek. It was not whiskey that made Geronimo change his mind once more: it was the veering compass of his eternal ambivalence. Four years later, when Crook asked him why he had fled the last time, Naiche denied that Tribolet had anything to do with it. "I was afraid I was going to be taken off somewhere I didn't like, to some place I didn't know," said the Chokonen chief. "I thought all who were taken away would die. . . . Nobody said anything to me that night; I worked it out in my own mind."

"Why did you get drunk?" Crook persisted.

"Because there was a lot of whisky there and we wanted a drink," answered Naiche.

Nineteen years after the event, Geronimo said simply, "We started with all our tribe to go with General Crook back to the United States, but I feared treachery and decided to remain in Mexico."

Geronimo had good reason for his fears. At that very moment, citizens all over Arizona, alerted to the surrender, were speculating as to the disposition of the captives once Crook brought them in. "The general belief is that the ringleaders will be executed," noted a journalist.

Maus and his scouts followed Geronimo and Naiche's trail for sixty miles through "the most impassable mountains." They found one horse, stabbed to death. Geronimo used his usual tricks, changing direction abruptly when his trail vanished on solid rock. With little food, the fugitives walked and ran sixty miles without stopping to camp. Near Fronteras in Sonora, the band split up, to rendezvous in some secret lair in the Sierra Madre. His horses played out and his rations thin, Maus gave up the chase.

Two warriors who had changed their mind fell in with Maus's returning scouts and gave themselves up. The band of fugitives now numbered only thirty-seven. In the initial outbreak, one of Naiche's wives had tried to flee to the soldiers' camp. The chief, probably still drunk, had shot her in the leg, then left her behind.

Meanwhile, at Fort Bowie, even before he learned the news about Geronimo and Naiche, Crook received a setback in a confidential telegram from Sheridan. President Cleveland would in no way consent to the terms Geronimo and Crook had bargained out. Sheridan ordered Crook to renegotiate for unconditional surrender, while somehow at the same time preventing ESCAPE OF THE HOSTILES, WHICH MUST NOT BE ALLOWED UNDER ANY CIRCUMSTANCES.

Now Crook had to wire the news of Geronimo and Naiche's flight. Sheridan was apoplectic. His telegrams over the next few days barely contain his annoyance and his second-guessing: IT SEEMS STRANGE THAT GERONIMO AND PARTY COULD HAVE ESCAPED WITHOUT THE KNOWLEDGE OF THE SCOUTS. With a deadpan patience, Crook explained the conditions of Apache warfare to Sheridan as he might to a cadet fresh out of West Point. Sheridan condescended in return.

On April 1, Crook summarized the whole logic of his campaign. The short telegram to Sheridan came as close to uttering an *apologia* as the laconic general was able to produce. He concluded:

I BELIEVE THAT THE PLAN UPON WHICH I HAVE CONDUCTED OPERATIONS IS THE ONE MOST LIKELY TO PROVE SUCCESSFUL IN THE END. IT MAY BE, HOWEVER, THAT I AM TOO MUCH WEDDED TO MY OWN VIEWS IN THIS MATTER, AND AS I HAVE SPENT NEARLY EIGHT YEARS OF THE HARDEST WORK OF MY LIFE IN THIS DEPARTMENT, I RESPECTFULLY REQUEST THAT I MAY NOW BE RELIEVED FROM ITS COMMAND.

Sheridan waited less than twenty-four hours to comply. Crook was reassigned to the Department of the Platte. Thus the country's ablest Indian fighter stepped down from the last Indian war in America, not with cheers and anthems in his ears, but with the murmur of official disappointment and the shrill condemnation of a hundred headlines drowning out his quiet statements.

On April 2 and 3, the surrendered Chiricahua, seventy-seven strong, rode into Fort Bowie. By now Chihuahua was bitter toward Geronimo, and blamed him for the fugitives' woes. His despairing mood continued. As Crook, in his last hours of service, questioned him, the warrior said, "I've thrown away my arms. I'm not afraid; got to die sometime. If you punish me very hard it's all right, but I think much of my family." Chihuahua said that he expected Naiche to come in to Fort Bowie fairly soon, but doubted that Geronimo would ever be seen again.

Among the surrendered band, the strangest figure was an eleven-year-old boy named Santiago McKinn. The summer before, with his older brother, Santiago had been herding cattle near the family ranch not far from Deming, New Mexico, when Geronimo swooped down. The warriors had killed his brother and taken Santiago captive. Now he served as living proof of the power the Chiricahua wielded to transform a captive into one of their own. Freckled and sandy-haired, the son of an Irish father and a Mexican mother, Santiago spoke Spanish and English; in only a little more than six months, he had learned quite a bit of Apache, too. At Fort Bowie, his rescuers told him he was about to be reunited with his parents. Santiago burst into tears and blurted out in Apache that he didn't want to go home—"he wanted always to stay with the Indians." The boy "acted like a young wild animal in a trap," according to one witness, and had to be forced into the wagon that took him home.

No journalist or historian ever bothered to interview Santiago about his months with the last free Chiricahua. Another priceless testimony escaped the documentary record.

Chihuahua and the other seventy-six renegades at Fort Bowie had given themselves up under the terms worked out with Crook: at most two years of exile somewhere in the East, then a return to the reservation. They had come to trust the Tan Wolf as one of the few among the White Eyes who would not lie to them. But at the moment, a double-cross as duplicitous as any ever perpetrated against American Indians was being cooked up in Washington.

On April 5, Crook learned from Sheridan that because Geronimo and Naiche's band had broken away, the President considered Crook's negotiated surrender null and void. Here was a pseudolegal dodge to rationalize the plan that Sheridan and Cleveland had already hatched. The banishment to the East was to be indefinite, not for a mere two years.

Despite his personal code of honesty, Crook did not have the heart to tell the Chiricahua that their deal was off. Rationalizing in turn, he wired Sheridan that it would be best to keep the Apaches in the dark, for if word got out there would be no hope of the surrender of Geronimo and Naiche's band. Sheridan rubber-stamped the deceit.

On April 7, the seventy-seven Chiricahuas boarded a Southern Pacific train at the whistle stop of Bowie, Arizona, ten miles north of the fort. All fifteen warriors, thirty-three women, and twenty-nine children assumed they would be back in Arizona within two years. A guilty and exhausted Crook wrote, "It is a big relief to get rid of them."

One of those children, Chihuahua's son, would look back many decades later:

> That day they put us on that train at Bowie . . . , we knew that we were facing two years of slavery and degradation, but my father was willing to endure that for the sake of the future when we were to be free again. Chihuahua did not know, nor did anyone else, that we were to be prisoners for twenty-seven years.
> It would have been a good day to die.

Crook lingered at Fort Bowie through April 11, when he formally passed over control of the Department of Arizona to his successor, General Nelson A. Miles. One of the Tan Wolf's last acts was to gather his loyal Apache scouts and tell them about the change. Shocked and alarmed, the scouts begged Crook to vouch for the character of this new *nantan*. "Is he a good man," they asked anxiously, "or will he lie to us the same way other people have lied to us?" Crook assured the scouts that General Miles was "a good and honest man."

The two generals performed the transfer with a show of courtesy, and Crook offered Miles all the knowledge he had gleaned of Apaches during his eight years of service in Arizona. On the afternoon of April 12, Crook rode away from Fort Bowie and the thankless campaign for good.

Crook went to his grave harboring a deep bitterness over Miles's arrogation of credit for ending the Apache war, when Crook knew that his successor's five months' service amounted to a feckless epilogue to an epic tale that better men had written. Miles, for his part, was privately scornful of Crook. Within weeks of his advent, he wrote his wife, "I am also annoyed by the statements thrown out by Crook. He made a dead failure of this, as he has every other campaign."

Miles had not had the benefit of graduating from West Point; in the Civil War, he was a volunteer. Twice wounded in that conflict, the second time at Chancellorsville, where he was shot in the abdomen and hip and not expected to live, Miles had nonetheless risen through the ranks faster than any officer other than Custer. By 1864, he was a brevet major general.

After the Civil War, Miles served with distinction against the Sioux and the Nez Perce. He had not damaged his prospects by marrying the daughter of a judge related to William Tecumseh Sherman, who a few months after the wedding became Commanding General of the Army. A natural rivalry had emerged between Crook and Miles: though Miles was about a decade younger than his predecessor, the two men had fought in many of the same wars, notably the struggle against the Sioux and Cheyenne. Their characters were utterly unlike: Crook with his taciturn, undemonstrative style, Miles with a smug and vainglorious charisma. In one respect, however, they were similar. In the words of historian Robert L. Utley, "[Crook] could entertain uncharitable opinions of rivals and bear a grudge almost as intensely as Miles, the champion grudge-bearer of the army."

Later, with the Apache war under his belt, Miles would preen himself to run for President. But he had made too many enemies along the route of his scrambling ascent to fame. "Too much circus, too little brain," wrote one veteran. Teddy Roosevelt considered him a "strutting peacock." Bourke, with his loyalty toward Crook, had formed a decade-long contempt for Miles, whom he considered "ignorant, almost illiterate." Likewise Britton Davis, whose memoir drips with irony on every page where Miles appears.

A journalist who greeted Miles at Fort Bowie in April 1886 found him impressive enough in person:

> He is a tall, straight, fine looking man, of 210 pounds weight, and apparently in the early fifties as to age [actually 46]. He has a well-modeled head, high brow, strong eye, clean-cut aquiline nose, and firm mouth. It is an imposing and soldierly figure, all around.

Although on his arrival in Arizona Miles stressed that he would carry on Crook's work with little change, almost at once he set out to un-do his predecessor's deeds. The most important reform was to put most of the Apache scouts out to pasture. Like many another officer, like Sheridan himself, Miles had never been comfortable with the idea of Indians enlisted to chase other Indians. He believed that the cavalry alone could perform more effectively. Crook's assertion from exile, that the "Chiricahua scouts . . . were of more value in hunting down and compelling the surrender of the renegades, than all other troops engaged in operations against them, combined," fell on deaf ears.

The general was also a gadgeteer. One of his first innovations in Arizona was to set up a heliograph system—large, movable mirrors that used the sun to flash signals in Morse code. Soon Miles had erected twenty-seven mountaintop stations all across southern Arizona. The general liked to show the Apaches his device, basking in their astonishment. Some of the Indians may have flattered the general's vanity, but the Chiricahua had been using mirrors for years to signal one another from mountaintops.

In five months, Miles later boasted, his heliograph network sent and received 2,264 messages. Not one of them aided in the slightest in finding Geronimo. Miles's "expensive toy," as one historian called it, served for little more than to keep troop movements sorted out.

The general's fundamental failing in Arizona was that he had no sympathy for Apaches. He was, in fact, afraid of them. It was one thing to ridicule his predecessor's decisions:

> Crook's policy was to treat those Indians at the Apache reservation more like conquerors than prisoners. . . . If that policy is continued, they will furnish warriors for the next twenty years, liable to break out and raid the settlements any time they go on a drunk.

It was another matter to exaggerate preposterously the tactical advantages of Geronimo and Naiche's small band: "The Indians have enough ammunition to last them five years, upwards of one hundred thousand rounds."

At the end of June, Miles made a trip to Fort Apache, where he met the Chiricahua who had declined to leave Turkey Creek in 1885. The visit deeply unsettled the general. As he later wrote,

I found at Fort Apache over four hundred men, women and children, belonging to the Chiricahua and Warm Springs Indians, and a
more turbulent, desperate, and disreputable band of human beings
I had never seen before and hope never to see again. . . . When I
visited their camp they were having drunken orgies every night, and
it was a perfect pandemonium. It was dangerous to go near them, as
they were constantly discharging pistols and rifles.

The shock and revulsion of that encounter spurred the fantasy of a
Final Solution in Miles's brain.

Except for Geronimo, Naiche, and the indomitable Lozen, the names
of the Chiricahuas in the final band of thirty-seven remain obscure.
Yet their five-month ride through the summer of 1886 can fairly be
regarded as the most remarkable campaign of guerrilla warfare ever
witnessed on the North American continent.

The warriors were such men as Fun, renowned among his people
for his bravery, who despite his youth was not afraid to stand up to
Geronimo; Perico, Geronimo's cousin, who had ridden in Nana's Raid;
Chapo, Geronimo's son, newly emerged as a warrior; Tissnolthos,
who had been a scout for Britton Davis; and Yanozha, who sat at
Geronimo's right hand in the council of warriors and was also reputed
for his courage. We know little about them individually.

The women and children among that band remain even more obscure, some even nameless in the white record. Geronimo's wife was
Yanozha's sister Shegha, whom the warrior had married around 1861,
cementing an alliance with Cochise's Chokonen. Naiche, who was
never short of women, had a young wife named Haozinne with him.
Tahdaste, a handsome young woman, had often served as Geronimo's
messenger. The children included two infant girls. Nothing reflects
the deep Apache reverence for family more eloquently than the tenacity with which this interrelated band hung together, babies and all,
through some of the most harrowing months any Apaches ever survived.

As Geronimo and Naiche fully knew, the band's constant flight
verged on a suicide mission. But surrender held out little promise of
a plausible world. As Naiche drily put it two years later, "We saw that
we were in for it and would be probably killed anyway, so we concluded to take our chances and escape with our lives and liberty."

Geronimo's fatalism ran just as deep: "We were reckless of our lives," he later remembered, "because we felt that every man's hand was against us. If we returned to the reservation we would be put in prison and killed; if we stayed in Mexico they would continue to send soldiers to fight us; so we gave no quarter to anyone and asked no favors."

As pursuit closed in from both Mexican and American armies, the band split into two units. Geronimo took six men and four women and slipped once more through the intensive border patrol, then raided north all the way to Ojo Caliente. Along the way, he killed his last white Americans, raising the pitch of terror among the settlers.

The best publicized of these depredations, the attack on Peck's Ranch on April 27, illustrates the difficulty of seizing the truth about an isolated encounter in the Apache wars. According to the most lurid version of events, Geronimo's small band attacked the lonely ranch in the Santa Cruz Valley of southern Arizona, "butchered several cowboys, and compelled the rancher, Peck, to witness the torture of his wife until he went temporarily insane. The crazed man was later freed by the superstitious Apaches and so he lived." But other versions insist that Peck was away from the ranch catching a steer when his wife and daughter were killed. He was captured in a separate action, then released with a warning not to go home, and "one of the Indians, for some unexplainable reason, gave him 65 cents in money."

A doctor on the San Pedro River, a herder in the Happy Valley, a miner in the Whetstone Mountains, a rancher near the Pantano Wash, another rancher near Greaterville, yet another in the Oro Valley, and so on—thus reads the litany of victims of Geronimo's last raid north of the border. It mattered little that only seven Chiricahuas performed these deeds: to the addled citizens, the bloodthirsty Apaches were everywhere.

As always, the object of the killings was to seize ammunition, without which every fugitive was as good as dead. Yet, pushed to the edge as the raiders were, they still bothered to kidnap two young Mexican-Americans whom they kept as captives, one the ten-year-old sister of Mrs. Peck, the other a young boy plucked from a ranch only fifteen miles from Tucson. These captives rode for several weeks with Geronimo. The boy reported that his captors "amused themselves by punching and teasing" him; but they also gave him the first rib from a freshly butchered cow.

Sometimes the boy rode in front of Geronimo on the same horse.

When he had been seized from his family's ranch, the captive's mother had been stoned and left for dead. Suddenly she had recovered consciousness and started running toward a ditch. Instead of shooting her, the Chiricahua watched her flee, remarking in Spanish to their captive, "Your mother is a good runner." Because he had lost his hat, the Apaches gave the boy a red handkerchief to wear, laughing, "Now you look like us."

The ten-year-old girl noticed that "a tall, slender, long-haired, sway backed young Indian ... seemed to give orders," suggesting that Naiche was with Geronimo during this American raid. She later complained that the Apaches "half-starved" and beat her, but at the same time seemed to be trying to teach her. An old man (probably Geronimo) struck her sometimes on the forehead: "He would tell me in the Apache language to do something, and I would not understand what he wished me to do, and then he would strike me."

What can Geronimo have been thinking, in the seizure of these captives? Did he still hope to live long enough at large to train them to become full-fledged Apaches? Were they not a further burden on the movement of his hard-pressed band? For theirs was indeed a desperate mission, in the heat of summer, with all the water holes guarded: once the Apaches went two days and nights without water, and their horses nearly died.

Both captives were freed in mid-June, in a surprise attack by a posse of about seventy Mexican vaqueros. The much smaller band of Chiricahuas managed to get away, all except for a single warrior who tried to retain the captive girl. The Mexicans shot his horse, yelled to the girl to run, then surrounded the warrior as he hid in the brush. It seemed certain that at least one Chiricahua was about to die for his sins. Perhaps it was Fun, or Yanozha, for the man was not only brave but a great marksman. He shot seven Mexicans dead, panicked the rest into flight, and made his getaway. When an American captain came across the battlefield shortly afterward, he found all seven vaqueros had been shot in the head.

Sometime in June, Geronimo's raiders reentered Mexico. Now the warrior's old hatred, undimmed despite all the Mexican blood he had shed, came surging into his heart. As he put it many years later, "On our return through Old Mexico we attacked every Mexican found, even if for no other reason than to kill."

There was nothing left to lose. There was only the fight to stay ahead of the game, to survive. Along with the constant worry, the ear cocked for the telltale footstep through each night's cold bivouac, Geronimo took a grim satisfaction in knowing that never before had the Chiricahua fought and ridden so well. Despite their differences in the past, he and Naiche had worked out an almost perfect partnership. Naiche was still the chief, ostensibly giving orders, but Geronimo was the strategist, the leader. Years later, Geronimo would praise Naiche for recognizing that "the life of his people depended upon someone who could do these things"—choose a fight or organize an escape or divine a distant event. "And I, rather than see my race perish from Mother Earth, cared little who was chief so long as I could direct the fighting and preserve even a few of our people."

Never before had Geronimo so relied on his Power. And his warriors believed utterly in it. In later days they would swear that in one nocturnal escape from an American command, Geronimo had sung to delay the dawn for two hours while his band crossed a naked basin.

And never before had Geronimo's sense of responsibility been so tirelessly exercised. As Kanseah, an eleven-year-old boy in the final band, put it decades later:

> Geronimo had to obtain food for his men, and for their women and children. When they were hungry, Geronimo got food. When they were cold he provided blankets and clothing. When they were afoot, he stole horses. When they had no bullets, he got ammunition. He was a good man.

Meanwhile General Miles had launched his grand campaign against the Apache menace. He requested and received two thousand additional soldiers, so that by early summer he had five thousand men— one quarter of the entire U.S. Army—in the field. Adding their numbers to the roughly three thousand Mexican soldiers scouring Chihuahua and Sonora, the several hundred Indian scouts still in service, and the numerous bands of vaqueros and volunteers out hunting Apaches, one arrives at a total of nearly nine thousand armed men pursuing eighteen Chiricahua warriors, thirteen women, and six children.

Miles deployed his men to guard not only every known water hole and pass, but every inhabited ranch in the vicinity of the border. And he chose a captain to press the chase whom he regarded as without peer for his "brilliant record" in the Civil War, his "splendid physique, character and high attainments as an officer." Henry W. Lawton was, in the eyes of one of his soldiers, "six feet four inches of brawn and muscle." The captain was put in charge of "one hundred of the strongest and best soldiers that could be found." Surely this picked force would settle Geronimo's hash.

For four months, by his own reckoning, Lawton's command traveled 3,041 miles on the fugitives' trail, nearly all of it in Mexico. They plunged south all the way to the Aros River, where Captain Crawford had met his death, then back north again. The conditions were debilitating in the extreme. As an officer wrote:

> One who does not know this country cannot realize what this kind of service means—marching every day in the intense heat, the rocks and earth being so torrid that the feet are blistered and rifle-barrels and everything metallic being so hot that the hand cannot touch them without getting burnt. It is a country rough beyond description, covered everywhere with cactus and full of rattlesnakes and other undesirable companions of that sort. The rain, when it does come, comes as a tropical tempest, transforming the dry cañons into raging torrents in an instant.

The men suffered badly from diarrhea. Lawton lost forty pounds. Miles insisted that at one point the soldiers' thirst was so terrible, they cut open their veins and drank their own blood.

And the campaign was a complete failure. The Chiricahua used their tricks to throw the army off the trail, sometimes going miles at a stretch hopping from rock to rock to leave no prints. Only once during those four months did Lawton strike the fugitives' camp, deep in the Sierra Madre. He seized some booty, but every man, woman, and child got away.

During their five months at large, the fugitives lost three of their number. One woman was killed in the surprise attack by the Mexican vaqueros. One warrior defected and showed up at Fort Apache. Another warrior was killed on an ill-advised trading mission to Casas Grandes. Three or four times the Chiricahuas lost their stock and supplies in attacks; each time they quickly reoutfitted themselves at the expense of other settlers.

On assignment for the Los Angeles *Times,* the flamboyant journalist

Charles Lummis was posted at Fort Bowie during Miles's reign. He reported sardonically on the only half-successful strike of the long summer:

> We have had but one "fair shake" with the hostiles in all these weeks. Captain Hatfield did come upon a little band of them, rout them and capture every whit of their camp outfit, even down to the frying pans. He pressed on in hot pursuit up a little cañon. Suddenly the bleak rocks spat fire and the sky rained lead. He had fairly walked into their trap. When the Apache gets you in that box there is but one thing to do, and that is to get out of it in the shortest way. To stay and fight is suicide—and Hatfield got out. He left upon the field all of the plunder just captured, and six of his men [actually two killed and two wounded].

In the wake of Geronimo's brief raid north of the border, Miles calculated fourteen Americans killed; Britton Davis put the figure at "near a score." The tally in Mexico was huge. Lawton's command came upon the corpses of as many as ten Mexicans a day. Though the number all but defies credibility, the governor of Sonora later claimed that in the summer of 1886 the tiny Chiricahua band took the lives of five hundred to six hundred people in his state alone. Miles repeated the claim as valid.

With five thousand soldiers and his vaunted heliograph system at his disposal, Miles managed to kill or capture not a single Chiricahua in five months of warfare. The general himself, unlike Crook, chose to command from the rear, staying put for the most part in various Arizona forts and never once entering Mexico. Apprehending it from a distance, Geronimo scorned the style of his new adversary. "What does Miles, though a general, know about chieftainship?" he railed to a young follower. Nearly all the top American officers were alike: "Don't they *send* their men into battle instead of *leading* them?" For an Apache, Miles's method amounted to pitiful cowardice. One of Crook's favorite colonels had long since earned the Chiricahua nickname "Always Too Late to Fight."

Lack of results did not keep Miles from basking in a fatuous complacency. Later, in his memoirs, with one eye cocked on the Presidency, he retraced the futile summer as though the army's hapless maneuvers carried out some shrewd plan in the general's head: "After this engagement the Indians continued to retreat. . . . The Indians were first driven north and then south. . . . By the 5th of July the Indians had been driven south of Opusara, Mexico."

In part to compensate for the emptiness of his net, Miles began to contemplate a drastic gambit. The germ of the idea came early in June, while the general was out on a hike with a fellow officer. On visits to Fort Apache, Miles's confidant had noticed that whenever news of a Geronimo raid swept the reservation, all the Chiricahuas, to ensure their innocence, assembled at the quartermaster's corral.

"I would suggest," the officer told Miles, "a false report of a raid be spread and when the Indians are in the corral, they be surrounded by the troops, disarmed, taken to the railroad and shipped east as prisoners of war."

Miles was taken aback. "Why, that would be treachery," he told his colleague. "I could never do that."

But the idea stuck in the general's head, where it danced with possibilities. With all his people banished from Arizona, Geronimo might be so demoralized as to surrender. It was a neat, efficient solution: no longer would anyone need to distinguish between good and bad Chiricahuas.

With his dismaying visit to Fort Apache at the end of June, Miles resolved on wholesale removal of the Chiricahuas from Arizona. The seventy-seven fugitives under Chihuahua and Nana who had surrendered at the Cañon de los Embudos had been taken by train to Fort Marion in Florida, where they were lodged in what amounted to a concentration camp. Miles at first thought Florida too alien a climate for the Apaches, warning that they might die there. He urged instead the Indian Territory of Oklahoma; but in time he grew reconciled to Florida. On July 3, via a confidential telegram to Washington, he aired his plan. Cleveland and Sheridan were receptive.

The first step was to invite a party of leading Chiricahua to Washington for a meeting with the Great Father. In July, a ten-man delegation led by Chatto and Kaytennae had a conference with the Secretary of War. It was one more attempt to awe the simple savages with the splendors of the white man's world: Miles hoped to soften the leaders up so that they would docilely accept whatever fate he decreed for their people.

Chatto was indeed impressed with the buildings of Washington. He was pleased to shake President Cleveland's hand, to be given a silver peace medal, and to receive a piece of paper that said "Washington" at the top. But all he wanted, and all his people wanted, was to stay on the White Mountain reservation. His earnest plea was translated through the Spanish and rendered by a stenographer in the third person:

> He came here to ask for his country; to ask for his land, where he lives now. . . . At Camp Apache what he plants grows up very well; the water that runs there is very good; that is why he wants to stay there; that is why he wants to have that land; and from the place where he lives it is only half a mile to where there is grass, and with that he can earn five cents, and with that he can take care of his land and his people. . . .
>
> He cannot make big houses like this [the War Department Building], but can only take small sticks and make a house; but still, even if his hands ache, he wants to live that way.

The conference ended indecisively, and the Apaches were sent back toward Arizona. This had never been Miles's intention, and he intercepted the entourage by telegram in Kansas, where the Apaches were held prisoner at Fort Leavenworth. Two months later the whole delegation was shipped to Florida. Incensed at the betrayal, Chatto threw away his silver medal, asking why he had been given it in the first place.

Through July and August, Miles surreptitiously sent troops to Fort Apache to bolster security there, as he planned how to trick the more than four hundred Chiricahuas into a mass removal. If he had a bad conscience about this plot, it does not emerge in his writings. Miles had perhaps convinced himself of his own specious justification:

> The indolent and vicious young men and boys [on the reservation] were just the material to furnish warriors for the future; and these people although fed and clothed by the Government, had been conspiring against its authority. They had been in communication with the hostiles, and some of them had been plotting an extensive outbreak.

The general summed up this bleak vision in a pithy phrase: "Their boys of to-day will become the Geronimos of a few years hence."

Yet even as he schemed their removal from the territory, Miles turned to the Chiricahuas for help. He had begun to recognize that without the aid of Apache scouts, white soldiers were virtually helpless to locate the fugitives, let alone defeat them. It would not have been the general's style, of course, to admit that Crook was right after all. The action that he began in mid-July was carried out almost in secret, and Miles managed to see to it that the officer in charge—the savvy Lieutenant Charles B. Gatewood—got almost no credit for his pivotal deeds.

Miles went to a trusted Chiricahua and asked his advice in making contact with Geronimo. The man in turn recommended two young Chiricahuas named Kayitah and Martine as emissaries. The former was a Chokonen and a cousin of Yanozha, the superb warrior in Geronimo's band; the latter was a Nednhi who had fought under Juh and was well known to Geronimo. It was reasoned that if any reservation Chiricahua had a chance of approaching Geronimo and living to tell about it, these men did. Gatewood was picked because he was the officer whom the fugitives knew best, and one of the few they respected.

Martine insisted many years later that the general had promised him and Kayitah $3,000 apiece if they were successful. No reward was ever paid, but Miles was in fact desperate for results. Gatewood organized a small party that included George Wratten, a former store clerk on the reservation who had learned Apache, probably better than any other white man before him. Wratten's whole life would intertwine with Geronimo's when he subsequently became the warrior's "guardian" and interpreter in exile.

Miles had ordered Gatewood, for his safety, never to go near the "hostiles" with fewer than twenty-five soldiers as escort. The lieutenant knew that such an entourage would prevent contact, but he set off into Mexico in July determined to make a show of compliance. As he passed one strung-out command after another, he found none that could spare twenty-five soldiers. Eventually Gatewood made his way two hundred fifty miles south to the Aros River, where Lawton was thrashing around looking for a Chiricahua trail.

No sign of the fugitives had been found for weeks, and Lawton was in a bad mood. Gatewood's arrival alarmed him, for he had heard rumors that "the General contemplates relieving me by some other officer." With a disingenuous show of objectivity, he wrote a senior officer to express concern that Gatewood's mission had not been entrusted to "an older and more experienced officer." (Though Lawton was ten years older than the lieutenant who caught up with him on the Aros, by 1886 Gatewood was the most experienced Apache fighter among the officers still in service in Arizona.)

Gatewood was disappointed to learn that Lawton had no idea where Geronimo was, but he attached himself to the captain's command. For almost two weeks, the soldiers floundered on, deep in the Sierra Madre. Suddenly, out of the blue, Lawton and Gatewood were blessed with a great stroke of luck.

Lawton's ignorance was hardly his fault. By early August, no one, Mexican or American alike, knew where Geronimo and Naiche were. The fugitives in fact had holed up in one more of their secret places in the Sierra Madre, on a mountain near the great bend of the Bavispe River, fully two hundred miles northwest of Lawton's hapless sleuthing.

The Chiricahua had eluded all their pursuers. They may have been short of food as well as ammunition: it was not easy to hunt while hiding, and plundered goods always ran out sooner or later. Constant flight and the many battles had taken their toll. At some point Naiche had been shot, the bullet passing completely through his chest, but leaving him alive and able to fight. Geronimo may have been shot in the right arm. An Apache scout returning alone to the United States from Lawton's command made a dubious claim to have run into thirteen Indians under Geronimo and Naiche, had a long conversation with them, and escaped to tell about it. The scout said the fugitives "looked worn and hungry," and that "Geronimo carried his right arm in a sling, bandaged."

Perhaps Geronimo had begun to accept the hopelessness of the fugitives' situation. More likely, what happened next was just one more trick to play on the Mexicans. Around the middle of August, he sent two women from the mountain hiding place into the town of Fronteras; some say they were Lozen and Tahdaste. The women who undertook this perilous mission told the town officials that the whole band wished to surrender. The officials seized the messengers, confined them briefly, then sent them back with three ponies laden with mescal and food and a promise of peaceful negotiations.

Historian Dan L. Thrapp, who has pondered this strange business deeply, argues that the women's errand to Fronteras was a calculated ruse on the part of Geronimo, which won the fugitives not only food but precious bottles of the fiery whiskey some of them—not least the two leaders—craved. The Chiricahua had no intention of surrendering, Thrapp concludes, but guessed the Fronterans would send the women back out with a peace offering, in hopes of luring them all into town where they could be massacred. It is known that in the interim, two hundred soldiers quietly slipped into Fronteras.

In any event, the governor of Sonora telegraphed Miles with the news, and Miles got word to Lawton and Gatewood on the Aros River. At once the soldiers packed up and headed by forced marches toward the northern bend of the Bavispe. By August 20, they were camped in the general vicinity of the mountain hideout of the Chiricahuas. Now Gatewood waved his orders from the general in Lawton's face, insisting on going ahead with his small, almost unarmed party. Perhaps Lawton was glad to let him go, for he knew from bitter experience how useless a charge on the Chiricahuas' camp would prove, and he cannot have envied Gatewood his dangerous sortie.

The lieutenant, only thirty-three years old, had been fighting Apaches for seven years, since the inception of the Victorio campaign. In Britton Davis's eyes, Gatewood was "cool, quiet, courageous . . . with a thorough knowledge of Apache character." Unlike virtually all the other officers in Arizona (including Crook), Gatewood had taken the trouble to learn a little of the Apache language. He was almost surely the only officer Geronimo might trust enough to talk with. The Chiricahua had given Gatewood a relatively unpejorative name: "Nantan Long Nose" (his fellow officers had nicknamed the lieutenant "Beak").

Kayitah and Martine picked up the Chiricahuas' trail. With six to eight soldiers in addition to the scouts and George Wratten as translator, Gatewood followed the trail for three days. The party carried a flour sack mounted on a stick as a peace signal. "The white flag was high up on a century plant pole all the time," wrote Gatewood later, "but that don't make a man bullet proof." The lieutenant was not ashamed to acknowledge his fear, as he insisted that the two Apache scouts march at the front of the party.

On the third day, as they descended a canyon perfect for ambush, the party suddenly discovered a pair of faded canvas pants hanging on a bush. As Gatewood put it, "A cañon like that with such a banner at its head would make anybody halt. In the discussion of the matter, everybody gave his opinion, but nobody knew how to interpret what the pants had to say."

Their nerves at a ragged edge, the party reached the bank of the Bavispe, where they camped in a canebrake, their flag of peace planted as prominently as possible. Gatewood sent Martine and Kayitah out to scout.

On top of their mountain, the Chiricahua had posted the eleven-year-old Kanseah as lookout. For several years now, the fugitives had been equipped with the best field glasses the American army could supply. Kanseah saw two moving specks on the plain below; deer, he mused, then realized they were too small for deer. He called out to Geronimo.

As the specks resolved into human beings, Kanseah saw that they were Apaches; remarkably, within minutes he recognized Martine and Kayitah by their walks. The warriors assembled at the lookout point.

"It does not matter who they are," said Geronimo grimly. "If they come closer they are to be shot."

"They are our brothers," Yanozha objected; Kayitah was in fact his cousin. "Let's find out why they come. They are very brave to do this."

Geronimo sneered that the scouts must be out for reward money. "When they get close enough," he ordered, "shoot."

"If there is any shooting done," Yanozha answered, "it will be at you, not them. The first man who lifts a rifle I will kill."

"I will help you," said Fun.

"Let them live," grunted Geronimo.

As the two scouts approached the mountaintop, their blood hummed with the danger of their mission. "We knew they might shoot us at any moment," they said later. Kayitah went first. Finally one of the scout's relatives stood up on a rock and shouted: "Come on up. No one is going to hurt you."

Geronimo led the two emissaries back to the fugitives' main camp, where they settled on the ground with the warriors. Kayitah gave a forceful speech:

All of you are my friends, and some of you are my brothers-in-law. I think a lot of you Indians, and I don't want you to get killed. The troops are coming after you from all directions, from all over the United States. You people have no chance whatever.

Geronimo had heard this before. But Kayitah went on:

At night you do not rest as you should. If you are awake at night and a rock rolls down the mountain or a stick breaks, you will be running. The high cliff even is your enemy. At night you go around, and you might fall off the cliff.... You even eat your meals running. You have no friends whatever in the world....

I live at the agency. I live peaceably. Nobody bothers me. I sleep well; I get plenty to eat. I go wherever I want, talk to good people. I go to bed whenever I want and get all my sleep. I have nobody to fear. I have my little patch of corn. I'm trying to do what the white people want me to do.... So I want you to go down with me when the troops come, and they want you to come down on the flats and have a council with them.

Kayitah's evocation of sleep, ease, plentiful food, tugged at the weary warriors' hearts, even Geronimo's, where it clashed with his contempt for that "little patch of corn." The men discussed their feelings. Finally Geronimo agreed at least to meet Gatewood for a talk. Beside the campfire lay a heap of freshly cooked mescal hearts. With both hands, Geronimo gathered a lump of the sticky agave "about the size of a man's heart" and gave it to Martine, telling him to take it to Gatewood as a pledge of his sincerity. But the mistrustful leader insisted on keeping Kayitah as hostage.

Martine reached the army camp by evening. He gave the mescal to Gatewood, who "took it, sliced it up and handed it to his soldiers who ate it between bread." Geronimo had demanded that Gatewood leave his soldiers behind when he came to talk. Here was the most dangerous moment in the lieutenant's long career. The next morning, with only George Wratten to translate and one or two other men, Gatewood agreed to meet the fugitives at a clearing on a bend of the Bavispe.

As the small party approached the rendezvous, they saw the Chiricahuas coming down the mountainside. "We were very anxious for a few minutes," Martine remembered, "thinking that maybe Geronimo had changed his mind and meant trouble for us." Then they saw Kayitah leading the descent.

Gatewood had brought fifteen pounds of tobacco with rolling papers, and also several days' rations of "jerked horse meat & other delicacies." The fugitives came in slowly, by ones and twos, with Geronimo among the last to arrive. He laid his Winchester rifle on the ground, walked up to Nantan Long Nose, and shook his hand; there was no sign that his right arm was crippled. Then, as Wratten translated, Geronimo teased the lieutenant about his thinness and apparent bad health "& asked what was the matter with me."

The two leaders sat on saddles laid across a fallen log. All Geronimo's warriors, still armed, watched carefully. "We did begin to feel a *little* creepy," Wratten reported; and Gatewood admitted to "feeling chilly twitching movements." The lieutenant passed the tobacco; soon every warrior was puffing on a hand-rolled cigarette. At last Geronimo asked for the substance of General Miles's message.

Gatewood blurted it out: "Surrender and you will be sent to join the rest of your people in Florida, there to await the decision of the President as to your final disposition."

In fact Miles would not execute his mass removal of the reservation Chiricahua for another two weeks. But Gatewood, whom the general had armed with knowledge of the plot, believed it had already been carried out.

The news stunned the fugitives. "A silence of several weeks fell on the party," Gatewood later wrote, trying to defuse the intensity of the moment with jocular hyperbole.

Geronimo passed his hand across his eyes, then held both hands forward. Gatewood saw that his fingers were trembling. Instead of responding to the lieutenant's words, he asked if Gatewood had brought anything to drink. "We have been on a three-day drunk," Geronimo confessed; all the mescal from Fronteras was gone. "Now I feel a little shaky," he added.

Finally the war leader gathered his wits. His people would surrender only if they could go back to Turkey Creek and live as they had two years before, with full amnesty for their misdeeds. Gatewood interrupted, saying that he had no power to negotiate: only General Miles could discuss terms.

All day the conference lasted, with the warriors gathering now and again to discuss what to do. The pall of Gatewood's announcement lay heavy over the camp. Every man, woman, and child in the fugitive band had relatives on the reservation; Geronimo had two wives and a son there, Naiche a wife and a daughter. Where was Florida? The distant place seemed as unimaginable as Alcatraz.

Geronimo would not give up his terms. He looked Gatewood square in the eye and laid down his ultimatum: "Take us to the reservation or fight." But he also asked a score of questions about the new general:

He wanted to know Gen. Miles' age, size, color of his hair & eyes, whether his voice was harsh or agreeable to listen to, whether he

talked much or little, & if he meant more than he said or less. Does he look you in the eyes, or down on the ground, when he talks?...
Do the soldiers & officers like him? Has he had experience with other Indians? Was he cruel or kind-hearted? Would he keep his promises?

By sunset, Geronimo was weakening. He asked Gatewood what the lieutenant would do in his place. "I would trust Gen. Miles & take him at his word," Gatewood barked.

The warriors talked through the night. According to Betzinez, whose relatives later told him of that fateful parley, it was Perico, Geronimo's cousin, who first broke down. "I am going to surrender. My wife and children have been captured. I love them, and want to be with them." Fierce individualists to the end, the Apaches knew that each man had to decide for himself. Another warrior echoed Perico, then another.

Geronimo stood in silence, then spoke: "I don't know what to do. I have been depending heavily on you three men. You have been great fighters in battle. If you are going to surrender, there is no use my going without you. I will give up with you."

In the morning, the Chiricahuas told Gatewood of their capitulation. It was the terrible news of the deportation that had turned the tide. The image of Florida in the fugitives' minds was a featureless dark hole, like the notion of slavery in the Mexican south. It was an unknowable void into which their people had vanished.

The formal surrender to General Miles was to take place at Skeleton Canyon, about twenty miles north of the border in Arizona, almost on the New Mexico line. Gatewood brought the thirty-four Chiricahuas up to Lawton's command, which had camped nearby. Lawton escorted the Apaches to Arizona. The journey was not without tribulations, for a Mexican force of two hundred soldiers wanted to finish off the fugitives before they could leave Sonora, and some of Lawton's soldiers, whose brothers-in-arms Geronimo's band had liquidated, were all for a massacre in the middle of the night.

Lawton did his best to assign himself credit for the "capture." In his official report, he claimed that Gatewood had failed to secure a surrender, and that only he had prevailed upon Geronimo. Miles himself subsequently recounted the surrender in accents that made it sound as though the whole thing had been handled by puppet strings from the general's desk at Fort Bowie. In his list of tributes to officers who had served gallantly in the Apache campaign, Gatewood's name does not appear. As for Kayitah and Martine, who had performed the boldest task of all: they had the misfortune to be Chiricahuas, and were shipped to Florida with the "hostiles" whose surrender they had assured.

On September 5, Miles finally put in action his mass removal from the reservation. The commander at Fort Apache called a conference of all the Chiricahua warriors, at which he told them that their people had been invited en masse to go to Washington to meet the Great Father and discuss their future. Inexplicably, the men believed this lie and turned in their arms. A caravan of 434 Chiricahuas, twelve hundred horses, and almost three thousand dogs wound north to the railroad depot at Holbrook. It was only after days aboard the train that the Chiricahuas realized they were not going to Washington after all. They finally disembarked at Fort Marion in Florida, where they joined Chihuahua and Nana's people as prisoners of war.

Meanwhile, the thirty-four fugitives arrived at the mouth of Skeleton Canyon on September 1. As Lawton scribbled one nervous telegram after another, Miles procrastinated. I DO NOT INTEND TO GO DOWN THERE SIMPLY TO TALK, he loftily wired Lawton. Miles's fear was that the Apaches would repeat the fiasco at the Cañon de los Embudos, which had cast so much discredit on Crook. Somehow the general wanted a priori guarantees that nothing could go wrong.

It was not until late on September 3 that Miles arrived. Geronimo at once rode down from his campsite in the rocks overlooking the stream. He dismounted from his horse, approached the general, and shook his hand. The interpreter said, "General Miles is your friend."

"I never saw him," the warrior replied, "but I have been in need of friends. Why has he not been with me?" The tension broke as everyone within earshot burst into laughter.

Miles later described his first look at Geronimo: "He was one of the brightest, most resolute, determined looking men that I have ever encountered. He had the clearest, sharpest, dark eye I think I have ever seen, unless it was that of General Sherman when he was at the prime of life."

Skeleton Canyon had been named for a massacre of Mexican smugglers by American volunteers in 1881 or 1882. The bodies of as many as fifteen of the slain were left unburied; cowboys later collected their skulls to use as soap basins. This grisly legacy was belied by the serene landscape of the gentle canyon, whose stream wound lazily from the low Peloncillo Mountains down to the arid San Simon basin.

Surrounded by their retinues, Miles and Geronimo sat on the ground near the junction of two forks of the stream. Giant sycamores shaded their colloquy. Though Geronimo was unarmed, his warriors retained their weapons. The general said, "Lay down your arms and come with me to Fort Bowie, and in five days you will see your families now in Florida, and no harm will be done to you."

Miles was irked by the laborious process of translation, through Spanish into Apache and back again. He picked up some stones from the river bed and addressed Geronimo as one might a child. He drew a line in the dirt, saying, "This represents the ocean." He placed a stone near the line: "This represents the place where Chihuahua is with his band." Two more stones at some distance from the line stood for the reservation Chiricahua and the thirty-four fugitives. Miles picked both up and placed them next to Chihuahua's stone. "That is what the President wants to do," he said unctuously—"get all of you together."

The next morning Miles made a ceremony of the formal surrender. As Geronimo remembered it,

> We stood between his troopers and my warriors. We placed a large stone on the blanket before us. Our treaty was made by this stone, and it was to last until the stone should crumble to dust; so we made the treaty, and bound each other with an oath.

Miles swept his hand dramatically across a patch of ground. "Your past deeds," he promised, "shall be wiped out like this and you will start a new life."

On September 5, on horses and in wagons, the entourage started for Fort Bowie, sixty miles away. At one point Geronimo glanced at the Chiricahua Mountains, whose every fold and wrinkle he knew, and said, "This is the fourth time I have surrendered." Miles promptly rejoined, "And I think it is the last time."

At Fort Bowie, the general repeated his promises. The Apaches would join their families in five days. (It would be eight months before

the warriors in the final band actually saw their loved ones again.)
Once more Miles resorted to parables in sign language. He held out
an open palm, traced the lines in it with a finger, and said, "This
represents the past; it is all covered with ridges and hollows." Then
he rubbed his palm with the other: "This represents the wiping out of
the past, which will be considered smooth and forgotten."

Meanwhile, the general was exchanging telegrams with Washington.
President Cleveland wanted the fugitives turned over to civil authori-
ties in Arizona—which would have meant speedy trials and execution
of all the warriors, if they were not lynched first. The President cabled
Miles: I HOPE NOTHING WILL BE DONE WITH GERONIMO WHICH WILL PREVENT
OUR KEEPING HIM AS A PRISONER OF WAR IF WE CANNOT HANG HIM, WHICH I
WOULD MUCH PREFER.

Such a betrayal, however, exceeded even Miles's capacity for dou-
ble-dealing. He raised objections and planted doubts; to the President's credit, he eventually sent an officer to ask the Apaches
themselves under what terms they had surrendered. Cleveland relented: Geronimo and his warriors would be deported, not hanged.

Unaware of these machinations, Geronimo and Naiche's band loitered among the adobe buildings at Fort Bowie. As far as they knew,
Miles was a good man and the promises would be kept. The Chiricahuas believed further that Crook's promise of a return to Arizona
within two years still held good: no one had told them differently.
Rather than contradicting Crook's pledge, Miles had equivocated over
the length of the stay in Florida, and he had promised Geronimo's
people a reservation of their own.

The sun burned down on the parched saddle near Apache Pass.
Geronimo drank once more from the spring that, twenty-four years
before, he had fought so hard under Cochise and Mangas to keep the
White Eyes from capturing. Some sixty-three years old, the warrior
posed for his photograph. The soldiers gawked at him as they encour-
aged him to buy new clothes from the trader's store. As souvenirs of
the campaign, Miles had confiscated for his personal collection Geronimo's rifle and spurs. Already the great warrior had begun the
transformation that the rest of his life would accomplish, from an
enemy whose very name could chill a settler's spine to a curiosity, a
totem of conquest. The Wild West Show was not far in his future.

On the morning of September 8, Miles packed the band of Chiricahuas into heavily guarded wagons and started them north toward the

railroad stop at Bowie. As they departed, the camp band broke out the tune of "Auld Lang Syne." The soldiers sang, "Should auld acquaintance be forgot, and never brought to mind. . . ." Geronimo was left to wonder why the music set the soldiers jeering and laughing.

At Bowie, on the bare plain of the San Simon Valley, scored with dry washes, shimmering in the late-summer sun, the train was ready for boarding shortly after 2 P.M. Geronimo looked around, strode to the doorway of a passenger car, whose windows had been locked shut to prevent escape, and climbed aboard.

That short step upward marked the first time in his life that he had been on a railroad train. And it was the last time Geronimo's feet would ever touch the soil of his native land.

Epilogue

■

> To be sure, we have taken their land from them, but in its place
> we have given them something worth infinitely more. We have
> given the [Apaches] a new religion and a Savior.
>
> —FORMER RESERVATION SCHOOLTEACHER
> MRS. ANDREW ATKINSON *(ca. 1974)*

*A*s the train hurtled them eastward, the members of Geronimo's final band felt a gathering sense of doom. Kanseah, the eleven-year-old boy who had served as lookout in the last camp, recalled many years later, "When they put us on that train at Bowie, nobody thought that we'd get far before they'd stop it and kill us."

In San Antonio, the train halted and the prisoners were allowed a closely guarded liberty. As the stop stretched into days, then weeks, the Chiricahua grew deeply apprehensive. Still certain that his vision from Ussen protected him, Geronimo told his people that he himself would not die at the white soldiers' hands, but that he feared for his warriors' lives. The unarmed Apaches expected a massacre at any moment. Kanseah's mother exhorted him that when the attack came, he must "show the White Eyes how an Apache can die."

The cause of the long delay was the usual dithering in Washington. It took President Cleveland and his advisors forty-two days to decide the fate of Geronimo's band. During those six ominous weeks, as sightseers gawked at the guarded captives, no one bothered to explain to the Apaches why they were being delayed.

Meanwhile, aboard a separate train, the 434 Chiricahua who had been tricked into removal from Fort Apache rode east toward their own unknowable destiny. To add to their misery, the windows were barred and locked shut, and the Apaches had access to no toilets: in the heat of September, the railroad cars steamed with the inevitable human stench. Thirty-eight years later, the commanding officer wrote, "When I think of that trip, even at this time, I get seasick." The odor inside the cars was so intense that, in his opinion, "no human being, other than an Indian," could have borne it.

One warrior, a young man named Massai, spent three days furtively loosening the bars on a window. Choosing his moment, as the train slowed to a crawl on a long hill, he slipped through the window and leapt to the ground. No soldier saw his escape.

During the following weeks, Massai walked back to western New Mexico, where he hid in the Black Range. He was never recaptured, spending years as a solitary fugitive. Some say he was finally killed by a shot from ambush near Ojo Caliente; others, that a party of white men trailed him near the Mescalero Reservation and slew him.

A handful of Chiricahua had managed to escape the American dragnet. According to Betzinez, they numbered fewer than ten. For decades they, and their descendants, hid out in the Sierra Madre, occasionally terrorizing an isolated ranch, while surviving by means of a constant ordeal of vigilance and discipline. Of these "lost Apaches," as they have been romantically called, almost nothing is known by whites today, although some historians believe their grandchildren, intermarried with Mexicans and acculturated to a Mexican life, linger on in Sonora and Chihuahua. Present-day Apaches in Arizona and New Mexico guard a secret lore pertaining to these ultimate fugitives.

At last the destination of Geronimo and his "renegades" was fixed by the bureaucrats in Washington. The women and children were to be sent to Fort Marion, near St. Augustine in Florida, where the bulk of the Chiricahua were to be confined. But the "hostile" warriors were to be kept separate, at Fort Pickens, on the tip of a long sandy island offshore from Pensacola, across Florida on the Gulf coast. The rationale was security. As the Secretary of War intoned in his declaration: "These Indians have been guilty of the worst crimes known to the law, committed under circumstances of great atrocity, and the public safety requires that they should be removed far from the scene of their depredations and guarded with the strictest vigilance."

Miles's promise was torn up and discarded like a piece of waste paper. It was in order to be reunited with their relatives that men such as Fun, Perico, Yanozha, Naiche, and Geronimo had finally capitulated. Now even the children who had ridden with them through the desperate summer of 1886 were taken away. For eight months, the Chiricahua warriors were kept as prisoners, 350 miles from their families, with almost no communication between the groups.

At Fort Pickens, however, the dangerous "hostiles" became a public sideshow, as the army led tours for citizens who behaved as if they were visiting a zoo. Journalists who edged close to Geronimo were awed by the scowling visage that bespoke his dark thoughts. "He is the picture of diabolical impassiveness," concluded one; "He has the coldest eye ever beheld in the face of a human being," wrote another.

George Wratten, the former trading-store clerk who had become the Apaches' interpreter and "guardian," wrote letters at Geronimo's dictation, translated into English. One was addressed to his two wives at Fort Marion. The newspapers got hold of it and published it under the title, "A Love Letter from Geronimo." In careful phrases, Geronimo is at pains to paint himself a "good Indian," working hard at the menial jobs his captors have assigned him, hopeful of soon earning the reservation Crook and Miles had promised. But the grief of separation—from his wives and children, and from his homeland—seeps into the homely English of the letter.

> Talking by paper is very good, but when you see one's lips move, and hear their voice, it is much better. I saw Gen. Miles, heard him speak, and looked into his eyes, and believed what he told me, and I still think he will keep his word. He told that I would see you soon; also see a fine country and lots of people. The people and the country I have seen, but not you.

As soon as they arrived in Florida, the Apaches began to die in alarming numbers. Before the end of the year, eighteen deaths were recorded at Fort Marion. One of them was that of Geronimo's four-year-old daughter, whom he had sent to the reservation with the soldiers the previous spring. In September, however, the wife Geronimo had stolen from the Mescalero Reservation in 1885 gave birth to a daughter. She had conceived the child at about the time Captain Emmet Crawford was so doggedly harrying Geronimo's people far south in the Sierra Madre, near the Aros River. Geronimo learned of his newborn daughter only months after her birth.

The Chiricahua kept insisting that the Florida climate was unhealthy for them, a claim their captors dismissed as idle complaining. But Fort Marion was surrounded by marshes that bred malarial mosquitoes. Having never encountered the disease before their forced residence at San Carlos, the Apaches had built up no resistance to the shaking sickness.

Exacerbating the punishment of separating Geronimo's men from their families, the commander at Fort Marion now concocted another outrage in the name of improving the Indian. All the children between the ages of twelve and twenty-two were to be rounded up and shipped to the Carlisle Indian School in Pennsylvania, despite their parents' tearful pleas to leave them with their families. At Carlisle, the Apaches had their hair cut short, and they were dressed in trousers, skirts, and jackets. They were lined up in a row by height and given American names by alphabetical order: Daklugie became "Asa"; Naiche's daughter, "Dorothy"; Betzinez, "Jason"; and so on. Arbitrary birthdates were pinned to them.

These children began to die, too—of tuberculosis, which was rampant, though only dimly suspected, at Carlisle. Before the epidemic ran its course, thirty students were fatally infected.

In April 1887, the Apaches lodged at Fort Marion were moved to Alabama. The impulse was humanitarian: to relieve the captives of their cramped confinement and of the daily ordeal of being stared at by tourists. But their new home was even more alien to the Chiricahua than the coastal prison near St. Augustine. Mount Vernon Barracks was a military post on the Mobile River, some thirty miles inland. It lay in dense pine woods, on swampy ground. At Mount Vernon, the Apache craving for the sun and space grew so intense that men climbed to the tops of trees just to see the sky.

To Mount Vernon came also, by ones and twos, the children who had contracted tuberculosis at the Carlisle School. Sometimes relatives rushed to the train depot to greet a beloved son or daughter; the child, disembarking, would totter and fall to the ground. Parents lifted children into wagons, carried them back to the village, and watched over their deathbeds. Their small corpses were taken far into the forest to be buried, like Cochise's, in a place the White Eyes might never find.

These deaths confirmed the Apaches' worst suspicions: the white men in charge took their sons and daughters a thousand miles north to a place called Pennsylvania, only to send them back emaciated and coughing blood, beyond the ability of the most gifted Chiricahua to heal. And still the officers sought out more children, as they turned twelve, to ship to Carlisle. When a new removal was announced, mothers frantically tried to hide their offspring to save them from the fatal exile.

Meanwhile the contagion the dying children had brought with them from the north spread insidiously through the Chiricahua at Mount Vernon. One of the first to die was Lozen. The woman warrior, who had survived the annihilation of her brother Victorio's people at Tres Castillos, who had ridden with Geronimo until the end, succumbed to a yet unknown bacillus, an enemy too microscopic for her vaunted Power to locate.

In October 1887, Geronimo and Naiche enlisted their interpreter, George Wratten, to write a letter on their behalf to the general in charge of their custody. The tone of this plea is almost fawning, yet the sharpness of the Chiricahua disappointment lies just below the surface.

> You told them [Wratten wrote] they [would] be here no longer than a year at the outside. The year is almost up and they now wish to hear from you. . . . They would like to know when they are going to see the good land and farms Gen. Miles told them about.
>
> They have behaved better under the circumstances than any other lot of people could have, I think.

Though the letter went unanswered, it helped to loosen the bureaucratic logjam in Washington. At last, in May 1888, Geronimo's "hostiles" were delivered from their imprisonment at Fort Pickens and allowed to rejoin the rest of the Chiricahua at Mount Vernon. The reunion in Alabama stirred the deepest emotions among the Apaches, although dignity required that they mask their feelings in the presence of their white jailers.

For six more years the Chiricahua languished in the gloomy pine woods at Mount Vernon. A makeshift schoolhouse was set up for children too young to send to Carlisle. The curriculum was strong on Christian piety. Half a decade before, Apache youngsters had run through the woods playing at hunting and war; now they knelt in the schoolhouse, bowed their heads, and prayed in English:

> Dear Savior, make me good,
> And help me every day;
> Forgive me my sins
> For Jesus' sake, I pray.

At Christmas, George Wratten dressed up as Santa Claus and gave the children bags of candy and marbles.

A party of Boston society women—"Indian lovers" of the kind veterans of the Apache wars could not abide—made an ostensibly sympathetic visit one December. The women were surprised at the depth of the Chiricahua longing for Arizona, "a country which the Apaches almost worship," as one later wrote. The women found the lame-footed chief Nana, well over eighty, especially disconsolate. "Do you *love* your own HOME?" he thundered at them through an interpreter. One of the women seized a globe and tried to instruct the chief: the whole world was covered with people, she soothed, thus the Indians could no longer roam at will, but must live and work as brothers with the white man. She tried to give the globe to Nana, but the chief sat with his head in his hands and sighed, "I'm too old to learn that."

Early in 1890, General Crook, by now a staunch advocate for the Chiricahua he had spent his best years fighting, paid a visit to Mount Vernon. It was the first time Geronimo had beheld the Tan Wolf since he had fled the Cañon de los Embudos four years before. Most of the Apaches were delighted to see Crook, but Geronimo held him personally responsible for the promises his government had broken. The feeling was mutual. "I don't want to hear anything from Geronimo," Crook told Wratten. "He is such a liar that I can't believe a word he says."

One by one other leading Chiricahua men pressed their grievances upon Crook. The general listened with his characteristic implacability, and left without committing himself. Yet he had been moved. In his report, though he stopped short of recommending a return of the Apaches to Arizona, he pleaded that they be given a reservation in the Indian Territory of Oklahoma, and condemned the practice of sending the children to Carlisle.

Only two months later, Crook was dead of a heart attack, at the age of sixty-one. Geronimo never forgave his old antagonist. Fifteen years later, as he dictated his autobiography, he spoke in words so black with bitterness that his amanuensis felt he had to disclaim them in a footnote. "I think that General Crook's death," said Geronimo, "was sent by the Almighty as a punishment for the many evil deeds he committed."

Malaria, tuberculosis, and malnutrition took an appalling toll among the Chiricahua. At the end of 1889, General Howard—like Crook now an Apache champion—sent his son to evaluate the captives' state. Bare statistics told the story. In a little over three years in the East, 119 of the Chiricahua had died—nearly one quarter of the number that had been carried to Florida on the sealed railroad cars in 1886.

The younger Howard recognized that disease alone did not account for the death rate. His report spoke with plain eloquence of the "grief-stricken" parents of dead children, of the "depression" and "hopeless feeling" so pervasive among the Apaches in Alabama. Howard strenuously urged giving the Chiricahua a reservation of their own, to be established by March 1, 1890. "Another year's delay would be criminal," the young officer concluded. It would take Washington four years to respond.

The impact of Chiricahua despair was epitomized, in March 1891, in the demise of Fun. The once-blithe warrior, arguably the bravest of all in Geronimo's final band, became infuriated one night at his wife's attentions to another man. Perhaps Fun was drunk, though liquor was not easy to come by at Mount Vernon. Perhaps the woman was guilty of adultery, and therefore, in Apache eyes, deserving of death or disfigurement. In his rage, Fun shot the woman with his rifle. He thought he had killed her, though she would soon recover. Certain that the army officers would hang him for his deed, Fun walked alone into the forest. He took his shoes off, leaned against a tree, propped the rifle so that the barrel touched his head, and pulled the trigger with his toes.

It was not until October 1894 that the Chiricahua were at last resettled in Oklahoma. Along with bureaucratic lethargy, other obstacles had conspired to delay the removal. The post commander at Fort Sill was extremely loath to receive the Apaches, and the Kiowa and Comanche who already lived there—and out of whose land the Apache settlement would be carved—were uneasy about a tribe of strangers who had never had close relations with them.

After eight years of imprisonment in Florida and Alabama—so much longer than Geronimo or Naiche or Nana had bargained for in 1886—a special train carried the Chiricahua west again. Not west to their homeland, but at least west to a place where the sky lay open above and low granite mountains loomed in the distance and a man could ride a horse.

Notorious at the time of his surrender, Geronimo had only grown more famous during his years of obscure penance in the Alabama forest. As the train crept through Louisiana and Texas, he became the star of the procession. Crowds gathered at whistle-stops to cheer the celebrated warrior. Geronimo responded with his canny pragmatism. Wratten had taught him to print his name in bold but childish capitals: soon Geronimo was selling his autograph at twenty-five cents a copy. On subsequent train journeys, he cut the buttons off his coat and sold them each for a quarter, then between stations sewed new buttons on. His hat went for five dollars.

At Fort Sill, the Kiowa and Comanche overcame their qualms and poured out to greet the Apaches. They tried to converse with them in sign language, unaware that the Chiricahua had never learned the lingua franca of the Indian plains.

For the first time in eight years, the Apache women gathered brush and built wickiups, using army canvas for covering in place of the traditional hides. At night, when they heard coyotes howl for the first time in eight years, the women wept. Learning that mesquite bushes grew only forty-five miles away, the Chiricahua begged permission to harvest the beans, which they had not tasted in almost a decade. In forty-eight hours, walking and jogging the ninety-mile round trip, they gathered three hundred bushels of the tiny brown fruit.

But Fort Sill was not a reservation: the Apaches were still prisoners of war. They would continue to be so for another nineteen grinding years. To be sure, they were not locked inside a palisade or guarded by armed sentries. The Apaches were given a loose freedom to wander about the grounds and to make trips to the nearby town of Lawton, but they had no privilege to venture farther afield.

Each family was allotted a plot of land under the cottonwoods, along the meanders of Medicine Bluff and Cache Creeks. The Chiricahua built serviceable wooden cabins, giving up their wickiups for good. They settled down, as the government had always insisted they must, to become farmers. A late photo of Geronimo shows him standing in his melon patch with his wife Ziyeh and three small children. He holds his hat in his right hand, a giant melon cradled in his left arm. There is no pride in his countenance as he squints into the sun and the camera: he looks worn out and sleepy in his dusty clothes. Is this the face, one wonders, that launched eight thousand troops?

For years, the authorities at Fort Sill worried that the Apaches might yet break out. That any of the Chiricahua might be permitted to see their homeland again, even on a supervised visit, was a thought beyond the wildest whims of their guardians' leniency. Yet by now Geronimo was world renowned; with the death of Chief Sitting Bull in 1890, the Bedonkohe warrior had become the most famous Indian in America. As a trophy of conquest, his jailers reckoned, Geronimo might be allowed to travel.

His first experience in such a role came in Omaha in 1898, when Geronimo attended the Trans-Mississippi and International Exhibition. There he did a good business selling autographed photos of himself and toy bows and arrows he had crafted. Then the promoters of the exhibition pulled their surprise: Geronimo was brought face-to-face with General Nelson Miles.

For Crook, eight years after the man's death, Geronimo still harbored a dark anger, but it was tempered with the respect the Chiricahua had always granted their finest enemy. In the case of Miles, Apache hatred was deepened with contempt for this general who led from the rear, who played with his sun-flashing toy, who hid behind his desk at Fort Bowie—"a coward, a liar, and a poor officer," as Juh's son Daklugie would insist sixty years later.

The sudden encounter, before a large and eager audience, sent a paroxysm of rage through Geronimo's breast. His hands trembled, he broke into a sweat, and at first he could not find his words. For twelve years he had ached for the chance to confront the man who had betrayed his people. At last, through an interpreter, he spat out, "When we surrendered to you in Skeleton Canyon in Arizona you said we would see our families in Florida within five days; you said that all would be forgiven. You lied to us, General Miles."

Playing to the crowd, Miles rejoined, "I did lie to you, Geronimo, but I learned to lie from you, Geronimo, who is the greatest of all liars."

In an effort to convey the pain of his people's separation from their homeland, Geronimo spoke in the animistic tropes of Apache oratory. "I have been away from Arizona now twelve years," he said. "The acorns and piñon nuts, the quail and the wild turkey, the giant cactus and the palo verdes—they all miss me. They wonder where I've gone. They want me to come back."

Miles chuckled. "A very beautiful thought, Geronimo. Quite poetic. But the men and women who live in Arizona, they do not miss you.

They do not wonder where you have gone; they know. They do not want you to come back. . . . The acorns and piñon nuts, the quail and the wild turkey, the giant cactus and the palo verde trees—they will have to get along as best they can—without you."

As Miles smirked, Geronimo stormed out of the room. The two men never saw each other again.

At Fort Sill, the soldiers who daily rubbed elbows with Geronimo belittled the old warrior, nicknaming him "Gerry." Yet in the larger world he grew to mythic proportions. The most absurd stories about him gained general credence. He was supposed to be the possessor of a blanket he had stitched together out of the scalps of ninety-nine of his victims. At the same time, having been driven insane by his years of imprisonment, he was purported to pace a cell at Fort Sill, confined as "a raving maniac."

Geronimo's Power had not failed him in old age. At Fort Sill he continued to treat fellow Chiricahua who fell ill. For a man who had contracted coyote sickness, Geronimo sang in the darkness for four nights, handled an eagle feather and a bag of pollen, and blew smoke to the four directions. According to his people, he cured an old woman whom a wolf had bewitched. He also treated those afflicted with ghost sickness.

The Chiricahua had need of his efforts: even at Fort Sill, the death rate held high. To walk today through the serene Apache cemetery set on a shelf of land above Cache Creek is to be smitten by this legacy of loss. Here in a line stand the headstones of six sons and two daughters of Naiche, all young when they died. Here lie three of Geronimo's children, the children of Fun, the widow of Juh, the relatives of Chatto and Kanseah, and many others. There stands the stone of Nana, who succumbed, worn out but unreformed, in 1896. Nearby lies Loco, the chief who wanted no part of Geronimo's rebellion, dead in 1905.

In regimental rows and columns, some three hundred identical white headstones range across the level grass. The inscriptions are terse, or nonexistent. Above the name of the deceased, each stone bears a cross inside a circle. On the back of each is carved a location marker, such as "SW5055"—a cold reminder of the number tags the Apaches were issued at San Carlos.

Through the first decade of the twentieth century, Geronimo continued to be trotted out for fairs and exhibitions. Pawnee Bill, an imitator of Buffalo Bill Cody, featured him in his Wild West Show. Geronimo was alternately billed as "the tiger of the human race" and as "the worst Indian that ever lived." On an Oklahoma ranch, before an audience of tens of thousands, he performed in "The Last Buffalo Hunt," despite the fact that the Chiricahua had last hunted the buffalo centuries before Geronimo was born. From the front seat of an automobile, the warrior opened fire. Then he leapt to the ground, sprang upon the wounded beast, and cut its throat with a hunting knife.

Geronimo's grandest show came at the World's Fair in St. Louis in 1904. For weeks on end, he lived in an "Apache village" erected on the grounds. He was now charging—and getting—two dollars for his autographed photo. Despite an age of some eighty-one years, Geronimo responded to the other exhibits with the probing curiosity that had marked his life. He rode a Ferris wheel, watched a puppet show, stared in amazement at a trained polar bear that carried a log and seemed to understand the speech of its handler. ("I have never considered bears very intelligent, except in their wild habits, but I had never before seen a white bear," he said later. "I am sure that no grizzly bear could be trained to do these things.") Geronimo focused his most penetrating attention on the magic acts—he was determined to figure out how the man passed his sword through the body of the lady in the basket without killing her—and on the "primitive" peoples of other lands (Turks, Filipinos, and the like) displayed in other booths.

For all the trivializing effect of such spectacles, Geronimo's name continued to resonate with the threat it had once sounded in the ears of the nation. One day during their stay at the Omaha Exhibition in 1898, Geronimo and Naiche and a few other Apaches hired a wagon to take a ride in the countryside. They got lost among the endless cornfields. Darkness fell. As word of their disappearance spread across eastern Nebraska, farmers bolted their doors and sat with rifles ready. By the time the Apaches regained Omaha, the headline of the extra read: "GERONIMO AND NACHEE ESCAPE. APACHE MURDERERS THOUGHT TO BE ON THEIR WAY BACK TO ARIZONA."

Even in old age, Geronimo was fiercely vain of his physical skills. In 1905, on a walk near the warrior's cabin, a historian visiting Fort Sill decided "to test Geronimo's agility" by jumping across a creek that lay in their path; the historian had been a broad jumper in college. Geronimo at once vaulted the stream, landing a foot beyond the other man's mark. An artist who came to paint the warrior's picture found himself challenged to a shooting contest with the artist's own .22 rifle. The target was a small piece of paper pinned to a tree yards away. Geronimo proposed a wager of ten dollars per hit, but the artist, pitying the old man's "bleary eyes," said, "No, we'll shoot for fun."

"It was lucky for me that I did that," the artist later wrote, "for he hit the paper every shot, and once hit the pin that held it. I never made a hit."

Another day, in "a most peculiar mood," Geronimo told the artist that no human being could kill him. The painter looked skeptical; suddenly Geronimo pulled off his shirt.

> I was dumfounded to see the number of bullet holes in his body. . . .
> I had never heard of anyone living with at least fifty bullet wounds on his body. Geronimo had that many scars.
>
> Some of these bullet holes were large enough to hold small pebbles that Geronimo picked up and placed in them. Putting a pebble in a bullet wound he would make a noise like a gun, then take the pebble out and throw it on the ground. Jokingly I told him he was probably so far away that the bullets didn't penetrate him, but that if he had been nearer they probably would have killed him.
>
> "No, no," he shouted. "Bullets cannot kill me!"

In 1905, Stephen M. Barrett, Superintendent of Schools for Lawton, Oklahoma, determined to record Geronimo's autobiography. The warrior himself was wary of Barrett's invitation, and the army, whose prisoner Geronimo remained, forbade the effort. Barrett appealed all the way to President Teddy Roosevelt, who gave his blessing.

Geronimo's Story of His Life, published in 1906, is an invaluable book, albeit a quirky and unreliable one. In his sensitivity to army outrage, Barrett sprinkled the text with editorial caveats: "These are the exact words of Geronimo. The Editor is not responsible for this criticism." What punches Barrett pulled via silent emendation, no one will ever know.

There were also, of course, the usual problems of translating Apache into English. The tone of Apache rhetoric is impossible to render in an Indo-European tongue. Miles had thought Geronimo was waxing sentimental when he spoke of the acorns missing him; but all Apaches recognized the mystic shorthand in a phrase, handed down over the centuries—the furthest thing from boasting—that imputed sorrow to the very trees. English imported its own vanities. Geronimo, like other Indian spokesmen, was often reported to allude to the President as the Great White Father. The best rendering of the phrase Geronimo actually used would be One in Washington.

As translator, Barrett enlisted Juh's son Daklugie, fresh from his schooling at Carlisle. Many years later Daklugie revealed that Geronimo had feared that Barrett was a spy for the government, trying to trick him into making confessions for which he would be further punished. The warrior thus approached the writing of "his" book with deep caution. It is not surprising that many of the pivotal episodes in his life go unrecorded in *Geronimo's Story*.

If the short memoir published in 1906 remains elusive, Geronimo managed to make it the vehicle for an eloquent plea. In the closing pages, pondering the grievance that had lain heaviest on his heart during the previous nineteen years, he appealed explicitly to President Roosevelt, who he hoped might prove his friend and benefactor. It was upon the chance that his people might at last be suffered to return to Arizona that Geronimo had brooded night after night.

> It is my land, my home, my fathers' land, to which I now ask to be allowed to return. I want to spend my last days there, and be buried among those mountains. If this could be I might die in peace, feeling that my people, placed in their native homes, would increase in numbers, rather than diminish as at present, and that our name would not become extinct.

In Roosevelt, Geronimo indeed found a sympathetic ear—so much so that the Rough Rider invited the Apache to ride at the head of his inaugural parade in March 1905. This was an honor far removed from the tawdry glory of serving as a performing aborigine at the World's Fair, and many an army veteran burned with indignation at the procession. Seizing his chance, Geronimo won a private audience with Roosevelt, where he made his Arizona plea with all the force he could muster. "My hands are tied as with a rope. My heart is no longer bad. . . ," he closed. "I pray you to cut the ropes and make me free. Let me die in my own country, an old man who has been punished enough."

"I have no anger in my heart against you," answered Roosevelt. But the President warned that the hatred that still seethed in Arizona would issue in further bloodshed if the Apaches returned. "It is best for you to stay where you are.... That is all I can say, Geronimo, except that I am sorry."

Upon its subjugated foes, a conquering nation projects its fantasies of the just order. The Apaches, so often likened to tigers, were now caged animals in a zoo, paraded to elicit the *frisson* that wildness always harbors. White America's fantasy of the Indian, in all its bluff Yankee optimism, had at its core the belief that savages could be cured of their wild benightedness, turned into farmers and citizens and Christians. Whence the haircuts and the long pants and skirts of the Carlisle School.

Central to that fantasy was the conviction that in time, the Indians would thank their teachers. It is not surprising that observers who visited Geronimo at Fort Sill sometimes reported him to be, as one put it, "an agreeable, amiable old man..., happy as a bird." Sometimes, whether to charm his tormenters or in an abject swing of his ever-vacillating temper, Geronimo himself spoke words that fed the fantasy. "I do not consider that I am an Indian any more," he said as early as 1894. "I am a white man and w[oul]d like to go around and see different places. I consider that all white men are my brothers."

To their decades as prisoners of war, the several Chiricahua leaders responded in different ways. Nana lapsed into a bitter and unrepentant gloom. The dreamy Naiche took up painting (his deerskin scenes from Apache life, preserved at the Fort Sill Museum, are among the most remarkable Indian artworks); around the turn of the century, he joined the Dutch Reformed Church, keeping a steadfast faith till his death in 1921.

Geronimo's response was more complex. The great labor of his last twenty-three years was a metaphysical quest to understand what had happened to him and to his people. He gave his captors only glimpses of this dark intellectual struggle, preferring to humor them with the vignettes from the Wild West Show. Even now, for non-Apaches, the traces of those decades of wrestling with fate can only be teased out of the record.

Geronimo, too, flirted with Christianity; he was even baptized. The triggering event was a fall from a horse in 1903 that left him badly injured. One day thereafter he came to a prayer meeting conducted by missionaries at Fort Sill, sat down next to Naiche, and spoke through an interpreter: "He says that he is in the dark. He knows that he is not on the right road and he wants to find Jesus."

Cynics thought Geronimo's Christian experiment just another charade to curry favor. The sense of doom, however, that hung over the old warrior's soul seemed to make him doubt the power of Ussen. If the white man had won in the end, perhaps the white man's god was stronger. For Naiche, once converted, faith was a clear light, and for twenty years he rose in church and testified with an unconflicted heart to the bounty of a Christian god. For Geronimo, with his itch to understand the cosmos, the strange god of the Bible was an idea that must be plumbed.

His utterances, as he puzzled over Jesus, reveal no simple piety, but the flickering shadows of doubt and wonderment. "Is that all I have to do," he asked one missionary, "just believe?" Ussen required more. Much of Geronimo's anguish had a moral root. His dreams were haunted by memories of the killing he had done, particularly that of white children. "Often I would steal up to the homes of white settlers and kill the parents," he confessed in an unguarded moment. "In my hatred I would even take the little ones out of their cradles and toss them in the air. They would like this and would gurgle with glee, but when they came down I would catch them on my sharp hunting knife and kill them." Now, he added, "I wake up groaning and very sad at night when I remember the helpless little children."

Yet even as he sought a Christian revelation, Geronimo continued to exercise the healing Power Ussen had given him. Near the end of his life, he uttered a sly paradox: "I am praying to the White Man's God to let me live," he said, "for my people need me and He does not."

After twenty-seven years as prisoners of war—a servitude unparalleled in the Indian annals of the United States—the Chiricahua were freed in 1913. Perhaps twelve hundred strong in Cochise's prime, they had dwindled to about five hundred when they were shipped to Florida. By 1913, only 261 Chiricahua were still alive.

Yet even then they were not allowed to return to Arizona. Space had been offered them on the reservation of their sometime allies, the Mescalero, east of the Rio Grande in New Mexico. About two-thirds of the Chiricahua chose to move there; the other third stayed in Oklahoma. In those two places, the Chiricahua live today, among them a few direct descendants of Geronimo and, through Naiche, of Cochise.

But the decision to free the Apache came too late for Geronimo. On a cold day in February 1909, he had ridden to Lawton, sold some bows and arrows, and gotten drunk. Heading home after dark, he fell off his horse and lay all night on the ground. Now eighty-five years old, he contracted pneumonia, and lingered in a delirium for several days. In this state he thought he saw a young Chiricahua who had recently died; the boy approached Geronimo and begged him to become a Christian, but he refused, saying he had been unable to "follow the path" in his life, and now it was too late. Geronimo died on February 17.

His people buried him in the cemetery beside Cache Creek. His memorial, a pyramid of brown granite stones topped by a carved stone eagle, is the only one in the graveyard that escapes the rigid anonymity of the numbered white headstones. At Geronimo's funeral, an old woman broke out wailing in Apache: "Everybody hated you: white men hated you, Mexicans hated you, Apaches hated you; all of them hated you. You [have] been good to us. We love you, we hate to see you go."

In this last years, Geronimo was haunted with an apocalyptic vision of the extinction of the Chiricahua, not unlike the one that had wafted out of a blue cloud before Juh's men in the Sierra Madre so many years before. Occasionally, in his pessimism, he voiced his gloom to white listeners, as in Omaha in 1898: "The sun rises and shines for a while and then it goes down, sinking out of sight and it is lost. So it will be with the Indians."

In the last years, no one was closer to Geronimo than Daklugie, who held his hand as the great warrior lapsed into his final coma. Daklugie knew his deepest thoughts. They were not, ultimately, of despair and extinction, so much as of an acid regret. He should never have surrendered, he told his young protégé, should never have believed "the lies told by Miles." He should have stayed in Mexico and fought until the last man died.

His thoughts came back often to the massacre of his family near Janos; sixty years later, his fury at the Mexicans was undimmed. Now, on his deathbed, he raved upon these obsessive themes. If only he had died like Victorio, fighting his enemies to the last bullet. He should never have weakened. He should have fought to the end with his last allies; how well they had eluded the eight thousand soldiers who had scoured Mexico in search of them! Again and again, as his feeble fingers clutched Daklugie's hand and his brain grew dim, Geronimo spoke out loud the names of the warriors in that final band: Naiche, Lozen, Perico, Chapo, Tissnolthos, Yanozha, Fun. . . .

. . .

Eighty years on, it seems unfathomable that white Americans could have found no way to coexist, in all the empty magnificence of the Southwest, with a mere twelve hundred Chiricahua—roughly the population today of such wayside Arizona hamlets as Pima or Morenci. The heartland of the Apache, upon which even the caravans of modern tourism have left little mark, pulses with the absence of the people who knew and used that wilderness best.

Along the rocky terraces above Aravaipa Creek, the saguaro blooms; its green fruit bulbs and withers, untasted by the human tongue. In the Dragoon Mountains, close by Cochise's bones, the mesquite branches load each August with beans that drop ungathered. The junipers and piñons yield their crop on slopes where only ground squirrels scavenge. Each May the agaves swell with the moisture of the soil, but no women come to dig their roots and bake the fleshy mescal hearts beneath the ground.

The sacred pool at Ojo Caliente brims in the silence, spilling toward the canyon where a thousand swallows dart and sing; the red face-painting clay sleeps in its geologic bed. In Apache Pass, the spring that Mangas nearly gave his life to hold seeps in its shadowy cranny, drunk only by the animals. Over Turkey Creek the hawks soar on spirals of wind, while the tall pines drift and toss and no one sees them.

Upstream from Cañon de los Embudos, the chipped flakes, black and gray and ruddy, disappear under each summer's shifting sand, where no fingers shape the flint. High in the Sierra Madre, the zigzag trail to Juh's Stronghold lies covered in the swaying grama grass. The deer flit safe beneath the cottonwoods along the blue Bavispe River, where, with no human ear to wonder what they say, at dusk the coyotes yip and howl.

Notes

■

Preface

Page

14 "They hurl themselves at danger": Sonnichsen, *Mescalero,* 46.

14 "In character they resemble": Cozzens, *Explorations,* 83.

14 "The most rascally Indian": Thrapp, *Victorio,* 60.

14 "An [Apache] only knows": Thrapp, *Conquest of Apacheria,* 155.

14 "A miserable, brutal race": ibid., 234.

14 "The cowardly Apache creeps": Bell, *Tracks,* 184.

14 "None of the Pacific Coast": *History of the Arizona Territory,* San Francisco: 1884, 181.

14 "They are the keenest": Skinner, *Rock,* 46.

14 "An [Apache] can stoically suffer": Skinner, 89.

One: Cut the Tent

Page

21 A Kentuckian by birth: Thrapp, *Conquest of Apacheria,* 16; Sweeney, *Cochise,* 427. A good photograph of Bascom is preserved in Arizona Historical Society.

21 Tall for an Apache: Sweeney, *Cochise,* XV, 118–19; Cozzens, *Explorations,* 86

21 "his glance being enough": Hughes, *"History:* Cochise, the Chiricahua Chieftain," *Arizona Star,* January 31, 1886.

22 "it was as much as anyone's life": Ball, *Indeh,* 23–25.

22 Arriving at Siphon Canyon: Governor A. P. K. Safford, *Tucson Citizen,* 1872, in Miller, *The Arizona Story,* 55; Lockwood, *Apache Indians,* 101.

22 he may even have contracted: Sweeney says the firewood story "lacks documentary evidence" (*Cochise,* 129–30); but Bourke claimed in 1891 that he was often told of the contract by oldtimers (*Border,* 119).

22 Thus he came to Bascom's: Sweeney, *Cochise,* 150–51.

23 So quickly had he made his escape: Turrill, "A Vanished Race," 14–15.

23 The chief's six relatives: Sweeney, *Cochise,* 151–52.

23 He would live on in Arizona: ibid., 427.

23 "a wandering, aged, unkempt": C. T. Connell, "Micky Free," 43.

23 The truth seems rather: ibid., 43–44.

23 Some said it was a birth defect: Griffith, *Mickey Free,* 20–25; C. T. Connell, "Micky Free," 50.

23 Some say the boy had run away: Poston, *Building a State,* 97; C. T. Connell, "Micky Free," 44.

24 In high dudgeon: Sweeney, *Cochise,* 144–46.

24 Some claimed he had been driven out: Poston, *Building a State,* 96; Farish, *History,* v. 2, 30.

24 "in all respects": Farish, *History,* v. 2, 30.

24 "was probably not of as much importance": Ball, *Indeh,* 25.

24 It was members of: John Rope narrative, in G. Goodwin, *Raiding,* 135.

24 In 1874 Felix Ward: Thrapp, *Al Sieber,* 185.

24 "an indolent creature": C. T. Connell, "Micky Free," 50.

24 "incapable of loyalty": James Kaywaykla, in Ball, *In the Days,* 155.

24 "the coyote whose kidnapping": Debo, *Geronimo,* 222.

24 "could not be printed": Davis, *Truth,* 37.

25 Before dusk that February 4: Sweeney, *Cochise,* 152–53.

25 Bascom ordered his soldiers to fire: Sacks, "New Evidence," 266.

25 One of the Butterfield men: Sweeney, *Cochise,* 153–54.

26 Coyuntara, a great fighter: ibid., 141.

26 His scouts had spotted: ibid., 155–56.

26 Yet Bascom's own official report: Sacks, 266.

27 Some witnesses reported: Sweeney doubts this story, but see Russell, *One Hundred and Three Fights,* 24–27, and Utley, "The Bascom Affair," 65.

27 Was it, as one scholar suggests: Sacks, 275–78.

27 He retreated south: Sweeney, *Cochise,* 158–63.

28 Two days later a detachment: Utley, "The Bascom Affair," 67.

28 Wallace's corpse could be identified: Oury, "To the Society," [n. p.].

28 Bascom could not tell whether: Sacks, 267.

28 On their way to relieve Bascom: Sweeney, *Cochise,* 163.

28 Bascom bound his captives: Sacks, 267.

28 Six soldiers tossed their lariats: Sweeney, *Cochise,* 163, 167; Oury, [n. p.].

29   One of them, Naiche: Ball, *Indeh,* 25.

29   In his official reports, Bascom: Sacks, 266–67.

29   the Apaches later admitted to: Barrett, *Geronimo's Story,* 115.

29   For his efforts, Bascom: Sweeney, *Cochise,* 165; Thrapp, *Conquest of Apacheria,* 16.

29   Among Apaches, the catastrophe: Sweeney, *Cochise,* 144; Betzinez, *I Fought,* 41.

29   One of Cochise's warriors: Barrett, 117.

Two: The Black Pot

Page

30   For about a month: Sweeney, *Cochise,* 170–76.

31   Agitated survivors swore: The American observation, born of terror, lives on in the obligatory Western movie scene: a wagon trundles along a canyon floor; on the rimrock above, a solitary Apache on horseback appears, glaring down; all at once, hundreds of other mounted Apaches ride into view, surrounding the hapless travelers.

31   An Arizona pioneer reckoned: Charles D. Poston to C. E. Cooley, May 17, 1866, cited in Ogle, *Control,* 45.

31   "Bascom's stupidity": Farish, *History,* v. 2, 32–33.

31   Cochise's biographer, Edwin R. Sweeney: Sweeney, *Cochise,* 132–41.

31   James Tevis, a gold miner: Tevis, *Arizona,* 165.

31   "the Abraham Lincoln of Indians": Neil Goodwin, personal communication, 1990.

31   Tevis, who knew the chief: Tevis, *Weekly Arizonian,* July 14, 1859, cited in Sweeney, *Cochise,* 129.

31   Yet in the heat: Sweeney, *Cochise,* 191–92.

31   Tevis, who at different times: Tevis, *Arizona,* 111–13, 147–52, 220–28.

32   The summer of 1861: Cole, *Chiricahua,* 91.

32   For the Apaches, lightning was the visible: Opler, *Life-Way,* 38, 195, 240–41, 281–84.

32   A whole class of shamans: Cole, 91.

33   As early as March: Thrapp, *Victorio,* 75.

33   The Apaches rejoiced: Ball, *In the Days,* 45.

33   A decade earlier, when his Chiricahuas: Sweeney, *Cochise,* 178.

33   By late 1861, only two: ibid., 190; Ogle, 45.

33   "If the world were searched over": Browne, *Adventures,* 134.

33   "Innocent and unoffending men": Cremony, *Life,* 117.

34   Then, in the winter: Terrell, *Chronicle,* 224.

34   Cochise never fully absorbed: Turrill, "A Vanished Race," 20.

34   Through early 1862, a western campaign: Terrell, 223–29.

35   Some ethnographers would eventually: Opler, *Life-Way,* 1–3.

35   Among his people, he was a giant: Sweeney, *Cochise,* 44.

35   "As noble a specimen": Cozzens, *Explorations,* 118.

35   "the poetic ideal of a chieftain": Edward H. Wingfield, cited in Thrapp, *Victorio,* 32.

35   "the greatest and most talented": Cremony, 176.

35   Uniquely in the known history: Wellman, *Death,* 58; Thrapp, *Conquest of Apacheria,* 13–14.

35   To cement an affiliation: Sweeney, *Cochise,* 45.

35   "The life of Mangas Colorad[as]": Cremony, 177.

35   "as black-hearted a murderer": Thrapp, *Conquest of Apacheria,* 10–11.

36   Johnson was motivated, not by: Sweeney, *Cochise,* 32; Ball, *In the Days,* 46; Thrapp, *Conquest of Apacheria,* 9.

36   At the head of a party: Sweeney, *Cochise,* 33–34.

36   Not only was Mangas: Ball, *In the Days,* 46.

36   "The White Eyes are superstitious": Nana, quoted ibid., 32.

36   Gold was too soft: Ball, *Indeh,* 10, 15.

36   The old chief took it: Cremony, 173; Ball, *In the Days,* 47.

37   "It was the greatest insult": Wellman, 57.

37   In May 1861, Mangas focused: Sweeney, *Cochise,* 181–82, 186–87; Terrell, 222–23.

37   By feigning peace with: Sweeney, *Cochise,* 196–98.

37   To ensure victory, he enlisted: Thrapp, *Conquest of Apacheria,* 23; Ball, *Indeh,* 249; Barrett, *Geronimo's Story,* 47–48.

37   In mid-July, a command of sixty-eight: Sweeney, *Cochise,* 198.

38   Cochise and Mangas let the troops: ibid., 198–99, 436.

38   The captain in charge: Cremony, 161.

38   The battle lasted three hours: Sweeney, *Cochise,* 199–201; Cremony, 164; Ball, *In the Days,* 47.

38   "After they turned cannon loose": Daklugie, quoted in Ball, *Indeh,* 52.

38   A private leading a played-out horse: John Teal, quoted in Cremony, 159–60.

39   The Apaches carried Mangas: Ball, *Indeh,* 20.

39   In early 1862, Jefferson Davis: Baylor, *John Robert Baylor,* 2, 10–14.

39   "a devout Christian, a good": Sweeney, *Cochise,* 203–4.

40   "All Indian men of that tribe": Sonnichsen, *Mescalero,* 110–11.

40   In January 1863, a party: Conner, *Walker,* 34–35.

40   According to Geronimo, who told: Barrett, 119–20.

40   Apaches have carried down: Cole, 96.

41   Only one reliable account: Conner, 36–41.

42   The skull was sent to: McClintock, *Arizona,* v. I, 177; Wellman, 89.

42   West subsequently reported that Mangas: Wellman, 89.

42   The Apaches who had warned: Barrett, 121.

42   Somehow the news contained: Ball, *In the Days,* 48; Ball, *Indeh,* 20.

42   "perhaps the greatest wrong": Barrett, 119.

Three: Torture

Page
43   In the 1970s, an ethnohistorian: Cole, *Chiricahua,* 97.

43   Three generations afterward: Ball, *Indeh,* 20; Ball, *In the Days,* 13, 206.

44   "There was no greater punishment": Ball, *Indeh,* 12.

44   "In the fury of the onslaught": Pfefferkorn, *Sonora,* 148–49.

44   "savagely cruel" Apaches: *Rudo Ensayo,* 88.

44   "After fattening her for several": Cozzens, *Explorations,* 125–26.

45   "They find out from the shaman": Opler, *Life-Way,* 252.

45   "to propitiate the Great Spirit": Cozzens, 125.

45   He also tied them spread-eagled: Cremony, *Life,* 267.

45   And he liked, we are told: Sweeney, *Cochise,* 256.

46   cut the hearts out: Thrapp, *Conquest of Apacheria,* 65.

46   some insisted the Indians: Thrapp, *Victorio,* 130.

46   staked them out to ant hills: Wellman, *Death,* 177.

46   tied them to cactuses: Thrapp, *Conquest of Apacheria,* 134.

46   slit their skin in strips: C. T. Connell, *Apache,* [n. p.].

46   cut off limbs: Sonnichsen, *Mescalero,* 46.

46   smashed heads: Thrapp, *Conquest of Apacheria,* 35; C. T. Connell, *Apache,* [n. p.].

46   "A favorite mode of mutilating": Poston, *History,* 53.

46   "Old Eskimi[n]zin says": ibid., 53.

46   "saw squaws stick pieces": Thrapp, *Conquest of Apacheria,* 320.

46   "Their savage and bloodthirsty": Cremony, 266.

46   "Every nation has practised": Amnesty International, *Report on Torture,* New York: 1975, 27.

46   Apache children growing up: Ball, *In the Days,* 133.

47   American soldiers not only scalped: Terrell, *Chronicle,* 249.

47   bridles, for instance, braided: Raphael Pumpelly, quoted in Terrell, 261.

47   In his first year of army duty: Bourke, *Diary,* 92:65, quoted in Porter, *Paper,* 10–11.

47   In 1864 a group of Arizonans: Conner, *Walker,* 266–67.

48   They would be taught: Opler, *Life-Way,* 69–73.

48   They were given captured birds: Ogle, *Control,* 17; Cremony, 227.

48   "When a brave warrior": Opler, *Life-Way,* 351.

48   his slayers skinned: Ogle, 17.

Four: The Unknown Cochise

Page

50   "Cochise was undoubtedly the bravest": Poston, *History,* 30.

50   "the very worst Indian": John Sanford Mason, quoted in Sweeney, *Cochise,* 231.

50   "For twelve years he": ibid., xxii–xxiii.

51   After a battle between: ibid., 272.

51   As early as 1860: The agent was Dr. Michael Steck. See Sweeney, *Cochise,* 140; Thrapp, *Victorio,* 65–66, 85–86.

52   In his fanatic optimism: Sweeney, *Cochise,* 220.

52   After all, a single: The Bosque Redondo tragedy is well summarized in Sonnichsen, *Mescalero,* 109–33, and in Brown, *Bury My Heart,* 20–35.

52   "In secret councils": Sonnichsen, *Mescalero,* 133.

53   The Yavapai Rangers were: Thrapp, *Conquest of Apacheria,* 37–40.

53   "The body was dried": Browne, *Adventures,* 102.

53   Another of Woolsey's: Thrapp, *Conquest of Apacheria,* 27; Terrell, *Chronicle,* 244.

53   In 1864, Woolsey led: Conner, *Walker,* 171–76.

54   "the most notable": Bert Fireman, *Historical Markers of Arizona,* v. II, quoted in Thrapp, *Conquest of Apacheria,* 27.

54   After the war, however: Faulk, *Campaign,* 26–31; Rickey, *Forty Miles,* 4, 20–27, 143.

54   The U.S. census for 1860: Thrapp, *Conquest of Apacheria,* 79; Sweeney, *Cochise,* 265.

54   The best estimates place: Thrapp says the total number of Apaches never exceeded six thousand *(Conquest of Apacheria,* viii); Utley claims there were eight thousand Apaches in the sixteenth century *(Clash,* 9). John Clum, a contemporary, estimated the Apache population at seven thousand in 1864 (W. Clum, *Apache Agent,* 123).

54   One traveler who tried: Bell, *Tracks,* 184, 188.

54   Of the six thousand to eight: Opler, *Life-Way,* 4; Sweeney, *Cochise,* 140.

54   The most important was Victorio: Ball, *In the Days,* 41.

55   "America's greatest guerrilla": Thrapp, *Victorio,* ix.

55   But in 1865, Victorio sought: Sweeney, *Cochise,* 223–25.

55   One suggestible traveler: Bell, 260.

55   Charles Poston, the Arizona: Poston, *History,* 43–49.

56   One settler swore: John Spring, quoted in Sweeney, *Cochise,* 266.

56   "Chase them and they": ibid., 251.

56   An 1858 traveler insisted: Cozzens, *Explorations,* 84.

56   Carleton himself: Sweeney, *Cochise,* 223, 265.

57   Only in 1991, after a: ibid., 240.

57   One of the threats: Cole, *Chiricahua,* 98, 104; Spicer, *Cycles,* 65–67.

58   In early 1871, the Territorial: Arizona Legislature, *Memorial,* 4, 9.

59   Cushing was the best: Bourke, *Border,* 29–30.

59   On April 26, with a column: The best account of Cushing's 1871 campaign is in Thrapp, *Conquest of Apacheria,* 63–78.

Five: 1871

Page

60   On the morning of May 5: John Mott to Alexander Moore, May 20, 1871, quoted in Thrapp, *Conquest of Apacheria,* 72–77.

62   "The Indians were well handled": ibid., 76.

62   Thirteen years later: Ball, *Indeh,* 26–27.

62   *Juh* is a corrupt: ibid., 6.

62   yet another insisted: Thrapp, *Juh,* 6, 9; McClintock, *Arizona,* v. I, 246.

62   As a young man, Juh: Ball, *Indeh,* 3.

62   The liaison, which made: Debo, *Geronimo,* 76–77.

63   At the same time, Juh: Ball, *Indeh,* 26–27.

63   By now there were nine thousand: Sweeney, *Cochise,* 265.

64   In February of that year: *Arizona Miner,* March 20, 1869, quoted in Sweeney, *Cochise,* 262–64.

64   A year later, Cochise: *Weekly Arizonian,* July 23, August 6, August 27, 1870, quoted in Sweeney, *Cochise,* 281.

64   At the end of August 1870: ibid., 283–84.

64   In October, William Arny: Argalus Hennisee to William Clinton, October 31, 1870; William Arny to Henry Parker, October 24, 1870; quoted in Thrapp, *Victorio,* 129–30, and in Sweeney, *Cochise,* 297–300.

66   In April, the Chokonen: Sweeney, *Cochise,* 312–14.

66   Once more, in September 1871: Ellis, "Reflections," 391–92.

68   As early as 1859: Walker and Bufkin, *Atlas,* 38.

68   In February 1871, the camp: Thrapp, *Conquest of Apacheria,* 80–81.

68   One day in February: Royal Whitman to J. G. C. Lee, "Report of the massacre," in Colyer, *Report,* 31–32.

70   William Bell, an adventurer: Bell, *Tracks,* 301–11.

70   In April 1871, the waters: Whitman to Lee, in Colyer, 32.

72   "Many valiant but frothy": William Oury, *Arizona Star,* June 29, 1879, quoted in Thrapp, *Conquest of Apacheria,* 88.

72   Organized in great secrecy: Oury, "To the Society," 4–10.

73   "glorious morning of April 30th": ibid., 12.

73   The attackers had shot: Whitman to Lee; C. B. Briesly, "Testimony"; both in Colyer, 33, 34.

73   "in the full satisfaction": Oury, "To the Society," 11.

73   Seven of these children: Lockwood, *Apache Indians,* 181.

73   Overcome by the catastrophe: Whitman to Lee, in Colyer, 33

74   "the blackest page": Lockwood, *Apache Indians,* 178.

74   "such massacres are necessary": quoted in Schellie, *Domain,* 172.
74   "purely murder": Terrell, *Chronicle,* 279.
74   In the May 1871 elections: Schellie, 187–88.
75   In December 1871, Lieutenant: Thrapp, *Conquest of Apacheria,* 93–94, 111.
75   Near the end of May 1871: Schellie, 189; Wellman, *Death,* 98.

Six: The General on Muleback

Page
76   The appointment was not a popular: Schmitt, *Crook,* 90, 100, 101, 122, 136, 160, 183. Crook remains the lowest-ranking West Point cadet ever to attain the rank of major general in the U. S. Army.
76   Yet before Crook's career: Bourke, *Border,* vi.
76   And Crazy Horse, whose warriors: Schmitt, xi.
77   By now, Crook was: Schmitt, 169.
77   Crook stood just over six: Bourke, *Border,* 109–11.
77   Crook sums up: Schmitt, 82, 98, 141, 306.
78   At Winchester, Virginia: ibid., 126–27.
78   Sheridan, ironically: E. S. Connell, *Morning Star,* 179–80.
78   Two years after the battle: Schmitt, 129–30, 134. Posterity has uncritically handed down Sheridan's deception. *The Encyclopedia Britannica,* for instance, says, "In the Third Battle of Winchester, Va. (September), [Sheridan] drove Gen. Jubal A. Early out of Winchester. . . . " (15th Edition, v. IX, 136).
78   "Intellectually, [Sheridan]": quoted in Schmitt, 130.
78   "The adulations heaped": ibid., 134.
78   Crook, it may be pointed: Bourke, *Border,* 109.
78   Obeying orders he thought: Schmitt, 135–36, 303–4.
79   In 1857, in the northeast: ibid., 39–40.
79   In 1867, for example: ibid., 149, 307–8.
80   As he came to Arizona: Thrapp, *Conquest of Apacheria,* 95.
80   "General Crook was admitted": Bourke, *Border,* 112.
80   As he fought against: Schmitt, 15, 52, 69, 73.
80   On the Columbia River: ibid., 63–64.
80   In Arizona, Crook's first: Bourke, *Border,* 108–9.
80   His first interview: Schmitt, 163–65.
81   Sherman himself grew: Sherman to William K. Belknap, January 7, 1870, quoted in Terrell, *Chronicle,* 265.
81   Crook had never thought: Schmitt, 105–6, 146.
82   "He made the study": Bourke, *Border,* 150–51.
82   Having dismissed his feckless: Schmitt, 165–66.
83   "The white people were": Bourke, *Border,* 142–44.

83   From Fort Apache, Crook: ibid., 145–49.

84   As he read his first: Schmitt, 167.

84   Four years earlier, a Board: Thrapp, *Conquest of Apacheria,* 102–3.

84   "The Apache Indians were": Colyer, *Report,* 3.

85   "fanatic pacifist": Bancroft, quoted in McClintock, *Arizona,* v. I, 420.

85   "that spawn of hell": Bourke, Diary, quoted in Thrapp, *Conquest of Apacheria,* 129.

85   "He harangued the Indians": Schmitt, 168.

85   "cold-blooded scoundrel": John Marion, *Arizona Miner,* quoted in Sweeney, *Cochise,* 321.

85   Now Colyer repeated: ibid., 329.

86   "We are tired of living": W. Clum, *Apache Agent,* 79–80.

86   Before Colyer left: Thrapp, *Conquest of Apacheria,* 105; Terrell, 286.

86   "I have visited seven-eighths": Colyer, 13.

86   Biting his tongue: Thrapp, *Conquest of Apacheria,* 106.

87   On September 4, at the very: Sweeney, *Cochise,* 323–24.

87   "the worst of all": Schmitt, 176.

87   "an uncompromising enemy": Crook to Adjutant General's Office, July 10, 1871, quoted in Sweeney, *Cochise,* 319.

Seven: This Is the Man

Page

88   Now, as he conferred: Sweeney, *Cochise,* 325, 334–36.

88   Sometime between 1867 and 1870: Farish, who interviewed Jeffords, gave 1867 as the date of the meeting (Farish, *Arizona,* v. II, 228). Sweeney, however, argues convincingly that this is too early; he thinks 1870 the most likely date (Sweeney, *Cochise,* 293–96).

89   Although he lived: Forbes, Untitled; Farish, v. II, 228–40.

89   Late in life, he told: Forbes, 3.

89   Around 1859, Jeffords: Sweeney, *Cochise,* 292.

89   "I made up my mind": Farish, v. II, 228–29.

90   In the Apache version: Ball, *Indeh,* 27–28, 31.

90   Nor, indeed, did Jeffords: Farish, v. II, 229.

90   He sent a runner: Sweeney, *Cochise,* 324–34.

91   During his visit, Colyer: Thrapp, *Victorio,* 138–39.

91   Now, in order to reconcile: Sweeney, *Cochise,* 325–38.

91   he would rather talk: Turrill, "Talk," 67.

91   From September 1871, when: Sweeney, *Cochise,* 325–38.

92   The meeting got off: Turrill, "Talk," 64.

92   it was a color: Opler, *Life-Way,* 38, 241, 476–77.

92   "I have fought long": Turrill, "Vanished Race," 20–21.

93   For Apaches, a strong: Opler, *Life-Way,* 330–32.

93   If Cochise would not: Turrill, "Talk," 65–67.
93   At the end of the talk: Turrill, "Vanished Race," 21.
93   The obtuse Granger: Sweeney, *Cochise,* 340–42.
94   Crook claimed he had: Schmitt, *Crook,* 176.
94   Years later Crook complained: ibid., 177.
94   An eyewitness recorded: Royal Whitman, untitled typescript, New York Public Library, quoted in Thrapp, *Conquest of Apacheria,* 110.
95   "General Howard was fond": Schmitt, 169.
95   In turn, Howard privately: Howard, *Life,* 151–52.
95   The party of Indians: ibid., 164–76.
96   Meguil, a White Mountain Apache: Crook calls this Apache Miguel or McGill, but Howard, who knew him better, insists on Meguil.
97   In a Presbyterian church: Howard, *Life,* 178.
97   Meguil's glass eye: ibid., 182–84. The White Eyes' mysterious writing had a somewhat magical power for the Apaches: among the raiding booty they kept and carried with them were letters mailed to frontier residents.
97   During Howard's journey: Sweeney, *Cochise,* 340–46.
98   From Fort Apache, the general: Howard, *Life,* 184, 186.
98   From the moment he arrived: Howard, "Account," 4.
98   While he was at Tularosa: Howard, *Life,* 187–88.
98   Chie was a nephew: Ball, *Indeh,* 28–29; Sweeney, *Cochise,* 354, 457–458.
99   Near Silver City, New Mexico: Howard, *Life,* 192; Sweeney, *Cochise,* 354.
99   When they were still seventy: Howard, "Account," 5.
99   During the following days: Howard, *Life,* 196–203; Howard, "Account," 5.
100   In the morning, as the: Howard, "Account," 6.
100   With Jeffords interpreting: Howard, *Life,* 206–9.
101   With Chie guiding day: Howard, "Account," 7.
102   In fact, Chie's sorrow: Ball, *Indeh,* 28; Sweeney, *Cochise,* 457–58.
102   At Fort Bowie Howard: Howard, "Account," 7–8.
102   He was right: the bear: Ball, *In the Days,* 55–56.
102   Howard accepted Chie's: Howard, "Account," 8.
102   Back in the stronghold: Howard, *Life,* 212–19.
102   The next day Cochise: Tom Jeffords, untitled manuscript, Arizona Historical Society, quoted in Sweeney, *Cochise,* 363.
102   Cochise announced his: Howard, *Life,* 220.
103   Yet something else: Ball, *Indeh,* 29; Safford, Untitled, 58.

Eight: Geronimo Ascendant

Page

104 By his own testimony: Ball, *Indeh,* 249.

104 The Bedonkohe were: Cole, *Chiricahua,* 9–10.

104 By 1905, there were: Debo, *Geronimo,* 12.

104 The name means: Cole, 10.

104 Geronimo was born sometime: Barrett, to whom Geronimo dictated his autobiography in 1905, tried to match events with calendar dates; he concluded that Geronimo was born in June 1829 (Barrett, *Geronimo's Story,* 17). Debo, however, argues cogently that Geronimo was born earlier, perhaps as early as 1823 (Debo, 7). Sweeney uses other evidence to corroborate this earlier date (Sweeney, "Carrasco," 47). As for the birthplace, Debo construed Geronimo's ambiguous designation (as recorded by Barrett) to mean a site near Clifton, Arizona. This, I believe, is erroneous. Juh's son Daklugie forcefully insisted on the Middle Fork of the Gila River (Ball, *Indeh,* 177), a site independently vouched for by other Chiricahua descendants (Ball, *In the Days,* 137).

105 Like all Apaches, Geronimo: Opler, *Life-Way,* 10.

105 Geronimo's mother taught: Barrett, 17–21.

105 There was tobacco: Opler, *Life-Way,* 8–9, 220–23, 440–42.

105 In a sense, an Apache: Ball, *In the Days,* 28.

106 To learn accuracy: Opler, *Life-Way,* 34, 46–50, 66–74; Cortés, *Views,* 68; Ball, *Indeh,* 93–94; W. Clum, *Apache Agent,* 42.

107 Another vital piece: Ball, *In the Days,* 54.

107 The Chiricahua themselves: Opler, *Life-Way,* 40.

107 At age seven a boy: ibid., 66, 70, 74.

107 Geronimo achieved this milestone: Barrett, 37.

107 One day during his: Betzinez, *I Fought,* 15.

108 Not until he was: Barrett, 18.

108 While he was still a: ibid., 38–39.

108 As late as 1849, Chihuahua: Thrapp, *Victorio,* 19.

108 Despite the official: Moorhead, *Frontier,* 284–85.

108 Recognizing that the bounty: Sweeney, "Carrasco," 35, 39–40.

109 With Alope, his mother: Barrett, 43–44.

109 The party that accomplished: Sweeney, "Carrasco," 40, 45–47; Sweeney, *Cochise,* 87.

110 Geronimo's grief left: Barrett, 44–46.

111 "He had gone out": Sam Haozous, quoted in Debo, 38.

111 According to Geronimo's: Barrett, 47–53.

113 By the Mexicans' own: Sweeney, "Carrasco," 42, 44.

113 According to Apache: Debo, 39.

113 The only version: W. Clum, *Apache Agent,* 28–29.

113   Geronimo's biographer, Angie Debo: Debo, 13.
113   but Geronimo's account: Barrett, 49; Sweeney, "Carrasco," 42.
113   In any event, according: W. Clum, *Apache Agent,* 29.
113   "all the other Apaches": Barrett, 55.
113   Edwin R. Sweeney, the only: Sweeney, "Carrasco," 42, 44.
114   Geronimo claimed that: Barrett, 43, 47.
114   Sweeney further documents: Sweeney, "Carrasco," 40.
115   Geronimo's is the only: Ball, *Indeh,* 80; Betzinez, 1, 17.
115   Hispanic accounts of: see, for instance, Jeff Long, *Duel of Eagles,* New
        York: 1990.
115   He remarried: Debo, 47; Betzinez, 17.
115   In his home in the Gila: Barrett, 113–14.
116   With only bow and arrows: ibid., 55–64.
118   Well into his seventies: Burbank and Royce, *Burbank,* 23.
118   One of his larger: Barrett, 69–77, 80–81.
119   "He was by nature": Ball, *Indeh,* 14.
119   To cure an old man: Opler, *Life-Way,* 40.
119   It was probably in the winter: Ball, *Indeh,* 13, 181.
120   It is odd, perhaps: When Geronimo dictated his autobiography to Bar-
        rett in 1905, he was still deeply apprehensive that the government
        might use his own story to justify his further punishment. This alone
        would have been a cogent reason to minimize his account of battles
        and raids against white Americans.
120   We know with reasonable: Debo, 68; Barrett, 119–27.
120   We do know that Geronimo: Barrett, 128; Howard, *Famous Chiefs,* 112–
        136.
120   He had three wives: Debo, 47, 50.
121   Geronimo was nonetheless: Sweeney, *Cochise,* 422.
121   A livid crease: W. Clum, *Apache Agent,* 221.
121   "I have killed ten": Howard, *Life,* 206–9.

Nine: The End of Cochise

Page
122   "I never could get": Schmitt, *Crook,* 177.
123   When hostile Apaches: Bourke, *Border,* 182.
123   "no nook or corner": ibid., 181.
123   As each patrol moved: ibid., 186, 203.
124   Like Tom Jeffords, none: The only exception, Tom Horn, penned his
        autobiography in jail in 1903 as he awaited execution for the murder
        of a fourteen-year-old boy; his "Vindication," as Horn called it, is so
        full of self-serving lies as to be almost worthless. *Life of Tom Horn,*
        Norman, Oklahoma: 1964.

124   Born in Ontario of a Scot: Thrapp, *Sieber,* 88–89.
125   Like other chiefs of scouts: Schmitt, 147, 150–51.
125   Born in Germany, Sieber: Thrapp, *Sieber,* vii–97 passim.
125   In 1891, an Arizona: Lockwood, "Grijalva," 1–2, 8.
125   This was a common: see, for example, Stone, *Sonora,* 23–24.
125   But Grijalva escaped: Lockwood, "Grijalva," 8–11, 23.
126   He knew Cochise's people: Sweeney, *Cochise,* 345.
126   He knew that the Chiricahua: Lockwood, "Grijalva," 11, 22.
126   The day after Crook's: Bourke, *Border,* 181, 184–87.
127   Bourke calculated: Thrapp, *Conquest of Apacheria,* 144.
127   "overhauling": Bourke, *Border,* 207.
128   "the worst reputation": Schmitt, 176, 180.
128   "a great chief": Mike Burns, quoted in Corbusier, *Verde,* 60.
128   An Indian told Crook: Bourke, *Border,* 184.
128   Some of them had come: Burns, in Corbusier, 59–60.
128   In late December: Bourke, *Border,* 188–93.
129   He sent a small contingent: ibid., 194–99.
130   Seventy-six Yavapai: Thrapp, *Conquest of Apacheria,* 129.
130   According to a boy: Burns, in Corbusier, 77, 81.
130   Sixty-one years later: J. M. Barney, *Tales of Apache Warfare,* [?]: 1933, [n. p.].
130   Eventually a party: Smith, "My Father," 3.
130   The bullet scars: Corbusier, 82.
130   As the various patrols: Bourke, *Border,* 207, 212–13.
130   "You see, we are nearly": Schmitt, 179–80.
131   Every Indian was issued: Bourke, *Border,* 215–19.
132   When a man persisted: ibid., 221.
132   Nantaje, the scout: ibid., 178, 184.
132   A seven-year-old Yavapai: Burns, in Corbusier, 72.
132   Matters came to a head: Thrapp, *Conquest of Apacheria,* 152–54.
133   As the Apaches thronged: Schmitt, 181.
133   Army patrols hunted: Thrapp, *Conquest of Apacheria,* 156–61.
133   "Being satisfied that both": Schmitt, 182.
134   "The Apaches of Arizona": Bourke, *Border,* 220.
134   "a fine looking Indian": Bourke, Diary, v. I, 130–32, quoted in Thrapp, *Conquest of Apacheria,* 146.
135   "are liable to go down": Bourke, Diary, quoted in Sweeney, *Cochise,* 379.
135   "His height is about": Safford, Untitled, 57–58, 60–63.
137   "some of the Chiricahuas": Bourke, *Border,* 236.
137   Appealing to his own: Cole, *Chiricahua,* 122.
137   The fault lay almost: ibid., 114–25.
137   Even worse, Walker pressured: Cramer, "Jeffords," 271.
138   Yet he grew so: Cole, 138.

138 "he did not care": *Arizona Citizen,* November 29, 1873, quoted in Sweeney, *Cochise,* 379.

138 newspapers feverishly claimed that Howard: Sweeney, *Cochise,* 375–376, 380.

138 Of the more than one: Cole, 125.

138 In March 1873, Cochise: ibid., 381–82.

139 About a year later, a trader: Lockwood, *Apache Indians,* 125–26.

139 Perhaps the oddest: Cole, 137.

139 "It is this stuff": Ball, *Indeh,* 10.

140 Dispirited, he resorted: Sweeney, *Cochise,* 393; Lockwood, *Apache Indians,* 125.

140 Late in May a government: Sweeney, *Cochise,* 392.

140 As the chief lay: Hughes, "History," [n. p.]; Williamson, "Reminiscences," 4–5.

140 Indeed, for the Chiricahua: Opler, *Life-Way,* 242.

141 On June 7, 1874, Jeffords: Farish, *History,* v. II, 236–37; Forbes, Untitled, 6.

141 Cochise was dressed: Lockwood, *Apache Indians,* 129–30; Cole, 142; *Army and Navy Journal,* July 11, 1874, 758.

141 The ceremonial mourning: Cole, 142.

142 "the howl that went": Hughes, [n. p.].

142 Only a few Chiricahuas: Ball, *Indeh,* 29; Sweeney, *Cochise,* 397. In November 1895, an eccentric would-be writer named Alice Rollins Crane reported to a newspaper that Jeffords had taken her to the burial site. Her account of the outing is so romantic and improbable, however, that it may be doubted that Jeffords did more than guide her into the Dragoons. See *Arizona Star,* November 21, 1895.

Ten: Turkey Gobbler

Page

145 Some scholars explain: Thrapp, *Conquest of Apacheria,* vii.

145 Others believe that the name: Sonnichsen, *Mescalero,* 36; Haskell, *Athapaskan,* 78–79.

145 It has even been: Davis, *Truth,* 1.

145 They are Athapaskans: Haskell, 9–16.

145 The early date postulates: Cole, *Chiricahua,* 4–5.

146 When Coronado rode: Spicer, *Cycles,* 229.

146 The Apaches who came: A new approach to the problem of dating prehistoric migrations comes from the field of glottochronology, which uses differences in related languages as a yardstick of how long ago the people speaking them separated from one another. So far, however, the premises of this science are untested, so that it cannot

yield reliable dates. Two students analyzing the same data for the divergence between the Apache language and those of Canadian Athapaskans came up with dates three centuries apart. See Haskell, 16–19.

146   Their only domesticated: Haskell, 71–76.

146   "coarse, vile, and wicked": Hammond and Rey, *Obregon's,* 19–20, 305, quoted in Haskell, 77–78.

146   They drank its blood: Haskell, 77–78.

147   It seems likely that: Clark, *They Sang,* 3–9.

147   "well formed, lively, warlike": Hammond and Rey, *Obregon's,* 305, quoted in Haskell, 77.

148   "gentle people, not cruel": Hammond and Rey, *Narratives,* 261, quoted in Haskell, 74.

148   They hunted deer, antelope: Moorhead, *Frontier,* 6–7; Sonnichsen, *Mescalero,* 19–20.

148   The Apaches named the seasons: Opler, *Life-Way,* 354–55.

148   Acorns and mesquite beans: Basso, *Cibecue,* 3.

148   All four were vital: Sweeney, *Cochise,* 131.

148   "If you meet a bear": Eugene Chihuahua, quoted in Ball, *Indeh,* 63.

148   "because hogs ate animals": Skinner, *Rock,* 6.

148   Apaches ingeniously made: Sonnichsen, *Mescalero,* 219.

148   By the eighteenth century, Apache: Opler, *Life-Way,* 19–22.

149   The bow, about five: Ogle, *Control,* 20–21.

149   To supply the venom: Mike Burns, quoted in Corbusier, *Verde,* 21–22.

149   Apaches were so skillful: Ball, *Indeh,* 15.

149   Their range was easily: Thrapp, *Conquest of Apacheria,* viii.

149   The lance—the weapon: Ogle, 22; Opler, *Life-Way,* 341.

149   By the eighteenth century: Cortés, *Views,* 69.

149   The name is a corruption: Ball, *Indeh,* 22.

149   Some say the name means: Cole, 2, 10; Skinner, I.

150   "The Indian follows": Ball, *Indeh,* 32.

150   The Chiricahua have their own migration legend: Cole, 2–3.

150   Ussen, who is usually: ibid., 14–15; Opler, *Life-Way,* 197–98.

150   "There are so many": Cole, 15, 144.

151   "Comparative peace now reigns": Safford to Arizona legislature, January 6, 1875, quoted in Wellman, *Death,* 152.

152   "the ancient curse": Cruse, *Days,* 185.

152   In April 1865, in Virginia: Schmitt, *Crook,* 138–39.

152   Custer's record at West Point: E. S. Connell, *Morning Star,* 107.

153   Clum's parents had: W. Clum, *Apache Agent,* 103.

153   "that notorious nation": ibid., 122.

153   With a Christian fervor: ibid., 128, 133–36, 139–40.

154   "my personal body-guard": J. Clum, "Geronimo," I, 21.

154   For days at a time: W. Clum, 202.

154   "novel proposition": ibid., 135, 142, 170, 203.

154   The Chiricahua, once they: Ball, *Indeh,* 39.
154   Ignorant of tribal: Cole, 160.
155   In 1875, at Fort Apache: W. Clum, 150–63.
155   As Crook had left: Terrell, *Chronicle,* 314.
155   In March 1876, matters: Cole, 156–57.
156   Clum received a telegram: W. Clum, 172.
156   Clum set out from: J. Clum, "Geronimo," I, 26.
156   At Fort Bowie in Apache Pass: ibid., 33; W. Clum, 179–84.
156   Even as he was relieved: Cole, 159–60.
156   Jeffords went back to: Sonnichsen, "Jeffords," 396–400.
156   As Clum had parleyed: W. Clum, 180.
157   According to Clum: Ball, *Indeh,* 33, 38.
157   "When he loafed around": C. T. Connell, *Apache,* [n. p.].
157   President Grant rubber-stamped: Cole, 160.
157   As he strutted around: W. Clum, 130, 148, 277.
158   In his 1875 report: J. Clum, *Truth,* 14.
158   "that wonderful reservation": W. Clum, 245.
158   "San Carlos! That was the": Ball, *Indeh,* 37.
158   "It is because of": Ball, *In the Days,* 32.
158   The agent had a sweetheart: W. Clum, 185–88.
159   "When their people saw": Ball, *In the Days,* 51.
159   As they boarded: W. Clum, 191–92; J. Clum, "Thespians," 17.
159   Clum thought the acting: W. Clum, 193–94.
159   "when the knife": unspecified St. Louis newspaper, September 9, 1876,
        quoted in J. Clum, "Thespians," 17.
160   "Although the best medical": J. Clum, "Thespians," 19.
160   Clum left "his" Indians: W. Clum, 196–97.
160   Now the Chiricahua believed: Ball, *In the Days,* 51–52.
160   "The illness and death": J. Clum, "Thespians," 20.

Eleven: Geronimo in Irons

Page
161   With his new bride: W. Clum, *Apache Agent,* 198, 202.
161   Meanwhile a new spate: Thrapp, *Victorio,* 186.
161   Now he believed that the fresh: W. Clum, 171, 205, 228; J. Clum, "Ge-
        ronimo," II, 15–16.
162   A lieutenant under General Kautz: Thrapp, *Victorio,* 186.
162   IF PRACTICABLE: W. Clum, 204–5.
162   He recruited an additional: Thrapp, *Victorio,* 186.
162   A month earlier: Harte, *San Carlos,* 351.
162   When he later learned: Thrapp, *Victorio,* 186–87.
162   One of their leaders: W. Clum, 100, 129, 141.

163   In his memoirs, Clum: ibid., 199–201.

163   It was some four hundred miles: ibid., 206–12.

164   According to Clum: W. Clum, 215–18; J. Clum, "Geronimo," I, 37–40.

165   Another version: Griffith, *Mickey Free*, 71–72.

166   When Geronimo had finished: W. Clum, 218–28; J. Clum, "Geronimo," I, 40–43.

167   Juh's son Daklugie: Ball, *Indeh*, 38–39.

167   In the words of a Chihenne: Ball, *In the Days*, 50.

168   Late in life he denied: "Corralled Geronimo," *Washington Evening Star*, March [?], 1905.

168   "I do not think": Barrett, *Geronimo's Story*, 132–33.

168   Among the records: in Clum Papers, Special Collections, University of Arizona.

168   Soon after the capture: W. Clum, 229–46.

168   Protocol demanded: Thrapp, *Victorio*, 190.

168   Another tragedy besides removal: W. Clum, 246–50, 285.

T w e l v e :   V i c t o r i o

Page

170   Clum later claimed: W. Clum, *Apache Agent*, 250–53; J. Clum, "Geronimo," II, 15.

170   Behind his back: Lockwood, *Apache Indians*, 225–26.

170   Meanwhile he appointed: W. Clum, 252–53.

171   "Therefore, at high noon": J. Clum, "Geronimo," II, 15.

171   Eventually he found his way: "Corralled Geronimo," *Washington Evening Star*, March [?], 1905.

171   He died: Thrapp, *Victorio*, 355.

171   "Who cut the rivets": J. Clum, "Geronimo," II, 16.

171   "Upon whose orders": W. Clum, 263.

171   "Had I remained": J. Clum, "Geronimo," II, 15–16.

171   There is one other explanation: Ball, *Indeh*, 39–40.

172   Geronimo's most careful biographer: Debo, *Geronimo*, 114.

172   "I was kept": Barrett, *Geronimo's Story*, 132–33.

172   Eighty years later: Sam Haozous, quoted in Debo, 110.

173   There is evidence: Thrapp, *Victorio*, 193.

173   "That is a good country.": Toclanny, quoted in Ball, *Indeh*, 187.

173   The hunting was wretched: Thrapp, *Victorio*, 193–94.

173   The White Mountain people: John Rope, in G. Goodwin, *Raiding*, 103, 116.

173   On September 2: Thrapp, *Victorio*, 195–205.

174   all along the rims: Ball, *Indeh*, 34.

174   Some 143: Thrapp, *Victorio*, 207.

174   "that they are happier": Charles Steelhammer, quoted ibid., 208.
175   According to an eyewitness: *Tucson Star,* April 6, 1880, quoted in Thrapp, *Conquest of Apacheria,* 179.
175   The captain insisted: Thrapp, *Conquest of Apacheria,* 179.
175   In late October: Thrapp, *Victorio,* 209–17.
175   When Victorio presented: Ball, *In the Days,* 61–62.
176   As a result of Chihenne raiding: Thrapp, *Victorio,* 218–19; Sonnichsen, *Mescalero,* 180–81.
176   "Victorio was not": Ball, *In the Days,* 41, 53.
177   "His long black hair": W. Clum, 230.
177   Though the photographer: Thrapp, *Victorio,* 8.
177   Atypically for a great chief: ibid., 15, 58.
177   "Drunkards are": McKenna, *Black Range,* 183.
177   Fearing the treachery: Ball, *In the Days,* 74.
177   As a young girl: ibid., 9, 11, 14–15, 21, 73, 76, 87, 115, 143.
179   Seventy years old: ibid., 8, 91.
179   He had the odd: Thrapp, *Conquest of Apacheria,* 212.
179   Yet Nana: Ball, *In the Days,* 7, 16, 57, 66, 71, 108.
179   When Victorio's band: Thrapp, *Victorio,* 218–46.
180   A pioneer who helped: C. T. Connell, *Apache,* v. II, [n. p.].
180   Sometimes the Chihenne came: Ball, *In the Days,* 64–67, 73–74.
180   One day, frantic: Thrapp, *Conquest of Apacheria,* 187.
180   At the time of his breakout: Thrapp, *Victorio,* 237, 246–47; Ball, *In the Days,* 66, 73–74.
181   At its largest: Ball, *In the Days,* 75; Wellman, *Death,* 184.
181   Sometimes women and children: Ball, *In the Days,* 66, 73–74.
181   According to one American: Cruse, *Days,* 81.
181   Sometimes in the middle: Thrapp, *Victorio,* 242–44.
181   "the only noise": Charles B. Gatewood, quoted ibid., 250.
181   The major in charge: ibid., 250.
182   But Kaywaykla and the other: Ball, *In the Days,* 72.
182   "We were essentially": ibid., 75–76.
182   Their success depended: ibid., 12–13.
183   Lulled into overconfidence: Thrapp, *Victorio,* 253–55.
183   Even Kaywaykla—so accustomed: Ball, *In the Days,* xiii, 77–78.
184   The major in charge: Thrapp, *Victorio,* 252–66.
184   Victorio even made good: ibid., 275–76; Cruse, 81–83.
185   Thomas Cruse, one of: Cruse, 67–68, 86.
185   In May 1880: Thrapp, *Victorio,* 277–82.
185   Thomas Cruse later admitted: Cruse, 157–58.
186   It was during these grim: Ball, *In the Days,* 58, 86.
186   During the next weeks: Thrapp, *Victorio,* 286–302.
187   Kaywaykla offers: Ball, *In the Days,* 89–90, 93.
188   For once, Victorio miscalculated: Thrapp, *Victorio,* 301–4.

188   Mauricio Corredor: Faulk, *Campaign,* 22.
189   But the Chihenne themselves: Ball, *In the Days,* 102; Ball, *Indeh,* 83.
189   A month after Tres Castillos: Thrapp, *Conquest of Apacheria,* 209.
189   Some Chihenne escaped: Ball, *In the Days,* 94–101.

Thirteen: The Dreamer

Page
190   "might easily have been death": Barrett, *Geronimo's Story,* 133.
190   Clum's successor: Debo, *Geronimo,* 117.
191   It was not until April: ibid., 117; Betzinez, *I Fought,* 47–48.
191   "instead of being in sympathy": Debo, 122–23.
191   "What [Geronimo] wanted": W. Clum, *Apache Agent,* 264.
191   "No warrior," remembered Kaywaykla: Ball, *In the Days,* 102–3.
192   One day a solitary: ibid., 115–19.
193   "a short, fat, wrinkled": Lummis, *Poco Tiempo,* 137.
193   "palsied, aged": Charles B. Gatewood, "Campaigning against Victorio,"
        The Great Divide, v. XI, no. 4, 102; quoted in Sonnichsen, *Mescalero,*
        210–11.
193   For the Chiricahua: Opler, *Life-Way,* 336.
193   As Kaywaykla put it: Ball, *In the Days,* 103, 108–14.
194   In two months, the chief: Lekson, *Raid,* 32; Wellman, *Death,* 204–5.
194   The confident colonel: Lekson, 9–32.
195   About thirty-six years old: Cruse, *Days,* 93–94, 105–6.
196   In the dance: Bourke, *Medicine Men,* 500–505.
196   Cruse thought the "smattering": Cruse, 94.
196   Juh and Geronimo: Ball, *Indeh,* 53–54.
197   "trouble with White Mountain Indians": Kelton to Adjutant General,
        August 15, 1881, *Records of the Adjutant General's Office* 94, 4327
        (hereafter cited as *RG*).
197   Cruse sent his trusted: Cruse, 95; Carr to Tiffany, August 10, 1881, *RG*
        94, Witness no. 86.
197   "Of all the encounters": Ball, *Indeh,* 52.
197   "[The] Indians think": Carr to Tiffany, August 10, 1881, *RG* 94, Witness
        no. 86.
197   Cruse was similarly: Cruse, 94.
197   Near the end of his life: Ball, *Indeh,* 54.
197   IT WOULD BE WELL: Tiffany to Carr, quoted in Thrapp, *General Crook,* 12.
198   Carr claimed: Carr to Assistant Adjutant General, Nov. 2, 1881, *RG* 94,
        Witness no. 51.
198   Al Sieber: *Arizona Enterprise,* May 12, 1892, quoted in Thrapp, *General
        Crook,* 21.
198   "I watched": Ball, *Indeh,* 54.

198   Finally Carr started: Carr to Assistant Adjutant General, Nov. 2, 1881, *RG* 94, Witness no. 51.

198   Daklugie claimed later: Ball, *Indeh,* 54.

198   The captain who had: Carr to Assistant Adjutant General, Nov. 2, 1881, *RG* 94, Witness no. 51; Thrapp, *General Crook,* 25.

199   According to one witness: Mike Burns, quoted in Farish, *History,* v. III, 335–39.

199   According to another, Nochedelklinne: Iton, quoted in Robert Frazer, *The Apaches of the White Mountain Reservation,* Philadelphia: 1884, 11.

199   Daklugie said: Ball, *Indeh,* 54.

199   Cruse estimated: Cruse, 128.

199   Carr's shellshocked command: Thrapp, *General Crook,* 28–31.

200   "I have never": Bourke, Diary, quoted in Porter, *Paper,* 145.

200   The scouts who had deserted: Thrapp, *Conquest of Apacheria,* 230.

200   "declined to interfere": Lincoln to Secretary of Interior, March 2, 1882, *RG* 94, 778B.

200   Six thousand rounds: Willcox to Adjutant General, March 2, 1882, *RG* 94.

200   Under the headline: *Arizona Star,* March 3 and 4, 1882.

201   "The day of the hanging": Mazzanovich, *Trailing Geronimo,* 201.

201   On the same day: Cruse, 139; Ball, *Indeh,* 55.

Fourteen: In the Stronghold

Page

202   On September 30: Lockwood, *Apache Indians,* 243–44.

202   But according to Geronimo: George Wratten to Charles Connell, October 2, 1905, quoted in Connell, *Apache,* v. II, [n. p.].

202   The government had in fact: Debo, *Geronimo,* 131.

203   "Geronimo was pretty much": Betzinez, *I Fought,* 58.

203   "the worst Indian": General Nelson Miles, quoted in Wellman, *Death,* 233. See also headline of Warren: "Geronimo, the Wickedest Indian that Ever Lived, Crazed by Imprisonment."

203   The census taker: George Stevens, quoted in C. T. Connell, *Apache,* v. II, [n. p.].

203   "On their way to the border": Debo, 132.

204   "news made business men": Grossman, "Grossman, Tells of . . ."

204   But John Clum: W. Clum, *Apache Agent,* 265–67.

204   "hardy pioneers": Grossman, "Grossman Tells of . . ."

204   It was the homeland: Ball, *Indeh,* xvii, 2, 78.

204   Now, in the autumn: Ball, *In the Days,* 22, 33, 62, 123.

205   Thomas Cruse insisted: Cruse, *Days,* 90.

205   Kaywaykla, who met Juh: Ball, *In the Days,* 123–26.

205   Juh had several Powers: Ball, *Indeh,* 61.
205   At the dance: Ball, *In the Days,* 125–28.
206   Geronimo took charge: Ball, *Indeh,* 86.
206   "The young men": Ball, *In the Days,* 125, 129.
207   "He was extremely credulous": Opler, "Implications," 617–18.
207   As long ago as 1876: Ball, *Indeh,* 34, 76.
207   It was Geronimo, the worrier: Ball, *In the Days,* 136–39.
208   Like Nana, he walked: Ball, *Indeh,* 87; Ball, *In the Days,* 28, 56, 139; Davis, *Truth,* 112.
208   At last the council: Ball, *In the Days,* 139.
208   On the morning of April 19: Betzinez, 56.
209   Despite the severed: Thrapp, *Conquest of Apacheria,* 236.
209   This deed convinced: Betzinez, 56–57.
209   At one point, to feed: ibid., 58.
209   The ranch belonged: Santee, *Land,* 167–71; Williamson, *Reminiscences,* 2–3; John Rope, in G. Goodwin, *Raiding,* 143–44.
210   According to an unreliable: unspecified San Francisco newspaper [n. d.], quoted in Thrapp, *Conquest of Apacheria,* 237–38.
210   Near the border: Grossman, "Grossman Tells of . . ."
211   In the midst of the fugitives': Betzinez, 60–62.
211   Before they could reach: ibid., 62–70; Thrapp, *Conquest of Apacheria,* 244–48; Thrapp, *General Crook,* 80–90.
212   A man named Fun: Ball, *In the Days,* 143–45; Ball, *Indeh,* 155; Betzinez, 72–74.
212   It may well be a suspect: Debo, 152.
213   By Garcia's own admission: Thrapp, *General Crook,* 93; Betzinez, 75–76.
213   Juh's son: Ball, *Indeh,* 40.
214   "We took care": Ball, *In the Days,* 12.
214   A group of Chiricahua: Ball, *Indeh,* 4–6, 10–11.
214   Flushed with overconfidence: Betzinez, 77–80; Bourke, *Campaign,* 6. This account basically follows Betzinez, who was there. But Geronimo believed the attackers were soldiers from another town (Barrett, *Geronimo's Story,* 103–4).
214   Geronimo escaped, but: Debo, 47, 157.
214   During this year, Juh: Ball, *In the Days,* 146–47; Davis, 70.
215   In November 1882: Betzinez, 93–96; Ball, *In the Days,* 134–35.
216   Daklugie remembered: Ball, *Indeh,* 73.
216   One day, as the band: ibid., 75–76.
216   Later the gossip: Cruse, 90.

Fifteen: The Tan Wolf Charges

Page
217   "he 'slid' ": Cruse, *Days,* 179.
217   It was these that gave: Ball, *Indeh,* 125–26.
218   At the Rosebud: Brown, *Bury My Heart,* 276–77; E. S. Connell, *Morning Star,* 88–92.
218   "My troops beat": Schmitt, *Crook,* 195–96.
218   "Ducks, geese": Bourke, *Border,* 429.
218   Immediately after the Rosebud: E. S. Connell, 92.
218   Only a week after: Schmitt, 199.
219   The general had served: ibid., 197–240.
219   Eighty-six army officers: Johnson, *Crook's Resume,* 27–28.
219   In particular, he felt: Schmitt, 229.
219   Crook learned that government rations: Davis, *Truth,* 33, 41–44.
219   Crook also discovered: Thrapp, *General Crook,* 106–7.
220   "Everywhere the naked": Davis, 31.
220   Six weeks after arriving: *Arizona Star,* October 17, 1882; Davis, 39.
220   He paid the Apaches: Davis, 44–46.
221   In a revolt linked: ibid., 9–28; Cruse, 158–70.
221   For years after: Fred W. Croxen, "The Battle Ground Ridge or Dry Wash Fight," typescript, 1929, University of Arizona Special Collections, 6.
221   By the time of Crook's advent: Davis, 40.
221   "They are an incorrigible": Thrapp, *Conquest of Apacheria,* 269–70.
221   In a manifesto: Crook, "Problem," 14.
221   For years: Ball, *Indeh,* 249–50.
221   Among his people, he was: Ball, *In the Days,* 86, 126, 142.
222   Geronimo was disappointed: Ball, *Indeh,* 61, 249.
222   Apaches told Britton Davis: Davis, 71–72.
222   When warriors went out: Ball, *Indeh,* 104–5; Opler, *Life-Way,* 138.
222   As they laid waste: Betzinez, *I Fought,* 105.
222   Newly orphaned: Ball, *Indeh,* 89–90.
223   Disheartened by the occasional: Ball, *In the Days,* 148–50.
223   He and Bourke covertly: Bourke, Diary, October 30, 1882, v. 61, 13–15.
223   Crook recruited: Davis, 38–39.
223   Crook also sent Indian: Thrapp, *General Crook,* 108–10.
223   In July 1882: ibid., 59, 123–26.
224   In less than a week, riding: Thrapp, *Conquest of Apacheria,* 270–71.
224   If, in the words of Kaywaykla's: Ball, *In the Days,* 126, 136, 138, 147; Ball, *Indeh,* 83.
224   He was said to be short: Wellman, *Death,* 207.
224   At San Carlos: Davis, 57.
224   In Tombstone, John Clum: W. Clum, *Apache Agent,* 265, 278.

224 "the breeding pen": *Tombstone Republican,* March 29, 1883.
224 "Those fellows with passes": *Tombstone Epitaph,* March 29, 1883.
225 "the remorseless savages": *San Francisco Examiner,* March 26, 1883.
225 The feeling against the reservation: Davis, 55–56.
225 The newspapers reported the bodies: *Albuquerque Review,* April 5, 1883.
225 Chiricahuas later maintained: Ball, *Indeh,* 51.
225 Newspapers at the time: unidentified Tombstone paper, April 1883; *Tombstone Republican,* [date?].
226 As late as 1938: *San Diego Evening Tribune,* February 16, 1938.
226 It was the Chiricahuas': Betzinez, 109.
226 In the middle of the night: Davis, 57–59.
226 A year before, he had: Debo, *Geronimo,* 154; Ball, *In the Days,* 147; Davis, 58.
227 Among the free Chiricahua: Ball, *In the Days,* 147–48.
227 Yet at the time, Tzoe's: C. T. Connell, *Apache,* [n. p.]; W. Clum, 278–79.
227 The White Mountain Apache: Bourke, Diary, April 7, 1883, v. 65, 20–30.
227 "the most important": Thrapp, *General Crook,* vii.
227 His expedition was large: Crook, *Report,* 1883, Appendix E, 3, 11–12.
228 Crook's aide: Porter, *Paper,* 4.
229 For three days: Crook, *Report,* 3; Bourke, *Campaign,* 44.
229 Bavispe was: Bourke, *Campaign,* 49–51.
229 Bacerac, population 876: Bourke, Diary, May 5, 1883, v. 67, 3.
229 It was Saturday night: Bourke, *Campaign,* 54–56.
229 "a squalid hole": Bourke, Diary, May 5, 1883, v. 67, 9.
230 At once, the trackers: Crook, *Report,* 4; Bourke, *Campaign,* 59.
230 Before the expedition had: John Rope, in G. Goodwin, *Raiding,* 154.
230 "To look at the country": Bourke, Diary, May 10, 1883, v. 67, 24.
230 A number of mules: Bourke, *Campaign,* 46–48, 58, 67.
230 The owl was the most: Opler, *Life-Way,* 30, 229–31.
230 One day a medicine man: Bourke, Diary, May 8, 1883, v. 67, 19.
231 By May 10: Bourke, *Campaign,* 65, 68–69.
231 "if they had a fight": Bourke, Diary, May 11, 1883, v. 67, 30–31.
231 Privately, they lived: Rope, in G. Goodwin, *Raiding,* 156.
231 "a formidable place": Crook, *Report,* 4.
231 They had left all kinds: Bourke, *Campaign,* 71–72.
231 "Some of the scouts were afraid": Rope, in G. Goodwin, *Raiding,* 159.
232 In the morning, the scouts stripped: Fiebeger, "Campaign," 30.
232 Then they went down: Rope, in G. Goodwin, *Raiding,* 159.
232 As John Rope guarded: ibid., 160.
232 At the moment, Geronimo: Betzinez, 113–14, 118–20.
233 Among the booty: Bourke, Diary, May 16, 1883, v. 67, 55–56.
233 Crook, who persistently: Crook, *Report,* 6–7; *Arizona Star,* June 13 and 19, 1883.

233   Five months later: "The Captive Boy!," Deming, New Mexico, *Tribune,* ca. October 4, 1883.

233   Oddly, though speculation: C. T. Connell, *Apache,* [n. p.]. Geronimo said, however, that Charley's death came before Crook's expedition, and that his body was "left in a tepee and the whole thing burned." Ruey Darrow, a latter-day Chiricahua, claimed Charley was hit by a stray bullet during the May 15 battle, and that a woman tried to save him before he died (Ball, *Indeh,* 51).

233   Through an interpreter: Bourke, *Campaign,* 78–79; Rope, in G. Goodwin, *Raiding,* 163.

234   "The Indians were so": Crook, *Report,* 5–6.

234   Bourke observed: Bourke, *Campaign,* 79–80.

234   "A more charming spot": Bourke, Diary, May 14, 1883, v. 67, 40.

234   "The troops stated": *New York Herald,* June 13, 1883, 3.

234   He was angry: Rope, in G. Goodwin, *Raiding,* 164.

234   "He was tired": Bourke, *Campaign,* 82.

235   One woman warned: Rope, in G. Goodwin, *Raiding,* 165.

235   On May 20: ibid., 167.

235   "as daring as any": Thrapp, *General Crook,* 158. See also Thrapp, *Conquest of Apacheria,* 295–302.

235   "the most supremely": Debo, 183.

236   Once he was caught: Bourke, *Border,* 430.

236   "Gradually their fears": Bourke, *Campaign,* 85.

236   "All the chiefs": Crook, *Report,* 7.

236   A garbled version: e. g., Silver City, New Mexico, *Enterprise,* July 6, 1883.

236   Geronimo certainly believed: Skinner, *Rock,* 90.

236   The Chiricahua descendants: Ball, *Indeh,* 154.

236   According to Rope: Rope, in G. Goodwin, *Raiding,* 167.

236   "The Chiricahuas are almost": Bourke, Diary, May 22, 1883, v. 68, 3; May 15, 1883, v. 67, 50–51.

237   "The best thing": Crook, *Report,* 7.

238   "did not include": Robert Hanna, "With Crawford in Mexico," Clifton, Arizona, *Clarion,* July 7 and 14, 1886.

238   On May 22 or 23: Rope, in G. Goodwin, *Raiding,* 168–69.

238   Bourke watched: Bourke, *Campaign,* 102–3.

Sixteen: Turkey Creek

Page

239   Tucson hosted: *Arizona Star,* June 21, 1883.

239   Journalists took Crook: e. g., *Arizona Citizen,* August 28, 1883.

240   In his parleys: Crook, *Report,* 1883, Appendix E, 7–8.

240 "If the government fails": *Arizona Star,* June 17, 1883.

240 "Feared and hated by": Davis, *Truth,* 72.

241 The women told Bourke: Bourke, *Campaign,* 92.

241 The women also swore: Bourke, Diary, May 22, 1883, v. 68, 3–4.

241 Nor had the Sonorans: Faulk, *Campaign,* 76.

241 Increasingly anxious, Crook: Davis, 77–80; Debo, *Geronimo,* 196.

242 With their gift for ironic: Ball, *Indeb,* 116.

242 "The thought of attempting to": Davis, 80.

242 Two months earlier: Deming, New Mexico, *Tribune,* ca. October 4, 1883; unidentified newspaper, ca. October 4, 1883.

244 Chatto finally came: Davis, 82–101.

246 "Soon after we arrived": Barrett, *Geronimo's Story,* 135.

246 In "The Apache Problem": Crook, "Problem," 13.

246 As early as 1885: Faulk, 184.

246 To the end of assimilation: Davis, 50–51.

247 By the end of June: ibid., 102–7.

247 And the Chiricahua went at: ibid., 103–4, 108–14.

249 In September, a delegate: Robert Frazer, *The Apaches of the White Mountain Reservation,* Philadelphia: 1884, 7–8.

249 "I am hunting": quoted in Porter, *Paper,* 165.

249 One day an astounding: Ball, *In the Days,* 168–69.

249 Davis thought the five: Davis, 140.

249 The Chiricahua on Turkey Creek: Ball, *In the Days,* 169–74.

250 The lieutenant had enlisted: ibid., 156–57.

250 Now Davis, who had taken: Davis, 73, 106, 136–37, 142.

250 Thomas Cruse swore: Cruse, *Days,* 207.

251 "Geronimo's appearance": C. T. Connell, *Apache,* [n. p.].

251 On Turkey Creek, Davis: Ball, *In the Days,* 155, 162–64.

252 "an indolent creature": C. T. Connell, "Micky Free," 50.

252 "the most curious": Bourke, Diary, v. 59, 67–68, quoted in Porter, 180.

252 The simmering trouble boiled over: Davis, 123–25.

252 The Chiricahua version: Ball, *In the Days,* 162, 165.

252 Davis came to Kaytennae's wickiup: Davis, 126–30.

253 The shock: Ball, *In the Days,* 166.

253 The appearance of calm: Cruse, 205–6.

253 Later Davis would try: Davis, 139–45.

253 Suddenly Nana stood up: Ball, *In the Days,* 176.

254 Mickey was afraid: Davis, 145–46.

Seventeen: Canyon of the Funnels

Page
255 Britton Davis: Davis, *Truth,* 147–49.
256 "I was living quietly": ibid., 200–1.
256 Chatto had adopted: Ball, *In the Days,* 175.
256 In the middle of the night: The numbers, which were obtained by counting the remaining Chiricahua on Turkey Creek, vary from source to source. Among the warriors who broke out, as many as eight were still teenage boys. See Faulk, *Campaign,* 222.
256 The leaders of the exodus: Lozen's presence is verified in Ball, *In the Days,* 119.
256 Geronimo and Naiche: Ball, *In the Days,* 177.
256 It would take weeks: Davis, 149–51. Davis says the telegraph wire was repaired the next day, but this claim is contradicted by other evidence. The lieutenant's memoir was written at a distance of more than forty years from the events.
257 In the Mogollon Mountains: Ball, *In the Days,* 177–79.
257 Davis later claimed: Britton Davis, "Difficulties of Indian Warfare," *Army-Navy Journal,* October 24, 1885, quoted in Thrapp, *Conquest of Apacheria,* 314–16.
257 "After my father": Eugene Chihuahua, quoted in Ball, *Indeh,* 98.
258 Using the network: Debo, *Geronimo,* 241; Thrapp, *Conquest of Apacheria,* 318–25; Faulk, 62.
258 Near Silver City: unidentified newspaper, May 28, 1885, quoted in Thrapp, *Conquest of Apacheria,* 319–20.
258 Lieutenant Charles B. Gatewood: Charles B. Gatewood to Mrs. Gatewood, June 30, 1885, quoted in Faulk, 64.
259 "BRAVE CAPTAIN CHAFFEE": [?] *Morning Journal,* May 31, 1885.
259 The people of Pima County: People of Pima County to the President, June 13, 1885, *RG* 94, no. 2057.
259 "The truth is, there is": "The Arizona Apaches," [unidentified newspaper], December 12, 1885.
259 "Dont throw this away": Sam P. Carusi to President Grover Cleveland, June 15, 1885, *RG* 94, no. 3693.
260 In 1876: E. S. Connell, *Morning Star,* 230, 316.
260 "the wickedest Indian": Warren, "Geronimo."
261 "When Geronimo left": "Crook Speaks for Himself," *Tombstone Record-Epitaph,* October 16, 1885.
261 Near Oputo: Davis, 161–62.
261 "The Indians lured us": Daly, "Capture," 42.
261 The observant Davis: Davis, 166–70.
262 Nana was at first: Thrapp, *Conquest of Apacheria,* 330.
262 Encumbered by women: Davis, 177–95.

262   Geronimo was not finished: Debo, 245–47.
263   One of the kidnapped: Charlie Smith, quoted in Ball, *Indeh,* 102–4.
263   Like his brother, Ulzana: Wellman, *Death,* 243.
263   The sheer statistics: ibid., 243–47; Thrapp, *Conquest of Apacheria,* 339; Faulk, 70–73.
264   "Crawford was born": Davis, 31–32.
264   On December 11: Faulk, 75–82; Greene, "Crawford," 144–49; Maus to Crook, January 21, 1886, *RG* 94, no. 544; Opler, "Chiricahua," 375; Lummis, *General Crook,* 79, 95. The identification of Geronimo's messenger as Lozen is in Ball, *In the Days,* 182.
266   The Mexican side: Greene, 150–52.
266   Many years later: Daly, "Scouts," 70.
266   As the fighting had broken out: Sam Haozous, quoted in Debo, 250.
267   Nevertheless, a few days: Debo, 250–52.
267   Ranchers and miners: McKenna, *Black Range,* 199; Elizabeth McFarland, *Wilderness of the Gila,* Silver City, New Mexico: 1974, 25.
267   Maus had tried: Ball, *In the Days,* 183.
267   "Geronimo knew": Ball, *Indeh,* 104.
268   The warrior had lost: Crook to Sheridan, March 27, 1886, quoted in Davis, 199.
268   In prison, Kaytennae: Bourke, *Border,* 473.
268   His first twelve months: Bourke, Diary, March 22, 1886, v. 87, 108–9.
268   During the conference: Davis, 211.
268   "The whole ravine": Bourke, *Border,* 474, 476.
269   "the only known photographs": Van Orden, "C. S. Fly," 319.
269   Geronimo began the conference: Davis, 200–203.
269   Throughout Geronimo's speech: Daly, "Campaign," 97.
269   This so nettled: Davis, 202.
269   Bourke was surprised: Bourke, *Border,* 476.
269   Now Geronimo summoned: Davis, 201–7.
270   "so excited and wild": Crook, quoted in *Arizona Citizen,* April 2, 1886.
270   On the morning of March 27: Bourke, *Border,* 478.
270   "not an ounce": Mobile, Alabama, *Register,* June 19, 1888, quoted in Skinner, *Rock,* 226.
270   "as pleasant a face": Lummis, *General Crook,* 42.
270   "It seems to me": Davis, 207–8.
271   "a tall, loose-jointed": Wellman, 206.
271   "What Chihuahua": Davis, 209.
271   The Bedonkohe warrior: Bourke, *Border,* 478.
271   "Crueller features": Lummis, *Poco Tiempo,* 135.
271   Geronimo was much subdued: Davis, 210–11.

Eighteen: Canyon of the Skeletons

Page

273   That night: Bourke, *Border,* 480–81; Debo, *Geronimo,* 264–65; Thrapp,
      Conquest of Apacheria, 345–47.

274   "If it had not been": Crook, quoted in Lummis, *Dateline,* 75.

274   Four years later: *Senate Executive Document 35,* 51 Congress, 1 sess.,
      33, quoted in Debo, 267.

274   "We started with": Barrett, *Geronimo's Story,* 139.

274   "The general belief": Lummis, *Dateline,* 20.

274   Maus and his scouts: ibid., 34.

275   In the initial outbreak: Debo, 265–66.

275   Meanwhile, at Fort Bowie: Johnson, *Crook's Resume,* 16–19.

276   By now Chihuahua was bitter: Lummis, *Dateline,* 33.

276   Chihuahua said that he: Lummis, *General Crook,* 32.

276   The summer before: McKenna, *Black Range,* 197–98; Lummis, *Date-
      line,* 57–58.

276   On April 5: Faulk, *Campaign,* 96; Schmitt, *Crook,* 265–66.

277   "That day they put us": Eugene Chihuahua, quoted in Ball, *Indeh,* 100.

277   One of the Tan Wolf's: Lummis, *Dateline,* 64–65.

278   "I am also annoyed": Nelson Miles to Mary Miles, [ca. June 1886],
      quoted in Tolman, *Search,* 139.

278   Miles had not had: Tolman, 23–25, 30.

278   "[Crook] could entertain": Utley, "Crook and Miles," 82.

278   "Too much circus": ibid., 82.

278   "strutting peacock": Faulk, *Campaign,* 193.

278   "ignorant, almost illiterate": Bourke, quoted in Porter, *Paper,* 174.

278   "He is a tall": Lummis, *Dateline,* 70.

279   "Chiricahua scouts": Johnson, 23.

279   Some of the Indians: Ball, *Indeh,* 66.

279   In five months: Wellman, *Death,* 259.

279   "expensive toy": Faulk, 190.

279   "Crook's policy": Nelson Miles to Mary Miles, May 17, 1886, and [ca.
      June 1886], quoted in Tolman, 137, 140.

280   "I found at Fort Apache": Miles, *Recollections,* 496–97.

280   The warriors were such: Stanley to Adjutant General, October 11, 1886,
      RG 94, no. 1066. Debo's heroic attempt to straighten out the identities
      of the thirty-seven Chiricahuas in the final band is the best we are likely
      to have (Debo, 304–8). On the basis of Stanley's list, which does not
      include Lozen, Debo argues that the woman warrior was not in the
      band. But the young Kanseah, who was there, swore that Lozen fought
      with Geronimo to the end (Ball, *Indeh,* 110); so did Kaywaykla, who
      though not in the band knew every member of it (Ball, *In the Days,*
      184). Their testimony seems to outweigh Stanley's list.

280   "We saw that we were": *Chicago Tribune,* March 5, 1888, quoted in Skinner, *Rock,* 204.

281   "We were reckless": Barrett, 140–41.

281   According to the most lurid: Wellman, 260.

281   But other versions: M. P. Freeman, "The Dread Apache—That Early Day Scourge of the Southwest," *Arizona Star,* November 7, 1915.

281   The boy reported: Freeman, "Dread Apache"; Ruth B. Fitzgerald, "Pioneer Tells of Capture By Geronimo and His Band," *Arizona Star,* September 22, 1929.

282   The ten-year-old girl: Leighton Finley, "Story of Trinidad Berdine (As told to Lieut. Finley)," typescript, Gatewood Collection, Arizona Historical Society.

282   Both captives were freed: ibid.; Fitzgerald, "Pioneer Tells"; Freeman, "Dread Apache"; Wellman, 260.

282   "On our return": Barrett, 141.

283   Years later, Geronimo: Ball, *Indeh,* 136.

283   And his warriors believed: Opler, *Life-Way,* 216.

283   "Geronimo had to obtain": Kanseah, quoted in Ball, *Indeh,* 105.

284   "brilliant record": Miles, *Report,* 6.

284   "six feet four inches": Stout, "Soldiering," 163.

284   "one hundred of": Faulk, 107.

284   For four months: Lawton, "Report," 4–6.

284   "One who does not know": Leonard Wood, quoted in Robert M. Utley, "The Surrender of Geronimo," *Arizoniana,* Spring 1963, v. IV, no. 1, 4.

284   Miles insisted: Miles, *Recollections,* 491.

284   The Chiricahua used: Lawton, 1–6.

284   One woman was killed: Stout, 162.

284   One warrior defected: Davis, *Truth,* 218; Debo, 270–71.

285   "We have had but one": Lummis, *General Crook,* 144.

285   In the wake of Geronimo's: Miles, *Report,* 12; Davis, 219.

285   Though the number: Wellman, 263.

285   "What does Miles": Ball, *Indeh,* 85, 136. The officer was Colonel George Forsyth.

285   "After this engagement": Miles, *Recollections,* 490, 491, 493.

286   The germ of the idea: James Parker, quoted in Davis, 236.

286   Miles at first: Faulk, 153–56.

286   Chatto was indeed impressed: "Transcript of Stenographer's Notes of a Conference between Honorable William C. Endicott, Secretary of War, and Chato . . . ," July 26, 1886, *RG* 94, no. 6101.

287   This had never been Miles's: Faulk, 158–61, 165.

287   "The indolent and vicious": Miles, *Report,* 12.

287   "Their boys of to-day": Faulk, 155.

288   Miles went: Opler, "Chiricahua," 372.

288 The former was a Chokonen: Barrett, 144; Debo, 280.
288 Martine insisted: Faulk, 203. Martine's son claimed the promised reward was $35,000 apiece! (Ball, *Indeh,* 109).
288 Miles had ordered Gatewood: Gatewood, "Surrender," 54.
288 "the General contemplates": Lawton to Thompson, August 15, 1886, Gatewood Collection, Arizona Historical Society.
289 At some point Naiche: Burbank and Royce, *Burbank,* 34.
289 An Apache scout: O. O. Howard to Adjutant General, August 19, 1886, *RG* 94, no. 1066. See also Forsyth to Thompson, August 21, 1886 (Arizona Historical Society): "The entire party is pretty well broken down; Geronimo is in bad health, nearly blind and badly wounded in right arm, and is nearly helpless." The source of Forsyth's information is not specified.
289 some say they were Lozen: Ball, *Indeh,* 107.
289 Historian Dan L. Thrapp: Thrapp, "Surrender," 17–34.
290 It is known that: Gatewood, 56.
290 "cool, quiet": Davis, 223.
290 "Nantan Long Nose": Ball, *Indeh,* 110.
290 Kayitah and Martine: Gatewood, 58–60.
291 On top of their mountain: Ball, *Indeh,* 109–10.
291 "We knew they might shoot": Boggess, "Final Surrender," 2.
291 Finally one of the scout's: Opler, "Chiricahua," 76.
292 Beside the campfire: Boggess, 3.
292 "We were very anxious": ibid., 3.
292 Gatewood had brought: Gatewood, 60–61.
293 "We did begin": Huddleson, "Interview," 5.
293 and Gatewood admitted: Gatewood, 61–63.
294 According to Betzinez: Betzinez, *I Fought,* 138.
294 Lawton did his best: Faulk, 176–78, 194.
295 In his list: Miles, *Recollections,* 532.
295 On September 5: Faulk, 161–65.
295 I DO NOT INTEND: Miles to Lawton, August 31, 1886, Arizona Historical Society.
295 Geronimo at once rode: Barrett, 172.
295 "He was one of the": Miles, *Recollections,* 520–21.
295 Skeleton Canyon: Barnes, *Place Names,* 410.
296 Though Geronimo was unarmed: Debo, 292.
296 He picked up: D. L. Stanley to Adjutant General, October 27, 1886, quoted in Welsh, *Prisoners,* 29.
296 "We stood between": Barrett, 146–47.
296 At one point Geronimo: Miles, *Recollections,* 526–27.
296 At Fort Bowie: Stanley to Adjutant General, quoted in Welsh, 29–30.
297 I HOPE NOTHING: Cleveland to Miles, August 25, 1886, quoted in Miles to Acting Secretary of War, September 29, 1886, *RG* 94, no. 1066, 21.

297   The Chiricahuas believed: Barrett, 138–40, 145–46.
297   As souvenirs: Faulk, 169.
298   As they departed: Miles, *Recollections,* 527–28.

Epilogue

Page
299   "To be sure, we have taken": Ball, *Indeh,* 223.
299   As the train hurtled: ibid., 131.
300   To add to their misery: Faulk, *Campaign,* 164–65.
300   One warrior: Ball, *Indeh,* 251–60; Betzinez, *I Fought,* 143–45.
300   According to Betzinez: Betzinez, 145.
300   For decades: Ball and Sanchez, *Lost Apaches,* 10–17.
300   "These Indians": Secretary of War Endicott to General Sheridan, October 19, 1886, quoted in Faulk, 173.
301   "He is the picture": *Pensacola Commercial,* December 22, 1886; *The Pensacolian,* November 13, 1886; quoted in Skinner, *Rock,* 129, 133.
301   One was addressed: Skinner, 151–52.
301   Before the end of the year: Debo, *Geronimo,* 314–17, 326.
302   At Carlisle: Ball, *Indeh,* 13, 144.
302   At Mount Vernon, the Apache: ibid., 139.
302   To Mount Vernon came: Skinner, 227.
303   One of the first to die: Ball, *Indeh,* 154.
303   "You told them": George Wratten to Brigadier General D. S. Stanley, October 3, 1887, *RG* 94, no. 7141.
303   A makeshift schoolhouse: Skinner, 235, 238.
304   A party of Boston: Debo, 339–40; Ball, *Indeh,* 157.
304   Early in 1890: Schmitt, *Crook,* 293; Debo, 347.
305   "I think that General Crook's": Barrett, *Geronimo's Story,* 139–40.
305   At the end of 1889: Debo, 344; Skinner, 269–70.
305   The impact of Chiricahua despair: Ball, *Indeh,* 155.
306   Wratten had taught him: Corum, "Geronimo Smiled," 6.
306   On subsequent train journeys: Burbank and Royce, *Burbank,* 22–23.
306   At Fort Sill, the Kiowa: Debo, 365.
306   At night, when they heard: N. Goodwin, *Resistance* (film).
306   Learning that mesquite: Debo, 365.
307   His first experience: Santee, *Land,* 171–74; W. Clum, *Apache Agent,* 287–90.
307   "a coward, a liar": Ball, *Indeh,* 111.
308   At Fort Sill, the soldiers: Debo, 379–80.
308   At the same time: Warren, "Geronimo." The belief that Geronimo was locked behind bars at Fort Sill so endures that many visitors today ask to be shown his cell.

308   At Fort Sill he continued: Debo, 434–35.
308   Pawnee Bill: Debo, 423; Roberts, "Geronimo," 67.
309   On an Oklahoma ranch: Debo, 423–24; Turcheneske, *Prisoners,* 117.
309   Geronimo's grandest show: Barrett, 197–206.
309   One day during their stay: Santee, 174–76; W. Clum, 290–91.
309   In 1905, on a walk: Debo, 387–88.
310   An artist who came: Burbank and Royce, 23, 30–31.
310   In 1905, Stephen M. Barrett: Barrett, 139.
311   Geronimo, like other: George Wratten, quoted in Skinner, 72.
311   Many years later Daklugie: Ball, *Indeh,* 12, 173–74.
311   "It is my land": Barrett, 215.
311   "My hands are tied": Debo, 421.
312   "an agreeable": ibid., 412.
312   "I do not consider": ibid., 360.
312   around the turn of the century: Lockwood, *Apache Indians,* 327–28.
312   Geronimo, too, flirted: Debo, 431–32.
313   "Is that all": Corum, 7.
313   "I am praying": Huddleson, "Interview," 8.
313   By 1913, only 261: Debo, 448.
313   On a cold day: ibid., 439–41.
314   "Everybody hated": Lawton, Oklahoma, *Constitution,* April 10, 1913, quoted in Turcheneske, 142–43.
314   "The sun rises": "Geronimo's Doleful Plaint," *Denver Times,* October 10, 1898, 3.
314   In the last years: Ball, *Indeh,* 23, 81, 101, 134, 179–81.

Bibliography

■

(*Note:* In the case of a reprinted or newly translated work, the date of original publication appears in parentheses.)

Primary Sources

Arizona Legislative Assembly. *Memorial and Affidavits Showing Outrages Perpetrated by the Apache Indians.* San Francisco: 1871.

Ball, Eve. *Indeh: An Apache Odyssey.* Norman, Oklahoma: 1988 (1980).

———. *In the Days of Victorio.* Tucson: 1970.

Barnes, Will C. (edited by Frank C. Lockwood). *Apaches & Longhorns.* Tucson: 1982 (1941).

Barrett, S. M. *Geronimo's Story of His Life.* New York: 1906.

Bell, William A. *New Tracks in North America.* Albuquerque: 1965 (1870).

Betzinez, Jason, with Wilbur Sturtevant Nye. *I Fought with Geronimo.* Lincoln, Nebraska: 1987 (1959).

Bigelow, John. *On the Bloody Trail of Geronimo.* Tucson: 1986 (1958).

Boggess, O. M. "The Final Surrender of Geronimo." Typescript. Arizona Historical Society.

Bourke, John Gregory. *An Apache Campaign in the Sierra Madre.* Lincoln, Nebraska: 1987 (1886).

———. Diary, 1869–1896. University of New Mexico library. Microfilm; original manuscript in library of the U. S. Military Academy, West Point.

———. *The Medicine Men of the Apache.* Glorieta, New Mexico: 1983 (1888).

———. *On the Border with Crook.* Lincoln, Nebraska: 1971 (1891).

Browne, J. Ross. *Adventures in the Apache Country.* New York: 1869.

Burbank, E. A., and Ernest Royce. *Burbank Among the Indians.* Caldwell, Idaho: 1944.

Clum, John P. "Apaches as Thespians in 1876." *New Mexico Historical Review,* January 1931, vol. VI, no. 1.

———. "Geronimo." 3 parts. *Arizona Historical Review,* July and October 1928, January 1929; vol. 1, nos. 2–4.

———. *The Truth About Apaches.* Los Angeles: 1931.

Clum, Woodworth. *Apache Agent: The Story of John P. Clum.* Lincoln, Nebraska: 1978 (1936).

Colyer, Vincent. *Report on the Apache Indians of Arizona and New Mexico.* Washington: 1872.

Connell, Charles T. *The Apache, Past and Present.* Typescript. University of Arizona Special Collections.

———. "Micky Free." *Arizona Magazine,* December 1906, vol. 2, no. 4.

Conner, Daniel Ellis (edited by Donald J. Berthong and Odessa Davenport). *Joseph Reddeford Walker and the Arizona Adventure.* Norman, Oklahoma: 1956.

Corbusier, William T. *Verde to San Carlos: Recollections of a Famous Army Surgeon and His Observant Family on the Western Frontier 1869–1886.* Tucson: 1968.

Cortés, José (translated by John Wheat). *Views from the Apache Frontier: Report on the Northern Provinces of Spain.* Norman, Oklahoma: 1989 (1799).

Corum, Fred T. "When Geronimo Smiled." *Pentecostal Evangel,* December 11, 1988 (1977).

Cozzens, Samuel Woodworth. *Explorations & Adventures in Arizona & New Mexico.* Secaucus, New Jersey: 1988 (ca. 1858).

Cremony, John C. *Life among the Apaches.* Lincoln, Nebraska: 1983 (1868).

Crook, George. *Annual Report, U. S. Army Dept. of Arizona.* Prescott, Arizona: 1883.

———. "The Apache Problem." Typescript. Arizona Historical Society.

Cruse, Thomas. *Apache Days and After.* Lincoln, Nebraska: 1987 (1941).

Daly, Henry W. "The Capture of Geronimo." *The American Legion Monthly,* June 1930.

———. "The Geronimo Campaign." *Journal of the United States Cavalry Association,* October 1908, vol. XIX, no. 70.

———. "Scouts—Good and Bad." *The American Legion Monthly,* August 1928.

Davis, Britton. *The Truth about Geronimo.* Lincoln, Nebraska: 1976 (1929).

Ellis, A. N. "Recollections of an Interview with Cochise, Chief of the Apaches." *Collections of the Kansas State Historical Society,* 1913–1914, vol. XIII.

Ewing, Russell C. "New Light on Cochise." *Arizona and the West,* Spring 1969, vol. 11, no. 1.

Farish, Thomas Edward. *History of Arizona.* 4 vols. Phoenix: 1915.

Fiebeger, G. J. "General Crook's Campaign in Old Mexico in 1883." *Proceedings of the Annual Meeting of the Order of Indian Wars of the United States,* February 20, 1936.

Finley, Leighton. "Geronimo Campaign: Story of Trinidad Bertine." Type-script. Arizona Historical Society.

Fitzgerald, Ruth B. "Pioneer Tells of Capture by Geronimo and His Band." *Arizona Star,* September 22, 1929.

Forbes, Robert H. Untitled typescript: interview with Tom Jeffords. Arizona Historical Society.

Gatewood, Charles B. "The Surrender of Geronimo." *The Journal of Arizona History,* Spring 1986, vol. 27, no. 1.

Goodwin, Grenville. *The Social Organization of the Western Apache.* Tucson: 1969 (1942).

——— (edited by Keith H. Basso). *Western Apache Raiding and Warfare.* Tucson: 1971.

Grossman, A. G. "Grossman Tells of . . ." *Arizona Republic,* April 14, 1926.

Hammond, George Peter, and Agapito Rey. *Narratives of the Coronado Expedition, 1540–42.* Albuquerque: 1940.

———. *Obregon's History of Sixteenth Century Exploration in Western America.* Los Angeles: 1928.

History of the Arizona Territory. San Francisco: 1884.

Howard, Oliver Otis. "Account of General Howard's Mission to the Apaches and Navajos," *Washington Daily Morning Chronicle,* November 10, 1872.

———. *Famous Indian Chiefs I Have Known.* New York: 1907.

———. *My Life and Experiences among Our Hostile Indians.* Hartford: 1907.

Huddleson, S. M. "An Interview with Geronimo and His Guardian, Mr. G. M. Wratt[e]n." Typescript. Arizona Historical Society.

Hughes, Fred G. "History: Cochise, the Chiricahua Chieftain." *Arizona Star,* January 31, 1886.

Johnson, Barry C. *Crook's Resume of Operations against Apache Indians, 1882 to 1886.* London: 1971.

Lawton. H. W. "Report of Capt. Lawton." Typescript. Arizona Historical Society.

Lummis, Charles Fletcher (edited by Dan L. Thrapp). *Dateline Fort Bowie.* Norman, Oklahoma: 1979 (1886).

———. *General Crook and the Apache Wars.* Flagstaff, Arizona: 1966.

———. *The Land of Poco Tiempo.* Albuquerque: 1980 (1893).

McClintock, James H. *Arizona: Prehistoric—Aboriginal—Pioneer—Modern.* 3 vols. Chicago: 1916.

McKenna, James A. *Black Range Tales.* Glorieta, New Mexico: 1963 (1936).

Mazzanovich, Anton. *Trailing Geronimo.* Los Angeles: 1926.

Miles, Nelson A. *Annual Report, U. S. Army Dept. of Arizona.* Albuquerque: 1886.

———. *Personal Recollections and Observations of General Nelson A. Miles.* Chicago: 1897.

Miller, Joseph. *The Arizona Story.* New York: 1952.

Opler, Morris Edward. *An Apache Life-Way.* Chicago: 1941.

———, ed. "A Chiricahua Apache's Account of the Geronimo Campaign of 1886," by Samuel E. Kenoi. *The Journal of Arizona History,* Spring 1986, vol. 27, no. 1. (1938).

Oury, William S. "To The Society of Arizona Pioneers." Typescript. Arizona Historical Society.

Pfefferkorn, Ignaz. *Sonora: A Description of the Province.* Albuquerque: 1949 (ca. 1794–1795).

Poston, Charles D. (edited by John Myers Myers). *Building a State in Apache Land.* Tempe, Arizona: 1963 (1894).

———. *History of the Apaches.* Manuscript. University of Arizona Special Collections.

Records of the Adjutant General's Office, Record Group No. 94. Arizona Historical Society. Microfilm; original in National Archives.

Rudo Ensayo ["by an unknown Jesuit Padre, 1763"]. Tucson: 1951 (1863).

Safford, A. P. K. Untitled. *Arizona Citizen,* December 7, 1872; reprinted in Miller, *The Arizona Story.* New York: 1952.

Santee, Ross. *Apache Land.* Lincoln, Nebraska: 1971 (1947).

Schmitt, Martin F. *General George Crook: His Autobiography.* Norman, Oklahoma: 1946.

"Soldier in the California Column: The Diary of John W. Teal" (edited by Henry P. Walker). *Arizona and the West,* Spring 1971.

Stone, Charles P. *Notes on the State of Sonora.* Washington: 1861.

Stout, Joe A. "Soldiering and Suffering in the Geronimo Campaign: Reminiscences of Lawrence R. Jerome." *Journal of the West,* January 1972, vol. XI, no. 1.

Tevis, James H. *Arizona in the '50's.* Albuquerque: 1954.

Turrill, Henry Stuart. "A Talk with Cochise." Prescott, Arizona, *Miner,* 1872; reprinted in Miller, *The Arizona Story.* New York: 1952.

———. "A Vanished Race of Aboriginal Founders." *Publications of the Order of the Founders and Patriots of America,* no. 18, 1907.

Warren, James G. "Geronimo, the Wickedest Indian that Ever Lived, Crazed by Imprisonment." *New York World,* August 5, 1900.

Welsh, Herbert. *The Apache Prisoners in Fort Marion, St. Augustine, Florida.* Philadelphia: 1887.

Williamson, Dan. *Reminiscences of the Early Days of Arizona.* Typescript. Arizona Historical Society.

Secondary Sources

Ball, Eve, and Lynda Sanchez. "The Lost Apaches." *True West,* January 1982.

Barnes, Will C. *Arizona Place Names.* Tucson: 1988 (1935).

Basso, Keith H. *The Cibecue Apache.* Prospect Heights, Illinois: 1986 (1970).

———. *Portraits of "The Whiteman."* Cambridge, U. K.: 1979.

———. *Western Apache Language and Culture.* Tucson: 1990.

Baylor, George Wythe (edited by Odie B. Faulk). *John Robert Baylor: Confederate Governor of Arizona.* Tucson: 1966.

Brown, Dee. *Bury My Heart at Wounded Knee.* New York: 1971.

Clark, La Verne Harrell. *They Sang for Horses: The Impact of the Horse on Navajo and Apache Folklore.* Tucson: 1966.

Cole, D. C. *The Chiricahua Apache, 1846–1876: From War to Reservation.* Albuquerque: 1988.

Connell, Evan S. *Son of the Morning Star.* San Francisco: 1984.

Cramer, Harry G. "Tom Jeffords—Indian Agent." *The Journal of Arizona History,* Autumn 1976, vol. 17, no. 3.

Davisson, Lori. "New Light on the Cibecue Fight: Untangling Apache Identities." *The Journal of Arizona History,* Winter 1979, vol. 20, no. 4.

Debo, Angie. *Geronimo: The Man, His Time, His Place.* Norman, Oklahoma: 1976.

Faulk, Odie B. *The Geronimo Campaign.* New York: 1969.

Freeman, M. P. "The Dread Apache—That Early-Day Scourge of the Southwest." *Arizona Star,* November 7, 1915.

Goodwin, Neil. *Geronimo and the Apache Resistance.* Film. Peace River Films, Cambridge, Massachusetts: 1988.

Greene, Jerome A. "The Crawford Affair: International Implications of the Geronimo Campaign." *Journal of the West,* January 1972, vol. XI, no. 1.

Griffith, A. Kinney. *Mickey Free, Manhunter.* Caldwell, Idaho: 1969.

Harte, John Bret. *The San Carlos Indian Reservation, 1872–1886: An Administrative History.* 2 vols. Ph. D. dissertation, University of Arizona: 1972.

———. "The Strange Case of Joseph C. Tiffany: Indian Agent in Disgrace." *The Journal of Arizona History,* Winter 1975, vol. 16, no. 4.

Haskell, J. Loring. *Southern Athapaskan Migration, A. D. 200–1750.* Tsaile, Arizona: 1987.

Lekson, Stephen H. *Nana's Raid: Apache Warfare in Southern New Mexico, 1881.* El Paso: 1987.

Lockwood, Frank C. *The Apache Indians.* Lincoln, Nebraska: 1987 (1938).

———. "Marijildo Grijalva—Guide, Scout, and Interpreter." Manuscript. Arizona Historical Society.

Moorhead, Max L. *The Apache Frontier.* Norman, Oklahoma: 1968.

Nabhan, Gary Paul. *Gathering the Desert.* Tucson: 1985.

Ogle, Ralph Hedrick. *Federal Control of the Western Apaches, 1848–1886.* Albuquerque: 1970 (1940).

Opler, Morris E. "Some Implications of Culture Theory for Anthropology and Psychology." *American Journal of Orthopsychiatry,* October 1948, vol. XVIII, no. 4.

Porter, Joseph C. *Paper Medicine Man: John Gregory Bourke and His American West.* Norman, Oklahoma: 1986.

Radbourne, Allan. "The Naming of Mickey Free." *The Journal of Arizona History,* Autumn 1976, vol. 17, no. 3.

Rickey, Don. *Forty Miles a Day on Beans and Hay.* Norman, Oklahoma: 1963.

Roberts, David. "Geronimo." *National Geographic Magazine,* October 1992, vol. 182, no. 4.

———. "Going After Geronimo." *Outside Magazine,* June 1990.

Russell, Don. *One Hundred and Three Fights and Scrimmages: The Story of General Reuben F. Bernard.* Washington: 1936.

Sacks, Benjamin H. "New Evidence on the Bascom Affair." *Arizona and the West,* Autumn 1962, vol. 4, no. 3.

Salzman, M. "Geronimo: The Napoleon of Indians." *The Journal of Arizona History,* Winter 1967, vol. 8, no. 4.

Schellie, Don. *Vast Domain of Blood: The Story of the Camp Grant Massacre.* Los Angeles: 1968.

Skinner, Woodward B. *The Apache Rock Crumbles.* Pensacola, Florida: 1987.

Smith, Lula B. "My Father, Survivor of the 1872 Cave Massacre." Typescript. Arizona Historical Society.

Sonnichsen, C. L. "From Savage to Saint: A New Image for Geronimo." *The Journal of Arizona History,* Spring 1986, vol. 27, no. 1.

———. *The Mescalero Apaches.* Norman, Oklahoma: 1958.

———. "Who Was Tom Jeffords?" *The Journal of Arizona History,* Winter 1982, vol. 23, no. 4.

Spicer, Edward H. *Cycles of Conquest.* Tucson: 1962.

Stockel, H. Henrietta. *Women of the Apache Nation.* Reno: 1991.

Stout, Joseph A. *Apache Lightning: The Last Great Battles of the Ojo Calientes.* New York: 1974.

Sweeney, Edwin R. *Cochise: Chiricahua Apache Chief.* Norman, Oklahoma: 1991.

———. "'I Had Lost All': Geronimo and the Carrasco Massacre of 1851." *The Journal of Arizona History,* Spring 1986, vol. 27, no. 1.

Terrell, John Upton. *Apache Chronicle.* New York: 1972.

Thrapp, Dan L. *Al Sieber, Chief of Scouts.* Norman, Oklahoma: 1964.

———. *The Conquest of Apacheria.* Norman, Oklahoma: 1967.

———. *General Crook and the Sierra Madre Adventure.* Norman, Oklahoma: 1972.

———. "Geronimo's Mysterious Surrender." *The Westerner's Brand Book,* Los Angeles Corral, no. 13, 1969.

———. *Juh: An Incredible Indian.* El Paso: 1973.

———. *Victorio and the Mimbres Apaches.* Norman, Oklahoma: 1974.

Tolman, Newton F. *The Search for General Miles.* New York: 1968.

Turcheneske, John A. *The Apache Prisoners of War at Fort Sill, 1894–1914.* Ph. D. dissertation, University of New Mexico: 1978.

———. "The Arizona Press and Geronimo's Surrender." *The Journal of Arizona History,* Summer 1973, vol. 14, no. 2.

Tyler, Barbara Ann. "Cochise: Apache War Leader, 1858–1861." *The Journal of Arizona History,* Spring 1965, vol. VI, no. 1.

Utley, Robert M. "The Bascom Affair: A Reconstruction." *Arizona and the West,* Spring 1961, vol. 3, no. 1.

———. *A Clash of Cultures: Fort Bowie and the Chiricahua Apaches.* Washington: 1977.

———. "Crook and Miles, Fighting and Feuding on the Indian Frontier." *MHQ: The Journal of Military History,* Autumn 1989, vol. 2, no. 1.

———. "Geronimo." *MHQ: The Journal of Military History,* Winter 1992, vol. 4, no. 2.

Van Orden, Jay. "C. S. Fly at Cañon de Los Embudos: American Indians as Enemy in the Field, A Photographic First." *The Journal of Arizona History,* Autumn 1989, vol. 30, no. 3.

Walker, Henry P., and Don Bufkin. *Historical Atlas of Arizona.* Norman, Oklahoma: 1979.

Wellman, Paul I. *Death in the Desert.* Lincoln, Nebraska: 1987 (1935).

Acknowledgments

■

*T*o previous scholars of the Apache, I owe a great debt—particularly to such perspicacious and original researchers as Dan L. Thrapp, Edwin R. Sweeney, Eve Ball, Angie Debo, Grenville Goodwin, Morris Opler, Keith Basso, Robert M. Utley, and C. L. Sonnichsen. From the buried veins of Southwestern history, these writers have mined many a lode of hard-won fact; the conclusions I draw from their ore remain the product of my own milling and smelting.

On the various Apache reservations, I was greeted with good will by a number of informants. Ouida Miller, Geronimo's granddaughter, gave me her trust and her insight, as did Berle Kanseah, Edgar Perry, and Elbys Hugar, Naiche's granddaughter. Wendell Chino, tribal chairman of the Mescalero Apache, facilitated my research, as did Ronnie Lupe and the tribal council of the White Mountain Apache reservation. Mildred Cleghorn provided a generous vision of the Chiricahua legacy as it was handed down to the generations in exile from the heartland. Genevieve (Sunny) Wratten opened the coffers of her grandfather's remarkable knowledge as interpreter for the Chiricahua.

A trio of Tucson Apache experts, Jay Van Orden, Barney Burns, and the late Tom Naylor, did their best to steer me along the right paths as I commenced my work. Neil Goodwin likewise shared the understanding that informs his superb film, *Geronimo and the Apache Resistance,* as well as the heritage passed him by his father, Grenville Goodwin, the first ethnographer of the Apache.

The staff of the Arizona Historical Society gave unstintingly of the resources of the most important collection of Apache materials in existence; their cooperation and guidance seem to me to form an ideal model of how a great archive can help a scholar. The staffs of the libraries of the University of Arizona, the University of New Mexico, the University of Colorado, and Harvard University cheerfully came to my aid, as did Steve Wilson at the Museum of the Great Plains and the staffs of the Fort Sill Museum and the Fort Bowie National Historic Site.

Terry Moore made a splendid companion for an exploration of the Sierra Madre in search of Geronimo's footprints. Bruce Dale's own photographic enthusiasm made for a happy collaboration for *National Geographic.* Erla Zwingle, my editor at that magazine, and Mark Bryant and John Rasmus at *Outside* gave me early and faithful encouragement.

Jon Krakauer, Sharon Roberts, and my indefatigable agent, Max Gartenberg, read my manuscript chapter by chapter and offered valuable suggestions. My editor at Simon & Schuster, Bob Bender, oversaw four years of research with the benign patience and intelligent coaxing that enabled one more writer, facing the terror of the blank page, to pick up his pen at last and begin.

Index

■